THE HOPI INDIANS OF OLD ORAIBI

ORAIBI ROCKS. Some informants say that Oraibi means "place of the rocks" and is named for these boulders. A Katcina shrine is located here.

The Hopi Indians
of
Old Oraibi
Change and Continuity

———

Mischa Titiev

Ann Arbor
THE UNIVERSITY OF MICHIGAN PRESS

Published with the assistance of a grant
from the Horace H. Rackham School of Graduate
Studies of The University of Michigan.

Dedicated, with affection,
to the memories of my parents-in-law,
SARAH and MAX BERMAN

Preface

The main purposes of this book are to provide descriptions of Hopi [HOE-pea] culture at Oraibi in the early 1930s and the changes that have since taken place. Unlike most studies of culture change, this one undertakes to make a detailed, longitudinal approach to its subject, based on information obtained in the course of more than three decades during which numerous visits to the same pueblo were made.

Every study of culture change, unless it is to be impressionistic, requires a firmly established baseline in the past from which changes of culture can be determined. In this case the required baseline consists of a day-to-day diary that was kept in 1933–34, while I was residing in Old Oraibi. All entries were written late at night, while the pueblo was asleep. No Hopi even suspects that this journal exists, and no part of it has ever been published.[1]

An awareness that this diary, like all diaries, might be regarded as a personal document has led the author scrupulously to eliminate all entries of a purely personal nature. Every effort has been made to retain only those passages that show how the Hopi lived and thought, together with some ideas that occurred to the author in 1933–34.

The method followed has been to present the diary, expurgated and edited wherever necessary, and to insert, at appropriate places in the text, accounts of such later events as are relevant. All material that has been added to the original journal has been placed within square brackets. A summary of the principal activities and ceremonies that take place in a particular month precedes the diary entries. Several important ceremonies, dances, and other performances which have been summarized in the diary are more fully described in chapter X. A discussion of the general nature of culture change is given in the concluding chapter.

Since the Hopi have no way of writing their own language, and since they have no semblance of a permanent calendar, it is often impossible to determine exactly when a given change took place. Luckily, frequent returns to Old Oraibi have enabled me to make close approximations. In broad terms the starting date for the culture and its changes here described is the summer of 1932, and the close falls between 1960 and the summer of 1966. This study does not deal with the effects of electricity, which was introduced to several Hopi towns around 1964. Before that, only Moenkopi had had the use of electric power.

Most living people have been given pseudonyms, although some true names have been kept. Hopi words, with the exception of those that begin with a capital letter, have been italicized; all kinship terms are uniformly prefixed by "i" which means "my"; and all plurals are formed by the addition of the English "s." A glottal stop is indicated by an apostrophe; "ö" has the value of "oy" as in boy; "û" is usually intermediate between the "u" in hut and the "u" in put, but it may range from one sound to the other; "ñ" is pronounced like "ny" in canyon; "c" is sounded like "sh"; and "tc" is like "ch" in chair.[2]

It is hoped that this book will provide not only reliable accounts of specific changes in Hopi culture at Old Oraibi, but that it will also provoke a useful discussion and reexamination of the broad workings of culture change as a universal and inevitable process.

Without the generous help of a number of persons and institutions interested in the support and furtherance of anthropological research, the project reported in this book could not have been carried out. A fellowship in ethnology, provided by the Laboratory of Anthropology in Santa Fe, New Mexico, in the summer of 1932, first brought me to Oraibi[3] and, under the guidance of Professor Leslie A. White, of the University of Michigan, gave me an excellent introduction to fieldwork. About a year later, a grant from Harvard's Division of Anthropology enabled me to go back to the Hopi Indians, and an exchange of letters brought permission from Chief Tawaqwaptiwa to reside in the ancient pueblo atop Third Mesa[4] from August 5, 1933, to March 23, 1934.

The data obtained in 1932 were combined with the material gathered in 1933–34, and were subsequently published by me in "Old Oraibi: A Study of the Hopi Indians of Third Mesa," *Papers of the Peabody Museum of American Archaeology and Ethnology*, vol. 22, no. 1 (Cambridge, Mass., 1944). For the interested reader, this monograph furnishes further details on many aspects of Hopi culture touched on in this study. Page references to this monograph have sometimes been inserted in the text of the diary in brackets, and are preceded by the abbreviation O.O. After 1934, return visits were made in the summers of 1937, 1940, 1953, 1955, 1957, 1959, 1961, 1963, 1964, and 1966. Most of these field trips were financed by the Board of Governors of the Horace H. Rackham School of Graduate Studies at the University of Michigan.

In 1956, while I was on sabbatical leave from the University of Michigan, Dean Ralph A. Sawyer, of the Horace H. Rackham School of Graduate Studies, very kindly provided me with working quarters. It was there that this study began to assume its present shape.

In 1961 a Ford fellowship in the behavioral sciences allowed me to revisit the Hopi and to continue working on this manuscript; and the entire project was brought to completion by virtue of funds (GS–1100) supplied April 15, 1966, by the National Science Foundation.

During the summers of 1964 and 1966 Dr. Edward B. Danson, Director of the Museum of Northern Arizona in Flagstaff, graciously made available to me both living and working quarters in his Research Center. It is a pleasure to acknowledge the interest and help that he and his staff so cheerfully provided.

I am genuinely thankful and deeply grateful to the many institutions and persons who have supported and encouraged my work. I regret that I cannot list each individual by name, but I must mention Mrs. Marie E. Braden, Mrs. Lawrence A. Wren, and Mrs. Dora D. Malone, who typed the manuscript. Mrs. Braden and Mr. Charles D. Hall made all the necessary line drawings.

Above all, I am forever indebted to my patient wife, Estelle, who, since 1937, has accompanied me on all my trips to Oraibi. I very much appreciate her help and companionship, and I am sincerely thankful for her advice and encouragement as well as for her thoughtful criticism.

MISCHA TITIEV

Contents

CHAPTER I

Introduction

On the first day of July, 1932, four graduate students in anthropology assembled at Oraibi (pronounced, Oh-rye'-bee), Arizona, under the leadership of Professor Leslie A. White, of the University of Michigan. Professor White had been asked by the Laboratory of Anthropology, which maintained headquarters in Santa Fe, New Mexico, to take charge of a field party in ethnology, whose student members were Fred Eggan, of the University of Chicago; Ed Kennard, then of Columbia University; Jess Spirer, who was studying at Yale University; and the author, a graduate student from Harvard University (see Fig. 1).[1] Later, George Devereux came from France to join this group.

Professor White found a place for his party to live, in a freshly constructed house at New Oraibi or Kikötcmovi. The house, not yet completed at the time, belonged to Mrs. Rebecca Williams, whose family included some of the earliest converts to Christianity made by the Reverend H. R. Voth, a Mennonite missionary.[2] The actual building of the house was being done by her brothers, and during the owner's absence responsibility for preparing meals and otherwise looking after guests was entrusted to Lee, her younger sister. All of Mrs. Williams's family are full-blooded Hopi, and those who have remained on the reservation continue to live at Kikötcmovi.[3]

The immediate objectives of 1932 were to acquire information pertaining to Old Oraibi's kin and clan systems, and to gain as much insight as possible into the background and consequences of the Split of 1906. (During the last decade of the nineteenth century two parties arose at Oraibi. The Progressives or Friendlies, led by the Village chief, favored the acceptance of some "White" practices, such as schooling; but the Conservatives or Hostiles violently opposed everything that was not traditionally Hopi. On September 7, 1906, the Conservatives were driven out, and went north on Third Mesa about four miles to found Hotevilla. Several months later, an aging leader from Hotevilla took a small party back to Oraibi. When they were again driven out in October, 1907, they established Bakavi, about a mile east of Hotevilla.)[4]

Needless to say, one summer of investigation, fruitful though it was, did not suffice to answer all the questions in which the group was interested. Accordingly, the present writer resumed fieldwork in the following year while he lived in Old Oraibi. The 1932 party's interpreter and one of its principal informants, Ned, graciously set aside for the author's use a large room in his own house and made arrangements for his younger sister Ida (Fig. 2) to serve as housekeeper. As a joke, growing out of the presence of a man from France in the 1932 party, the street was called Bakwa ("Frog") Avenue; and the number 17½ was chosen at random (Fig. 3).

While advance preparations for the 1933–34 field trip were being made, Professor A. M. Tozzer, then the chairman of Harvard's Anthropology Department, asked me to supervise the initial ethnographic investigations of Miss Charis Denison, later Mrs. Crockett, a student at Radcliffe College. Miss Denison resided at New Oraibi while I lived on top of Third Mesa. It was understood that she would interview Lee and other members of her sex, while I would deal primarily with male informants. When she left the field several weeks later, Miss Denison kindly turned her notes over to me, and their substance was incorporated into "Old Oraibi."

Toward the end of July, 1933, I drove to Arizona with a cousin and a friend, who were planning to proceed to California. We stayed with Lee in Kikötcmovi until my quarters at Old Oraibi were ready.

After leaving Old Oraibi in 1934, I kept fresh my contacts with the Hopi and their culture by correspondence and numerous return visits. In the course of time, matters of cultural dynamics, including the important problem of change, had become of dominant interest, and on later trips information was elicited from a number of tribespeople whom I had known since 1932. In this work Ned again played a key part, and the bulk of his statements proved to be reliable when checked against those of other informants.

One piece of anthropological folklore that still is heard from time to time received what ought to be a fatal blow during the checking-up process. The belief is sometimes expressed that nonliterate natives have, perforce, better memories than those who use and depend on writing. This proved to be untrue. Ned, as well as many another Hopi, forgot much of what they had told me some decades earlier, and only my written notes preserved much that would otherwise have been lost. (Even so, Ned may well be an exception to the general rule, since in some matters he has a fantastic memory.)[5]

While I was residing in Old Oraibi, I was informally visited from time to time by Fred Eggan, who lived and worked at Shipaulovi but who was well known on Third Mesa. Together, we shared many experiences, exchanged much information, and discussed numerous ideas.

One of the most useful procedures employed in 1933–34, in addition to participation in the daily life of the pueblo, and apart from the conduct of systematic interviews on particular topics, was the collection of census data. A chart, supplied by the Museum of Northern Arizona in Flagstaff, made possible a house-to-house and street-by-street survey of the residents of Oraibi at the approximate time of the Split of 1906. Chief Tawaqwaptiwa furnished most of the data, and Ned served as interpreter and secondary informant. Ostensibly, the census was supposed to provide no more than the clan, ceremonial, marital, and residential affiliations of Oraibi's populace, in addition to the side that each person took at the time of the Split. However, informants were encouraged to pursue, while careful notes were taken, whatever subjects they wished. In this way a vast fund of undirected material was acquired. Indeed, so valuable did the "taking of a census" prove to be that the use of such a device is strongly recommended wherever it is feasible.

CHAPTER II

Diary for August, 1933

[*Various villages hold their annual Niman ("Homegoing") dances. These mark the end of the open* katcina *(see p. 6) season, and when they conclude, the* katcina *dancers are "sent home" until the next open season begins.*

In the third week of this month two pueblos perform Snake-Antelope dances and three conduct Flute rituals. (They will alternate every year.) This is also the season for such colorful social (maskless) dances as the Butterfly, in which both sexes participate. Also, at this time, men may run ñötiwa, *holding gifts aloft while they dodge in and out among groups of women.*

In the fields, an early variety of sweet corn is picked for the Niman, but other crops are not quite mature enough for harvesting.]

Tues. Aug. 1. Entered the Hopi reservation from Holbrook, Arizona, and called on Superintendent E. K. Miller at Keam's Canyon, who gave me permission to live and work at Third Mesa and offered help whenever necessary. At Kikötcmovi, visited Homer[1] at his store, and Horace[2] [at Hubbell's]. Drove up to Oraibi and saw Chief Tawaqwaptiwa, as well as Ned and his folks. Ned had just killed a sheep for his *itiwaiya* ("niece"), Delia, daughter of his deceased oldest sister, Gladys, of the Sun clan. The occasion was the birth of a girl, Duwawunsi, born to Delia and her husband, Nelson. [Delia died in childbirth around 1940, whereupon Nelson, who belongs to the Sand clan, returned to his natal village of Hotevilla and remarried. The children of his first marriage were brought up by Martha, Ned's sister, at Oraibi.]

Old Oraibi seems unchanged except for a sign warning visitors not to wander about the village or to take pictures without the head chief's permission. An arrow points to Tawaqwap-

4

tiwa's house, at the back of which there is another sign saying, "Head Chief." These signs were erected by Ernest V. Sutton, a friend of Ned.

Allen and Moe [sons of Edna] have moved to a different house, leaving Edna alone in the old one.[3] Moe met me and said that they had quarreled over property and therefore moved. Allen and his wife, Betty, were at Hotevilla (Betty's natal village, where she should have remained after marriage), and would stay there until after the Niman dance on Thursday.

Wed. Aug. 2. Met Ned on the way to his fields with Louis, brother of Kane, for an assistant. Ned complained that his best pulling horse had been eating loco, and the horse did act balky and restless.

Delia's baby was named early this morning and taken to the east edge of the mesa. A feast was spread at Ned's house, consisting of his sheep, another sheep contributed by his father, Duvenimptiwa; blue *piki* [paper-thin wafer bread, made with a cornmeal batter, baked in crisp sheets, and folded into multilayered loaves about 10 to 12 inches long and 1½ inches wide] (the *piki* served at naming rites must always be blue); *pikami* (a steamed pudding made of sweetened cornmeal and wheat sprouts); melons; mutton stew with hominy (*nukwivi*); coffee; and other items.

Visited Chief Tawaqwaptiwa and promised to have my cousin and friend take him to Hotevilla for tomorrow's dance.

Drove to Chimopovy with Homer who had business there. Hoped to make a contact, but Homer professed to know no one intimately and indicated that the Chimopovy people were as conservative and hostile to "Whites" as was the populace of Hotevilla.

Lee told a story of Walpi, whose people she claimed were half-Navaho and often fought in disguise with the Navaho against the Hopi from Oraibi.[4] One of these traitors cried, "Anai!" ("Ouch!" in the Hopi language) when he was shot, and the Navaho dumped his corpse into a corral. Next day the Hopi found the body and discovered it to be that of a Walpi tribesman.

Thurs. Aug. 3. Niman *katcina* dance–Jemez–at Hotevilla. [The word *"katcina"* has a number of meanings, including the spirits of deceased Hopi who have become Cloud People, supernatural personages capable of bringing rain. The Hopi distinguish more than 250 types, each one set apart by its colors, designs, costume, and accessories.⁵ Most often, *katcina* refers to a masked, masculine dancer who becomes deified as soon as he dons his mask.

Each Hopi village divides the year into an "open" *katcina* season, extending from late November to early August, and a "closed" one, during which *katcinas* may not appear. The final dance of each "open" season is called Niman ("Homegoing") at the close of which the *katcinas* are "sent home" until the following November. The Jemez type of *katcina* is frequently, but not invariably, portrayed at a Niman dance.]

The fathers of the *katcinas* were Puhunimptiwa and Qömaletstiwa, who assisted one another. This pair acted in the same capacity last year, but in 1932 Puhunimptiwa seemed primary, whereas the reverse was true this year. Met Allen at the dance and chatted with Albert, the policeman.

[In 1955 Albert was old and had retired. He was still resident at Hotevilla when he became mortally ill in 1964. There is no policeman currently at Hotevilla, as the people there are reported to want complete independence and to prefer to have no government connections. Among the Hopi, policemen are not greatly admired.] Also had a long talk with Coin, who told me that the government had sent a commission to investigate the Hopi demand that all Navahos should be driven from their reservation. [Coin was once town crier at New Oraibi. He had received a "White" education at Keam's Canyon many years ago and had served as an interpreter for Lololoma and Yokioma.⁶ He lived primarily as a cattleman and died soon after 1940. His son is employed by the Museum of Northern Arizona in Flagstaff.] Coin claimed that the Navaho held land needed by the Hopi and cited his own cattle as a case in point. He went on to say that the president of the Hopi council at New Oraibi is Otto Lomavitu, and that the council consists entirely of New Oraibi residents. [Otto was a leading resident of Kikötcmovi. Although he was a Christian and had been educated at a seminary, he was jailed around 1938 for statutory rape. After his release he moved to Parker, near Wickenburg, Arizona. Parker has irrigation and is a good spot for growing cotton. The settlement is said to be owned by the Mojave, but most of the farmers are Hopi and a few are Navaho. Otto was the only Third Mesa man at Parker and never returned to the reservation for ceremonies or other events. The other Hopi at Parker are chiefly from First Mesa. Otto died in the spring of 1964.]

On a return visit a government agent had told Otto and the Hopi that the government had agreed to separate the Navaho from the Hopi reservation, but had decided to cut the Hopi land by a third. Otto had protested, holding out for the whole reservation, independence from the Navaho, and a period of twenty-five years for all the Navaho to clear out. The agent promised to stir things up in Washington but made no definite commitments. It is thought that Mr. Collier, United States Commissioner of Indian Affairs, is coming to pay a personal visit to Oraibi.

When asked how the other villages were organized in this fight for Hopi rights, Coin replied that Second Mesa was in accord with Oraibi; but that Walpi, for reasons that he professed not to know, was in sympathy with the Navaho.

Just before the noon dance at Hotevilla I was accosted by a stranger who introduced himself as Ralph, and asked if I were Misch. He claimed to be a (ceremonial) son of the Oraibi chief and said that he was a Moenkopi man, living at Oraibi because he had quarreled with his wife over dancing as a *katcina*. Later he asked if I could get him a ride to Moenkopi and promised to show the way to my cousin and my friend, who were going to the Grand Canyon. When the chief was asked if he would care to go to the dance at Moenkopi, he jumped at the chance. After lunch, the travelers picked up Ralph and Tawaqwaptiwa, who were dining together.

Fri. Aug. 4. Visited Lorenzo Hubbell and his clerk, Fletcher Corrigan. [Fletcher left Hubbell's around 1935 and was killed in an automobile accident in 1954. He was buried beside his old friends, the Weatherills, who are well known throughout the Southwest.]

Allen and his wife left for Moenkopi, where there is to be a mixed *katcina* dance next Sunday and Monday.

During the afternoon Ned returned from his fields with his shirt spattered with blood. He explained that his loco horse had become unmanageable and had even reared up and tried to jump on him. Hence, he had brained it with his ax and had cut off its tail for making masks. He "sort of took pity on it," but felt that it was best to kill it.

Sat. Aug. 5. Ned called with a wagon for my equipment and helped me get established at 17½ Bakwa Avenue. He has rented me the large room which he generally uses for winter quarters. It is in the lower story of his house. [See Fig. 20, #16.] From it leads the "*katcina* home" in which Ned keeps his mask and sacred paraphernalia; there is another large room, usually used for storage, that he intends to make into his winter home during my stay. It was arranged that his wife Ruth would haul water for me and keep the place in repair; while his sister Ida would serve as cook and housekeeper. [As far as is known I am the only stranger to have spent a winter at Old Oraibi. There were no other "Whites" in the village while I was there, but today, especially in the summer, "White" visitors are not unknown.]

Sun. Aug. 6. Ned came down to Kikötcmovi to meet Miss Denison. He was dressed in a clean shirt, wore his best turquoise beads, and had on a fresh headband.

In the evening Ned and I had a long talk of a very general nature, including the matter of Oraibi relationships with Walpi. Ned repeated, in somewhat greater detail, a story similar to Lee's. [See p. 5.] Ned added that while the Third Mesa folk resented the intrusion of Navahos at their dances, as well as their habit of dropping in at mealtimes, the Walpi people didn't seem to mind such things. Moreover, he was of the opinion that the residents of Walpi were the first to adopt "White" folks.

Mon. Aug. 7. Ned went sheepherding. Just before he left, Grace, of the Bear-Piqöc clan at Chimopovy and wife of Martin, came in great excitement to ask Ned to catch a bull snake that had gotten into her corncrib. Ned showed no fear at all, catching the snake, holding it, and stroking it with saliva-wetted fingers, "just like the Snake dancers" [Fig. 4]. [Sometime later Ned revealed that he had once wanted to join the Snake society, but he never had.] All the women watched him fearfully, and he teased his wife by twirling the snake in her direction. He asked whether he ought to kill it, and I, knowing the native feeling toward snakes, replied in conventional Hopi fashion that it was up to him. He said that he "sort of took pity" on the snake, and was about to let it go when his mother (Hahai'i, of the Sun clan) appeared and told of an episode where a released snake had come back. She then urged Ned to kill the reptile. Again, he asked me what I thought, and I suggested that he ought to obey his mother. Without further hesitation Ned dashed the snake against a stone and killed it. He then took it to the west edge of the mesa (the Hopi believe that Maski, home of the dead, lies to the northwest) and dropped it into a deep crevice where buzzards could not get at it. [Hahai'i died early in 1938. Ned, who had loved his mother very much, thought that she was a witch because she had not made a greater effort to live.[7] In retrospect the sequence of Ned's covert thoughts seems to have run somewhat as follows: I love my mother very much. Her death has caused me great sorrow. One who brings sorrow on a relative is a witch. Therefore my mother was a witch.]

Tues. Aug. 8. Ned went sheepherding again. Allen and his wife returned late yesterday from Moenkopi. They have taken his wife's sister's daughter Marian to live with them. This little girl was the daughter of Allen's sister-in-law by her first husband, a Hotevilla young man whom she had married in a "White" ceremony while both were students at the Sherman Institute, an Indian school in Riverside, California. When her husband left her, Marian's mother secured a divorce and married Benjamin Waitiyauoma, Hotevilla's storekeeper and its richest inhabitant. Allen constantly refers to his own wife as Marian's mother. [Note the use of teknonomy and Crow terminology.] They are very kind and attentive to the little girl, the more so, I believe, since they lost their own first baby soon after its birth last year.

This morning Ida said that the real reason Allen and Moe had moved away from their mother was that she was always harping on their laziness.[8] Neither one will farm for her and she actually has to do her own farming, although she has a childless married son, Allen; a divorced adult son, Moe; and an unmarried son of seventeen, Francis. [Francis is now married to a woman at Laguna, where he lives. It is regarded as a disgrace for sons to neglect a widowed mother.]

[In 1933 Allen did very little work and even refused an opportunity to join a road-building crew, but his brother Moe, who was then living with him, did join, together with Baldwin, Ruth's brother, and Jim and Otto from Kikötcmovi. Road workers were usually employed for six months, at forty dollars a month, and they had to furnish their own food.

The mother, Edna, died suddenly at her home in Oraibi over a decade ago. Allen was summoned from Hotevilla, where he was then living, in order to bury her.]

It is true that Edna had led a dissolute life, but she is quite old and the village is sorry to see her so neglected. It is Edna who has quarreled with all her relatives, and who insists that she belongs to the Yellow Fox clan. Other Hopi do not regard Yellow Fox as a separate and distinct clan. To them the Yellow Fox is no more than one of several *wuyas* ("ancients") of the Coyote clan. Thus, everyone at Oraibi, with the exception of Edna and her children, claims that she belongs to the Coyote clan.

[Many years later it dawned on me that such quarrels may help to explain how some "new" clans came into being. Pearl Beaglehole cites the case of a Sun's Forehead woman on Second Mesa who, after a quarrel, called herself Reed, though Reed was not even a *wuya* either of her clan or phratry.][9]

Chief Tawaqwaptiwa returned from Moenkopi late in the afternoon. I promptly called on him and presented gifts. At the time he seemed quite cordial. But as soon as Ned got back he came to my house and, with Ned for an interpreter, he began to question me about my dealings with Ralph. From his manner I knew that something serious had gone wrong, so I replied very guardedly. Finally, it developed that Ralph was somewhat demented and that one of his ancestors, in a fit of insanity, had once tried to kill the chief. Since then Tawaqwaptiwa believes that all insane people are out to kill him. All madness is invariably attributed to the malevolence of *poakas* ("witches"),[10] and the chief somehow associates witchcraft with his enemies at New Oraibi.

It developed, further, that soon after their arrival at Moenkopi, following the ride that I had arranged for them, the chief and Ralph had gone into the kiva where the dancers were rehearsing. Here Ralph began to make himself obnoxious, arguing with the *katcinas* and telling them that they had mistreated him, possibly by denying him the right of participation. In the end Ralph had declared that his "White" friends—including me—had agreed and sided with him. Luckily, the chief had enough confidence in us to stand up and announce that Ralph was crazy and that we had never taken sides against the *katcinas.*

Apparently, Ralph had continued to make trouble during the next two days, quarreling bitterly with the chief over his manner of handling the *katcinas.* It so happened that there was a recently confined woman at Moenkopi and the *katcina* dancers had decided to bring her happiness by leaving the plaza and performing within her sight near her house. To this plan Ralph had objected strenuously, telling the chief that he had no business to let the *katcinas* leave the plaza. The chief replied that it was he who owned the *katcinas* and that he would not allow Ralph to interfere with his management.[11]

At last, when the final dance of the two days was over and the father of the *katcinas* was about to lead the performers to their shrine, Ralph again stood forth and shouted that he wanted to speak to the *katcinas.* Before he could go further the chief ordered the father to continue leading the dancers out of the plaza as he had begun to do. When this was done, the chief denounced Ralph, forbidding him ever again to meddle in *katcina* affairs and accusing him of being in league with the people of New Oraibi. "You want to kill me, just as they do," Tawaqwaptiwa claims to have said, "but you're not man enough to do it." [The chief's purported defiance of an opponent allegedly bent on killing him is a stock device in many Hopi narratives. It should not be given too much weight.]

The next day, badly disturbed and sick at heart, the chief had returned to Oraibi. Ralph did not accompany him, and the chief knew nothing of his whereabouts.

At the end of this long recital I made it plain to Tawaqwaptiwa that I had arranged a ride for Ralph only because he had claimed to be the chief's son. I pointed out that I had allowed my friends to spend money for gasoline only because I thought that Ralph was related to the chief, and I argued that I would not otherwise have taken so much trouble for a stranger. I also said that I had assumed the chief was Ralph's friend because I had seen them dining together at the chief's house. To all of this Tawaqwaptiwa made no objection, but he violently resented Ralph's having claimed to be his son. The chief admitted that through a ceremonial clan relationship Ralph was his "son," but he insisted that Ralph had had no right to give the impression that he was the chief's child. This brought the episode to an end, and I was warned to have nothing further to do with Ralph because he was crazy and bewitched. [In later years, Ralph was said to have "reformed," and is now regarded as such a good fellow that he is even allowed to dance as a *katcina*. He remarried but separated from his wife, and now lives alone at Moenkopi, where he farms on irrigated land. When he visits Old Oraibi he stays at the home of Louis.]

Wed. Aug. 9. Ned went to visit a Navaho friend (Nestcili) in order to get a replacement for his dead horse. In the forenoon the chief dropped in for a smoke, during which I questioned him about a man named Bill, who lives across the way. Tawaqwaptiwa was just expressing antagonism when Allen came in. Immediately, the chief changed the subject by telling Allen the whole story of Ralph's actions at Moenkopi. After the chief's departure Allen said that Ralph was crazy and bewitched. This turned our conversation to matters of insanity and witchcraft, and Allen spoke of one of his own uncles who had gone insane and had committed suicide by jumping off a mesa—a story that

Lee had told last year. I professed great interest and arranged to interview Allen on the dangerous topic of witches.

In the evening Bill called. His married sister Mary with whom he lives has proved very friendly and often sends little dainties to me—a courtesy which I endeavor to return.

Ordinarily, when anything is left over after a meal, Ida gives it to someone. Unless otherwise directed she always brings such items to her brother and sister-in-law, Ned and Ruth.

Thurs. Aug. 10. Dropped in on the chief and found Edna dining at his house.

Ned got back in the afternoon and after telling about his trip to the Navaho, he made out a list of Oraibi men who would give me data on their daily activities.[12] Also arranged to tour the entire pueblo with Ned, who promised to tell all about the people who had lived in each house before the Split of 1906.

I asked Ned to take supper with me after he had hobbled his horses. He appeared with his adopted son, George, and announced that George wanted to take his place. [See Fig. 5.] [During World War II George was killed in action in Luxembourg. His uterine mother, who had paid no attention to him, claimed the insurance money, but the government rightly awarded it to the adoptive parents.]

As we were to have chile con carne and sauerkraut I suggested that George come to breakfast the next day, when food more suitable for a young child would be served. When Ned translated this to him, George burst into loud and copious weeping. Instead of protesting, Ned took the child in his arms and tried to soothe him while George bawled and yelled. Of course, I soon offered George Ned's place at the table, and in due time he condescended to sit down and eat, while Ned dined at home. Ida, George's aunt, stood by in silence during the fuss, and his adoptive mother, Ruth, made only one or two gentle remarks to which George barked replies. Thereupon Ruth quietly withdrew. Ned subsequently explained that while he had been angry at George's behavior and would have liked to spank him, he preferred to control his own anger and not to show loss of temper before me.

After supper Tom came in and spoke of his troubles with Pawikya, from New Oraibi, about which Pawikya himself had once told me. It appears that Pawikya had built the store at Kikötcmovi which Tom and his brothers ran. He had also loaned them money, and these transactions ultimately led to a great deal of quarreling and enmity. [After the death of his brothers Tom gave up the store and devoted himself to farming and trading with other tribes. In 1955 he claimed that work out-of-doors made him feel better than ever and that under no conditions would he again work in a store. However, in 1963 Tom became so seriously ill that he had to leave his wife and family at Oraibi while he went elsewhere to live with a medicine man. Within a year he seemed to have been cured and returned home. Unfortunately, he died a few months later.]

During the evening I remarked on the beauty of the moon, and Tom said that he called it his uncle because of a ceremonial relationship. Checking revealed that Tom was a ceremonial child of the Sun clan, one of whose *wuyas* ("ancients") is the moon.

Fri. Aug. 11. Toured all of Old Oraibi with Ned, including the ruined area, and got much information about the former inhabitants of the pueblo. After lunch I interviewed Ned regarding George's initiation into Powamu.

Called on Bert Fredericks and got many expressions of antagonism toward the people of New Oraibi and toward those residents of Old Oraibi who were neglecting or profaning the old ceremonies. Bert claims to have quarreled with the chief, his brother, for having taken part in a masked *katcina* dance at the Grand Canyon at Fred Harvey's request. Bert also complained that the *katcinas* were presently unable to bring rain because their rites had been profaned. He also spoke slightingly of the inadequacies of Hopi "doctors" when compared to the wonders achieved by medicine men from the Rio Grande and the Eastern pueblos. He praised their magical performances and commended them for guarding their secrets from the "Whites." Bert takes a fatalistic view of the ancient myth that deals with Old Oraibi's destiny, and he regards the Split that led to the founding of Hotevilla as the first warning that Oraibi is fated to crumble away. [Bert Fredericks, a bachelor, is the brother of Chief Tawaqwaptiwa. While the chief was being forced to attend the Sherman Institute in Riverside, California [Fig. 6], from September of 1906 to 1910, Bert secretly carried out Tawaqwaptiwa's wishes at Oraibi.

When "Uncle Joe" Lomahongyoma [Fig. 7] led a splinter group back to Oraibi from Hotevilla in 1907, Bert, with the help of the Kwan society, drove them out of Oraibi for the second time, in October, 1907. This event led directly to the founding of Bakavi.

For a time, in the 1930s, Bert served at Oraibi as a silversmith and storekeeper. He used to live with Grace and Martin. Soon after 1934 he moved to Santo Domingo pueblo in New Mexico, where he resided for a few years. Later, he lived in Winslow and Flagstaff, supporting himself by silversmithing until his eyesight failed. Bert only rarely visits Oraibi.]

Sat. Aug. 12. Watched Betty making *piki* this morning, and interviewed Allen on witchcraft and insanity. Got an interesting sidelight. Allen thinks he caught the chief red-handed as an accomplice of Ralph in preventing rain. The chief had admitted that he knew Ralph to be insane yet, says Allen, he accompanied him to Moenkopi. Allen claims that rain clouds gather over the village but are blown away because the chief is indifferent to rain. He backs this up with the statement that the chief does not farm. [The chief made his living, primarily, by selling *katcina* dolls.] According to Allen, other Hopi chiefs on First and Second Mesas do farm. He is suspicious of Tawaqwaptiwa and feels that he is two-hearted.[13]

Allen also verified much of Moe's story about the death of their sister Gladys, as a protest against Edna's behavior, but Allen claims that boys as well as girls can die at will. Allen's word for such willful dying is *qövisyuta;* and his word for madness (angriness) is *itsivúyuta.* [Even contemporary Hopi believe that girls are "meaner" than boys, and give more trouble to their parents. However, both sexes are supposed to be capable of willful suicide (*qövisti*). Ned regards his near-death in an unstable sandpit [*Sun Chief,* p. 93] as a case of an attempt at such a suicide.]

Miss Denison came to supper and brought Lee along from New Oraibi. Lee wanted to order a bracelet for a friend. She was very much embarrassed while at Old Oraibi and refused to eat with us. When I casually told Ned next day about Lee's uneasiness, he remarked pointedly that *he* didn't feel ashamed when he went to New Oraibi.

In the evening Baldwin came in for tea and a smoke. When he left, he said that he slept on top of the Marau kiva. I walked with him, curious to see his sleeping arrangements. When my light revealed a sleeping form already there, I switched it off, thinking that since Baldwin is unmarried, it was his mistress.

(Later—I was wrong. It was not a woman.) [Not long after 1933 Baldwin married at Hotevilla. He switched his residence from Hotevilla back and forth to Lololoma's Spring, following the dictates of his sheepherding. Some years later he left the reservation for Phoenix where, for a time, he worked as a policeman.]

Dennis, a Masau'û clansman, Ruth's mother's sister's son, and a resident of Hotevilla, finds it convenient to sleep at Oraibi after herding sheep. He spends the night at Ruth's house and departs after breakfast. He feels free to follow this arrangement whenever he desires. [In the last few years Dennis, now a widower, has been living permanently with Ned and Ruth. Although his eyesight has been failing, he does odd jobs and helps Ned with his farming.]

Sun. Aug. 13. Worked with Ned on the household census of Oraibi as it was around 1906. In the afternoon I drove to Walpi to purchase pottery materials for the Laboratory of Anthropology. Miss Denison, Lee, and Charlotte, her sister's daughter, came along. En route we saw the Mishongnovi Snake society men off in the distance, hunting snakes. Lee, Christian though she is, hid in fear lest the Snake men see her and induct her as a trespasser into the Snake society.[14]

A Walpi potter, related to Lee, brought out her implements and was explaining their use when a village elder went by and ordered her to tell no secrets to "Whites," lest they begin to make "Hopi" pottery as they had already begun to manufacture *katcina* dolls. She obeyed reluctantly. At Oraibi, too, there is resentment whenever a Hopi deals with "Whites," and Bert berated the chief for having given us information for money.

Returning to Lee's house we found Ned waiting. He told me that people had been trying, in a nice way, to convert him to Christianity.

On the following day Ned teased his sister Ida about conversion; and I joined the fun by announcing that Ida was about to change her faith. Then Ned said, "No. She can't become a Christian. Only good people are wanted as Christians, and I know her heart. It's no good." To this Ida retorted, "I'm better than you are. My heart is much better than yours." [Brothers and sisters are expected to tease each other.]

Today Ned and Ruth entertained another distant relative. He is Lemuel Siyesva of Hotevilla, whose ceremonial father and his own wife are in Ruth's phratry. He had been chasing horses in the direction of Oraibi and had found it convenient to spend the night with Ned and Ruth. He left for home after breakfast. [Lemuel Siyesva was married at the time to Daisy Kyackwapnim, who subsequently divorced him and remarried. Lemuel had a partially crippled leg and thought it best not to marry again.]

Ned's old father, Duvenimptiwa, returned last night from three days of work on his farm. Nevertheless, he took his regular turn at herding sheep today, although it was very hot.

Mon. Aug. 14. Some tea was left over from breakfast this morning. Ida was unable to find Ned and Ruth, so she gave it to Sikyaletsnim, her older sister's mother-in-law.

Ned's older brother Sidney told him that he had better finish hoeing his corn, so Ned left to spend two or three days at his farm. He plans to return for the Mishongnovi Snake dance on the sixteenth. Ned said that he would rather see the Mishongnovi dance than the one at Walpi because the Walpi plaza is so narrow and gets overcrowded with tourists. [Compare p. 19.]

Ida reports that Baldwin and his father, Humingkwai'ima, were members of the Snake society and used to perform at Oraibi in the old days.

Interviewed Allen and Kane. The latter revealed that he had just sent fried bread and dried meat to Vera, his wife's sister's daughter, who had written from Riverside that she craved "Indian eats." Vera was being brought up by Kane and his wife, Jessie, Tom's sister, since her own mother had died.

Tues. Aug. 15. Kane remarked that "White" men often called the Indians lazy because they did not cultivate more ground. Then he pointed out how futile this was under local conditions. Lack of rain and suitable soil made large crops next to impossible, and there was no sense in growing more than could be eaten before it rotted. He told of planting and diligently tending a big field of beans, only to have it fail completely for lack of water. He spoke feelingly of the potentialities of irrigation.

Called on the chief and found that Ralph had returned last night. The chief had questioned him carefully, and when he found that he answered rationally, he allowed him to resume living at Oraibi.

A little Oraibi girl, daughter of Cedric and Juanita, came in with a rabbit given her by a Hotevilla man to whom she is *ikya'a*. [This term is widely used by the Hopi for all of a father's clanswomen, regardless of age. It does not apply specifically, as was once wrongly believed, to the father's sister.

Males are expected to give rabbits and natural salt, particularly, to their fathers' clanswomen. There is a bond of affectionate intimacy between an *ikya'a* and any son born to one of her clansmen (*imûyi*). A boy's *ikya'as* are required to resent his sweethearts. During his marriage they make a show of "hating" and "castigating" his bride.]¹⁵

After lunch, Cedric came in to report on his daily activities and to say that he is making a saddle blanket for Willie Coin of New Oraibi, in exchange for a bracelet. I had a chance to observe him at work and found him to be a skillful weaver. Cedric also engaged in conversation with a young boy named Lawrence, whose mother, Grace, had previously lived with her Sun clan husband at Second Mesa. She had later divorced this man and had come to live at Oraibi with Martin, her second husband. (To my knowledge Grace was three times married and violated the rule of matrilocal residence on each occasion.)

Cedric listed the six kivas that stage Bean dances at Hotevilla. Only three—Tawaovi, Powamu, and Marau—are active at Oraibi. [Following the death of his wife, Juanita, around 1935, Cedric held odd jobs as a builder of houses. He then moved to Moenkopi where he remarried and works as a stone mason.]

Wed. Aug. 16. Left at four in the morning to see the race prior to the Snake dance at Mishongnovi. [Footraces are held on the mornings preceding the public performances of the Flute and Snake-Antelope societies. Formerly, these races started from the plain as soon as shouting was heard from the mesa top. Spectators were expected to raise a cry at the moment the sun appeared on the horizon. Races now begin later in the morning, and some runners go by truck to the starting point.]¹⁶ Noticed one thing not seen last year. One Antelope and two Snake men drew a cornmeal line to the east; prayed to their fetishes; and, according to Ida, invited one and all to see the Snake dance that afternoon. The Antelope man spoke first and led the way back to the pueblo. Auditors replied, "So be it," and "Thank you."

The dance itself was rather dismal. Only three men actually danced with about fifteen snakes in all, and there was a heavy sandstorm throughout the ceremony. Participants wore turtle shell rattles about the right calf, snakes were gathered unceremoniously, and many women sprinkled cornmeal.¹⁷

Thurs. Aug. 17. Called on Tawaqwaptiwa this morning and discovered that he had "nine times eat" at yesterday's dance. Also, the Shipaulovi chief had invited him and several others to hold a talk about their lives and the lack of rain. [See O.O., pp. 251–52.]

There was to be a meeting of the council at New Oraibi. [On Third Mesa neither Old Oraibi nor Hotevilla, nor Lower Moenkopi on the plain, has a council, and these pueblos refuse to be bound by any decision of any council. New Oraibi, Bakavi, and Upper Moenkopi have councils. These are not traditional bodies, but were set up by the American government, beginning in the mid-1930s. Not all residents of the villages where they exist belong to them.

Lately, Ned and Martin have joined the council at New Oraibi. This has aroused the displeasure of their fellow villagers at Old Oraibi.]

It is said that the council was to hear a divorce action concerning Lily of New Oraibi, a clan sister to Mary, and her Moenkopi husband. The corespondent in this case is rumored to be Homer.

Fri. Aug. 18. Today the criers at New and Old Oraibi called out that work on the roads would be suspended until around the first of September. This means that Otto will have more time at home in Kikötcmovi, and I hope to interview him.

Cedric and Martin seem to be great buddies. Martin's nephew Sam is exceptionally fond of Cedric and accompanies him everywhere. [In due time Sam grew to manhood, married a Moenkopi girl, and moved to California. They have several children who are full-blooded Hopi but who cannot speak the language. Sam seldom visits Oraibi, but generally stays with his sister Margaret, or with her daughter, when he does come to the pueblo.]

Allen borrowed a horse from Cedric in order to chase one of his own. Later, Moe asked Allen to fetch some wood in his old Ford, but Allen made every sort of excuse to get out of the work. Moe had to drop his road job in order to bring the needed wood. This, despite the fact that Allen had once admitted that were it not for Moe he would have no money for buying such things as sugar or coffee.

Kane reported on his daily work, and we had a long talk. He speaks intelligently and seems to know what he is doing. [Ned, in company with other Oraibi people, regards Kane as well educated, but he has gone only through the fourth grade at school.] Kane hopes to get some choice land at a distance, but he does not want to sever his ties with Oraibi. He plans to increase his herd of sheep rather than devote himself to farming, which he regards as too precarious. His great ambition is to own a large flock, a ranch, and an automobile. [In 1955, Kane was reputed to be very wealthy, with much livestock and two cars. He was working as a carpenter at Piñon but was living in Oraibi. When the sheep-reduction program started, he began to accumulate cattle. Kane is one of the few Hopi to belong to a union (carpenters').]

Kane is very contemptuous of the Navaho for their lack of thrift. He resents the lavish manner in which they share food and other goods with friends and relatives, only to face want and starvation later on. He feels that a man should save his food for the use of his immediate family.

Kane tells of an incident that took place in his youth concerning some Hopi who had built a small settlement at a distance from Oraibi, only to be attacked and driven back by the Navaho. Kane says that in the event of an attack he would prefer to report the case to government officials rather than fight back.

Toward evening Mr. Sutton and another "White" friend of Ned's arrived and distributed costly presents freely.Their coming disrupted my program for the next day.

Sat. Aug. 19. Nothing much accomplished.

Sun. Aug. 20. Went to arrange an interview with Otto at New Oraibi, and found Edna dining there. Saw the Antelope dance at Walpi. Sutton hinted of an old affair between Tawaqwaptiwa and a woman from Moenkopi and spoke of a former prevalence of prostitution.

Mon. Aug. 21. Drove to the Snake dance at Walpi with several Oraibi people, including the chief, Frank Siemptiwa, who is Tawaqwaptiwa's lieutenant and Village chief of Moenkopi [Fig. 8]. At the suggestion of Dr. Jesse Nusbaum, head of the Laboratory of Anthropology, I sought out Dr. Breasted, the famed Egyptologist, and told him what I could about the full Snake society ritual. The dance itself was very disappointing. Spectators overflowed into the tiny plaza and interfered with the dancers, making the entire performance appear badly disorganized. Could see very little, learned nothing new, and decided it was not worth attending again. Tawaqwaptiwa said that there was a new Snake chief this year. He wore a cottonwood wreath about his forehead whereas the other dancers had armbands of cottonwood. The only difference of procedure that I noted was that the "huggers" who danced behind the carriers of snakes constantly brushed with their Snake whips the heads of the reptiles which their partners were carrying. (At other villages the "huggers" brush the backs of the carriers in time to the rhythm of the dance.)

Tues. Aug. 22. Butterfly dance at Walpi. Took most of the same crowd, plus Mary and two of her children. Her oldest daughter, Evelyn, aged about eight, stayed home cheerfully in order to prepare lunch for her *itaha* ("uncle" or "mother's brother"), who is Bill. All of Mary's children are fond of Bill. Frank planned to spend the night at Walpi. So did Ruth who has several real sisters there, with one of whom I had lunch.

The Butterfly dance was very pretty, but many native spectators made unfavorable comments because some of the male performers wore everyday store clothes. Ned didn't care to go as he doesn't feel very friendly to Walpi. Although the chief attended, he had only a single friend at Walpi, and I discovered that he went hungry during the dance. Despite these drawbacks and antagonistic attitudes, a large crowd of Oraibi and Moenkopi people was present. The dance was performed in the Sitcumovi plaza, and there was no "father," no sprinkling with sacred corn-meal, and no official kiva center.

Ned surprised me by offering for sale at one dollar the bow and arrows that George had received from his ceremonial father at the time of his Powamu initiation. To a comment that we didn't like to sell such things, Ned replied that the Hopi didn't feel sentimental about them, and he gladly sold the whole outfit, including the attached prayer feathers, because George was always pestering him for money.

Mr. Sutton had brought with him pictures of a young woman who had died since his last visit. He gave two copies to her mother but she returned them next day, sobbing out that although she liked them, they had reminded her so forcibly of her deceased daughter that she had been unable to sleep. [Grief is said to make one more susceptible to attack by witches.]

Ida says that Edna is her ceremonial mother, but that she finds the old lady to be so mean that she refuses to have anything to do with her or to call her "mother."[18] It seems that Edna's daughter Gladys had married Perry, a brother of Ned and Ida. Both young people had died soon after the birth of a baby daughter, whom Edna was said to have maltreated until the child's death. Ned, whose own children had died all in infancy, had asked to have the child but had been refused; and he was heartbroken when she died. Ida remarks caustically that Edna didn't even cry when her own daughter had died. Edna's love affairs are a standing joke in the village. One reason Allen is so angry at the chief may be that he occasionally feeds Edna. Possibly, the chief had once been her lover. [Edna was the woman whose own sons had refused to farm for her, p. 9.]

Ned complained of a buzzing and pain in his left ear.

Ned's older brother arranged to castrate some of their sheep to prevent them from breeding. Ned and Sidney are trying to improve the quality of their flock.

Jack met us at the Walpi dance. He had been looking for a man with whom he plans to go on a trading expedition to the Grand Canyon. [In 1953 and 1955 Jack was doing a great deal of trading outside Oraibi, with Tom as his partner. He did much less as he grew older.] Francis, Edna's youngest son, herded for Jack during his absence.

Wed. Aug. 23. Ned spoke of dreaming that his *dumalaitaka* ("spirit guide")[19] had told him that someone had sent the earache because of his friendliness to "Whites" and that he had advised him to seek the services of a medicine man. If he did this and continued straight ahead on the Hopi path of life, his pain would go away.

Visited the chief in the afternoon and learned that the large First Mesa village had once been known as "the seven Walpi folk," because that was the number of its earliest inhabitants. Later, so he said, Navahos began to mix with these people. He verified the story of Walpi men in disguise accompanying Navahos when they raided Oraibi.

The chief doesn't like Bill, primarily because he lets his cattle eat crops and then refuses to pay for the damage. The same holds for Albert, the policeman from Hotevilla, and Lorenzo Hubbell, even though Hubbell had made restitution and on the surface is considered to be a friend. The chief invited me to go with him to the Powamu at Chimopovy, which he claims is better than Oraibi's.

In the afternoon I drove Ned to Hotevilla to look for a medicine man. We passed one in whom Ned had no confidence, found another one out, and went on to the home of Polingyauoma in Bakavi. The old man served us with watermelon, chatted awhile, then had Ned sit on a chair with his back to me and his left side to the "doctor" who was facing me. The medicine man began by spitting on his fingers and massaging the affected ear with his left hand, occasionally blowing on his fingers or rewetting them with saliva. He kept this up for a few minutes while Ned continued to chat. Then he turned his back to me, blew into Ned's ear a few times, and resumed the massaging in lackadaisical fashion. After that he spoke to Ned and the treatment was over. Through it all his son continued to eat watermelon while his son's wife tended their small baby. There was no attempt at secrecy. Ned paid the "doctor" twenty-five cents, which he had taken along ostensibly for the purchase of chili peppers. [Polingyauoma, now dead, used to live primarily as a farmer, and only secondarily as a medicine man.]

On the way home Ned said that he was related to the "doctor," and asked if I had seen the medicine man "remove that bad thing." I said that I had, although I had not noticed that he had removed anything. Ned said it hurt a little when "that bad thing" came out, but that the ear felt better after the treatment. He then told me that he had received instructions for applying medicine, but as I had an appointment with Otto that night, I did not see the preparation of the medicine.

Ned recalled that Polingyauoma and two companions were once driving some loaded burros when lightning killed one of the animals and stunned the men. Ned said that they had really died and that on coming back to life they found themselves full of the power of the lightning. In a dream the Cloud People came to the "doctor" and told him to become a medicine man. This he did, but one of the other men refused and was accordingly afflicted with blindness.

Thurs. Aug. 24. This morning Ned remarked without anger that George had stolen a package of cigarettes from him and had sold it to older boys.

Yesterday, George spent some of his money to buy gifts for which the women chased him. This is the only survival I have so far noted of the four-day scramble for good things, *ñötiwa*, which is supposed to follow each Snake-Antelope and Flute dance. [When running *ñötiwa* men or boys would hold good things aloft and dodge about while females chased them and tried to snatch their presents. A spirit of good-natured fun always prevailed throughout the event. At the present time, no one runs *ñötiwa* at Oraibi, and the custom has elsewhere become, for the most part, a desultory, childish pastime.

It may be that running *ñötiwa* always had a covert sexual connotation, even though it was overtly regarded as an innocent sport. In some villages of today, however, it has become an open prelude to sexual indulgence. In such cases, girls who are prepared to grant their favors chase desirous boys and try to snatch money from their hands.]

Ida said that an Oraibi woman had given birth to a baby at Walpi during the Butterfly dance last Tuesday. She was very eager to get home, so yesterday she and the baby were driven back to Oraibi. [The mother proved to be Louise, and I later named the child Ann.] [In 1955 Louise was reported to have had an affair as a result of which her husband, on the advice of Jack, his older brother, left her.]

Ida made a dress for her *ikya'a*, Kane's mother, Kuwanmönim. There is no question of payment in such cases.

Ida calls Ned lazy because he won't rebuild his house as Kane is doing. Ned's is an old Masau'ü clan house that belonged to Sidney's first wife. After her death Sidney had married a New Oraibi woman, whereupon Ned and Ruth had moved into the house.

An old uncle of Ruth came to visit her, and a Hotevilla boy came to play with Sam.

The chief claims that neither Baldwin nor his father is interested in ceremonies, although Baldwin sometimes participates in *katcina* dances. The chief considers this rather crazy and expects the family to move to New Oraibi in the near future. [See p. 15.]

Frank Siemptiwa came in for a long chat. He said that about ten years ago he had been taken to New Zealand and Australia with a troupe of Hopi dancers. He had brought back about $1,500 and had spent about $800 on a truck for one of his sons, Ray Siemptiwa, at New Oraibi. This son's wife had committed suicide by taking strychnine, but Frank claimed to know no further details. [At present Ray lives and works in Flagstaff. Frank said that he himself had had three children by his first wife, Kikötcmana, who ran around too much and had had a bastard, but that she was otherwise all right. He divorced her and remarried. He pointed out that he didn't get angry and that he didn't worry or quarrel because this was no good and made a person ill.] In fact, Frank said that Ned got sick so often because he got angry too quickly and worried too much.

The chief calls Frank his Corn and Water Chief. [These are *wuyas* ("ancients") of Frank's clan.]

Later in the day Tawaqwaptiwa agreed to run *ñötiwa* with Ned and me. I purchased food and candy for all from Bert, and the three of us took turns running about while the women chased us and tried to snatch the dainties. I was surprised at the number of women who took part. A great deal of good spirit was aroused, everyone talked about the fun, and that evening I was showered with presents. Before dark Bill also ran *ñötiwa*.

Fri. Aug. 25. An old uncle of Ruth's came to visit her from New Oraibi. At noon Ruth invited her sister Clara's daughter Edith to eat with her, while Clara dined with Ruth's mother-in-law, Hahai'i. The latter are related in some way.

Ida and Ruth do not like Frank because they accuse him of watching women too closely, an expression of sexual interest, and because they say he is a storyteller (bearer of tales).

Allen has again discussed two-heartedness with the chief. He brought up an old belief that it would always rain if a village chief really wanted it to. Hence, Allen blames the lack of rain directly on the chief. He went so far as to say that the chief had had no comeback and that Tawaqwaptiwa had told him to hush up when he claimed to be sure that he was single-hearted. The chief insisted that he knew how to recognize a person's heart, but that Allen didn't.[20] This, Allen interprets as an attempt to cover up on the chief's part.

While I was talking to Allen, the topic of prostitution came up; and I explained that a prostitute was a woman who would accept any man for money. "Are you sure?" asked Allen with a queer grin. It turned out that while traveling with Billingsley's show, he and several other Indian men had been refused in bawdy houses on at least two occasions. At other times they had been accepted.

Sat. Aug. 26. Early in the morning Frank, though a visitor, did some work for Tom in his fields. (Tom is married to a Pikyas clanswoman of Frank and so works on her land.)

While Ned and I were working on the census of Oraibi, Lily Hamana, a Greasewood clanswoman, saw us and raised a fuss. It seems that Ned has several times had trouble because of his friendship with "Whites." He said that what he did was none of Lily's business and that the entire matter was up to the chief.

For the last two mornings I have been sending cereal to Louise, who was recently confined. Today her mother, Sikyaletsnim, came to thank me and brought a half-dozen ears of corn.

At noon Ned's "doctor," Polingyauoma, came over from Bakavi. He had lunch with Ned and then gave him another massagelike treatment. He also worked on Ruth who was suffering from toothache. I withdrew when I felt that my presence was interfering with the proceedings.

A little girl and her baby halfsister joined Ned, Ruth, and Polingyauoma at lunch. While Ruth was doing the dishes later, she wiped the baby's nose with her dishcloth and continued cleaning up.

In the afternoon Ned suggested that we visit the chief regarding my adoption into the tribe and then into the Sun clan. Tawaqwaptiwa not only agreed, but offered to do his part before sunrise tomorrow.

Hahai'i teases her daughter Ida and calls her no good because she is unmarried. Ned, too, is eager to have his sister wed because it would lighten his work load by bringing another man into the family. [When Ida finally married, it was to a Chimopovy man. They went to the Grand Canyon to live and work. This, coupled with the deaths of George and Ned's father, left Ned with a heavy burden in later life.]

Margaret (Parrot), the chief's adopted daughter, teased him about his well-developed breasts and said that her son Edward liked to play with them and to pretend that he wanted the chief to suckle him.

Sun. Aug. 27. Just before sunrise Ned brought me to Tawaqwaptiwa's house for adoption. The chief and his wife were still asleep outside their home, wrapped in one blanket. Sam was sleeping beside them, while Margaret slept indoors with her baby and two other small children. The chief got up, dressed, washed, and prepared a bowl of yucca suds. He shampooed my head, smeared cornmeal all over my face, gave me a full ear of corn as a "mother," and named me Honautiyo ("Bear Youth," as I was then single, hence not a man—*taka*). Ned then took me to his mother's house, where Hahai'i held my corn "mother" for awhile and then returned it. This made me a member of the Sun clan whose head woman was Hahai'i. Neither rite of adoption attracted much attention.

Ida told more about Bert's quarrel with Tawaqwaptiwa, his brother. She said that most people thought that the chief and his wife were mean. After their break Bert began to take his meals with his niece Grace, who was married to Martin. The chief is angry at this arrangement, but Grace and Martin continue to feed Bert, who pays nothing although he does contribute some food from his store.

It begins to appear as though Otto is not entirely wrong in his assessment of Tawaqwaptiwa's character. If, as Otto says, Lololoma [Oraibi's former chief] wanted to hasten Oraibi's split, he picked a suitable successor.[21] Apart from Ned and some of his own relatives, Tawaqwaptiwa does not seem to have a genuine follower, even among the residents of Old Oraibi. Of course, as he himself says, he can feel the walls closing in on him, so he is always suspicious and on the defensive. The chief feels, as Oraibi legends imply, that the cards are stacked against him and that he is waging a losing fight against Fate. What his character and behavior might have been under happier circumstances, it is hard to say.

More on the quarrel with Bert. Apparently, Bert often scolded Margaret's children. The chief objected and pointed out that Bert never scolded Martin's children. This is said to have caused ill feeling and to have led to a rupture between the brothers.

Went to the Flute dance at Hotevilla in Bert's car. (The chief once said that long ago he had had himself initiated into the Flute society.)

At Hotevilla I accompanied Ned, Ruth, and George to the home of one of Ruth's clan sisters, where we were well received and fed. Our hostess wore an old-fashioned Hopi dress which exposed her left shoulder and breast, but she was unconcerned. Baldwin also came here to eat.

There was a race for women in the afternoon during which a contestant fainted. [Races for women are things of the past at Hotevilla.] She was treated by a medicine man and was then carried home on the back of an *itaha* ("maternal uncle").

After a time Ned decided to visit Kiacwaitiwa, the Hotevilla medicine man who had treated the fainting racer. (Ned had been looking for him [see p. 21] before going on to be treated by Polingyauoma.) Kiacwaitiwa [now dead] is married to a Sun clanswoman who is Hahai'i's sister. [Kiacwaitiwa and Huminkwai'ima, father of Ned's wife, were the sons of two sisters.] After eating here, Ned and I went into another room where Kiacwaitiwa began to treat Ned with the customary manipulations. I then saw him rolling something in his fingers, after which he "extracted" it from Ned's ear. Ned was highly elated and motioned me to watch how skillfully "the bad stuff" had been removed without cutting the flesh. Kiacwaitiwa showed the object to Ned, who said it was some kind of an insect that he couldn't identify.[22] The medicine man put it in the fire and fetched a handful of leaves that he told Ned to brew and apply to the sore ear. Kiacwaitiwa then recited a long account of his travels and cures, and Ned assured me that Hopi medicine men were better than "White" doctors because they never amputated and never cut a patient's flesh.

Afterwards we went outside, and I bought a few objects with which Ned and the chief ran *ñötiwa*.

Mon. Aug. 28. Went to visit Louise and agreed to attend her baby's naming rites and to call it after my mother.

Ned thinks (read knows) that Edna used to take men for pay. He suspects that she may yet be doing it as she has little visible means of support.

Ida gossiped about Bill today. She claims that he had had many girls in the village, but that his sister had objected to his marrying any one of them because it would deprive her of his help. Bill finally got angry and said that henceforth he would make *dumaiya* calls only on married women.[23] (Some of his sweethearts were actually named.) [Bill later became rich, but remained a bachelor. He lived with his mother and was far from well.] Ned says Bill is too miserly to marry, and Tom calls him a troublemaker and refuses to talk to him. This is noteworthy because Tom is fat, friendly, and jolly. Even Joe, his brother-in-law, has quarreled with Bill. Nevertheless, his income from cattle and his store is said to be so large that he must pay a goodly income tax.

Ned got angry with Ida for telling me some of these things. He said that "White" people didn't "like" to hear things of this nature and that we were not to be told of Hopi "troubles."

Ned butchered a sheep and carried it on foot to his "doctor" in Bakavi. [Oraibi men seldom go afoot nowadays, even if it is only between pueblos on the same mesa.

During a Corn *katcina* dance that I witnessed at Moenkopi on June 14, 1964, my companions claimed to have seen one of the dancers "give out." He is supposed to have been led away to rest and recover.

It may well be that the modern Hopi neither walk, run, nor climb as did their forefathers, and that some of them find *katcina* dancing too strenuous.

Again, in June of 1966, I was told that some participants had "given out" during an arduous *katcina* dance at Moenkopi.]

Tues. Aug. 29. Roadwork started up again this morning.

Frank Siemptiwa was setting out for Moenkopi and Tom gave him a dollar.

Mr. Suderman, the Mennonite missionary from New Oraibi, invited Ida to go to a picnic. Although her mother encouraged her to go, she was reluctant until Mr. Suderman called for her in his car. She was the only guest from Old Oraibi, but she had a good time with girls of her own age only a few of whom were Christians. The only religious touches were the saying of grace and the singing of a few hymns.

Ruth's mother, the daughter of Oraibi's late chief, Lololoma, joined Ruth and Ned at lunch. [Ruth's parents were Huminkwai'ima, of the Real Badger clan, and Nawisoa, of the Masau'û clan. Huminkwai'ima was burned to death at Lololoma's Spring, around 1953, and Nawisoa died in March of 1957.]

In the evening I again ran *ñötiwa* with the chief, Ned, and another man. Allen merely looked on until Emily, a clan sister from New Oraibi, gave him two dishes with which to run. I observed that Emily did not join this chase, although she was very active in pursuing other runners.

After supper, the chief, Ned, Tom, and Kane dropped in. Had another long and interesting talk with Kane, who said that he herds in partnership with his brother Louis and two New Oraibi men, Seba James and Valjean, who has the same mother as Ray Siemptiwa. When Edna's last husband died and his sons had taken practically his entire flock, Kane invited Allen to herd with his outfit. Allen refused on the grounds that he would have to do a disproportionate amount of work in tending a large flock of which he would own but a tiny part. Kane told Allen that he would be paid in lambs, but Allen still refused. Thereupon, Kane made the same offer to Valjean who broke an earlier partnership to accept.[24] [Valjean is married to Elta, a daughter of Tom and Anita, and now lives in Old Oraibi.]

Kane also launched into an interesting discussion of Hopi psychology. He contrasted the Navaho custom of banding together in all emergencies with the Hopi lack of solidarity. Every Hopi, he said, must look out for himself and can expect little help from nonrelatives. Hence, where the Navaho can present a united front in such matters as land rights, the Hopi fail to support each other's claims. This, it seems to me, is the basic factor in Hopi disintegration. The spirit of individuality is so strong that no overall unity can be achieved. At the same time, as Kane points out, no laws are considered binding by the Hopi, who are free to defy public opinion if they are daring enough. When this attitude is linked to the Hopi distaste for physical violence, one can see why old customs, rites, and even whole villages may readily fall apart. Otto, who deplores the New Oraibi council's lack of power, says that what the Hopi need is law and order. Kane puts it slightly differently. He supports the remark made on one occasion by a government official who had said that the Hopi needed water and a law.

Perhaps the lack of fight among the Hopi may also be attributed to their lack of unity. Organized warfare, of all things, requires discipline and united action. This is entirely contrary to the Hopi emphasis on individuality. Even in important matters, as when Johnson of New Oraibi is supposed to have burned sacred paraphernalia, as well as in such trivial cases as when George refused to pose with his parents until he was paid a nickel, no Hopi ever takes it on himself to speak for another. Ceremonial secrets are jealously guarded from the general public by each society; and even calendrically scheduled rituals are performed or not at the option of their owners and leaders. Even the chief of a pueblo cannot control his people, who can move away if they please. In other words, with rare exceptions, no Hopi has the right to interfere with any one else's activities.

George continues to act like a little beast. At mealtime he rushed into the house, shouted angrily at Ruth, struck her with his fists, beat a puppy viciously, tore through his food, and rushed out again without a word. Ned, Ruth, and her mother were present, but no one made any comment.

Noticed that Ruth's mother, who was holding Edith's baby—both are of the Masau'û clan—soothed it by stroking its vagina.[25]

Wed. Aug. 30. Tawaqwaptiwa came to breakfast and seemed to enjoy the meal immensely. Betty [see Fig. 9], of course, hung about the table although no one encouraged her to stay. The chief's wife went past and called Betty out. She subsequently spanked the child for pestering me. [The chief and his wife, who were childless, adopted Betty (Parrot), even though she was frail and mentally retarded. She was the granddaughter of the chief's wife's sister.]

Martin has again quarreled with his wife, Grace. Ruth had given some plates for running *ñötiwa* yesterday, and Grace had seized them. Martin expressed jealousy and anger and ordered her to return them, which she did tearfully. [Compare p. 22.] Everyone pities Grace, and Ida calls Martin crazy because chasing men in this fashion is innocent fun, long sanctioned by Hopi tradition. Grace threatens to return to a sister at Chimopovy if Martin continues to quarrel over every petty trifle. [Not until 1953–54, though, did Grace divorce Martin and return to Second Mesa.] Some think that Martin is given to adultery himself and that is why he is apt to be overly suspicious of his wife.

While Ned was picking corn he came across three rattle-snakes. They showed no signs of anger and did not rattle, so he judged them to be "pretty good" and did not kill them. He continued harvesting but, as a precaution, he made George climb into the wagon and stay there.

The chief came to supper and again had a good time. He entertained us with a sprightly story of how he had once been cutting a steak in Tucson when it slipped and upset several coffee cups. On another occasion, at the Grand Canyon, he had unthinkingly gathered all the silver near him in his right hand, while eating with his left. (Like all orthodox Hopi, the chief eats most of his food by hand. It was the use of tableware that put him in mind of these stories.)

Thurs. Aug. 31. Ned refused an offer to be foreman of a dam construction crew because he felt duty-bound to serve as my interpreter and informant.

Ida, supported by Ned, states that missionaries are active at all government schools for Indians.[26] Albuquerque students are said to accept Christianity more readily than pupils at Phoenix.

Ida says that her mother, who had spent the night at Hotevilla, had been told by Kiacwaitiwa that he liked me because I ate Hopi food in the real Hopi fashion. [On several occasions I noticed that this trait attracted more favorable attention than anything else.]

I have been told that the only Kikötcmovi men who take part in Old Oraibi rituals are Ned's brother Sidney; Tom's father; and, on occasion, Nick, Tom's brother-in-law. Not all the New Oraibi people are Christians, yet they want the chief to give up his Soyal ceremony. Joe, who came from Hotevilla to wed Mary, thereafter gave up attending rites at his home pueblo. Yet, Louise went from Oraibi to participate in a Butterfly dance at Hotevilla. Of course, this is not a serious ceremony. [Interpueblo participation in rituals occurs occasionally even at present. For example, in spite of Joe's attitude, he took part in a Hotevilla *katcina* dance on May 22, 1966.]

Ruth showed me a pretty pottery bowl which her younger

sister Barbara had made. Barbara is now married, after two divorces, and lives on First Mesa. [Barbara is the true mother of George, whom Ruth and Ned adopted. She is rather dissolute.

More pottery is made by First Mesa women than anywhere else in Hopiland.]

Iona, a good-looking girl from Moenkopi and clan sister of Ida, had been made pregnant by a Zuñi man. Iona had wanted to marry him, but her parents objected so strenuously that she fainted and died while Hotevilla was staging a Patcava. Her intentional death had made the neighbors very resentful of her parents.

In connection with the psychological timidity of the Hopi, I can hardly consider it accidental that their most common rebuke for misbehavior of any sort is *ka-Hopi* ("un-Hopi," literally "un-peaceful"). This applies to restless horses, mischievous dogs, noisy or quarrelsome children, adulterous husbands, and in countless other cases where improper conduct is involved. [It seems to imply that if you don't do things "right," you are not a Hopi.]

When Ned returned from herding, he announced that his father had been unable, because of a rainfall, to track down a rabbit trap that had been dragged away. He considered the trap valuable enough to lead him to forego other duties while he looked for it. The trap cost about seventy-five cents.

Am planning to go on an overnight, wood-hauling expedition with Ned.

CHAPTER III

Diary for September, 1933

[*September is unofficially known as "the harvest month." No rites are performed by men, but any of the three societies for women may be active and may give a maskless public dance. (Women never wear masks.) Butterfly dances are also common.*

Some houses are being renovated, and some women are re-plastering floors.

Harvesting begins, and groups of relatives or friends enjoy a long picnic in the fields while sweet corn is picked and baked overnight in permanent ovens, dug in the earth.]

Fri. Sept. 1. In the morning the Oraibi crier, Kelnimptiwa (Sand), called out that Kane's house was ready for plastering and asked all the women who wished to help to report there. Although it was a scorching hot day, nearly all of the pueblo's women showed up. Practically all of them could trace some relationship to Kane or his wife. Sikyaletsnim failed to go because of her daughter's recent confinement, otherwise Grace and the Parrot clanswomen were the main abstainers. A feast for the workers was given at noon. It consisted of mutton stew, corn, *piki*, fruit, and coffee, and a good time was had by all.

Ida discussed with Lena, aged five or six, the possibility of her mother, Grace, returning to Chimopovy. Lena told her that Martin was to get another chance. One more outburst of temper, and Grace plans to leave.

Ned continues to worry about the seventy-five cent trap that was lost. Our wood-gathering trip will be delayed until he finds it.

Note.—Benjamin, the Hotevilla storekeeper, stopped to talk about an errand that Ida had asked him to do. She explained that he was partly her brother because he was an Eagle, although not a Sun clansman. When pressed, she repeated Ned's standby of last year—Sun and Eagle are connected because the Sun shield is surrounded with Eagle feathers. Can this be symbolic of a union for ritual purposes of two (originally) distinct clans? Merging might have occurred in some such fashion: a man of a given clan is needed in a ceremony. If none is available, the *husband* of a suitable clanswoman might serve, bringing together two unrelated clans. Thus, Ned once acted for the Masau'û clan because of his wife; and Puhunimptiwa, one of the heads of the Hotevilla Flute society, is married to a woman of the proprietary Spider clan. He himself is a Lizard clansman. [Likewise, Jack's activities regarding Oraibi's chieftainship rest on the fact that his wife is a Parrot clanswoman, the clan destined to succeed Bear, although he himself is of the Gray Badger clan.]

Louise's *imû'wis* ("female relatives-in-law") are all grinding corn for her. This goes to the baby's father's clanswomen (its *ikya'as*).

Little boys are swinging small bull-roarers (*tovokinpi*) as toys.

While Ned was lunching with me, his ceremonial mother, Solimana, came by, and he gave her such a hateful stare that she burst into tears. According to Ned she is an awful troublemaker who likes to cause sorrow just when people are happiest. (Part of the difficulty is her objection to Ned's dealings with "Whites.") He claims that she has no regard for him, and as she has never aided him, he feels under no obligation to her. [Compare Ida's repudiation of her own ceremonial mother, p. 20.]

During the evening several young boys went to sleep in Tawaovi kiva. [A kiva is a subterranean chamber wherein esoteric rites are held.] In total darkness, and with no grown-ups present, one of them pretended to be a father of the *katcinas* and made the proper calls while the others danced. [Inexperienced boys like to practice *katcina* dancing when there are no spectators before whom they might possibly feel ashamed.]

Sat. Sept. 2. Went to fetch wood with Ned. Returned in midafternoon and interviewed Ned. Later, the chief came over and said that his heart was troubled because Edward, Margaret's second youngest child, had that morning swallowed a piece of metal and had begun to run a fever. [Edward is now married to a Chimopovy girl with whom he lives at the Grand Canyon.] No doctor had been called, and the chief said that if they were lucky, the metal would be excreted. I suggested that a "White" doctor be summoned to hurry the child's bowel movement. The chief agreed that it was a good idea and left to consult the child's father. However, I don't believe anything was done about it. Ned says that is the way the Hopi are; they never hurry to seek medical aid. [So far as I can tell this is true, except for Ned and his own family. There is little doubt that Ned is a hypochondriac. Reluctance may stem from the belief that medicine men and witches are closely linked. Possibly, medicine men are called only when an ailment is thought to be witch-caused.][1]

Ned's sister remarked that she had again heard it said that people who were jealous of Ned's intimacy with "Whites" were circulating rumors to the effect that he sold corpses and sacred objects. Ned admitted that such rumors had formerly troubled him very much, but claimed that he now tried to laugh them off. He said that he knew better than to sell ceremonial things, because if he did, the punishment of sickness or death would fall either on himself or his sisters.

Joe chatted quite freely about Hotevilla affairs. He said that the pueblo's founder, Yokioma, had secured a following by holding out a false promise of more rain, better crops, and no "White" schooling for Hopi children. Joe is not impressed with Yokioma, and he feels that the Hopi Conservatives were deceived or deluded. He claims that the Bakavi contingent left Hotevilla because their children wanted to attend school, and that this was accomplished on their return to Oraibi. [A different version is given in O.O., pp. 212–13.] Then, when the people of Oraibi made fun of them, Kuwannimptiwa asked the American government to help them make a settlement at Bakavi; thus, several Bakavi houses were built by the government. Joe went on to say that during the first hard winter after the 1906 Split many folks at Hotevilla lived in caves and rock shelters and were fed by relatives who had stayed at Oraibi. His own family was aided in this way.

It was also pointed out by Joe that the only true Soyal objects had belonged to Tawaqwaptiwa and that the things used at Hotevilla and Bakavi were deliberate frauds. He claims that the Spider folk were troublemakers and had once seceded even before the Split. [This seems to refer to events described in O.O., pp. 75–83, but there is no verification.]

Joe separates his own clan, Pikyas (Corn), from Patki and

others in the same phratry. He says that Rain, Water, and others combined with Corn because they were needed for its growth. He also separates his wife's clan, Tobacco, from Rabbit and says that she, her mother, and one Moenkopi family are truly Tobacco and only partly Rabbit.

Joe also stated that Masahongva (Parrot), the *katcina* cult leader, had given up his office two years ago [in 1931] following a conversation with Tawaqwaptiwa who had told him to do as he pleased. Masahongva had then asked Siletstiwa, the Powamu chief from Moenkopi, to give up his functions at the same time, but Siletstiwa had refused. Despite all implications Masahongva did not turn Christian, and still resides at Oraibi. [Masahongva was the husband of Solimana, Ned's ceremonial mother. He had been a Tao society member, as well as Katcina chief. After the death of his wife many years ago, he had moved to the home of a daughter in Moenkopi and had died there.]

NOTE.—The Katcina chief, Masahongva, has charge of *katcinas* in summer. The Powamu chief, Siletstiwa, has charge in winter.[2] Now Tawaqwaptiwa is rumored to be training Sam (Parrot) to be the Katcina leader, possibly Village chief as well.

The reason there is no true chief at Hotevilla is that there was a quarrel between Yokioma's nephew, who *ought* to succeed, and his son, who *wants* to succeed [see p. 346].

The Hopi have no "State," i.e., no true political organization. [See O.O., pp. 59–68.] This is what we would expect from a society where individuality is allowed to run riot as it is here. This extreme laissez faire attitude is due largely, I believe, to fear of reprisals through witchcraft. The stress on individuality is an enemy to integration; so are the "clique" feeling among each of the clans and the secrecy practiced by each sodality. Thus Hopi society seems to be in an everlasting state of balance between integrative forces such as those of extended kinship and the disintegrative power of extreme individuality. It is the latter which explains the chief's inability to prevent important schisms, such as the 1906 Split; or ceremonial disruptions, such as Masahongva's relinquishment of the *katcina* leadership; or individual aberrations, such as conversions to Christianity or decisions to move off the mesa. This, too, may help to explain some of the clan groupings, for if an appropriate clansman had dropped a rite, a different clansman might have taken it up.

Sun. Sept. 3. Ruth and Kuwanmönim, who is Kane's mother and Ned's *ikya'a,* replastered the floor of my house.

Oliver La Farge and M. Burge came as representatives of the National Association of Indian Affairs, to sound out Tawaqwaptiwa for Mr. Collier on the possibility of setting up a single, tribal-wide council. Ned was interpreter, but the chief got only a vague idea of the whole business. He was confused by the New Oraibi council, whose members are Christians or enemies.

At about three in the afternoon the crier announced a Sunday school meeting in Voth's church. George bolted out to ·attend, and Ida went despite the protests of her parents. There were also present several young women, non-Christians, from the chief's own household at Oraibi. There was some reading of a Hopi translation of the Bible that Otto had once made, and a few hymns were sung. (I have the impression that the desire for a break in customary routine was all that attracted non-Christians to attend.)

NOTE.—La Farge backs up Kane's statement regarding Navaho organization and tribal unity.

Kane spoke in an autobiographical vein. He had tried several trades at school and had asked to transfer to Sherman because he was unhappy at Phoenix. The principal was surprised at this request because Kane had never before uttered a complaint. Hopi are unpopular among students at Indian schools because they are stolid pluggers, serious-minded, and never make trouble or fight back. For example, while he was at school, Kane was issued shoes that were too small for him. Despite his discomfort he wore them rather than make a complaint. Charles did the same. [See p. 254.]

After leaving school Kane clerked for Hubbell, but that winter an epidemic of card playing and gambling broke out at Oraibi. Nearly every man was concerned in the outbreak, gambling night and day and neglecting his duties. Officers from the government agency arrested most of the offenders. Kane worked out thirty days at Keam's Canyon, and Ned did a similar term on the road to Hotevilla. [The gambling mania broke out around 1915. The favorite game was poker, which was played in kivas by practically all the men on Third Mesa. It was terminated when the womenfolk complained to government officials that the men were neglecting their farming, herding, and other duties. Only a little, desultory gambling goes on at present.]

Following this, Kane clerked for Hubbell at Piñon; but he soon got lonesome, returned to Oraibi, married, and settled down to herding and farming.

Ned repeated the story that Voth had fooled the Hopi into building his church on Third Mesa by telling them that it was going to be a dispensary.

When Ned asked about Edward's condition, both Margaret and the chief's wife burst into tears; yet not even a native medicine man had been summoned. They had tried to get the child to eat, but he was feverish and had refused to take anything but water.

Mon. Sept. 4. Worked with Ned in the morning, and afterward Bill came over. He complained of trouble in tracking one of his horses and said that while he was not the main owner of his outfit's cattle, he had to do most of the herding. He sang a song that he had composed for a future Buffalo dance. The words were in English, Navaho, and Hopi. Ned admitted that Bill was a good musician.

Later, a friend of Ned, his Navaho "grandfather," dropped in. At the time, Ned was getting his head washed at his mother's.

Ruth is suffering from toothache. Her jaw is badly swollen, but nothing is being done about it. In the same way, Edward grows worse, but no aid is summoned.

Ned asked me to feed the Navaho. After feeding him we measured him for a winter coat to be ordered from Sears Roebuck. Ned will pay the cost of about six dollars. Ned claims that many Hopi have Navaho friends but are ashamed to admit it before their tribesmen lest they be charged with being vain—show-offs— *qwivi.* [It is bad form for a Hopi to brag or show vanity.]

Bill said that while his sister and her family are away, roasting sweet corn, the house is being kept for him by his *itaha,* Humiletstiwa (Rabbit), and his wife, Duwayesnim (Bakab).

Ida neither visited Ruth nor asked about her toothache. Ned carried water in place of his wife, although his sister Martha had volunteered to do so.

Kane narrated a story of killing a rattler in his youth, while he was in the company of a young member of the Snake society. The latter had shown Kane where the poison sacs were, how a snake could distend its jaws, and the way in which its poison flowed into the wound made by the snake's bite. Kane also related a prevalent belief to the effect that a badger could not be dislodged when halfway into its hole. On one occasion, believing the story, he had got all set for a hearty tug at a trapped badger, only to fall over backward when the animal was easily dislodged. Ned's comment was that the badger might not yet have penetrated far enough into its hole.

While we had been gathering wood, Ned's dog had chased a rabbit into its hole. Ned had dug until the rabbit was partly exposed, but he had been afraid to reach far in for fear of a snake.

Ned's interviews of September 2 to 4 suggested that he was impotent for a time because of gonorrhea, yet he insisted that he has not been unfaithful and his wife does not appear to be infected.[3] Ned claimed to have heard of students from Sherman resorting to houses of prostitution, but said it was strictly forbidden and that he knew nothing further about it. [Ned tells a different story in *Sun Chief*, pp. 263–64.] He knew about true female virginity, having heard of the hymen, and he said that in theory Hopi brides were expected to be virgin, but that this was seldom the case. This checks with what Allen has said and makes it likely that loss of virginity is no bar to a girl's marriage.

Louis caught a small coyote but let it go without killing it. It was too small to be valuable and might be worth more when it was full-grown. Unlike Ned, he had no ceremonial scruples about killing the animal.

As Ned and I came up the road this evening, we saw several children of both sexes at play. Two little girls were disheveled or partly nude, but Ned said nothing.

Tues. Sept. 5. Hired Bert's car and drove to a Butterfly dance at Mishongnovi. Chimopovy dancers had come over and were performing in relays with the Mishongnovi folk. One Shipaulovi woman got so excited that she got between the leader of one line and his partner, even though she was not in costume. An old man protested, but she went on and seemed to know the steps. Then another woman grappled with her and tried to pull her out of line, but she kept on until the formation ended. She did not participate in later dances. [Although I did not check the facts at the time, it is my guess that the women concerned were *ikya'as* to the men.] One of the Chimopovy formations contained a burlesque of American-style ballroom dancing, with males and females holding hands for a few steps. Then the drum beat a march rhythm, the singers chanted in English, "Left—left—left, right, left"; and the performers clasped each other about the waist.

It struck me as screamingly funny, but Ned commented afterward that he didn't like such innovations. He said that the whole thing had been done during a Butterfly dance at Chimopovy some years earlier. The song had been revived because the present dance had been called on such short notice that there was no time for composing and learning new tunes.

A strange thing took place during the afternoon's dancing. At one point the Chimopovy troupe began to perform before the Mishongnovi outfit had finished and withdrawn from the plaza. (I was in error. Such dual performances are customary whenever two competing groups perform.) When Ida was questioned about the seeming intrusion, she said it was so planned in order to give observers a chance to make direct comparisons. For the vigor of their performance I would have voted for the Chimopovy dancers. This seemed to be the crowd's consensus. Ida admitted she would have favored Chimopovy in any event because she had more relatives there and knew more of the dancers.

Some say that the same two groups will perform at Chimopovy tomorrow, but others say the Mishongnovi outfit will not take part because many of the men are preparing for a salt-gathering expedition to Salt Lake in New Mexico. Ned said Second Mesa folk always go there instead of to the Salt Canyon visited by Oraibi men.[4]

On the way home saw boys and girls again playing near the road. This time two small boys had their pants off. Ida was the one who drew attention to the children, but she seemed unconcerned and did not comment on their disheveled attire.

Met Lemuel Siyesva who had come by wagon from Hotevilla and was planning to spend the night with Ruth and Ned. When Siyesva returned from hobbling his horses, he joked about fearing the dark. Ned remarked that most men feared the dark because of Masau'û, god of death, but that he was not afraid of Masau'û. (Could this be because his wife is of the Masau'û clan?) Most men took a companion along if they had to perform a burial after dark. Ida also jokes about being afraid of Masau'û, who seems to be a sort of Hopi bogeyman. [Masau'û is widely feared. He has charge of the Underworld to which the spirits of the dead go; and it is a touch of his club that brings death. Men who impersonate Masau'û sleep by day and go about at night.]

Siyesva's wife told two stories. One concerned a Hopi girl from Walpi who had gone insane while in school and whose heart was found covered with a loco weed of a different variety than horses sometimes eat. The other dealt with a Walpi woman, wife of a bone-setting "doctor," who had broken a leg and suffered other injuries following a simple fall. Her injuries were blamed on witches either because they had a grudge against her or because they wanted to test her husband's ability. There was also an undercurrent of suspicion against the woman herself. In any event, I was told, "Good people wouldn't do such a thing."

Somiviki [little cornmeal cakes, wrapped and tied in corn husks] were being eaten for supper by Mary's family for no special reason. [A new bride was supposed to show her ability to cook by making *somiviki* for the groom's relatives.]

Ned thinks that the forthcoming Marau, scheduled to be given in Hotevilla, ought to have been called out earlier than usual because the summer has been exceptionally dry.

Wed. Sept. 6. Joe says that in the old days no man could go on a salt expedition until he had gone through Wuwutcim (Tribal Initiation). [This was later verified.] He also spoke of the difficulties of descending Salt Canyon. (Ned and Tawaqwaptiwa had likewise thought that this would be too tough a climb for me.) Joe told of one man who had made the journey but who didn't dare risk the descent.

Siyesva came in after breakfast with his wife and baby, Miller. [Miller is now full-grown, probably married and living on First Mesa.] The conversation turned to "White" schooling, and Siyesva complained of Mrs. Simpson, then a government matron at Hotevilla. He accused her of being mean and whipping pupils. He also objected to the policeman Albert for the rough manner in which he dragged truants off to school. Siyesva accused Mrs. Simpson of intercepting letters that contained money, because on one occasion he had failed to receive such a letter that had supposedly been sent him. He was likewise of the opinion that letters to Washington were held at Keam's Canyon and there answered as if the replies had come from Washington.

Siyesva spoke too of a baby that had died during the past winter. Its death had disturbed their other child, Miller, who had cried so bitterly that he himself (Siyesva) had shed tears of sympathy. Miller now cries less and likes to go with his father to the fields.

Siyesva told me further that he had lectured his sisters on thrift, saying that as a married brother he could not help them because he was duty-bound to work for his wife and children. (Yet, married men often help the households of their mothers, particularly if they are widowed.)

For some reason several men are building or repairing houses at this time. Baking sweet corn is the chief farming occupation, and whole families generally cooperate, spending one or two nights in the field.[5] Ed and Edith invited Allen and Betty to go along. Allen is a phratry brother to Edith. On her return Edith gave a tray of roasted sweet corn to Ruth, her mother's sister.

Edward is rapidly getting better, and Ruth's toothache is easing up.

Margaret and Nasingönsi, Margaret's adoptive mother, have been quarreling about Margaret's sister Clara, who is rather licentious. Grace and Martin are at it again, too.

Solimana and Masahongva invited Allen and Betty to dine. Masahongva and Betty are clan siblings.

Tom told of a recent trip to Winslow where he rolled a lucky number with dice. He had put up one dollar and should have won thirteen, but the concessionaire refused to pay. Tom snatched up a blanket and hung on to it till he got his dollar back. He said it wasn't right for the man to refuse him the thirteen dollars, but he made no fuss after he got his own money back. If even staid and fat Tom gambles, it looks like a widespread Hopi trait. [It is! (M.T.) Compare Ned's playing "Bingo" several years back, and the gambling outbreak described by Kane on p. 36.]

Thurs. Sept. 7. Most of the men are leaving for the annual sheep dip at Wipo Wash, near First Mesa. They will return late Friday or Saturday. Ned's old father [Fig. 10] will take their combined flock afoot as far as possible in the cool of the morning after which Ned, on horseback, will relieve him. Later still, Sidney plans to overtake and join Ned. Much cooperation is required of herding partners during a sheep-dip.

Chatted with Tawaqwaptiwa, who reported that several Second Mesa folk had ordered moccasins. He also said that he had called a conference to discuss the plan proposed by La Farge. Cedric, Ed, Louis, and Andrew were among those present. It was their consensus that nothing needed to be done as Washington annually made proposals that failed to materialize.

Got the chief started on lightning. He verified most of what has already been said and affirmed that the sky god, Sotukinangwû'û, lived just above and not in the San Francisco mountains. He revealed that his own ceremonial father, Ned's great-uncle Talaskwaptiwa (Sun), and his son had been split open by lightning. Ned's great-uncle had then heard a water bird (*patjiro*)[6] talking to Hahai'i, mother of the *katcinas*, saying that he would be put together again, which proved to be the case. It seems that this experience led the affected man to become a "doctor." [Subsequently, it turned out that the reference should have been not to Talaskwaptiwa but to Homikni, who was Ned's maternal grandfather. He was a Lizard clansman who prayed to the lizard for power. He began by massaging stomachs and then became an extractor. Homikni had offered to teach Ned his trade, but Ned had refused. [For more information, consult the references to Homikwina in the index to *Sun Chief*.]

Little Edward is still not entirely well. Tawaqwaptiwa admits that no medicine man was called. He rationalized it by saying that the child was not eating and so could not have a bowel movement. Edward expressed a desire for popcorn, and his father went all the way to Hotevilla to get some. This shows that the Hopi are far from indifferent to their offspring even if they are reluctant to summon medical help.

This morning Andrew, father of Louise, dragged home a sheep that is to be butchered at his granddaughter's naming party. Delia brought a batch of fresh *piki*. Her own mother had been Louise's ceremonial mother, and Ned had been the ceremonial father. Delia was now serving on her late mother's behalf. Delia's own ceremonial mother had turned Christian, so when Delia wanted to join a women's ceremony, Oaqöl, she had merely picked a member to be her new ceremonial mother.

Ruth calls Ida "George's *ikya'a*," a woman from George's father's clan; but Ida calls Ruth not George's mother, but *imû'wi* ("my female relative-in-law").

NOTE.—Connect the attitude toward dirt with the attitude toward excretion. We say, in our culture, "Cleanliness is next to Godliness." Thus we dislike dirt, fear excrement, dislike the organs of excretion and reproduction, and look upon sexual activity as dirty. On the other hand, the Hopi are utterly indifferent to dirt, think nothing of excretion, and lack our ideas of dirty organs and sex.

Went below to New Oraibi to call on the Corrigans and was told that dancers performing elsewhere must dance afterward in their home pueblo to placate the local spirits. [Checking reveals that this is correct.]

Fri. Sept. 8. Two Navahos had supper and spent last night at Ruth's. They made their own breakfast and left early this morning.

Got more on the marital difficulties of Lily from New Oraibi. She had had an affair with Homer, which had led her husband to leave her. When all this became public, she was very much ashamed, became ill with grief, and even fainted one night. She is now penitent and wants her husband back. There was no official divorce, and no punishment was meted out to Homer.

Ruth said today, in what seemed to be all seriousness, that she didn't like Oraibi and would rather move to Hotevilla or Walpi where there was more doing.

Ida sleeps at home in a room apart from her parents, who share quarters with Delia and Nelson.

At different times Ned, Tawaqwaptiwa, Jack, and Kane have made the same sort of comment regarding food. All say that whoever comes to a Hopi house may have a meal without payment, but in town the Hopi must always pay when they eat among "Whites." (The Hopi confuse public restaurants with private homes.)

> NOTE.—The power of public opinion is a strong force among the Hopi. The known fact that "people will talk" is an ever-present deterrent from wrongdoing. Ned, among others, worries about giving us information because "people are always talking about him." Ida often remarks that "the people are talking" about this or that, and even Lee is much concerned when she is talked about. In such a closely spaced community as a pueblo, privacy is next to impossible, and talk spreads rapidly throughout the village. Can it be that lack of privacy, coupled with public opinion, is a counterbalancing factor set against excessive individualism? Are people afraid to give free rein to their individuality because they lack privacy and do not want to be talked about? Is this another element of restraint on unusual behavior, like the fear of being branded a witch?[7]

In our culture the two most secret acts are sex and the excretion of body wastes. Among the Hopi neither of these is entirely private, especially for men. When a boy wants to make love to a girl, he does not take her out on a private date but sneaks into her house. The postdance picnics (*oveknaiya*) of long ago were clearly important for sexual affairs, but they were, to a large extent, public. This lack of privacy was intensified when the ancestors of the Hopi built villages in cliffs and on mesa tops. As it became more and more difficult to do anything without danger of observation and talk, the importance of kivas must have increased. This may explain why a kiva's major importance is the performance of a secret rite. Those who share in the performance of a kiva's principal ceremony tend to become members of the chamber where the observances are held. At the same time, each ceremony is shut off from all nonmembers and has a "whip" that afflicts unauthorized observers with a particular ailment. [See O.O., p. 241.]

Sat. Sept. 9. Louise's grandmother came from Bakavi to help with the naming feast. Many other women are bustling about and helping to get things ready.

Just how close does a man feel to an otherwise unrelated member of his secret societies or kiva? Not very.

In digging a chicken coop by the side of the western road near a ruined house, Allen found a little chocolate-colored stone [clay? terra-cotta?] animal, *tohopko,* much like a Zuñi fetish. He considers it a prize because such things were formerly used in ceremonies. Similar objects are still used in some Hopi rites. [Tohopkom were usually in the form of mountain lions or bears. Sometimes, they were fashioned in cornmeal dough (*qömi*) by Wuwutcim men on salt-gathering expeditions. They were placed in a cuplike depression into which water continuously dripped. A year later they were supposed to have turned to stone.

Tohopkom were sometimes tied about a patient's wrist. They were occasionally used for brewing medicine during ceremonies in kivas.]

Duvenimptiwa secretes his mask and other religious paraphernalia in Martha's house, in order to keep them out of the hands of Delia's two-year-old son, Milton.

In the evening Kane, Tom, Louis, and Ned came in. Conversation turned to a bone "doctor" from Mishongnovi who had saved the life of Tom's younger brother O'Ray. According to these men O'Ray had become suddenly lame at school, had been given up by "White" doctors, and had been sent home to die. The bone "doctor" had been called and had apparently pushed the head of the femur back into the acetabulum. Kane had held the boy, who had no anesthesia. He screamed with pain, but did not shed tears. In time O'Ray recovered, though still lame because one leg is shorter than the other. [Although his limp could not be disguised, O'Ray was permitted to dance as a *katcina*.] Kane once had had a dislocated shoulder set by the same medicine man and told of other cures that this "doctor" had made. Kane also commented on the "doctor's power" and the fact that the "doctor" was never touched by the pain he was sometimes forced to inflict on his patients.

Kane elaborated on his plans to increase his livestock, although he does not want to give up farming altogether. Still, he felt that in case of need he could always trade meat for farm products at Hotevilla.

Sun. Sept. 10. This morning Louise's baby Ann was named. Except for myself the active participants were women. Males slept on one side of the house and females on the other. One old woman had slept indoors. On awakening she had dressed under the blankets. Juanita [Louise's clan sister] was sleepy and seemed bored, but their mother, Puhumana, was most active and seemed to lead the proceedings. After the child had been named, its paternal grandmother, Puhumana, went to the east edge of the mesa with Louise and me, and the child was presented to the Sun. [A detailed account of the naming rites is given in chapter X, section A.]

Later, Cedric said that the child's father, Dick, had not yet been officially married to Louise. Nevertheless, he was living with her at her mother's house. Louise said that her Hopi wedding would take place after harvest when there would be time for making wedding garments.

Between the naming rites and the feast I went to get some *katcina* dolls from the chief. I found him urinating into a basin placed at the foot of a sheepskin on which his wife was sleeping.

Two naming feasts were held simultaneously. The main one was in Louise's mother's house; and the other was in Dick's mother's house, which Louise had supplied with food.

Coin, brother of Sikyaletsnim and uncle to Louise, came up from New Oraibi. Martha and her husband, Luke, half brother to Louise, were present, and many others stopped in, as Sikyaletsnim had announced that there would be open house for all. During the feast, Dick and Louise, with Andrew and Sikyaletsnim (Louise's parents), waited on the diners. Most of the guests were relatives, as only a few outsiders had responded to the invitation made to all. [Andrew and Sikyaletsnim separated around 1953. From then until he died a few years later, Andrew lived with Louise, his stepdaughter. Meantime, Sikyaletsnim lived with her granddaughter Ann. Around 1964 she took up residence with Louise, who had been divorced at that time from Dick. When Sikyaletsnim and her daughter shared a common residence, their household at Old Oraibi looked like the only remaining vestige of the former practice of unilocal, matrilocal residence. The first brides to live in their own homes, instead of with their mother, were the daughters of Tom and Anita, beginning around 1945. Their example was followed by Alice, daughter of Jack and Margaret, and others.]

Mon. Sept. 11. Got full details about Louise and Dick at breakfast. He had made *dumaiya* calls on her, but when talk of marriage began to spread, many people grew indignant because Dick was of the same clan as Louise's father. Technically, this made him her *ina'a* ("my father") and ineligible to marry her. When Louise found herself pregnant, however, she insisted on marrying Dick, but was ashamed to have the ceremony performed at Oraibi. Instead, she had it done in Hotevilla. She is expected to get her wedding robes this winter and may wear them when she presents her next baby to the Sun.

Ida repeats that a young woman used to make *dumaiya* calls on men.

Ada is the daughter of the Shipaulovi chief and Ned's late sister Gladys. She should have been named for her father's clan, but since there were no Bear clanswomen at Oraibi, she was named by Nasingönsi, wife of Tawaqwaptiwa (Bear). Nasingönsi named the child Kyachepnim for her own Parrot clan. When Ada's mother died and her father had returned to Shipaulovi, Ada had been reared by Martha, her mother's sister, and Luke, Martha's husband. After a time Ada became ill and was given to Luke's mother, Sikyaletsnim, for adoption. (If witches try to kill relatives, doesn't this kind of adoption disrupt their plans?)[8] When it came time to select a ceremonial mother, Mary was chosen, and Tom, a Rabbit-Tobacco clan brother of Mary, acted as ceremonial father. Mary's own brother Bill refused to be Ada's ceremonial father, it is said, because he did not want to observe the requisite taboos.

There are several other cases of sick children being given for adoption to unrelated clans. Most important of these is Bert Fredericks who, when ill, was adopted by the Sun clansman Talaskaptiwa, who was the chief's ceremonial father and who had been married to their aunt, a Bear clanswoman who was sister to the late chief Lololoma.

Ned said today that the oven in which witches are burned in the afterworld is laid out in the four cardinal directions like a pit oven for baking sweet corn.[9]

Cedric claims that he sleeps outdoors with his family because his house has too many chicken bugs inside. His brother Nick is married and lives at Kikötcmovi, but he comes to visit his parents at Oraibi now and then. He does not take part in any of Old Oraibi's esoteric rites, but he dances *katcina* at New and Old Oraibi, presumably to please his wife.

During the afternoon I left by wagon for Ned's sweet corn bake, together with Ned, Ruth, George, Edith, and her children. Ned's sweet corn field was supposed to be on "free" land—not held by a particular clan—but in the vicinity I noted farms run by Ned, Ed, and Jasper, who all had Masau'û wives. On the other hand, Ned's father and brother, Duvenimptiwa and Sidney respectively, are married into other clans but farm here. Jasper [husband of Patcavamana], father of Edith, is being cut out by Louis. Jasper herds five days at a stretch with a brother and avoids coming to Oraibi. [The area where these fields are located is called Patuwi. Joe also grows sweet corn here. In 1961 his oven was so flooded with excess rain that he could not bake his crop, but he grew enough for two bakings in 1965.]

Ruth laughingly drew my attention to Edith's three-year-old son, David, while he was urinating.

At the field the men slept outdoors while the women slept within. Ned slept with George next to me, Jasper slept with his grandson, Edith and her baby slept with Ruth, and Duvenimptiva made himself a bed in the horse corral. We dined on boiled mutton, coffee, chili peppers, watermelon, and other fruits that had been brought along. George ate the same foods as the adults. So, too, did David, except that his coffee was diluted with water.

Edith did not hesitate to slap David when he became unruly, but when George struck Ruth violently with his fists across the back, she merely cried, "Anai!" ("Ouch!") and nothing further was done by Ned or Ruth. [Ned and Ruth were so fearful of losing George as they had their other children that they were reluctant to thwart or punish him.[10] See p. 12.]

Tues. Sept. 12. While all the adults were picking sweet corn in the morning, George walked about or played and made no effort to help. Ned only remarked casually that George "was pretty lazy."

When Ned returned from hobbling his horses, both women in our party thanked him.

The men do not hesitate to urinate in view of the other sex; and when Ned took down his trousers to examine an insect bite on his buttocks, Ruth and Edith merely laughed.

Ned taught me the appropriate call to make at daybreak when the earth oven is about to be opened.

Wed. Sept. 13. Early in the morning Ned expressed the hope that Ruth would soon fetch George, as "the little boy" would be angry if he missed the excitement, but George did nothing but eat corn when he did arrive. Jasper held Edith's baby while she helped with the husking.

On our way back to Oraibi we stopped at another of Ned's cornfields to gather a few ears, partly for Sun clan use in the pueblo, and partly to pay Edith for her work. Ned almost stepped on a rattler coiled under some tumbleweed and shouted a warning to me. Ned killed the snake with some stones, but he would not cut off its rattles with his own knife. He insisted on using mine. He felt that he had been saved from a bad bite because he had a *nakwakwosi* ("prayer feather") in his pocket.

On the drive homeward Ned gave roasted sweet corn to various people, including the Bakavi chief, Kuwannimptiwa. Ned said that Kuwannimptiwa was our "father" because he was from the Sand clan to which Ned's own father belongs. Kuwannimptiwa was most gracious and invited Ned and me to act as clowns at Bakavi. I thought the idea good, but Ned cautioned me that it might offend Tawaqwaptiwa, who was not friendly to Bakavi's inhabitants.

Sikyaletsnim called on Ned after lunch to get some of the freshly roasted sweet corn. She offered to pay, but Ned refused her money, saying that this food was free to all.

Tom calls all Sun clansmen *ina'a* ("my father"), and he calls Duvenimptia *ikwa'a* ("my grandfather") because Duvenimptiwa is the husband of a Sun clanswoman whom he calls *ikya'a*.

Thurs. Sept. 14. When Ida heard about George's behavior, and especially about how he had struck Ruth, she gave the following explanation. George had been badly scalded when small, and Kiacwaitiwa had been called to save his life. The medicine man thought he could cure George but warned that the remedy would make him "mean" and ill-tempered in the future. George was adopted by Kiacwaitiwa at the time. Much the same is said of Kane's son Edmond, but it is not clear if Kiacwaitiwa adopted this child.

Allen and Betty had supper last night and breakfast this morning with Solimana and Masahongva. Allen said that although he and Moe had taken care of their stepfather, Kuwanwaitiwa

(Rabbit), in his last illness and had buried him when he died, they got very little of his flock, because his own children took practically all of it. There was no appeal because apparently no one has the authority to settle such disputes. [A burier is supposed to get a large portion of the deceased's estate.]

Spoke to Dennis about making a trip to Salt Canyon. [This trip never materialized.] He wanted to know about pay. Ned is willing to go for one dollar a day plus expenses, but Dennis probably will want more. While herding, Dennis stayed overnight with Ned and Ruth.

Most of the Oraibi children are at school. Sam has bad eyes and doesn't attend, Betty played hooky because her mother and father went to their sheep camp, and Lena refused to go because she was planning to live at Second Mesa with her mother's sister. People avoid scolding Betty because it induces crying spells that last day and night.

This month is harvest month, Huhulmuya, and people are supposed to eat as much as possible. (However, no special ceremony is connected with this custom.)

NOTE.—Is the absence of social taboos among the Hopi tied up with the idea of excessive individualism?

Fri. Sept. 15. Dennis spent a second night at Ruth's. Asked Bert some informal questions about fear of the dead. He confirmed Allen's statement that excessive handling of corpses causes the witch people to send an illness that makes the patient waste away until he resembles a skeleton. Bert reported that a Bear clan medicine man from Hotevilla, Kiachongniwa, was visiting the chief. [The man turned out to be Spider, the other clan in the Bear phratry. Spider clansmen played leading parts in the Spirit of 1906 that led to Hotevilla's establishment. They used to be bitterly opposed to Bear clan leadership of Oraibi.]

There is to be a Marau dance at Mishongnovi next Saturday, and a Lakon dance at Walpi Sunday. [These ceremonies are conducted by feminine societies. Note the tendency to hold dances on weekends. This characteristic has increased virtually to the point of a "must." Jack, claimant through his wife to Oraibi's chieftainship, is trying, without success, to get the Hopi to return to their traditional solar calendar.

It is interesting and amusing to note that when Ned first began attending school at the turn of the century, he was so ignorant of the "White" man's calendar that he used to show up for school on Saturdays and Sundays.]

Ned again showed his distaste for Walpi by commenting that their Lakon dance was being held too soon. Its "breath" is frosty, and it may cause an early frost that will damage unharvested crops.

Ned explained that he had not been adopted by the Navaho man whom he calls "grandfather." He uses this term in Hopi fashion. The Navaho's wife is Sand clan like Ned's father. This makes her Ned's *ikya'a* ("my father's clanswoman") and her husband *ikwa'a* ("my grandfather").

Betty's misbehavior came up in discussion. Ned said that she was badly spoiled as evidenced by her hanging around my house whereas his son never hung about me and even got angry with those who did. [Here Ned shows himself to be the proud father. Actually, his adopted son George was surly and behaved wretchedly. See p. 47.]

The Hopi name of Cedric's older daughter, the name that stuck, was given her by his father's mother's mother. The same woman contributed the name which is most likely to stick to the younger daughter, too.

There was much wind today, and everyone remarked that it was the Marau wind and that there was always much wind at the time of this ceremony. [Note how much more telling this makes Ned's statement that the Walpi Lakon might cause frost.]

Asked Ned the Hopi expression for urinating. He gave it with the remark that it was not "bad," and could be freely used by either sex in the presence of the other. Incidentally, he mentioned the belief that intercourse with a menstruating woman almost invariably resulted in pregnancy.

When a child was whipped on admission to the *katcina* cult, a ceremonial mother remained in her customary dress but a ceremonial father stripped to a G-string.

Cedric said that he had hauled wood for his mother, but the woman was really his mother's sister. [Hopi terminology does not separate mother from mother's sister, and even English-speaking Hopi regularly confuse the two.]

Sat. Sept. 16. Ned planned to fetch wood from a distance and to spend the night with Nestcili, his Navaho friend. While Ned was hitching up, Polingyauoma arrived, and Ned casually remarked that he had sent for him because his penis had been itching. Ruth served the medicine man some food, and after he had eaten, he treated Ned in a back room. Knowing that Ned was

Fig. 1. The 1932 Field Party at New Oraibi. *From left to right:* Ed Kennard, Jess Spirer, Dr. Leslie A. White (leader), Fred Eggan, and Mischa Titiev.

Fig. 2. Ida. The younger sister of Ned, who served as the author's housekeeper while he lived at Old Oraibi.

Fig. 3. 17½ Bakwa Avenue. The writer's residence in the pueblo of Old Oraibi.

FIG. 4. NED HOLDING A BULLSNAKE. Ned showed no fear of reptiles, and had even considered joining the Snake society.

FIG. 5. NED'S IMMEDIATE FAMILY. Ned is pictured in the doorway of his house at Oraibi, with his wife, Ruth, and their adopted son, George.

FIG. 6. TAWAQWAPTIWA AT SHERMAN INSTITUTE. The Chief stands in the center, wearing light suit.

FIG. 7. "UNCLE JOE" LOMAHONGYOMA. This photograph was taken at Alcatraz early in 1895. "Uncle Joe," then quite young, is the second man from the right, in the front row of men standing up. He had been taken prisoner at Oraibi on November 25 or 26, 1894, for "seditious conduct," although he knew no English. (Courtesy of Professor Robert C. Euler, who, by permission, copied a photograph that was in the files of the Southwest Museum.)

FIG. 8. Two Hopi Chiefs. *Left to right:* Frank Siemptiwa, Tawaqwaptiwa, and Betty
adopted daughter of Tawaqwaptiwa. The chiefs are enjoying a smoke in front of Tawa
qwaptiwa's house. This picture was taken in the fall of 1933.

FIG. 9. The Oraibi Chief and His Fa
ily. Tawaqwaptiwa (Bear), his wi
Nasingönsi (Parrot), and Betty who h
been adopted by the chief and his w
since they were childless. Betty was t
daughter of Margaret and the gran
daughter of Masamösi (Parrot), who w
the chief's wife's sister.

FIG. 10. NED'S PARENTS. Duvenimptiwa (Sand) and Hahai'i (head woman of the Sun Clan). Duvenimptiwa was considerably older than his wife, and was one of the most conservative men at Oraibi.

FIG. 11. RUTH'S WEDDING ROBES. She is showing how a bride goes home, wearing a large robe and carrying a smaller one, wrapped in a reed case, in her outstretched arms. She is not wearing the moccasins and attached wrapped leggings of white buckskin that traditionally are parts of a bridal outfit.

FIG. 12. A MATERNITY RUBBISH HEAP. All objects connected with a child-birth at home, and nothing else, must be thrown on this heap. Harm is supposed to befall anyone who tampers with it.

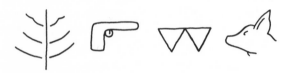

FIG. 13. A PICTOGRAPHIC RECORD. *From left to right,* there are pictured a reed (*bakap*); the male genital organs, in the form of a pistol; a conventionalized vulva; and a coyote's head. The inscription states, in effect: "Here a Bakap clansman had intercourse with a Coyote clanswoman." One cannot help thinking that many pictographs were meant to convey equally mundane messages. (*Drawn by Charles D. Hall.*)

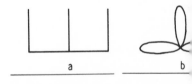

FIG. 14. MISCELLANEOUS DESIGNS AND SYMBOLS.

a. Design used by Eototo impersonator. It symbolizes the Oraibi domain.
b. Growing plant symbol, worn on the forehead by masculine Powamu
   katcinas (Bean dancers). Made with cornhusks.
c. Friendship mark. Stands for clasped hands.
d. Two embroidered designs, near the lower border of a Lakon maiden
   robe. They represent growing vegetation (corn?).
e. Lightning (?) marks on the bodies of male Buffalo dancers.
f. Star (*left*) and Crescent Moon (*right*) designs. Painted with white clay
   (*duma*) on the body of a foot-racer. The designs represent *wuyas* of
   the Sun clan.

(*Drawn by Charles D. Hall.*)

FIG. 15. AN AGAVE PLANT. It shows
the model for Kwan (Agave)
one-horned headdresses.

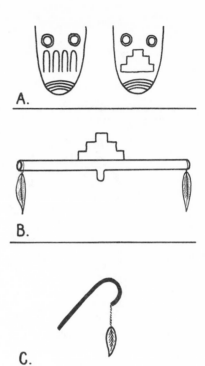

A.

B.

C.

FIG. 16. SUMAIKOLI PARAPHERNALIA.

A. Mask designs. B. Sumaikoli
object. C. Crook (ñalöchöya) with
prayer feather.

(Drawn by Mrs. Marie E. Braden.)

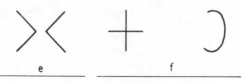

c

d

e

f

FIG. 17. A WUWUTCIM DANCE FORMATION. Observed at Hotevilla on December 2, 1933. (*Drawn by Mrs. Marie E. Braden.*)

FIG. 18. BUFFALO DANCE. The picture below was taken at New Oraibi in 1933. The one opposite was taken at Old Oraibi about twenty-five years later. Their close resemblance is noteworthy.

FIG. 19. SCREEN FOR THE 1934 PUPPET-DOLL DANCE AT HOTEVILLA. The dolls are a Shalakmana ("Shalako girl"), *at the left,* and a Palhikmana ("Water-drinking girl"), *at the right.* The figure of Muyingwa, an important germination deity, is painted on the central panel. At each corner there kneels a Hehea *katcina;* and cornsprouts, set in clay cones, represent a cornfield in front of the screen. A sandpiper may be seen above Muyingwa's head.

Explanation of Figure 20

All dwellings are indicated by similar rectangles, regardless of actual shapes and sizes, and all "streets" have been arbitrarily straightened out. Residences have Arabic numbers; but kivas are shown as squares with Roman numerals.

In the list below, names of principal occupants are followed in parentheses by their clans. Houses always belong to women and their clans. Widowers sometimes live on in the houses of their former wives.

True clan houses, that is, the houses that are supposed to contain each clan's basic fetish, are indicated in parentheses following the names of the occupants. Theoretically, these fetishes must never be moved, even if a house is abandoned. Many real clan houses are not indicated because they are no longer remembered.

DWELLINGS

#1. Jack (Gray Badger) and Margaret (Parrot).

#2. Tom (Rabbit-Tobacco) and Anita (Pikyas).

#3. Panimptiwa (Gray Badger) and Masamösi (Parrot). (True clan house)

#4. Ed (Pikyas) and Edith (Masau'û).

#5. Humiletstiwa (Rabbit) and Duwayesnim (Bakap).

#6. Andrew (Gray Badger). Later, at marriage, he moved to dwelling #23.

#7. Louis (Sand) and Clara (Masau'û).

#8. Poliyestiwa (Tep) and Kuwanmönim (Sand).

#9. Chief Tawaqwaptiwa (Bear) and Nasingönsi (Parrot). (True clan house)

#10. Ralph (Real Coyote).

#11. Lomanimptiwa (Bow). Later, Cedric (Pikyas) and Juanita (Gray Badger) lived here.

#12. Humingkwai'ima (Real Badger) and Nawisoa (Masau'û).

#13. Kane (Sand) and Jessie (Rabbit).

#14. Allen (Real Coyote-Red Fox [?]) and Betty (Parrot).

#15. Masahongva (Parrot) and Solimana (Tep).

#16. Ned (Sun) and Ruth (Masau'û). (True clan house)

#17. Puhamana (Gray Badger). (True clan house)

#18. Martin (Parrot) and Grace (Piqöc).

#19. Luke (Tep) and Martha (Sun).

#20. Kelnimptiwa (Sand) and Qöyawaisi (Pikyas). (True clan house)

#21. Real Badger house (?) slept in by Panimptiwa after 1950 (?).

#22. Duveyauoma (Patki) and Honanhönim (Piqöc).

#23. Andrew (Gray Badger) and Sikyaletsnim (Tep).

#24. Joe (Pikyas) and Mary (Rabbit-Tobacco). (True clan house)

#25. Edna (Real Coyote-Red Fox [?]).

#26. Duvenimptiwa (Sand) and Hahai'i (Sun). (True clan house)

#27. Harold (Sand) and Lily (Tep). (True clan house)

KIVAS

I. Tawaovi (active).

II. Wiklavi (inactive).

III. Powamu (active).*

IV. Marau (active).

V. Al, formerly Nasavi (inactive).

VI. Tao (Singers') (inactive).

VII. Hano (inactive).

*This kiva may formerly have been known as Hotcitcivi ("Zigzag kiva"). In that case, it is wrongly listed as a separate kiva in "Old Oraibi," p. 245.

The kiva called Hawiovi, not shown on this figure, was active in 1933 but inactive by 1964. It was situated just a few paces south of house #27, and just northwest of the abandoned Is ("Coyote") kiva. Possibly, Kyacsus ("Parrot-tail") kiva was located between Hawiovi and Is. Also, while the exact location of Sakwalenvi ("Blue Flute kiva") was not remembered, it was said to have been near No. III.

Immediately south of No. IV was the Tcu ("Rattlesnake") kiva, southeast of which there once stood the Kwan ("Agave") kiva. On the same "street," at its eastern limit, there used to stand Katcin ("Katcina") kiva, which was nicknamed Kwitavi ("Feces kiva").

Three other ancient kivas, none of whose locations is known, were Tcotcovi ("Bluebird"), Hemis, and Pakovi ("Water-settling"). All three were probably in the southern portion of the pueblo.

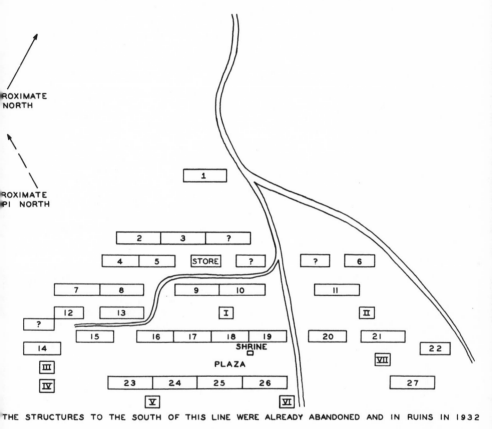

APPROXIMATE
NORTH

APPROXIMATE
HOPI NORTH

THE STRUCTURES TO THE SOUTH OF THIS LINE WERE ALREADY ABANDONED AND IN RUINS IN 1932

FIG. 20. HOUSE AND STREET PLAN OF OLD ORAIBI, 1933. (*Drawn by Charles D. Hall.*)

Explanation of Figure 21

In order to facilitate comparisons, drawings and notations, insofar as possible, are identical with those of Figure 20. New dwellings are marked with capital letters.

DWELLINGS

#1. Jack (Gray Badger) and Margaret (Parrot).
#2. Valjean (Chimopovy Sun) and Elta (Pikyas), daughter of Anita (dwelling #20).
#3. Neal (Hotevilla Tep) and Bessie (Pikyas), adopted daughter of Anita (dwelling #20).
#4. Ed (Pikyas) and Edith (Masau'û).
#5. Pete (Acoma Parrot) and Lomita (Masau'û), daughter of Edith (dwelling #4).
#?. Possibly Louis (Sand) and Clara (Masau'û). Occupants of dwelling #7, Figure 20.
#6. Dick (Gray Badger).
#7. Possibly Louis (Sand) and Clara (Masau'û).
#8. Unknown.
#9. Empty.
#10. Former house of Chief Tawaqwaptiwa (Bear).
#11. Sidney (Sun) and Martha (Sun). Brother and sister of Ned.
#12. Robert (Tep) and Dorothy (Masau'û), daughter of Clara (Figure 20, dwelling #7). They now live in New Oraibi.
#13. Empty.
#14. Louise (Tep), divorced from Dick.
#15. Empty.
#16. Ned (Sun) and Ruth (Masau'û).
#17. Lawrence (Moenkopi Water Coyote) and Ann (Tep).
#18. Martin (Parrot), divorced from Grace (Piqöc).
#19. Empty.
#20. Tom (Rabbit-Tobacco) and Anita (Pikyas). See also Figure 20, dwelling #21.
#21. Joe (Pikyas) and Mary (Rabbit-Tobacco).
#22. Wally (Hotevilla Tep) and Clarabelle (Piqöc). This couple is now divorced.
#23. Peter (Hotevilla Tep) and Eleanor (Rabbit-Tobacco), daughter of Mary (dwelling #21).
#24. Empty.
#25. Empty.
#26. Empty. Used for dances by a Chimopovy couple. Byron (Spider) and Sandra (Sun), mother's sister's daughter of Martha. Reared by Martha (dwelling #11).
#27. Harold (Sand) and Lily (Tep).

NEW DWELLINGS

A. Not in use.
B. Dave (Chimopovy Sun's Forehead) and Evelyn (Rabbit-Tobacco), daughter of Mary (dwelling #21).
C. Thomas (Rabbit-Tobacco) and Triva (Pikyas), daughter of Anita (dwelling #20).
D. Kane (Sand) and Jessie (Rabbit). See Figure 20, dwelling #13.
E. Courtney (Mishongnovi Eagle) and Mary Alice (Pikyas), daughter of Anita (dwelling #20).
F. Dalton (Chimopovy Sun) and Virginia (Tep), daughter of Lily (dwelling #27).
G. Second house of B.
H. Samuel (Rabbit-Tobacco) and Berdella (Real Coyote). This is a new house, built over Wiklavi kiva. He is the son of Mary (dwelling #21) and brother of Evelyn (new dwellings B and G).
J. Lonnie (Hotevilla Tep) and Anna May (Parrot). She is a daughter of Margaret (dwelling #1).

KIVAS

I. Tawaovi (active).
II. Wiklavi (inactive; house H built upon it).
III. Powamu (slightly active).
IV. Marau (active).
V. Al (inactive).
VI. Tao (inactive).
VII. Hano (inactive).

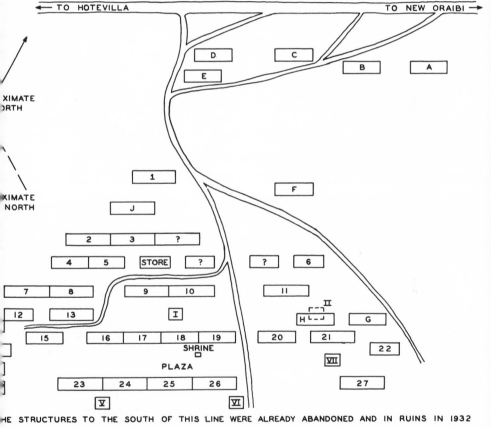

THE STRUCTURES TO THE SOUTH OF THIS LINE WERE ALREADY ABANDONED AND IN RUINS IN 1932

FIG. 21. HOUSE AND STREET PLAN OF OLD ORAIBI, 1964. (*Drawn by Charles D. Hall.*)

FIG. 22. GIRL CARRYING A BABY ON HER BACK. This mode of carriage was very common at Oraibi in the early thirties, but is now rarely seen.

FIG. 23. OLD MAN IN WINTER UNDERWEAR. This picture was taken at Old Oraibi in 1933. It shows Qöyayeptiwa, who was then in his nineties, wearing what used to be considered proper summer garb for elderly men. He is eating a lunch of watermelon; and his spindle rests beside him. Despite his advanced age he continued weaving a rug until he died.

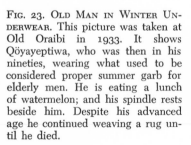

FIG. 24. BOY MOUNTED ON A BURRO. The animal's front legs are hobbled to keep it from wandering too far. Its clipped ears show that, in keeping with an old decree, it has been "punished" for having grazed on a farmer's crops.

FIG. 25. A PAIR OF BUTTERFLY DANCERS. Since they wear no masks, they are not *katcinas*. The girl has a tablita on her head; and the long bangs over her forehead are made of horsehair.

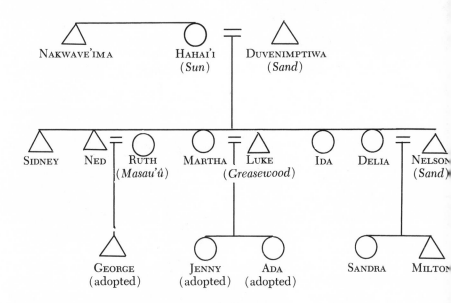

FIG. 26. NED'S FAMILY AT OLD ORAIBI, 1933–34.

touchy about this particular ailment I did not watch the treatment, but Ned told me afterward that Polingyauoma had "extracted" three "poison arrows."[11]

After the treatment we left in Ned's wagon, taking Polingyauoma as far as Hotevilla en route. All along the way Ned pointed out how the few Navaho cornfields that we passed were allowed to become overrun with weeds, and he constantly called attention to the state of the grass beside the road. (The condition of vegetation forms a large part of ordinary Hopi conversation.) During a stop for lunch Ned described more of his symptoms, which suggested that he might be suffering from a venereal disease. We reached Nestcili's hogan at about three in the afternoon.

Sun. Sept. 17. Spent the day with Ned among the Navaho.

Mon. Sept. 18. Returned on horseback, while Ned drove his wagon that was heavily loaded with wood. The trip back was uneventful. We stopped for a rest at the home of Siyesva in Hotevilla and were cordially received and given melon to eat. During our stay a young woman sat by, nonchalantly nursing a baby in our presence. [This custom persists. At the Mishongnovi Snake dance of 1955 a young mother, a former schoolgirl, suckled her child before me with no embarrassment and with no attempt at concealment.]

On starting for home we met Edna and offered her a ride back to Oraibi. At her brother's melon patch we stopped while she picked some fruit. Then, before getting back in the wagon, Edna stopped and urinated without lifting her dress. With a practiced foot she kicked a little sand over the wet spot and clambered into the wagon without a word. (No other Hopi woman ever acted thus in my presence. Is her indifference to excretion somehow connected with her easy morals?) [In 1966 an older woman was observed urinating without lifting her dress.]

When we got to the pueblo, Ned's mother was visiting his wife and both women thanked us for bringing wood.

During our absence a New Oraibi Sun clanswoman, Evelyn, had married Ray Siemptiwa in Holbrook. Ida was noncommittal, but Ned ventured the opinion that he didn't like Ray because it was his meanness that had caused his first wife, also of the Sun clan, to have committed suicide by taking strychnine. Ned thought that Ray was overly jealous because he was himself frequently unfaithful. At the same time Ned admitted that Ray was good to the baby daughter left by his previous wife. The child is being reared by its mother's mother, and Ned thinks it will remain there despite its father's remarriage. No one brought up the fact that Evelyn had a deformed leg. [Ray was still married to Evelyn in 1966. They live in Flagstaff, and their daughter Eunice is married to Supplee, a "White" man, who once taught at Ganado and is now teaching at Northern Arizona University.]

At night, when Kane and Louis came to report on their work, Kane said that he had been very ill last week. He had run a high fever but did nothing but bake in the sun. He did not call a medicine man. Kane also said that he had quarreled with one of his herding partners, Seba James from New Oraibi and an older brother to Tom. Kane had wanted Seba to do some extra herding so that he (Kane) might earn some cash by working on a dam-construction project. Kane argued that when Seba had been ill the preceding summer with boils on his buttocks, he (Kane) had done extra herding for him free of charge. Seba replied that he would repay the time if Kane were ill and that he was waiting for him to get sick. This, Kane says, so infuriated him that he told all the people Seba was waiting for him to get sick. (Does this mean that Kane now regards Seba as a witch? Possibly, although Kane has never openly said so.) Thereupon, Kane decided to break up his partnership with Seba. This put the third partner on the spot. He was Kane's father-in-law and Seba's father. In the end the older man pooled his flock with Kane, but promised to do extra herding for either one whenever necessary.

Tues. Sept. 19. Ned's mother and other Sun clanswomen are repairing the Sun clan house for use in future Sun ceremonials. [These ceremonials are supposed to take place in conjunction with the Niman *katcina* dance that used to occur not long after the sun had reached the summer solstice point. According to Ned, speaking in 1955, his old Sun clan uncle Talaskwaptiwa, his mother's mother's brother, used to have charge of these rites. Later, Ned succeeded him as Sun chief, or head man of the Sun clan, and carried on with the solar ceremonies. He may also have served as one of Oraibi's Sun Watchers, using *the* Sun clan house for his observations.

Early in the 1960s Ned retired and turned his post over to his older brother Sidney. Now, Sidney performs the traditional Sun clan observances at *the* Sun clan house during the summer solstice. As a rule, Sidney is aided by his nephew Milton (Sun), who lives at Hotevilla. Sometimes, while he was living, Pani-mptiwa (Gray Badger) used to lend a hand purely out of friend-ship because he hated to see any traditional custom lapse. He considered all Hopi ceremonies to be good for everyone.

At present Sidney watches the sun's apparent journey from the winter to the summer solstice. By word of mouth he tells his neighbors when it is the correct time to plant different crops, but some farmers prefer not to heed him and to rely on their own judgments.[12] For further details see pp. 134–35.]

A Marau dance is scheduled for Hotevilla, but neither Ida nor Ruth plans to attend. Ida says that it is not fitting for women to watch this performance except in their home villages; and Ned says that some of the performers are "half-naked" which doesn't "look right" to female spectators. [There is a surprisingly strong feeling of sexuality and shame connected with the Marau in the eyes of the Hopi. Some of the dancers wear kilts that expose their bodies from the thighs down, and native men call this dance "Knee-high." To a "White" American, however, there is nothing lewd about the costume nor suggestive in the performance. An opinion was expressed in 1955 that women were reluctant to view this dance away from home in order to discourage their husbands from attending and, perhaps, becoming infatuated with the dancers. Marau observances have long lapsed at Oraibi and are supposedly extinct on First Mesa, but they continue to be held at Hotevilla and the three Second Mesa towns.

In the summer of 1957 the town band of New Oraibi marched by daylight. It was led by two baton twirling majorettes from Walpi, wearing abbreviated skirts. No one commented on their costumes.]

Edith dined with Ruth and brought her a hand-sewn apron that she had made.

Nestcili's mother-in-law and her husband came on horse-back to shop at Hubbell's. They also brought some meat which they traded for *piki*. They were famished and ate heartily at Ruth's. Another woman and girl stayed overnight at the home of Puhumana.

Ned and Ida scolded two small children, not related to them, for stealing but did nothing more. They also scolded Betty for rarely attending school, and Lena for remaining away after her return from Chimopovy.

Two Hopi strangers, men from another Mesa, wandered about Oraibi this evening. They were supposedly on a govern-ment assignment dealing with insecticides, but Cedric was of the opinion that they were probably looking for girls. He went on to say that there were so few girls at Oraibi that the men would have done better in another village.

Cedric and Ida profess to "hate" each other because they are brother and sister. Their relationship stems from the fact that each has a Sand clan father. Cedric hit Ida with a small piece of melon rind, and in retaliation she snatched from his house a whole melon, which we ate at lunch.

Wed. Sept. 20. While working with the chief, Ned remarked that he had summoned Kiacwaitiwa by way of Nelson who had gone to Hotevilla to fetch wood for his mother. When Kiacwaitiwa failed to come, Ned remarked peevishly that the doctors weren't on the job these days. However, Kiacwaitiwa arrived after dark soaking wet from a rainstorm. He treated Ned by "extracting" several thin pieces of rabbit bone and a fragment of white shell from the Painted Desert. He then brewed medicine for Ned in a large seashell and gave him something to chew that would cause him to dream and thus learn the identity of the witches who were after him. Other details of the treatment Ned refused to divulge because Kiacwaitiwa had warned him that any further disclosure would bring victory to the witches.

Ida and Martha went down to New Oraibi to call on their recently married clanswoman Evelyn. Ida predicted that Evelyn would be "ashamed" to come out during the visit and said that if she had just been married, she, too, would feel "ashamed." [In retrospect, was Evelyn merely coy or was she ashamed because she had just married a widower and had become a basket-carrier? Compare p. 358, note 23.]

After making their call Ida and Martha did some shopping. They found Homer whistling and singing and teased him by asking if he were expecting Lily, his mistress. He replied in the affirmative, saying that he was going to marry a young girl, just as Ray had done. [Again, does this refer to the basket-carrying tradition?] Later, it turned out that Homer was not living with his wife, but it is hard to tell if this is a temporary separation or a divorce.

Thurs. Sept. 21. Ida accompanied her brother-in-law Nelson and his sister from Hotevilla when they went to pick beans and melons. She claimed that Superintendent Miller had "made" Delia and Nelson marry at the Agency before a minister; and that Mr. Marks had "insisted" on a "White" wedding for Martha and

Luke. [Most couples now go through a "White" ceremony in order to obtain written documents, whether or not they also have orthodox Hopi weddings.]

Ned paid Kiacwaitiwa for his treatment with some parakeet feathers.

Hahaiʼi went to New Oraibi to help Homer's mother plaster his house. When I showed surprise that she should help so unpleasant a man, I was told that Hahaiʼi was very friendly with Homer's mother and that he was always good to her. Yet, when Hubbell had once sold Ruth, Hahaiʼi's daughter-in-law, a teapot marked $1.50 for $1.25, it was Homer who made Ruth pay back the extra quarter.

George didn't come home from school this afternoon. Ruth wasn't greatly concerned, as she thought he would spend the night with an *ikya'a* at New Oraibi, but after dark he showed up.

Louise said that she had decided to use the Hopi name Qölmainmana for Ann. This was the name given the child by Puhumana, who had acted as mistress of the naming ceremonies.

Ida, Ned's sister, said with assurance that all of Ruth's babies had died young because she (Ruth) had neglected them. This statement strikes me as a case of sibling loyalty because Ruth is very devoted to her adopted son George, and bestows much affection on the babies of others.

I asked Mary to have supper with me. She seemed reluctant, but finally agreed. She explained that her children would tease her for having dined with a "White" man.

Ida reports that the New Oraibi people are sharply critical of Ned and his family for befriending "Whites." Strange that New Oraibi should be so concerned as it is supposed to be more "Americanized" than any other village at Third Mesa.

Lawrence is occasionally kept out of school to take Martin's turn at herding.

Joe has to do some extra herding for a brother who is working on a dam.

NOTE.—The freedom given to children may be what lays the foundation for the excessive individuality of adult behavior. Youngsters are seldom curbed and are generally indulged. For example, Ned and Ruth ate some cake that had been given them, without saving any for George. Afterward, Ned remarked that he was sorry to have forgotten about George, who was at school, but that he would give the child a nickel if he got really angry. On another occasion, the chief asked Betty to carry home another piece of cake, but she ate it on the way. People said that it didn't matter because he would have given it all to her in any case. At Hotevilla, while Siyesva was once skinning a little yellow bird, *sikyatci,* his young son had clambered all over him. Siyesva hardly reprimanded the child, addressing him in a soft tone utterly devoid of reproach or anger. [The *sikyatci* bird is supposed to be present at cornbakes.]

Thus children grow into adults, unaccustomed to criticism and entirely undisciplined in respect to control by others. One exception was noted. The other day, Evelyn had just climbed up the mesa after school when her uncle asked her to return to New Oraibi to fetch a parcel for him. She refused, but he insisted on her going; and she went. When Ida spoke about this episode, she was sympathetic with the child and indignant over the way Evelyn's uncle had "got after her."

Freedom of thought and action for each person explains why some members of a family turn Christian while others do not. Something of the same attitude may underlie Hopi unwillingness to intervene with regard to marriage and divorce.

Fri. Sept. 22. Ned reported that the diet the "doctor" had given him forbade him to eat muskmelon, beans, and onions because they had "too much iron." Nestcili had also told him not to eat muskmelon.

A Marau dance is scheduled at Chimopovy tomorrow. Hahai'i received a message asking her to come to Chimopovy to keep house for a clan sister who was planning to take part. Ida said that women who engaged in ceremonies often sought help from their kin.

This evening Ned voluntarily opened up on the subject of medicine. Before sunrise he had gone to the eastern edge of the mesa to pray for health to the sun. He is angry because he thinks Polingyauoma will no longer treat him. He suspects that Polingyauoma is jealous because he also uses Kiacwaitiwa, although the latter is not jealous of the former and even welcomes his cooperation. Ned says he is now on his guard and will wait and watch for Polingyauoma's next move. (Ned's attitude is probably based on the conceptual link between medicine men and witches.)

While Hahai'i is at Chimopovy, she is going to ask Jay Kuwanheptiwa to see Ned. [This helps to confirm the opinion that Ned is a hypochondriac.] Jay is a medicine man who, like Ned himself, was prenatally supposed to have been twins. (Ned here repeats exactly what he said last year about the circumstances surrounding his birth.) Ned says that this kind of "doctor" does not "extract poison arrows." Jay told the inhabitants of New Oraibi to call on him if they had trouble with their sex organs, as ordinary medicine men would only make them worse. Ned says that he had power like Jay's when he was young, but that he never became a medicine man because his grandfather had warned him it might arouse jealousy among other people and so lead to harm.

Just the same, Siyesva had heard of Ned's former power and had asked for his help when he was threatened with blindness. Ned took pity on him, examined him behind closed doors, thought that his eyes looked healthy and might improve, and decided to treat him. First he spat on his hands and rubbed Siyesva's eyelids "scattering the blood vessels," then he spat directly into the eye four times.

Here Ned digressed to say that there was a time when he used to chew *piki* before giving it to patients. Then he came to realize that this might spread such an infection as tuberculosis, whereupon he would stir *piki* in water with a spoon before feeding it to patients.

After treating Siyesva, Ned had said, "I'm not the one who can cure you. Go home and pray to your *dumalaitaki* ("guardian spirit") and my 'symbol,'[13] the sun." About two weeks later Siyesva came to thank Ned because his eyes were much better. He offered to pay but Ned refused, on the grounds that Siyesva might later regret having paid if he should ever be in want. Siyesva gratefully offered to call Ned his father, but Ned says that they now regard each other as brothers.

NOTE.—Too much success invariably arouses jealousy, gossip, and spite—thus leading either to injury by witches or the circulation of uncomplimentary remarks and nasty rumors. Hence the eagerness to avoid any show of success, to adopt a self-deprecating attitude, and to desist from boasting of one's power. Fear and suspicion still seem to be dominant factors in Hopi life.

Sat. Sept. 23. Several New Oraibi people have become ethnology-conscious. I suppose they think there is a mint of money to be made. It amused me to hear Amy's sophisticated son Oscar refer to the chief as his father, although the chief is really his father's brother, and then correct the term to uncle. This reveals that some of the old culture persists even after much "Americanization." [In later years Oscar worked for Fred Waring, and became the only Third Mesa Hopi to have taken a "White" wife. He also contributed much to Frank Waters, *Book of the Hopi*.]

Allen teased Ida, telling her that she was getting fat and that she must have been eating the vulvae (he used the crude Anglo-Saxon equivalent) of various animals. Ida seemed peeved but not particularly upset.

Drove to the Chimopovy Marau with Bert and others. Several other Oraibi men arrived later. [See chapter X, section B, for a description of this performance.]

Bert said that the Sun clan had first settled at Walpi, but had been kicked out because their women were prostitutes. The same thing happened when they moved to Chimopovy, whereupon they had come to Oraibi. Because of the same complaint some of the people at Oraibi had wanted to drive them out, but Lololoma had argued that the males were all right and were faithful to the ceremonies; thus, the whole clan had been allowed to stay.

Bert also said that at the time of the Split, Yokioma was supposed to go all the way to the Colorado River, but he had gone no further than Hotevilla because he had feared that his followers would not make so long a trek. Bert claimed that the Spider people, who had come to Oraibi from Chimopovy prior to 1906, had been prevented from splitting with the Bear at Chimopovy by government agents. (Tie this with the disintegrative tendencies in Hopi society, particularly at Third Mesa.)

When I got back to Oraibi, Ned was entertaining Nestcili, his wife, and a young Navaho boy. Polingyauoma was obviously awaiting his turn to eat after the Navaho. At this point Kiacwaitiwa arrived. Polingyauoma promptly became restless, muttered some excuse, and left. Ned said, "Let him go." Kiacwaitiwa then joined the Navaho at their meal.

When he had finished eating, openly before all who were present, Kiacwaitiwa went to Ned, who was lying on a sheepskin, and began his manipulations, massaging Ned's stomach and breathing on his right hand after every fourth stroke. I had been watching him closely as he ate, and this time I could not detect him preparing anything, yet he "extracted" three objects and called me over to see them. He identified them as a lump of paint pigment, a fragment of eagle bone, and a splinter of obsidian. Nestcili, himself a medicine man, and the Navaho boy crowded close and were much interested in the proceedings.

Kiacwaitiwa then explained that the pigment was of a kind Ned used when making Sun prayer sticks, that the eagle bone showed the jealousy of a phratry member, and that the obsidian was from a *yoisiva* ("lightning point") and gave power to the other two things. He warned Ned that some relative who was jealous of his ceremonial status was trying to harm him, but Kiacwaitiwa advised him not to weaken in the performance of his religious duties. Kiacwaitiwa then put the "extracted" things into the fire and gave Ned some medicinal herbs to brew and drink.

The Navaho medicine man was not impressed. He indicated that the objects had been previously palmed. Ned, however, was wide-eyed and excited. At a later time, when I asked Ned if he had noted that the "extracted 'arrows' " were dry and bloodless, he replied, "Yes. Aren't those medicine men wonderful? They can take things out of your body without cutting the flesh or getting them wet."

There is little doubt now but that Ned looks upon Polingyauoma with suspicion. His jealousy of Kiacwaitiwa and his uneasiness and withdrawal after the latter's arrival must make him appear guilty in Ned's eyes. It seems certain that if any injury befalls Polingyauoma, it will be interpreted as sure evidence of his being two-hearted, i.e., a witch.

Since it was late when Kiacwaitiwa had finished, I invited him to spend the night with me. He refused, saying that he didn't mind returning late to Hotevilla. [Next day I found out that he had spent the night in Hahai'i's house because he had been ashamed to sleep at a "White" man's.]

Sun. Sept. 24. There are numerous instances of urination and defecation, by members of both sexes, in full view of others.

Medicine men often express jealousy, claiming that their rivals don't know their business.

Went to a Yaiya'a [Ya-ya] dance at Walpi with Tom and his brother Quincy, from New Oraibi, in the latter's truck. The dance turned out to be a Hopi-Tewa performance at Hano. [See chapter X, section C.][14]

Mon. Sept. 25. Tom said that lots of Moenkopi boys had Ned's sickness, which he described as gonorrhea, and that his brother was having pain in urinating, even though his disease was different. Tom said that Kiacwaitiwa spent much time watching after his sick brother, and that he had once saved the life of his (Tom's) daughter by his treatment. This little girl used to fear her own father because of his long absences while trading with other tribes.

The salt-gatherers, who had left Mishongnovi after the Butterfly dance (p. 39), were due back today. Ned said that what they will bring back is tastier than store-bought salt.

Ida said that Kiacwaitiwa had told her Ned's illness was due to his worrying too much over things that people say about him. (Tie this with the diagnosis made by Frank Siemptiwa, p. 23.)

Everyone refers to the wind that has been blowing as the Marau wind, because a performance is to be held tomorrow at Hotevilla. Most of the Oraibi folk who are planning to go say that they are going primarily for such social reasons as visiting and feasting.

During the afternoon Jay Kuwanheptiwa came to treat Ned. He did not "extract" but merely massaged the affected area. His Antelope power is supposed to enter a patient through his hands. He also gave Ned some medicine and left some for Ruth to prevent her from becoming infected through intercourse. Ned said that this was hardly necessary as his sex appetite was "under control," and that even when he felt normal, he indulged only about once a week. Jay promised to prepare a more potent medicine if this one failed to work and cautioned Ned that it would have to be taken in secret. Ned, accordingly, hid it in his mother's house.

Bert asked Jim to repair his car. This is interesting because Jim is Bert's brother's son, but the New Oraibi branch is Christian and not especially friendly to the Old Oraibi branch.

Tues. Sept. 26. Tom took me to the Hotevilla Marau. Ned refused to go for fear of making himself more subject to the evil power of whatever witch was making him sick.

As soon as we had arrived, Edna's sister invited us to eat. A Navaho couple, total strangers, lingered in the doorway until someone finally asked them to eat.

At one place Tom met an *imûyi* ("grandson") who refused to shake hands with him, whereupon Tom pulled him off his seat. (This was proper because the two are in a joking relationship.)

One old man told of having been a good runner in his youth and claimed that if he got an early start, he could make Moenkopi for breakfast. He said that in the old days Oraibi men sometimes ran to Moenkopi (forty miles away) early in the morning, farmed during the day, and returned that same night. [Incredible as it may seem, there is every reason to believe the truth of this statement.]

The dance was not particularly impressive. There were

only about a dozen participants in the morning, but a few youngsters joined them after school was out. The performance closely
resembled the dance at Chimopovy, but there was only one "warrior," with a different female taking the part each time. Many
other features were curtailed, and there were no shooters.
[Compare chapter X, section B.] There was considerably more
byplay among the spectators than at Chimopovy. One of the
Marau songs made uncomplimentary remarks about various
young men who had recently gone through the Wuwutcim rites.
Another song thanked a Wuwutcim initiate called Piqöc ("Carrying-strap") for having composed a Marau song, but went on to
say that he was a Mexican carrying-strap because he had a snotty
nose.[15] The onlookers received all such quips with great merriment. As if in retaliation one of the recent Wuwutcim initiates
brought out a pair of large field glasses and ostentatiously trained
them on the kilt-wearing warrior, who happened to be Joe's
sister. Other initiates asked for a look, but the owner demanded
that they pay or go without. The poor "knee-high" warrior was so
abashed that she put the fox pelt that generally dangles from the
wrist directly in front of her.

When Ned heard about this, he replied that in November
the Wuwutcim men would get even by singing uncomplimentary
songs about the Marau women [pp. 301–3]. (If Wuwutcim men
happen to tease a non-Marau member, they must compensate her
with something like a rabbit.) This led Ned into a discourse on
various obscenities that clowns used to perform. He remarked
that these had shocked some teachers and school principals into
complaining, but he stoutly maintained that the antics of the
clowns were an important part of the rites and that what they
did was no business of the "Whites."

During the Hotevilla dance Ned was visited at Oraibi by
Jay, who gave him another treatment and reprimanded him for
harboring evil thoughts about his opponents. If Ned kept this
up, Jay told him, the witches would win out and cause him to
die. Then Jay urged Ned not to worry and so "put him on a
good road again."

Siyesva and his family were uncertain about coming to
George's birthday party next Friday. Ned was a little peeved. He
said it was "up to them," but he went on to comment that he
had twice invited them and would not do so a third time.

Wed. Sept. 27. Cedric and Juanita came to dine, whereupon
Ruth and Martha grew resentful because they said that Juanita's

mother, Puhumana, was among those spreading evil rumors about Ned.

NOTE.—Although the success of a ceremony requires complete cooperation, harmony, and good "hearts" among all the celebrants, no one takes it on himself to pass judgment on another's fitness. Each participant must make his own decision. Only when someone asks to *sponsor* a performance are his qualifications reviewed by others.

Martha married a sort of *imûyi* ("grandson") when she married Luke. His ceremonial father had been Perry, Martha's brother. Hence, she was a woman from the clan of Luke's ceremonial father and a ceremonial *ikya'a* to Luke. Such marriages are not unknown in Hopi practice.

A Shipaulovi man once came to live with a relative at Oraibi because he had a girl there. This affair did not result in marriage.

Ned paid Jay one dollar for his treatments and intimated that he would pay more if they resulted in a cure.

Tawaqwaptiwa called out for a meeting of Oraibi men this evening. They assembled at Bert's store but sat outside. The chief sat on the doorstep with Bert at his left. Martin faced them, and the others sat scattered in an irregular arc. Tawaqwaptiwa did most of the talking in a low, restrained voice, and Bert spoke up from time to time in a more excited and rapid manner. Other men contributed a few remarks. There was no special order observed, and two talkers now and then went on together. Most of the auditors sat in silence except for an occasional whisper. The subjects concerned Jack, Bert, Grace, and Martin. No women were present in the beginning, but soon the chief's wife joined the group, stood silently on the fringe for a few moments, then entered into the discussion. She was heard with as much attention as the masculine speakers. Soon three or four other women joined in and spoke up freely. Sam sat quietly for a time but grew impatient and withdrew. No concrete action resulted from the meeting.

Thurs. Sept. 28. Practically every woman in the village attended a sewing class in Voth's church that was conducted by Suderman and his wife.

NOTE.—There seems to be quite a heavy emphasis on the value of talk for its own sake. For instance, "doctors" use talk as part of their curing; good results were supposed to follow the talks that were held at the time of the Mishongnovi Snake dance; and last night's meeting was essentially a talkfest. Perhaps a good part of the chief's "ruling business" consists of talks.

NOTE.—There seem to be three basic factors in one's relationship to a clan-phratry. They are: (1) a feeling that one is a child of his father's clan; (2) a sense of relationship with the ceremonial and "doctor" father's clan; and (3) a tie with one's affinal clan. Any of these three factors makes possible substitutions whenever no one from an actual proprietary clan is available. This may be connected with the disintegrative aspect of Hopi society, as it provides a pool of eligible personnel for officers in the event of a split.

Why should not the same factors be assumed to have worked in bringing about clan groupings in times past?

Another factor to be considered is the taking in of clans that belonged originally to outside tribes. This is all the more possible since many tribes have clans with the same names as Hopi units. [It is also possible that mergers occurred for ceremonial reasons. For example, members of a substitute clan might offer to conduct a ceremony whose proprietary clan was allowing it to lapse.]

NOTE.—The Hopi have just a touch of the Trobriand idea of food display. They like to heap up bowls and bowls of food, particularly on feast days, and dislike doling out food in niggardly fashion. There may be more to this than appears on the surface.

Ned balked at giving complete information about yesterday's meeting. The chief said only that it wasn't interesting, and he claimed that the meeting was Bert's idea and was not a regular feature of Hopi life.

Throughout the afternoon George's female relatives prepared things for his birthday party tomorrow.

When Kane came over in the evening to report on his work, he told a long story about a Hopi who had taken wood from a Navaho hogan in which a death had occurred (*tcinti*). The man felt that it was safe to take the wood because he had a good team and strong harness. (Ned had once refused to dismantle such a hogan on the grounds that his team had weak harness.) While the wood-gatherers were camped for the night, the wood kept slipping off the wagon although there were no footsteps in the vicinity and no one was to be seen. Next day the horses had balked at every rise on the way, and their driver had had to unload and reload each time. As a consequence it took him two full days to complete a journey that is usually accomplished in a single day. The Hopi man had said that his horses had kept acting as though "something was holding them back," and vowed that never again would he take wood from a *tcinti* hogan.

Fri. Sept. 29. Joe said this morning that he was one of the Hotevilla children whom soldiers had rounded up after the Split and had forced to attend school at Keam's Canyon. His father had worked for and liked "Whites" and favored schooling even though he went to Hotevilla. Other inhabitants of that pueblo derisively called Joe and his siblings "White chiefs."

Kiacwaitiwa called on Ned, and Polingyauoma visited Clara. Polingyauoma will probably not be invited to George's party.

NOTE ON DISINTEGRATION.—Some of the chief's material suggests that village splits occurred even in legendary times. Sitcumovi is said to be an outgrowth of Walpi; and Shipaulovi is undoubtedly a branch of Chimopovy or Mishongnovi. The fact that these villagers are now friendly does not mean that there was no ancient rupture. After all, a Bakavi woman was seen dancing with a Hotevilla group, even though Bakavi was founded by people who had split from Hotevilla; Nelson, who lives at Oraibi as Delia's husband, joined Hotevilla's Wuwutcim; and even Tawaqwaptiwa, who drove out of Oraibi the people who founded Hotevilla in 1906, now has many friends there and eats frequently among them whenever he visits that pueblo. So do old antagonisms wear off after a rupture.

The party that went for salt from Mishongnovi on September 7 has just returned today after an absence of about twenty-two days.

Although George was allowed to leave school early on account of his birthday, he dawdled until overtaken by Lawrence. He seemed reluctant to get home and burst into tears when questioned. He stopped crying, however, when Lawrence "gave him a good talk." When Ruth asked why he was late, he again began to cry and said that he didn't want a party. When the guests began to arrive and gave him presents, George snatched them and never said thanks, despite the prompting of his father.

A first table was set entirely for relatives. Later, many other guests came, most of them from Oraibi.

During the feasting Jacob's Clara's youngest baby, who was stark naked, defecated on a mattress. This aroused quite a little chatter, and Clara carried out the soiled mattress. When the child continued its defecation on the floor, Clara removed the fecal matter with two pieces of cardboard. She then returned to the meal without washing, nor was the baby cleaned in any way.

> NOTE.—Possibly related to excretionary practices is the way men and women spit anywhere at any time.

Sat. Sept. 30. Old Qöyawai'ima came to Oraibi from Kikötcmovi to call on his Badger clan sister Juanita.

While I was working with the chief and Ned, Joe sat outside and openly listened to what was going on. After a time he couldn't restrain himself and came right in, breaking up the session. Curiosity and inquisitiveness about everyone else's business are typical for both sexes, and strike me as small-town traits. [Lack of space and an attendant lack of privacy may account for some of the distinctive features of pueblo "personality" and behavior.]

Hahai'i went about the village, securing the help of women for plastering the newly renovated Sun clan house. Ruth also got women, including Jacob's Clara, to help tidy up her winter quarters.

The chief said that Kiacwaitiwa was a good man and a good "doctor." He also said that Yokioma had had a stone picturing a decapitated man, which he is alleged to have shown to Theodore Roosevelt. Tawaqwaptiwa claimed that this meant Yokioma wanted to cut his (Tawaqwaptiwa's) head off, but the chief said Yokioma "wasn't man enough to do it." [Compare p. 11.] Without prompting, Tawaqwaptiwa went on to say that Yokioma was two-hearted. It is noteworthy that the chief insists that the whole Kokop clan—to which Yokioma had belonged—had consisted of witches.

> NOTE ON TOWN CRIERS.—Some of the ordinary announcements they make suggest that they occasionally act as agents to maintain discipline. Thus, the Oraibi crier, on being told that horses have been getting into the melon patch of Cedric's mother, called out to ask men to hobble their horses further off. [Horses often had to be hobbled so far away that it took

much time and energy to round them up when they were needed.]

Also, the crier had once asked for the return of a window that had been stolen from Edna's house. In another instance, Lee had seen that it was dangerous for youngsters to hang on the backs of trucks. She thereupon asked the New Oraibi crier to announce that children were to quit this practice.

A topic for jest at George's party was a fat man who was accused of being pregnant. Ned's father drew a big laugh when he asked a stout *ikwa'a* (husband of an *ikya'a* and a prime joking relative) when he was expecting to give birth and if he intended to hold a naming feast for his child.

When I asked how Kiacwaitiwa had started to be a medicine man, I was told that he had begun to practice following a vow made when he was very ill. As a Badger clansman he is thought to have known much about medicine all along, but he did not begin curing until after his illness. He was reported to have promised that if his own life were saved, he would pay for it by helping to prolong the lives of others. There is a feeling that if Kiacwaitiwa became lax in his business, he would surely die.

NOTE.—There is something contradictory about reputed witches seeking to prolong lives. This is undoubtedly related to the Hopi notion that life is the most important thing there is. Even witches are, under some circumstances, averse to terminating life.

More on Tawaqwaptiwa's suspicions toward all. He says he trusts the "White" sons he has adopted, but that he has no proof of how they will act in the future. He is waiting to see whether or not they will, in time, turn against him.

CHAPTER IV

Diary for October, 1933

[*Harvesting continues, especially the picking of watermelons and peaches for drying or canning. Children sometimes go from house to house, begging for food.*

The women's societies remain active; and small groups of women grind corn together, for the sake of companionship.

There is talk of a Masau katcina *dance that is soon to be performed at Hotevilla. It turns out that this* katcina, *because of its connection with Masau'û, the god of death, who does many things that are the opposite of normal expectancy, may appear even in the closed* katcina *season.*]

Sun. Oct. 1. Ida railed against Allen today, saying that he had appropriated many articles of his sister's that should have reverted, after her death, to Edna. He is also supposed to have wrongly taken two horses that had belonged to Perry. Everyone was indignant about these misdeeds and talked about them at length, but no one did anything. Ida remarked, rather naïvely, that Allen was as "mean" as a girl. She openly stated it as her opinion that girls are "meaner" than boys. [Relate this to the idea of *qövisti*, p. 14.]

On seeing a picture of Frank Siemptiwa, Joe remarked that he was no good. Apparently, Frank is disliked by most Oraibi men and women.

Ned told me that during the treatment Kiacwaitiwa had given him on the morning of George's party, he had "extracted" two bits of rabbit bone and a rabbit tooth fragment. Ned could think of no possible connection between these things and his sickness; but he felt that since these objects were far less powerful than those taken out the other day, it showed that his disease was getting better. I would guess that medicine men sometimes hit out blindly, hoping that their patients will make some sort of a connection that will satisfy them as to the "doctor's" wisdom.

(Just happened to remember that whenever George got a gift during his party, his mother and all his aunts would express thanks. [Compare p. 51.] There seems to be a feeling that a benefit to one woman is good for all her female kin.)

More on the small-town attitude at Oraibi. On hearing a dispute between Solimana and her husband, Ida deliberately went outside so that she could hear better. She took the best possible vantage point in full view of the couple but was careful not to leave the terrace of the house.

Ned recalled that while he was in school at Sherman Institute, he had fallen in love with a Moenkopi girl and had lived there for about a year and a half in 1908–9. He had stayed first with an *ikya'a* and then with a sister of his mother. There was no marriage because the girl's mother objected, presumably because a Sun clanswoman had years earlier stolen one of her sweethearts. The girl's father was the man Ned now calls his partner. This individual became a medicine man after he had been struck by lightning. He is supposed to have been a good-looking young man, who had had several wives and many mistresses.

Here Ned waxed a bit philosophical on the matter of sex attraction. He said that often feminine sweethearts who seemed perfect turned out to be bad wives on account of someone's jealousy. For his own part, he thought it was wrong to be jealous unless one caught a spouse in the act of adultery.[1] He did not approve of jealousy based only on hearsay evidence.

(Ned's data help to illustrate intervillage ties. If a man has a girl in another pueblo, he goes there to live; and matrilocal residence causes a husband to live in his wife's town. Thus do villages become linked.)

Mon. Oct. 2. Ned accompanied me to the house of Tawaqwaptiwa, who showed me a sacred stone that he claims to have inherited from Matcito, legendary founder of Oraibi. The chief says that when the Hopi originally emerged from underground, there were two such stones. One was kept by the ancestral Hopi and the other by the "White" man Bahana, who is supposed to have come out of the underworld together with the Hopi.[2] According to legend, says the chief, if ever the two should meet and show their respective stones, they would treat each other as brothers rather than mere friends. The chief says that he was instructed never to disclose his stone to outsiders unless he was in a tight spot and thought he had "White" friends who might help him. He speaks of another Hopi stone, smaller in size, that was held by Yokioma; and he refers to a third that was held by Lololoma's grandsons who had turned against him because they were partly Navaho. [I could never get confirmatory information about the other stones, or about the identity of "Lololoma's grandsons."]

In response to questions, Tawaqwaptiwa spoke about ancient medicine men who had practiced at Oraibi before 1906. He claims that the oldest and smartest was Dotuka (Kokop), who had belonged to the *real* curing society—now long extinct—that used to be called "Pocwimi." The second old-time "doctor" was Homikni, Ned's mother's father, a Lizard clansman who had died many decades ago and whom Ned had buried. He had begun his career as a stomach specialist, softening stomachs that had grown hard from "bad thoughts." Although Homikni did not "extract poison arrows," he was so successful that a Walpi medicine man, Nuvati, chose him for an assistant and taught him how to "extract." (Ned says that Homikni must have been a witch or he never could have learned the art of "extracting." Nuvati, himself a witch, is supposed to have known this before he selected Homikni for a helper.) Homikni had offered to transmit his craft to Ned, but Ned had refused because he was single-hearted and felt that he could never become a successful "extractor." The third of Oraibi's ancient "doctors" was Nasingainiwa (Eagle) who had started as a stomach specialist, had then become a bone "doctor," and finally took to "extracting."

Tawaqwaptiwa explains the shooting of arrows during Marau as a kind of exorcism designed to keep bad winds and other undesirable things away from crops. At Chimopovy the arrows had been shot at a bundle of vegetation made of *ma'ovi*,[3] which stood for crops.

NOTE.—Hopi ceremonies are by no means 100 percent rigid and fixed. Variations creep in (*a*) because of memory lapses, unchecked on account of the absence of writing; or (*b*) because of individual whim since no one takes it upon himself to dictate how another should behave; or else (*c*) because of the breakdown of traditional patterns of leadership frequently resulting in the transfer of ceremonial chieftainships from one clan or person to another.

Louis and two other Hopi left for Flagstaff to help harvest potatoes for the next two weeks. [Until quite recently Louis regularly went to Flagstaff to help a Mr. Burroughs harvest potatoes. The arrangement was simply a matter of convenience, and Louis generally picked his own helpers.]

Bill and Cedric joined a construction crew, and in their absence Cedric's brother Ed will stay home to keep things going.

Since Jacob's Clara, who helped Ruth prepare her winter residence, has no husband, she will be repaid with a load of wood.

Tues. Oct. 3. Nelson came to repair a window in Ruth's house. He said nothing, did his work in silence, and returned home without a word.

Ned decided to try active work for the first time in days. He got his horses, hitched up his wagon, and went to pick watermelon with Nelson. They made two trips, bringing the first load to Ruth and the second to Delia, Nelson's wife.

Many women are replastering their houses with the help of other females. Picking watermelon is the seasonal activity for men.

Joe said that he was supposed to help Louis pick potatoes, but that Louis had failed to notify him. He attributed it to Louis's jealousy, claiming that the "White" owner of the farm had once told him that Louis was lazy. Joe must have been mixed up, as the owner wrote directly to Louis.

Bill and Cedric did not get to work on construction because they had not taken a required physical examination. Later, Bill was examined and went to work, but Cedric did not. Joe said that Cedric was ashamed to strip in front of a doctor. He also said that only Navahos are being employed. [This is a standard Hopi complaint.]

(It looks as though Joe is not above spreading unfounded rumors. No one confirmed his charge that Cedric was too bashful to strip; and Joe's brother-in-law Bill, a Hopi, was hired on a crew made up, supposedly, of Navaho.)

Cedric and Juanita had had an "American" wedding and a Hopi wedding after their first child was born. The birth took place during the ceremonies, and Juanita was surely pregnant before either rite took place. Like Louise, Juanita was a teen-ager when her first child was born. Is her case, as was true of Louise, an instance of *dumaiya?* Probably.

Joe is somewhat contemptuous of Kane. He feels that all the talk of raising sheep and diminishing farming is just daydreaming.

In a discussion of Voth's disregard of Hopi conventions respecting the privacy of kiva rituals, Joe said openly that the Hopi were cowards. [Voth often went into places which he had been forbidden to enter.]⁴

Wed. Oct. 4. Joe has agreed to talk about Hotevilla tomorrow.

The chief chuckles whenever Edna's name is mentioned. He and Ned anticipate much fun when her name is reached on our census and they try to list her husbands. Her escapades are a ready source of merriment; and Puhumana is said to have been nearly as bad.

Andrew announced that an Oaqöl dance is to be held at Sitcumovi. Several Hopi greeted the news with the usual cracks about starving at First Mesa. "Even if people know you," they said, "they don't ask you to eat." [This notion was repeated in later years. Oraibi's inhabitants claim that all the Hopi towns are getting lax about inviting guests to eat, but that for unknown reasons Sitcumovi is the worst of all.]

At last Ida has again opened up the subject of *dumaiya*. She regarded a Hotevilla man as "crazy" because he publicly talked about his sweethearts. [The Hopi, as do we, frequently use the word "crazy" (*honakti*) for one who is excessively amorous. We often speak of a person being crazy over someone. Note too the dread of publicity.]

The Hotevilla man in question was supposed to have told Louis that he would make a *dumaiya* call on Ida during a Bean dance. Sure enough he showed up and openly asked Hahai'i if he could call on Ida. Ida was furious and indignantly refused to see him. (This man is now married to a Hotevilla girl whom he first made pregnant. His wife had borne an earlier bastard to Benjamin, but since her sister objected to Benjamin, the girl in question never married him.)⁵

(A surprisingly large number of premarital pregnancies have been noted. They seem to be a regular preliminary to marriage but are probably *not* tests of fertility. It is likely that whatever bashfulness the Hopi exhibit, as in the case of Marau dancers, results more from an aversion to publicity than from a sense of modesty.)

Several Zuñi visitors arrived in New Oraibi this evening. There seems to be a firm conviction that they really are related to Hopi of their own clans. Ned and Tom voluntarily added that the Hopi had lots of relatives in the New Mexico pueblos, and that they didn't even know all of them.

Superintendent Miller, it is alleged, sent Tom a letter asking him to kill all Hopi dogs. Knowing how much resentment this was likely to cause, Tom did nothing about it.

Trouble looms ahead. Some of the Hopi, Panimptiwa in particular, who had been taken to the World's Fair at Chicago saw a reconstruction of the Soyal climax in the Field Museum, now the Museum of Natural History. They claimed that it showed Ned as the Sun (Star) chief, about to twirl the plaque which is supposed to reverse the sun's course after the winter solstice. Ned is sure that he never revealed his part in the rites except to our party of last year. I suggested that the group in Chicago was a reconstruction made by Voth and promised to write for information that would put Ned's mind at ease.[6]

Thurs. Oct. 5. Went to Andrew's house and found him stringing a turquoise necklace. He expects to trade it to a Navaho for thirty or forty sheep.

Worked on Hotevilla kivas with Joe.

Ned was treated by Sami, chief of the Walpi Ya-ya'a society and a highly regarded "doctor" from Walpi. He did not "extract" but prescribed a medicinal brew after questioning Ned thoroughly about his symptoms. Ned was greatly impressed, found that the medicine "tasted good and strong," and paid for the call with groceries that cost him $2.25.

Ned revealed that he had dreamed that he was drowning but that he had somehow managed to struggle ashore. There I had met him, given him a corn "mother," made the Hopi naming speech that he had taught me, and called him "Napoleon." He then asked me to tell him about Napoleon, and when I did he was greatly impressed. He interprets the dream to mean that he will win out in his long struggle against disease.

Martha came to my place after supper and teased me about going *dumaiya*. It was certainly good to get a spontaneous use of the word and a free reference to the custom it describes.

Kane and Joe dropped in before bedtime. There was much talk of sheep and some joking about Joe's bad luck in trapping coyotes. [It is possible that this refers to his lack of success in obtaining the favors of a Coyote clanswoman.]

Fri. Oct. 6. Today Ned claimed that he had gotten the dream he described yesterday by putting cornmeal under his pillow when he went to sleep. [By 1955 he had become sophisticated enough to insist that cornmeal had nothing to do with dreaming. Instead, he asserted, dreams arise only from one's wish or will.]

The Walpi "doctor" treated Ned again, singing a song and scattering ashes in circular fashion, four times about his body and away.[7] He also used a "lightning point" (arrowhead), *yoisiva*, for doling out medicine. When Ned took his medicine, he stirred it with his fingers, drank most of the liquid, rubbed some on his penis, added more water, stirred with his fingers again, then drank and rubbed some more. Neither the "doctor" nor he saw anything wrong in this procedure.

Tawaqwaptiwa received a visit from a Christian nephew who resides at Kikötcmovi. No resentment was shown, and the chief even seemed pleased because his nephew had retained an interest in things Hopi.

Cedric and Juanita have been living at her mother's house for the last few days.

Practically all the women in town cooperated to help Solimana build a new *piki* house. Hahai'i was among the most active helpers, despite the fact that her son hates Solimana. (Hahai'i is very proud of her skill in dealing with *piki* ovens. Besides, Hopi individualism is so strong that a mother and son do not feel compelled to love or dislike one another's friends or enemies. On the other hand, Ida does not bring Solimana any surplus food because she fears her brother will "get after her.")

When boys who went through the *katcina* rites grow up, they generally learn the identities of the *katcina* impersonators who had whipped them. Thus Kane knows that he was whipped by Tom. No resentment is felt although everyone speaks of the severity of the whippings.

Kane is sometimes accused of taking little part in ceremonies. The reason may be that so few are available to him at Oraibi. The Wuwutcim (Tribal Initiation) had lapsed before he was of an age to join. Ned's group, which went through the rites when they were last held at Oraibi (around 1912), is still considered to be only incompletely initiated. Full initiation cannot be achieved by one set of men until a succeeding set has gone through the rites. Failure to pass through the Wuwutcim debars a man from full participation in the Soyal. This, coupled with Oraibi's extinction of the Snake, Antelope, and Flute societies, leaves Kane little chance to take part in much more than *katcina* activities.

A ceremonial father in the Tribal Initiation first takes his "son" to the Kwan kiva and then carries him on his back to the kiva that houses his particular branch of the joint observances. Since Kwan's patron is Masau'û, the Hopi god of death, does this bear on the notion of death and rebirth? [It does.]

Many families are picking and canning or drying peaches. No major harvesting of crops has yet begun. Subsequent observations reveal that harvesting is not performed at a single moment of time but goes on for weeks, as the condition of various crops dictates.

Sat. Oct. 7. Nelson again helped Ned bring in two loads of melons, one for each of their households. As the second load wasn't full, the men brought in beans, plants and all.

Poliyestiwa, who is Kane's stepfather, helped carry melons to Louis's Clara, who is his *ikya'a*.

Cedric explained why his family is living with Puhumana. They are to stay there until after Louise's wedding is completed in November. Cedric will do much weaving and will supply about fifteen sheep for feasts. He will be repaid with cornmeal to be ground by Louise's sisters and sisters-in-law. In other words, Louise's female kin, Greasewood women or those married to Greasewood men, will do the grinding; and men connected with Dick's Badger clan will weave the garments and provide meat. Phratry groups count the same as clan relatives, and spouses of men or women in the phratries concerned are expected to help. [Note should be taken of this instance of reciprocity.]

Cedric also explained that he had failed to return to construction work not for the reasons given by Joe. He had decided to begin harvesting because while home he had noticed Albert's cows were getting into his corn.

After dark, Cedric saw someone go by on the street. Casually, he remarked that it must be some fellow "who was trying to sneak in someplace." [This is probably a reference to *dumaiya*.]

Cedric and Ned spoke about a "White" visitor who went about only in shorts and whom the Hopi called "No-shirt-no-pants." Ned remarked that one could see his private parts when he sat down. Cedric commented that his wife had noted this and had kidded him about it. [In private, the Hopi frequently laugh and make contemptuous remarks about "White" tourists and their strange clothing.]

It is strange to hear Ned condemn marriages into one's

father's clan, because his own parents are so related. There is evidence for many similar marriages, some of them reaching far into the past.

Sun. Oct. 8.

NOTE.—During this morning's interviewing we came to the case of a Hopi who is supposed to have married a Navaho and taken her into *his* clan—Masau'û. This suggests another way that some clan groupings might have come about. (Consider this with reference to combinations like Real, Gray, and Navaho Badger.)

Little Milton's *ikya'a* jokingly offered to take him along to Hotevilla. He cried so bitterly when his mother, Delia, tried to take him away that he was allowed to go to Hotevilla with his *ikya'a*.

A Hotevilla girl named Asola (?) had a child by Benjamin and another by Haiyeva, whom she later married. Asola was also much desired (and possibly had) by Allen and Cedric. Ida teases them about it. Allen also was said to have been sweet on Jacob's Clara, and some say that is why Betty hurried to marry him.

Cedric told more about his "White" wedding to Juanita. It took place at the Agency, and the officiating clergyman gave some sort of a lecture that Cedric didn't understand. I suppose, though, that this counts as a Christian ceremony.

Contrary to my impression [p. 73], Tawaqwaptiwa was not pleased with his Christian nephew's visit. Although he treated his guest cordially on the surface, the chief fears trouble such as he had with his visitor's Christian father. [Chief Tawaqwaptiwa's own brother Charles was a zealous Christian, who had moved from Old to New Oraibi. The incident refers to a heated argument that once took place in Tom's store at New Oraibi when his Christian brother tried to convert the staunchly pagan Tawaqwaptiwa.]

NOTES ON CHILD TRAINING.—Joe tried to keep a five- to six-year-old daughter from interrupting during an interview. She persisted and he insisted, but I noticed that as he grew more angry, he lowered his voice instead of raising it. The chief does the same thing under similar circumstances. It has a soothing effect on a child.

Contrary to the frequent observations of indifference to genitalia is the manner in which older people invariably chide a youngster, particularly a girl, if she exposes her sex organs when clad.

This afternoon we planned to go to a Navaho Squaw dance. Ned refused to go along because he thought that one of his "doctors" might call and because he wanted to save his strength so that he could attend some of the Hopi women's ceremonies that are scheduled for the near future.

NOTE.—Don't overlook the obvious fact that the clan system is sometimes an integrative factor; namely, when it keeps ceremonies going that would die out if limited families failed.

Mon. Oct. 9. Cedric had planned to haul wood today but decided instead to harvest his beans because Albert's cattle had been getting into them.

Sutton wrote Ned that he would like to spend a week or so at Oraibi and suggested that he would like to stay at Edith's. Ned is trying to get Martha to take Sutton in, presumably so that he may keep in closer touch with his "White" friend, as well as to give his sister a chance to earn some money.

Ray Siemptiwa and Evelyn are Christians but do not seem to take their conversions very seriously. [Yet, by midcentury Evelyn was a devout Christian and an ardent Sunday school teacher.] Ray takes part in *katcina* dances, and Evelyn watches many rituals. Ida repeats that girls who go to school in Albuquerque tend to become Christians. It is also frequently said that some students "used to be Christian" while they were at school. Now and then, too, one hears of an adult who "used to be a Christian" for a time.

More small-town stuff. Ida shushed me so that she could the better hear what Mary, across the way, was saying. Mary was gossiping about an old lady at Hotevilla who was considered "mean" and was generally disliked.

Couldn't pin Ned down to an explanation of why all the Ya-ya'a and Somaikoli members were not branded as witches since all "doctors" and "powerful people" are supposed to be two-hearted. Ned and the chief seemed to be utterly dumbfounded by such questions.

Hahai'i, Ida, and Jenny ground corn till late at night. Delia did not join them presumably because there was no more room, but Ida accuses her of being lazy.

Jasper came in for a smoke. He said that he had heard Edna was up in arms at the rumor that I was going to get the names of her ten husbands. (The names of only eight were given.) Edna threatened that she would claim whatever money was paid for information about her marital affairs. It is amazing how this kind of thing spreads. The villagers appear to be so eager for something to talk about that they cannot keep still, even in matters that may be detrimental to themselves.

THOUGHTS ON BASTARDY.—New Oraibi's leading citizen took calmly the news that his sister had just had her third bastard. Informants said, "Oh, he won't do anything about it. He's just as bad himself." Apparently, bastardy is rife everywhere. The common attitude seems to be something like this. When an illegitimate child is born, everyone says that the mother did wrong, and there is much talk but no action. If the same woman bears another bastard, people say, "Oh, that's the way she is. Last year she had a bastard, this year she's got another, and I suppose she'll have one every year." When a third child comes, it is unnoticed or simply joked about.

Tues. Oct. 10. Joe and Cedric said this morning that they didn't like Solimana because she said "mean" things about them. Yet, their wives helped make her *piki* house.

At noon the Sudermans held a sewing class at Voth's church on the mesa. Ida jumped up when it was announced by the crier. She was all excited and fearful lest she be late. Practically every woman at Oraibi went.

Ned and Ruth lunched with Betty, wife of Allen. He is a phratry brother of Ruth, and she has been helping Betty do some plastering.

Ned admitted today that he has abstained from telling me about the obscene pranks performed by clowns because he didn't think they would sound good to me. Also, when the chief revealed an incestuous marriage that concerned the Sun clan, Ned had refused to translate until he had asked the chief if he thought it would be all right to tell such things to a "White" man. (He must be watched and checked on very carefully in the light of these revelations.)

In the beginning of work on the Oraibi census, for example, Ned and the chief had claimed that there were no divorces and no remarriages. After a time the same man was found to have been listed as the husband of two different women. Tactfully, I said that I must have made a mistake, whereupon Ned and Tawaqwaptiwa began to laugh and admitted that the man had been divorced and remarried. From that point on they gave numerous instances of "brittle monogamy."

Wed. Oct. 11. Siyesva came to visit Ned. He has a new name given by his ceremonial father, a Kokop, when he went into the Wuwutcim at Hotevilla. Ned said that the name referred to Masau'û, and he let fall a hint that the Kwan are supposed to "kill" the boyishness of an initiate, so that he drops his baby name. (This seems to relate to the "death and rebirth" procedure that was already noted in the Tribal Initiation [pp. 73–74]. It is very important and should be investigated further.) [See especially O.O., p. 136, fn. 47.]

During the course of today's work, the chief several times cried out in mock anguish when certain names were mentioned. All had reference to past love affairs. He had been a handsome youth and had enjoyed the favors of many girls and women. Ned says that if a man makes love to an *ikya'a,* a green lizard will chase and urinate on him. This is said to be painful but not poisonous.

At night Kane got talking about clan groupings and said that he couldn't make anything out of them. He is Sand and claims that only one real Sand man whose ancestors came to Oraibi long ago is now alive. His own Sand forebears came from somewhere near Sikyatki. Of course, all the Sands then combined, and Kane says that he feels very close to all Sand people, whether or not he can place them in his own line of direct descent or lineage; but he adds that he is "only a little bit connected" with Snake and Lizard (other clans in his phratry), which he clearly differentiates from Sand. Apart from his own mother and Ned's father, Duvenimptiwa of the Sand clan, and perhaps one other man, practically all of the Sand people went to Hotevilla in 1906.

This business of a close tie with one's own clan, but of being "only a little bit connected" with the others of one's (phratry) group, is a universal attitude expressed also by Ned, Tawaqwaptiwa, Allen, Ida, and others. Possibly, too, this kind of differentiation is an indication of something that might apply to lineage groupings within a single clan, somewhat in keeping with Parsons's idea.[8]

It was curious to find Kane expressing satisfaction over the fact that since 1906 Oraibi had split into five villages (Hotevilla, Bakavi, Old Oraibi, Kikötcmovi, and Moenkopi) because, says Kane, it made land less scarce and made it easier than in the past to graze flocks. In the old days there was much congestion.

Kane says that Louis had taken a Hotevilla man, Kenneth, and a New Oraibi man, Lucas, to pick potatoes with him at Flagstaff. Contrary to what Joe had told me, these men were mentioned specifically in the letter that Louis got. A smaller crew than usual was wanted this year, and Joe does not seem to have been left out because of Louis's jealousy.

Thurs. Oct. 12. Ned disclosed that he had been making daily prayers to the sun at dawn. He said that he prayed hard, telling the sun that he was feeling better, thanking it for its help, and asking it to look at his path and to see that it was good. This morning he had notified the sun that he was going to give up his daily visits for the time being because if he said that he was giving them up altogether, it would be *qwivi* ("vain" or "presumptuous") and might keep the sun from listening to him the next time he prayed. (People of any clan may pray to the sun.) [Around 1960 Mary said that she had wanted her children to make similar morning prayers (*kuivato*) but that they preferred not to arise so early.]

Siyesva, hoping to repay Ned for having treated his eyes [p. 57], sought and sought for a special plant that he knew about from his father, a medicine man. (It is not known why Siyesva did not ask his father for help when his eyes were troubling him.) This plant is rare around Third Mesa but is said to be common at the San Francisco mountains where, the Hopi believe, all sorts of medicinal plants abound. At last Siyesva's prayers were answered and he found the plant whose virtues were known only to him and his father. He gave it to Ned when they were alone and asked him to use it in secret. Siyesva explained that the plant was "alive," and told Ned that it had an unpleasant taste but was very potent. Ned is to chew one stem at a time. Although he feels better, Ned will still use this plant. He believes that the best policy is to use everyone's medicine, on the theory that if one remedy fails, another may work.

An old Hotevilla uncle of Ruth, merely a phratry relative from the Coyote clan, came with a bag of chili peppers that he traded for sugar. Ruth took half and her sister, Louis's Clara, took the rest. The old man also brought some home-knitted stockings which Ned bartered for groceries. Ned intends to use them in trading for turquoise with San Domingo or other New Mexican Indians who might come this winter.

NOTE ON INDIVIDUALITY.—It is most startling to learn that even the performance of an important ritual is left entirely to the will of its owner. Also, the ceremonial father who puts a boy through *katcina* cannot force the boy to join any of his other societies. The most such a father can do is to urge his "child" to follow in his footsteps, but the final decision is up to the youngster. Beyond any doubt this custom is a disintegrative feature.

This noon Ned ate some chili peppers and remarked that they tasted hot to those with jealous temperaments but not to people of even temper. Later, someone suggested that Ned kill a sheep for making tamales. He replied jokingly that he would do so as soon as he was able to sleep again with his wife. "I've kept out of her a long time," he explained.[9]

The Walpi "doctor," Sami, today released Ned from his diet. "All food is beneficial," he said, "and should be eaten freely." This "sounded good" to Ned, so now he eats everything.

Ned butchered a sheep for Siyesva, who will pay for it by helping Ned with his harvesting.

An important fact came to light while I was listing ceremonial affiliations. Moenkopi people rarely join religious societies. [It is now evident that Moenkopi never had a full ritual cycle of its own; and that it was most inconvenient for its inhabitants to come all the way to Oraibi for ceremonies, even though the Oraibi rites were open to qualified residents of Moenkopi.][10]

When, in our house survey, we got to Puhumana and her marriages, Ned refused point-blank to list her husbands, even though he admitted that he knew their names. Perhaps he feared the same sort of trouble from her that Edna had threatened to make [p. 77].

NOTE ON PROSTITUTION.—Prostitution is certainly not unknown even in so small a pueblo as Oraibi. Besides the suspicion I have of Edna, I was told of another woman (unnamed) who took lovers for money.

The orthodox Hopi generally accuse Fred Johnson, of Kikötcmovi, of having burned the sacred paraphernalia of the Al ("Bow") society. Duvenimptiwa claims to have seen the stuff being removed while most of Oraibi's populace was away watching a dance at another village. Men from New Oraibi are usually blamed for having destroyed the things, but Ida says it was a Chimopovy Christian who did the burning. [Another version is given in O.O., p. 208.] This man is now dead, and it is "natural," therefore, for Ida to regard him as the culprit. Before he died, she says, he constantly dreamed of Al men, and at the time of his death he is said to have been haunted by a host of Alaitakam ("Al men") who swarmed about him.

Ida was badly frightened last night by the howling of a dog that sounded like the call of Masau'û.

Fri. Oct. 13. Tawaqwaptiwa is hard at work preparing a field for next season's planting. He does a reasonable amount of farming these days [in spite of what Allen says].

NOTE ON INTEGRATION AND DISINTEGRATION.—The location of villages on mesa tops may further disintegration among the Pueblo Indians because it forces farmers to reside at a distance from their farms. This may encourage farmers to move near their fields, to establish a new settlement that may achieve independence, and so to break away from the parent community. This seems to have happened at Moenkopi and Acomita. Overcrowding and farming convenience may also work toward similar results even if the original pueblo was not on a high mesa, as in the case of the new towns outside of Laguna and Zuñi.

If Hopi society is *potentially* disintegrative at all times, why do not pueblo splits occur more often? The answers may begin with inertia, together with lack of leadership resulting from fear of witchcraft accusations.

Also, while membership in secret societies tends to divide a pueblo's populace into small cliques, no clan performs major rites exclusively for its own benefit or only with its own members. On the contrary, each ceremony draws on people of various clans and so serves to bind them together. Exogamy, phratry ties, and kinship extensions that are binding on a host of relatives also help hold together large numbers of people. Just the same, the Hopi are not unaware of the disintegrative *potential* of their own society, as witness their frequent pleas for pueblo unity and harmony.

During the afternoon Joe showed me a rock [Sowika, O.O., Pl. III c] where parents bring sick children for cures. (Must get more on this.)

Joe also showed me the shrine used by Sand clanswomen. It is sacred to the founder of the Lakon society, and he definitely calls her a witch.[11]

Joe states that clans sometimes meet as units and that all officers are supposed to train their successors. He feels that the proper altars are the most important part of rituals. [Others disagree. Ned emphasizes singing and the use of sacred corn-meal.] Ordinarily, there is no difficulty about a successor, who should be a chief's brother or his sister's son. However, if a leader dies suddenly or has never trained an heir, the head woman of the proprietary clan generally talks the situation over with her clansfolk and then makes a selection. [It is said that in the old days, when tribal warfare was common, the feminine heads learned their clan's ceremonies so that they might serve as repositories in the event that a masculine successor had to be trained to replace a suddenly slain ceremonial leader.]

So far I have noted that the following are the items concerning which clans function as units: land ownership, names, possession of common *wuyas* ("ancients"), certain houses, cisterns, snow deposits (for water), shrines, and ceremonies. [In ancient times, melted snow was often an important source of water.]

Sat. Oct. 14. One of Lee's brothers drove a bunch of young men to Winslow to see a football game between the Phoenix Indian School and the Winslow High School. After the game we went to the Santa Fe Railroad's workyards and ate with a clan sister of Ruth, who asked about Ned's illness. Some of the New Mexican Indians were staging a dance that night, and I was told that "Whites" could not attend. Thus, discrimination works both ways, for public restaurants would not serve even 3.2 percent beer to the Indians.

Jay Kuwanheptiwa, the medicine man from Second Mesa, visited Ned and spent the night at Oraibi. Although he knew much about Ned's illness and was aware that there had been a discharge from his penis, he crept into Ned's sleeping bag without a qualm. [The sleeping bag had been given to Ned by a "White" friend.]

Half a dozen men dropped in for a chat before bedtime. Ned read them a letter from Sutton, asking for details of damage done to crops by Albert's cattle. Cedric reported that at a recent meeting of the New Oraibi council Albert had been fined twenty-five dollars for letting his cattle damage crops. (I doubt if Albert ever paid the fine.) [He did not.]

Sun. Oct. 15. At Sunday school there was the customary large turnout of women and children.

Ida is sewing for Kane's wife, and Hahai'i is making *piki* for Evelyn. Evelyn is not planning a Hopi marriage and may not repay Hahai'i, but this doesn't seem to trouble the older woman.

Mon. Oct. 16. Heard some choice gossip today. Mary is supposed to have had a bastard (now dead) by some man before she married Joe. Before his marriage Joe had had an affair with Edith, who had likewise had a bastard by another man. She attributed the child, who has since died, to her husband.

Ida is to grind corn today for her sister Martha.

First Tom, and then Allen, invited Jay to have breakfast with them even while a meal was being prepared by Ida. Ned says that it isn't right to try to hold a guest when he is invited elsewhere.

Cedric claims to have harvested only two wagonloads of corn. He normally gets as many as eight loads. This year he feels that he would have gotten a third load were it not for the damage done by Albert's cattle.

More instances of public urination, especially by males. At Hotevilla, one little boy was observed micturating from a housetop to the plaza.

Little Sandra was sick and cried all of last night. Her folks did not plan to call a "doctor," but as Jay happened to be in Oraibi, he was asked to treat her for earache.

Yesterday George had had his head washed for the first time since Ruth and Ned had adopted him. Hahai'i gave him the Sun clan name Tawawuyioma, but he will continue to use the name he got at his *katcina* initiation. Other Sun clanswomen did not name him but laid hands on his head to express their participation in the rites. Hitherto, George had refused to have his head washed because he did not like cold water. Ned had refrained from force and had used only gentle persuasion, "talking good" to him several times.

Tues. Oct. 17. A death by witchcraft was attributed to Laura, but there was some doubt of it because the victim was not related to the witch.

NOTE.—Not only does the horror of witchcraft acquire greater emphasis from the fact that the two-hearted must work on relatives, but the same belief [that witches can harm none but relatives] serves to keep disputes and quarrels "within the family," as it were. Squabbles over witchery might have more serious consequences if one were free to go about accusing total strangers. [When I checked on witchcraft notions in 1966, I was told that most of the old beliefs still prevailed. The more sophisticated tend to give them up, yet witchcraft may be invoked to "explain" any mysterious or extraordinary phenomenon.]

Sandra was taken to be cured to the chief, who treated her in his capacity of Soyal leader. The treatment made her feel better and she slept well.

NOTE ON OBSCENITY.—Don't forget that "White" interference has done much to force the people to conceal such activities as much as they can. They have not really changed their ideas about sex and excretion but have learned to hide them from "White" observation. It is even possible that "White" teachings about the dirtiness of sex have made them self-conscious. This may account for the seeming contradiction between their easy sex behavior and the painful bashfulness of participants and women onlookers during the open-to-the-general-public performance of the Marau. For instance, Ned teases freely about sex with other Hopi, but he gets angry if Ruth or Ida tease me, a "White" man, about sex.

Some Hotevilla women came to Oraibi to trade chili peppers for siva'api ("rabbit-brush"). The dried fibers of this plant are used for weaving plaques and baskets. [Third Mesa plaques and baskets always have raised centers. They are made by twining or weaving, wherein the fibers that form the weft are passed over or under fixed warp elements. Most of Third Mesa's feminine population continues to make various objects by the weaving technique.]

Ned gave watermelons to some Navaho and asked them to have Nestcili bring his horse. Now that he feels better, he thinks that he can herd from horseback.

In the course of the afternoon's interviewing, Tawaqwaptiwa again made reference to a former sweetheart. Cedric was present and he was kidded about having at least four girls at Hotevilla, as well as an adult [married?] mistress at Bakavi.

There may well be much truth to those jests as Cedric is very good-looking.

Ida gets angry whenever I refuse to eat all the food that she has prepared. On one occasion when I protested that I would get sick if I ate any more, she exclaimed, "Who ever heard of such a thing? Getting sick from food!" (This is a typical Hopi attitude.) [See p. 8o.]

During the evening Tawaqwaptiwa and several men assembled informally and began to chat about the possibility of an airport at Kikötcmovi. The chief said that the land was his, but Otto claimed it was New Oraibi's. All that the chief would say was that he was "kind of waiting" to see what Otto would do about it. (This is typical of the Hopi way. They never act to prevent an enemy or an opponent from carrying out a threat. Instead, they wait until he has made his move, and then they *may* try to get retribution.) [Compare the chief's remark on p. 66.]

Joe insists that the brother of Frank Siemptiwa refuses to be trained as successor to the Pikyas chieftainship in the Soyal. He says, half seriously, that the man is "powerful with the ladies" and that he may not want to observe such taboos on sex as the office entails.[12] [Frank's brother Qopilvuh, now a very old man, still lives at Moenkopi. He is a helper to the pueblo's chief.]

Wed. Oct. 18. Tawaqwaptiwa said that he had often cured people, including Ida when she was little, of earache. He described the treatment he had given Sandra as follows. He first sang a Soyal song. Then he exhaled, breathing gently into her ear; and sucked hard as he inhaled. He repeated this four times, after which he chewed a combination of cornmeal and cedar ashes, took a pinch of the mixture in his left hand, waved it four times around the affected area, and then threw it away from him over his left shoulder. (This is like the act of discharming and is the standard manner in which ceremonial officers effect cures.) He was tickled silly when I called him a good doctor.

The Walpi medicine man, Sami, called on Ned again this morning. Like Jay he pronounced Ned better. Both men, however, left medicine for Ned to take—supposedly to make assurance doubly sure.

Joe gave some gossip about Bert. He had once married and had left a Navaho woman in New Mexico; had got into some sort of trouble there; had returned to Oraibi; and had hidden out in the fields until the atmosphere cleared.

On another occasion, says Joe, he was weaving in the kiva when he overheard Andrew and Jasper attacking Tawaqwap-tiwa's ability as composer. In disgust Joe left and told no one but Louis. Since Louis was then in the process of "cutting out" Jasper, he promptly told the chief who grew very angry with Andrew and Jasper. As a result of the trouble Andrew thought for a time of moving to Kikötcmovi, but when things blew over, he decided to remain in Oraibi. (Joe says that Louis was "power-ful" with women, although he doesn't look it. When he cut out Jasper, he cut out a phratry brother, as he is Sand and Jasper is Lizard-Snake. This is supposed to be less serious than cutting out a man in one's own clan.) ["Cutting out" still goes on among the Hopi, but no recent cases have been reported at Oraibi.]

Kane, Joe, and Allen came in after supper and got on the subject of trapping. Kane spoke of a time when Fred and he had sought shelter in a deserted hogan but left at once when they found it to be *tcinti*. On a later occasion when Kane and Cedric were fetching spruce for a Niman dance, they passed the spot and went in. There they found the skull of a Navaho, and they judged that he had been stricken with the flu and had stag-gered into the hogan to die.

Other stories of dead Navahos followed, and the moral was drawn that one should never take anything from a corpse. The men also spoke of cremation among other tribes, and all agreed that a puff of white smoke arose if the deceased were one-hearted but not if he were a witch.

Before he left, Kane told of a trading journey he had once made to New Mexico. He went to San Domingo by train; then walked to various other pueblos with a pack of trade objects that included *katcina* kilts, belts, and *mantas* (Hopi dresses); and finally returned by way of Zuñi.

Thurs. Oct. 19. Ned had a couple of Navaho to breakfast. They had probably spent the night at his place.

The Katcina kiva at Oraibi used to be called Kwitavi ("Feces Place"). It is the name first used by all informants who refer to it. Allen says that the word connotes jealousy and means that the members of this kiva had a reputation for being overly jealous. Allen commented further that "the Indians" like to joke about such things but that "White" people don't.

This morning, for the first time since we visited Nestcili on September 16, Ned is going to try herding because his brother Sidney has blisters on his feet. In the presence of others Kane asked if I knew the nature of Ned's disease. I professed utter ignorance, whereupon everyone laughed. Kane said that Seba James, at New Oraibi, had the same disease. (Seba is the man whose herding partnership with Kane was broken with bad feelings.)

Sikyaletsnim and Juanita are helping Mary grind corn. This is just a neighborly act for which Mary will probably reciprocate. Louise will soon start grinding corn for her wedding.

This is the season for women to grind corn and men to go harvesting. Ida ground for Mary and Jessie, who gave her a big dish of cornmeal in exchange.

Joe told me that his little daughter Lois was ill and had nearly died. Knowing that Kiacwaitiwa was away, Joe had gone afoot to Bakavi to get Polingyauoma, only to find that the medicine man had left for Oraibi. In succession Joe had then returned to Oraibi, walked to Kikötcmovi, and returned to Bakavi before he located the "doctor" and brought him to the patient in Oraibi. Polingyauoma asked for a piece of paper with which he then "extracted" a heap of supposedly graveyard sand from the sick child. Thereupon he announced that she would recover if her parents continued her cure at Sowika [p. 81]. Polingyauoma did not adopt Lois because he was already her phratry uncle. Unlike Kiacwaitiwa, Polingyauoma does not (is not allowed to?) reveal the names of suspected witches.

About two years ago Mary, Joe's wife, became very sick. The whites of her eyes turned yellow, but Kiacwaitiwa saved her by "extraction." On another occasion Kiacwaitiwa had similarly saved Mary's life when she was so ill that her stomach became swollen and her feet began to grow cold. A medicine man from Moenkopi assisted on the case, and this time Kiacwaitiwa named the witch who was responsible for Mary's ailment. It proved to be one of Mary's clan mothers, and Joe repeated what I had so often already heard, that a witch can do harm only to a relative.

Joe described the proper treatment of a witch. He said that one must disarm her with kindness and courtesy, otherwise she might inflict even greater injuries on a sufferer. Constant watchfulness was also necessary. When asked if anything had happened to the witch who had attacked Mary, Joe replied, "No, not to her, but her husband died shortly after, *and some day she'll die.*" He assured me that he was "still watching her." Joe confirms others who have said that the victim of a witch must never show anger and that bewitching goes on all the time among the Hopi.

NOTE.—What is the effect of their witchcraft beliefs on the Hopi? This may be the essential factor of Hopi psychology that keeps these people from resorting to violent or daring action.

It is said that the Hopi like fat *katcinas* like Tom and Joe rather than lean and scraggy ones. Informants could offer no explanation, but I suppose there is a suggestion here that a *katcina* should appear plump and well fed, and that a fat man is supposed to be jolly. [Compare our ideas of Santa Claus.]

Fri. Oct. 20. Left after breakfast to help Ned fetch wood. Stopped to greet the Coltons and Miss Bartlett, who were camped near Hotevilla. [Dr. Colton was founder and head of the Museum of Northern Arizona, and Miss Bartlett was his secretary. When Dr. Colton retired from his position, he was succeeded by the present director, Dr. Edward B. Danson. Miss Bartlett is now the Librarian of the Museum's Research Center.]

The Colton party is traveling through the Hopi pueblos. They are trading corn for long-staple cotton. They use the corn for feeding poultry, and they hope that the cotton will encourage the natives to maintain or revive weaving and perhaps some of their other arts and crafts. [The Coltons made these trading trips for a number of years but ultimately gave them up. They were, however, highly successful in stimulating a revival of Hopi interest in arts and crafts. Now, annually, the Museum of Northern Arizona puts on Hopi and Navaho shows in which a great many native craftsmen compete for prizes and offer their wares for sale. A number of demonstrators are also brought to the Museum from the reservations to show people how various objects, such as pieces of pottery, basketry plaques, silver ornaments, or rugs, are made.]

Saw Edna drying peaches just outside of Hotevilla, and asked Ned why she didn't move to Hotevilla where she spent so much time and seemed happy. He answered that the Hotevilla "ladies" were jealous and did not want her to settle there because she was still sexually attractive to men.

Stopped at Hotevilla to give a picture to Haiyeva. His sister is albino, but is normally accepted in the community. The Hopi lack explanations of this phenomenon, but do not ascribe it to the supernatural.[13] [More than two decades later Ned repeated the same ideas on albinism but added that he

knew of one case where a man had had an albino child because
he had stolen a sacred doll.]

Ned confirmed Joe's description of Sowika and added
that he had taken George there to be cured. On the night before
the fourth visit the spirit of Sowika, a male deity, had appeared
to Ned in a dream and had assured him that George would
recover. Although the Hotevilla people lack a Sowika shrine, it
was said that they can get the same results by praying to the
sun. The Hopi concept seems to be that their gods and spirits
are ubiquitous. Hence they can be reached anywhere. This
makes possession of shrines and ritual paraphernalia less essential
than the proper songs and prayers with which supernatural
agents can be reached. That is why Hotevilla could get along
with no original kivas or shrines and only a few "genuine" religious objects. Ned states flatly that the songs are the most essential aspects of Hopi rites, although Joe still claims that altars are
more important. [Compare p. 82.]

In talking of marriages Ned repeats the names that go
with marital status and tells more about basket-carrying beliefs.
In this connection there is a story of a girl who had married a
previously wed Hopi off the reservation. She did not know of his
former marriage and was furious when she found out about it—
not at her husband, but at her folks for having failed to tell her.
At the time, this story seemed to have but little significance. Now
I understand the cause of the bride's anger. [See n. 23, p. 358.]
A few elaborations were added. One man said that the carrying-
strap that had to be used by a basket-carrier was so narrow that
it cut into the flesh of the forehead; and another thought that the
pieces of gravel which a basket-carrier had to carry were in the
shapes of the genital organs of the opposite sex.

Before reaching Nestcili we stopped at the hogan of his
wife's sister, who served us tortillas and coffee. Ned left eight or
nine watermelons. He asked for nothing in immediate exchange,
but after we had left, he commented that we would stop in next
day on our way home. There was a young girl in the hogan who
had recently had her first baby with no other attendant than
her husband. Nestcili received us cordially, although he was
feeling ill and nauseous. He neither treated himself nor called
another "doctor." He spent a good part of the evening teaching
his sister's son the proper songs to use in a curing rite soon to
be performed over a sick baby. Nestcili again showed me his
paraphernalia. He was glad to get a gift of turtle meat from Ned,

because this was [and still is] regarded as a powerful medicine. Nestcili openly stated the opinion that Hopi medicine men did not really extract anything. To what extent will this shake Ned's confidence? Not much, probably. [Not long after his first wife had died around 1952, Nestcili married a much younger woman. Even when he was very old, he remained in great demand as a singer.

Ned stopped visiting him for the overt reason that sight of him might have reminded Nestcili sorrowfully of his first wife.

At the time of this diary I was utterly unaware that Ned was carrying on a love affair with Nestcili's (Neschelles's) late wife. He discusses this affair in *Sun Chief*, p. 320.]

Nestcili also spoke of witches who often take the guise of coyotes or wolves in Navaho belief. Unlike the Hopi, who are taught to be kind to suspected witches, the Navaho do not hesitate to take pot shots at them.

Sat. Oct. 21. Slept last night in Nestcili's hogan, after having loaded the wagon with wood. In the morning Ned butchered a sheep. A wet stick was used for manipulating the intestines of the butchered animal. One of the Navaho moistened it with spittle, and Ned used it without a word. We then set out for Oraibi.

On the way back to Oraibi Ned spoke further about Hopi "doctors" and their links with witches. He repeated much that was already known but added that only the medicine men who "extract" are two-hearted.

Ned then asked about hypnotism. Told him what I could and asked if the Hopi had hypnotists. In reply he spoke of *duskyavu*, people of either sex who can lure partners to them for amorous purposes. Such "hypnotists" are not necessarily witches, but they may learn the procedures from witches. Their activities are often dangerous since they are unlikely to know the proper "discharming" songs. Storekeepers may entice customers by similar means; and dance sponsors may even ask a kiva member or friend to use this technique for getting a good turnout. It strikes me that here we may have the answer to my questions about Ya-ya'a and Somaikoli. [See p. 76.] Apparently, it is possible to learn from witches without becoming a witch one's self. Indeed, when I later discussed this whole subject with Joe, he told me of a man—not *duskyavu* himself—who accompanied a "hypnotist" and followed his directions for luring two girls to them. Everything went as planned, but before the men could enjoy the girls, someone came by and broke the spell.

Thereupon the girls, who had not known what they were doing, suddenly became aware of their situation and ran off in tears. [Present-day Hopi still know about and believe in this kind of hypnotism. They also believe that there are ways of luring game animals, such as rabbits, to their deaths.]

On our return we found that the baby of Sam Jenkins, a Christian at New Oraibi, had died. All the school children went to view the body in the church. Hahai'i scolded Jenny, not for having entered a church, but because she was too young to look at corpses.

NOTE ON TOOTHACHE STORIES.—Ned says that old-timers believed an exposed bone from a graveyard, placed in the mouth, would cure toothache. (For himself Ned thought such a bone would cause all of a person's teeth to fall out.) One sufferer spotted such a bone, but when he went for it after dark, a dog howled. He took it for the call of Masau'û and was so frightened that he forgot all about his aching tooth. He was very grateful to the dog and said that had he recognized it, he would have made a prayer stick for it at the next Soyal.

Another story concerned a man who had suffered a violent toothache while in a kiva during a Bean dance. He agreed to yank out the bad tooth, looped a string around it, but lacked the nerve to pull. His ceremonial father talked soothingly to him and suddenly touched his elbow with a hot iron. The man involuntarily jerked his arm away—and out came the tooth. Despite the pain of the burn he thanked his "father."

A third story dealt with a man who had been advised to tie a string around an aching tooth, weight the string with a heavy stone, and throw it from a high spot. At the crucial moment the man lost his nerve and jumped, but as he hit the ground, the stone bounced and out came the tooth.

These stories led Joe to tell how his mother had once developed a bad toothache while they were on a cornbake. He got a pair of pliers and pulled out the bad tooth. "That must have hurt a lot," I said. "You bet it did," answered Joe. "She almost cried from the pain." [Today, people with toothaches go to dentists.]

The sons of Martin, who live with their mother at New Oraibi, joined Calvin and Sam in reviving an old custom tonight. While women ground corn, the boys went about the streets, singing a song that asks for *piki*. In the old days, unmarried girls used to beg for rabbits in this way. The boys got *piki* from some of the women, store bread from others, a melon from Kane, and so forth. They took the food to a kiva and enjoyed a feast.

Sun. Oct. 22. Ned went herding today. He feels so much better that he is gradually resuming his customary duties.

Anita invited Ida to have lunch with her. Ida had been helping her grind corn.

NOTE ON CLAN GROUPS.—Did Hopi clans come singly to their present locations, as their legends state? That is, was each clan once a distinct entity, something like a "tribe"? I doubt it. Exogamy seems too deep rooted for such a possibility, and there is too much similarity of physical type and culture. More likely, the Hopi saw many ruins in the Southwest and in trying to account for them somehow struck on the notion that each clan had arrived in Hopiland separately. This is all the more probable in view of the emphasis on individuality. Each clan could thus have its own migration legend to go with its own *wuya* and ceremony.

Then, again. How about the five Hopi towns that the Spaniards found? Was there once a parent village from which the others branched off? Could the five Hopi pueblos have resulted from past disintegrations? Did they arise from a series of splits? Is the same situation found in other Pueblo tribes? Do they also have one language, one religion, and one pattern of general culture, but five distinct places of residence? [This problem looms large in Hopi ethnological studies but, since one or more ancient splits are postulated, the problem can be solved only by the use of archaeological techniques. This shows the great need for a combination of the two subdisciplines of anthropology. Southwestern anthropologists must bridge the gap that has developed between archaeology and ethnology.

Material from the detailed account of the Split of 1906 given in O.O., chapter 6, may serve as a guide.]

Ida says that while we were at Nestcili's, there was a big fuss at Oraibi. Several women pitched into Jacob's Clara, accusing her of being no good and allowing her children to misbehave. In the end Tawaqwaptiwa took a hand and ordered Clara to stay home more and to keep closer watch on her children. (It is significant that Clara's own sister Margaret was one of her leading critics. This is also the first evidence of the chief, who is Clara's maternal uncle, exerting authority in secular affairs.)

Joe, backed up by Ned, affirms that "mother" ears of corn, which are given to children when they are named, should be planted the following spring without ado. Both men also say that no distinctive ceremonies are observed either for planting or harvesting.

Today Ida remarked offhand that her cold must have come from Masau'û. Thus, in spite of negative answers to all direct questions on the topic, it does seem as though Masau'û can send illness.

NOTE.—Part of the preparation of *pikami* consists of pre-chewing meal.

There is a tendency to rationalize the grouping of clans on the basis of their associated ancients and associations of meaning. Thus the Navaho Wood clan, in the absence of a similar Hopi unit, is equated with Cedar.

There is an account of an ancient occurrence when a man who was walking along a road was accidentally shot by someone in a wagon who was fooling with a gun. Somehow, it was decided that the shooting was truly accidental, and the whole matter was dropped.

Ever since I discovered the basket-carrying notion, Ned always says when the census reveals boys or girls who have married previously wed spouses, "He (or she) will have to carry a basket." No longer is there any attempt to conceal this belief.

Mon. Oct. 23. Several women ground corn for Hahai'i in the forenoon. They were all invited to lunch.

When the chief was told that Mr. Collier was coming to New Oraibi and that he ought to speak to him there, he replied, "No. The Hopi at New Oraibi don't like me." It was pointed out that he could speak directly to the Commissioner without regard to the other Hopi. His face lit up and he agreed to go down, taking Ned as his interpreter. However, he'll probably back out when the time comes. [He did.]

Tawaqwaptiwa referred to two Sun clansmen as his "fathers." This results from the fact that his ceremonial father was a Sun clansman, and that his name means "Sun's movements." He also revealed that his Christian brother had visited him yesterday and had told him that his ceremonies were no good and that he would soon have to give them up. To this Tawaqwaptiwa claims to have replied: "No. This is my way of life. You're a Christian and Jesus is for you. That's all right, and I don't get angry. But I'm a Hopi, and the Hopi way is for me."

In some respects the chief's wife is even more conservative than he. He had agreed to make me a head scratcher, such as novices use in ceremonies, but his wife stopped him because she ruled it would be a religious object that ought not to be made public.

Tues. Oct. 24. More corngrinding on the part of women.

Ned and Ruth left for four days of harvesting at his fields in Patuwi.

Kane arrived early and stayed for breakfast. His conversation ran along the usual lines of sheep and cattle herding. He cited his own brother Harold as a careful herder; and Albert, the Hotevilla policeman, as a careless one who allowed his animals to spoil crops. The conflict of herders and farmers plays so great a part in Hopi life and seems to go so far back in their history that it may well be an important factor in their cultural development. If so, it should be given greater emphasis. At this writing it looks like a constant irritant and cause of local disturbances. It may be reflected in the lack of pueblo harmony, a sort of conflict of differing interests.

Most of the women attended the missionaries' sewing class in Voth's church.

Cedric has a badly infected finger and may have blood poisoning. He was going to a Hotevilla medicine man for treatment but was persuaded to see a "White" doctor. His brother Charles did not hesitate to take aspirin and other remedies for a cold.

Ruth seems not to approve of Ned's dealings with Nestcili. Before departing for Patuwi Ned had left some watermelons that were to be given to Nestcili if he happened to show up. Ruth frowned, picked out a few of the best melons, and put them back into her own storeroom. On another occasion, when I was bringing Nestcili a can of beans, a box of crackers, and some bread that Ida had baked, Ruth grumbled and said, "Make him give you meat for it."

Wed. Oct. 25. Most men are out of the pueblo, harvesting for a few days at a stretch. The women continue to grind corn for each other. George is staying with Louis's Clara while his parents are away. Evelyn is staying with relatives at New Oraibi while Joe and Mary are at his fields.

Next Sunday three villages are going to have women's dances. Chimopovy and Mishongnovi will do Lakon, and Sitcumovi will do Oaqöl. What a rotten break! [As time went on the Hopi staged more and more of their ceremonies on weekends. [See p. 49.] This was influenced by the "White" calendar. At first weekends were chosen to accommodate school children; later, they proved to be the only days convenient for men who had jobs.]

Ed has been helping his brother-in-law Tom to harvest, and Andrew is lending a hand to some Bakavi people.

Little Sandra has fainted once or twice in the last few days. On the surface Ida, the child's aunt, doesn't show that she is at all worried. The baby's grandmother Hahai'i gave it some medicine. Hahai'i remarked that Ida and some of her other children had been similarly afflicted in infancy.

Thurs. Oct. 26. Met Jay in the morning just as he was about to walk home to Chimopovy. He had treated Sandra. He said that her heart was at fault and that he had left some medicine for her.

Questioned Bert about the extra fertility that is supposed to be imparted to a field if it is struck by lightning. He professed to know nothing of such a belief. In his opinion all whose fields are struck are witches who deliberately ask lightning to hit their corn, probably in atonement for some sin that they have committed. Bert says it is strange that lightning splits corn down the middle just as it does if it hits a man. (Is there a connection between corn and people which makes a request for lightning to strike one's field the same as bewitching a relative? This may or may not be true.) [It was never verified.]

Tried to feel Bert out on ties between Kwan and Masau'û. He says the connection is due to the Kwan clansmen's ability as warriors. They are better fighters than Coyote clansmen. (To me the link is that warriors cause deaths, and Masau'û is the god of death.) Bert says that part of the Kwan society's initiation consists of having candidates visit graveyards and handle bones to "give them bravery." (This is a direct tie with Masau'û. He is their patron deity, so they must not be afraid of death and the dead.) Also, at Wuwutcim time a meal of tortillas and beans, cooked without salt or fat (these are usually tabooed during ceremonies), must be set out on the roof of every house.[14] (It is clear that Masau'û, Kwan, and Wuwutcim all play a part in the cult of the dead.)

Cedric's infected finger grows worse. He did go to see

Dr. Burgess at New Oraibi, but he found the doctor out and went to Hotevilla for treatment by a medicine man.

Hahai'i would like to have Kiaciwaitiwa treat Sandra, but says that she has no one to send to Hotevilla. (I find this hard to understand, as messages between Hotevilla and Oraibi go back and forth regularly.)

Was very much surprised to find the chief chatting amiably this afternoon with Ray, the insane man who had caused him so much trouble at Moenkopi. (Like every other Hopi the chief believes that one must disarm suspected witches by treating them with every show of kindness.)

NOTE.—What, if anything, can be the significance of the fact that the Hopi have so many ceremonies that are similar in many details? Has this anything to do with disintegration? Was there once a central ceremony from which others branched or split off, retaining many features of the original? Again, why is there no central religious authority, with the possible exception of the Soyal? Some say that even an ordinary member of the Soyal may be called a *mongwi* ("chief"); and at Oraibi its leadership is in the hands of the Village chief or his delegate, and the chamber in which its esoteric rites take place is called the chief's kiva. But, then, why is there no formal priesthood? Is it due to individuality that practically every man can be a "priest" at one time or another? [Possibly, though, there is a minimum of full-time specialists, including priests, at this level in the evolution of Hopi culture.

Can it be that there was once a Pan-Hopi ceremonial calendar maintained by a Pan-Hopi group that lived in one place, and that variants of this uniform calendar were set up as various villages came to be settled? Were there sometimes two competing ceremonies in a single pueblo, as at Oraibi between 1898 and 1906, one of which later moved to a new town? These are the kinds of questions that can be answered, if at all, only by archaeological investigations. See p. 92.]

Fri. Oct. 27. A little girl, Cedric's daughter Euberta, had a very bad running nose. Mucous ran on to some melon that she was eating, but no adults who were present, including her parents, made any effort to stop her from eating the melon or to clean her up.

Cedric's finger is worse. Some say that he had had it diagnosed by Jay, who thought it was a case for the Snake society to cure. One rumor has it that he went to see Puhunimptiwa, Hotevilla's Snake chief; and Ida says that Luke had once had a similar swelling which the Snake men had cured. She thought that joining a society which cures a patient with part of its rites is optional. However, I think joining is compulsory, but active participation is optional.

Ned and Ruth returned from harvesting at Patuwi. His first concern was for Nestcili, who had not come to Oraibi in his absence. While he was at work, he had had the assistance of several helpers from Hotevilla. [Ned said long afterward that his wife had done no fieldwork with him for several years. This may be the result of the government money that she had received when George was killed in action.

For a time Ned was aided by Duwan, a distant relative and a bachelor who made his home at New Oraibi. Ned and Ruth offered him a chance to live with them, but he did not accept. In 1961 Duwan moved back to Kikötcmovi. Ned had bought Duwan a pickup truck, but he had acquired it for himself when Duwan left. Now Dennis lives with Ned and Ruth and does various odd jobs for them.]

Cedric says that there is to be a Masau *katcina* dance at Hotevilla soon. I cannot understand how a real *katcina* can be impersonated in the closed season, but Ned assures me that Cedric is not joking and that he will tell me all about it. Ned is too tired to be interviewed today. [As later proved to be the case, Masau *katcina* is a real, masked impersonation; and it is the only kind of *katcina* that may appear in the closed season. Because death is the opposite of life, the *katcina* that stands for the god of death may therefore appear in public when all regular *katcinas* are locked up. Moreover, as F. J. Dockstader pointed out, death may strike at any moment in either season. See O.O., pp. 184–87.] Ned also said something about a harvest-time appearance of the deity Masau'û himself.

Several Navaho traveled by cart in the moonlight to New Oraibi. They had come from beyond Keam's Canyon and were on their way to Hotevilla to do some trading for peaches.

Sat. Oct. 28. Sandra has been sick again, and her father left very early this morning to fetch Kiacwaitiwa from Hotevilla. Ida ascribed the child's sickness to the fact that her mother had once been struck by lightning. Several girls had been grinding corn

at the time, and when Delia's aunt had bathed her four days
later, she discovered a scar. Polingyauoma and another Al man
were supposed to have cured Delia but are said to have done so
erroneously. Moreover, some of the stones from the stricken
dwelling had been used for making a new house, and Ida said
that this wasn't right (Polingyauoma and the other man, Masa-
ve'ima of the Rabbit clan, were members of the Al society which
was supposed to deal with lightning.)

Ned, Ruth, and George went to their melon patch for some
preliminary work that had to be done before Ned again would
have the use of his team. At present Sidney has it for the next four
days, while he is harvesting. Ruth and George were on horseback,
and Ned went afoot. A barking dog frightened the horse, and
Ruth nearly fell off but was saved by George. She cried from
fright. In contrast to Navaho women, Hopi women very rarely
ride horseback and are poor horsewomen.

Joe and Mary came back from harvesting late in the afternoon. Joe's right forearm and left eye are badly swollen. He
doesn't know the cause and is doing nothing about a cure.

During an interview tonight Otto revealed that in former
times the town War chief (Kaletaka) could assign anyone who
misbehaved to the most dangerous spot in the next conflict.

Otto also stated that if a Hopi found anything, he was supposed to say, "Thank you." [This custom is still prevalent. The
thanks are supposed to go to one's guardian spirit, or spirit guide,
for having brought one good luck.]

Be sure to check on the duties of the official Town Crier
and on any ritual characteristics that pertain to his office. (There
are no special forms of behavior that the crier is supposed to observe in his daily life. Many of the calls he made, even in the
old days, seem to have been of a secular nature.)[15]

Several Oraibi dogs are in heat, and small children openly
watch their sexual activities. [There were noticeably fewer dogs
at Oraibi in later years. Some native women regarded this as a
victory for chicken raisers. However, it may have resulted from
the decline of sheepherding, or from some other cause.] Hopi
youngsters are much more accustomed to nakedness and sex than
are "White" children. Does this have any bearing on their adult
behavior?

Valjean (Sun) was married to Elta (Pikyas), daughter of
Tom and Anita. Neither principal is Christian, but the wedding
took place in the schoolroom of New Oraibi and the Reverend
Mr. Suderman officiated.

Sun. Oct. 29. Went to the Lakon dance at Chimopovy this morning. We had scarcely arrived when we were asked to eat by Grace's sister. Grace's little boy Barney was fitful and cried a great deal. Grace seemed indifferent and even rude, but her sister soothed and petted the child. As a rule Hopi mothers tend to be overindulgent to their children, but they do lose their tempers on occasion and once in a while they may even strike an obstreperous youngster.

From the house of Grace's sister, Ned and I went to call on Jay, the medicine man. On the way I recalled that Kane had suggested Ned's ailment might not have been a venereal disease but might have been the aftermath of a severe strain suffered by Ned in his youth when he used to break in and ride wild horses.

Among interesting people we met during the day was a young man named Lemuel, who had spent most of his life at school. His mother had died when he was a baby, and his sisters had taken him along to school so that they could care for him. Lemuel is quite up to date and talks of electricity and telephones for Chimopovy. [Neither of these had been installed in the pueblo at the time. It was as late as 1964 before Chimopovy agreed to accept electricity. Even after the necessary poles had been erected, the pueblo's officials changed their minds and refused to go any further. About a year later they reversed their stand and permitted the village to have electricity.]

We also met Susie, a young lady known jokingly as "the girl with a saddle." She got the title because one night while she was entertaining a lover who had come by horseback, someone had taken the saddle from his mount and turned it loose. Informants thought the deed might have been done by a jealous rival, a brother, or an uncle. Susie's story was told freely, with no indication of wrongdoing because she had been sleeping with a lover.

Chimopovy's Lakon was not very impressive. Only five appearances were made by the society throughout the entire day, and the intervals between dances were exceptionally long. All the Oraibis say that this is the way it always is on the other mesas, but that when Lakon used to be given at Third Mesa, there were many appearances and short intermissions. Is this the usual pueblo or in-group loyalty?

The following features of the performance were especially noteworthy. Each of the two Lakon maidens had on her head a bunch of feathers on the right side and a single blue horn protruding from the left. Bert interpreted this in terms of bisexualism—a topic that ought to be fully studied in Hopi religion—with the feathers representing, whether it be a *katcina* dance or a pair of prayer sticks, female on the right and with the horn representing male on the left.

At the last dance of the day all the performers had their faces smeared with cornmeal. A male officer deposited prayer sticks at a shrine, asperged from a bowl, poured the remaining liquid into the shrine, and threw two plaques far out over the housetops. After their final appearance in the plaza the members of the Lakon society took many babies and small children into their kiva for purification, some say, or else for initiation, blessing, or cure. Then the performers came to the top of the kiva and distributed whatever gifts remained. Some gave the plaques that they had carried in the dance to young men whose *ikya'as* they are. At Oraibi, in times past, this was invariably and universally done. [See chapter X, section D, for a detailed description of this performance.]

NOTE.—The striking similarities of the women's rites in the Marau, Lakon, and Oaqöl performances raise an interesting question. Why should there be three rites that are so nearly identical? It seems likely that Hopi ceremonialism was once more limited than it is today. Possibly there was a time when the ritual calendar consisted only of the Tribal Initiation (Wuwutcim)—Soyal; Momtcit; Katcina-Powamu; and, perhaps, Snake or Flute. It may be that the clans which controlled rites were somehow set apart, and this led others to seek equivalence by "inventing" new ceremonies which nevertheless ran along lines similar to the originals. For example, Snake-Antelope and Gray Flute–Blue Flute rites are so much alike that they are interchanged in alternate years. Were they originally a single ceremony and then divided or were they first distinct and later combined?

I am particularly struck by the parallels between the Wuwutcim and the Marau, and Ned tells me that the shrine used by women performers at Chimopovy is the same one used by Wuwutcim men. It looks as though the women, being excluded from the Wuwutcim, have a tribal initiation of their own.

[I wonder if there is any place in the primitive (nonliterate) world that duplicates the Hopi in having a single tribal, cultural, and linguistic group whose members live in at least five different autonomous towns, within a space of less than twenty-five miles, each of which gives independent performances of a nearly identical but highly intricate and elaborate religious calendar? If not, what does the Hopi situation mean? Were the Hopi once a single group that split into five in ancient times, as was suggested on page 92? It strikes me as impossible that five towns in close proximity to one another should have independently evolved the same elaborate complex of rites. This means that the ancestors of those who now occupy the Hopi villages had probably once lived together in the past. They might have become separated either through enemy action or through the workings of environmental or sociocultural disintegrative forces. Enemy pressure is scarcely acceptable, since it is more likely to have been a cause for consolidation rather than of separation such as that which followed the Split of Oraibi in 1906. One could think of an original unit that divided into a number of parts, each of which, from a common base, developed local variations of ritual and other practices. I believe that this is what the Spaniards first found and that all we have today is a further development of the same process of earlier times.]

Kane again talked about sheep. Cedric wants to sell his sheep, and several men are anxious to buy them. Cedric refused to consider offers other than the one made by his half brother Nick, who lives in Kikötcmovi and has a full-time job with a road-working crew. [In the end Cedric sold his flock to Nick for $300, and Nick additionally paid him several dollars a month to do the herding. At the time this looked like an excellent arrangement for Cedric, but all the Hopi disagreed. "Money is round," said the old-timers, "and it soon rolls away from one." This is exactly what happened in the case of Cedric. As soon as Nick had paid him, he ordered a new rifle, and his wife bought dishes, dresses, and other luxury items. In a short time Cedric had neither sheep nor money.]

As usual, Kane then brought the conversation around to the conflict between herders and farmers. He cited with approval the case of Laguna which, according to him, had seven settlements that cooperated under a single authority, unlike the Hopi. He said that when it came to rearing fences, each of the Laguna communities did its share until the whole territory was properly fenced in. He contrasted this with Hopi individuality and lack of central authority.

Joe reported that he got a dollar a day whenever he took his brother's turn at herding.

Louis returned from Flagstaff today and plans to begin harvesting immediately. He says that cattle owners are anxious for him to gather his crops so that they may turn their herds loose to graze on the stubble.

Mon. Oct. 30. Sandra is still ailing, yet Kiacwaitiwa was at the Chimopovy dance yesterday. He must have passed by Oraibi, but he may not have known that he was wanted as Nelson missed him at Hotevilla. In the absence of Kiacwaitiwa nothing was done about the sick child.

Joe remarked that it wasn't very pleasant to eat at Chimopovy because, he claims, these villagers do not bury their dead in the ground but put corpses into crevices on the edges of the mesa. He is particularly disturbed at midsummer when the Niman is held, because there are swarms of flies that might have been eating the bodies of the dead. [It is said that during the smallpox epidemic of 1898, people at Chimopovy died in such numbers that the bodies were put into crevices instead of being properly buried in the ground.]

Mary is busy grinding corn to make up for the days she missed when she was harvesting with Joe, her husband. While she was out of the house for a short time, one of the Oraibi children is thought to have set fire to some of her dry cornstalks. Ida and I helped put out the blaze. It was pitiful to be sprinkling water when a good dousing was needed. It is surprising that there are so few fires in the pueblo. Probably the hazard is none too great because the houses are built primarily of stone.

Ned left alone on horseback to do some more harvesting. His father is helping Sidney, who has no paid assistants. If Sidney has to miss his herding turn, however, he will have to hire someone to take his place. Undoubtedly, though, while Ned was laid up, his father and brother shared his herding duties without getting extra compensation.

At lunch Ida remarked pointedly that Ruth was all alone and that she had asked her to eat with us. Ruth is on good terms with her sisters-in-law who call her *mû'wi* ("female relative-in-law"). Yet, while Ned regularly frequents his mother's house, Ruth very seldom goes there.

Tues. Oct. 31. Cold today. Women and children, less often men, still go barefoot.

When I asked Dennis about the Masau *katcina*, he said that it was a real *katcina*, but it was not "locked up" with the others. He believes (wrongly in my opinion) that it appears in the fall (closed season) because it is associated with foods made of cornmeal that is more abundant in the fall. (This is a patent rationalization, as the Hopi eat cornmeal foods throughout the year.)

Dennis, who is from Hotevilla, reports that the Masau *katcina* dance was requested by a woman named Salome (Parrot-Crow). She vowed to sponsor it if she were safely delivered of her first child. Since the baby was expected in the closed season, she had to make it Masau *katcina*.

The dancers are to wear masks, and those who are going to take part, about fifteen in all according to Dennis, are now busy repainting the masks they wore at last summer's Niman. They will use Tcu kiva as a center. Instead of the conventional *katcina* collars of spruce they are to wear *katcina* dance kilts about the throat and shoulders, leggings made of cottontail rabbit skins, and the customary turtle-shell rattles bound on the right calf. Their appearance is ghastly, Dennis says, and they would certainly frighten anyone meeting them in the dark. They are to have a conventional type of father, who will probably be Puhunimptiwa, and they will come and go in the dance plaza like ordinary *katcinas*.

Dennis also gave a good deal of miscellaneous information about Hotevilla (Third Mesa) rituals. Of all secret societies, only Snake men are allowed to eat meat while they are in session. [This was verified in 1955.] Niman sponsorship in 1934 will be from Al kiva, and subsequently it will go in successive years to Tcu, Sakwalenvi, Kwan, and Hawiovi. The masks (a mask?) from a Niman that has just been concluded are (is?) taken over to the kiva which is to sponsor the Niman a year later. The Wuwutcim and Marau are brother and sister. He knows of no other ties between specific women's societies and particular branches of the Tribal Initiation. Oaqöl is a "late" introduction, open to all women, and not a real ceremony (?) but a composite of bits taken from other rituals. Dennis refused to take part in the Wuwutcim at Hotevilla because, he says, having been initiated at Hawiovi in Oraibi before the Split, he felt that his ties with the ceremony were severed when he moved to Hotevilla. He now participates only in *katcina* dances. He took a female part in Hotevilla's Niman in 1932.

According to Dennis, people look askance at a man who never dances *katcina*. During a performance a dancer cannot hear the singing of others because of his mask. Hence the need for so much practice. The only way to keep exact time is to have every man know the song and rhythm perfectly. Otherwise, there would be utter confusion.

Dennis says that conditions were frigid during the Patcava that followed Hotevilla's Wuwutcim initiation in November, 1932.[16] It was so cold that the performers, especially the girls, were nearly frozen. Some of the girls wore gloves. Because of the weather the men in charge of the rites had a hard time rounding up enough feminine volunteers. Their troubles were compounded because schoolgirls who had returned to Hotevilla refused to take part. [This is a striking example of the effects of acculturation. Those who have been to school off the reservation commonly refuse to participate in what they call "old-fashioned" ceremonies.]

At death a Kwan *mongwi* ("chief") is supposed to be buried with his full costume. Does this apply to all members of the Kwan society? [Later information showed that all Kwan men are buried not in costume but with chiefs' sticks and markings.][17]

I asked Dennis for an English translation of *wimi*. He said that it means ceremony, but it may also refer to special ceremonial objects. Dr. Parsons often uses the word in this sense.

Ruth, Dennis, Delia, Milton, Ida, and I had supper together. There was a good deal of joking and teasing about Masau'û and *poakas* ("witches"). There was no restraint on the choice of words. Ida said that if one met Masau'û, he would be unable to speak to him, as his mouth would begin to stiffen immediately at sight. All this talk went on freely in front of little Milton, who is about three years old. That explains how youngsters come to be imbued with a dread of Masau'û, and to believe in the omnipresence of witches.

Dennis remarked that while horses, burros, and sheep (all useful animals economically) went to Maski at death, dogs did not. (Joe, in a subsequent interview, said the same.) As the source of his information Dennis cites evidence from people who had "died" (become unconscious), gone to Maski prematurely, returned to life, and told of their adventures in the other world. Ned and Joe's mother had reported seeing burros, horses, and sheep in the other world, but no mention had ever been made of dogs. Ruth then disclosed that during one of her confinements she had "died," gone to Maski, and met Kwanitaka. He had refused to wash her head because she had arrived prematurely and had sent her back to the world of the living. (Thus does Ned's account of such an episode in his life take on the aspect of a tribal pattern rather than that of an individual experience.[18] This puts the event in a new light and confirms Ed Kennard's remark that Dr. Benedict had said that visits to the world of the dead were fairly common in various primitive cultures.) [Does the *dumalaitaka* always play a prominent part, or is the reference to a "spirit guide" a personal idiosyncracy of Ned?]

In the course of the jesting about witches Dennis said that he'd like to know exactly where their meeting place was. He used the same term, Palungwa, that Ned had used for describing the place where witches gather.

CHAPTER V

Diary for November, 1933

[*The weather is turning cold, and wherever people can do so, they are moving into the lower quarters of their houses which are easier to keep warm. Societies for women are still active, and late harvesting goes on.*

Before this month ends, the lone Soyal katcina appears as the first act in opening the year's katcina season.]

Wed. Nov. 1. There is a real cold snap in the air this morning, and the families of Solimana, Mary, and Ruth are moving into winter quarters in the lower stories of their dwellings. This will put Ruth, Ned, and George right next to me with only a thin door between us and may lead to numerous complications. For example, this very morning Ida paused in her work to overhear what Ruth was saying to Dennis. When Ida went so far as to put her ear to the door, I couldn't help telling her to mind her own business; whereupon she sulked for the rest of the morning. Later on she made a pretense at reading something so that she could remain motionless, the better to hear what Ruth was saying.

Such all-devouring curiosity and greed for gossip are symptoms of the small-town atmosphere, and lack of space and privacy that were already noticed, and that all-pervading eagerness to pry into each other's affairs may be what makes a kiva an absolute necessity in a pueblo. [Curiosity and gossip seem characteristic of closed corporate communities everywhere.] The Hopi avoid interfering with someone else's actions, but they do love to spy on and gossip about them.

Several Moenkopi men made a visit to Oraibi. They paid a good deal of attention to the chief and gave him a ride in their truck to the Lakon dance at Chimopovy. Apparently, the Moenkopi people who sided with him in 1906 have remained more loyal in some regards than those who live with him in Oraibi. On one occasion, for instance, Tawaqwaptiwa wanted to go to Mishongnovi to trade for onions, because, people said, he didn't want to do business with his brother at Oraibi. (People meant Bert Fredericks, who runs a small store at Oraibi.)

During the morning the crier called out requesting volunteers to begin grinding corn for Louise's wedding. Martha was one of the first to go because Luke, her husband, is Louise's half brother and a member of her (Greasewood) clan. Many other women also helped to grind, and all were rewarded with a good lunch. (A Moenkopi girl has begun to grind corn at the home of her sweetheart in Bakavi.)

Hahai'i is *ikya'a* to the prospective groom, and when his father brought the news, Hahai'i playfully hit him with a tin can. This is part of the "antagonism" that an *ikya'a* is supposed to show toward the parents and bride of an *imûyi*, and this is the attitude that is given fuller expression later on in a mud-fight. Ida, who is also *ikya'a* to the boy, confided, "We make believe we don't like the girl." [Compare p. 17, and n. 15, p. 357.]

Cedric dropped in during the afternoon and said, with verification from Charles, that the Masau *katcina* is a real *katcina* even though it is never locked up with the others and does not appear until after the Niman. [This is not so. The Masau *katcina* may appear at any time.] His mask portrays him with only two upper and one lower tooth and big round eyes and mouth, painted red. He wears a necklace of goat horns and is draped in a mantle of woven rabbit skins. Since these items are now scarce, an ordinary blanket may be substituted. Masau *katcinas* used to appear frequently when Cedric was young. They do not rehearse in a kiva but practice in some isolated spot near the village. Nonparticipants are not supposed to watch them, but Cedric happened to overhear a takeoff on a Butterfly song that is scheduled to be used at the forthcoming performance in Hotevilla. [Cedric was right. This performance did include a burlesque of a Butterfly dance.]

Cedric has completed the deal for his sheep. Nick is to pay him $300, and Nick will hire him to herd the flock.

Charles came in after supper. He told how lonesome he is at Oraibi in the absence of age-mates, and that is why he often goes to Hotevilla. He is unmarried, although he is in his late twenties. His case is one of several in which younger brothers marry before an elder. The underlying idea seems to be that an older brother starts being helpful to his father and household while his male siblings are small. He then continues with his duties, leaving his juniors free to marry and work for their wives.

[Charles was said to have had many love affairs while he was single. He was once married to Florine, daughter of Harold, around 1946, but the marriage did not endure. Florine remarried a Moenkopi man and moved to Flagstaff, where she now works.

Charles became a veteran of World War II. He then returned to Oraibi to live with Anita, his sister, and Tom. He drinks heavily and has caused much concern to all the villagers. When his brother-in-law died in 1965, he lived with his sister for a time, then he moved in with a niece. Charles's eyes are bad. He works as a farmer when he can.]

Thurs. Nov. 2. Tom came in early this morning with the news that Homer had been discharged by Hubbell. His marital troubles are supposed to have brought matters to a head. Tom does not like him, even though he is a brother-in-law since he is married to a Rabbit-Tobacco clanswoman. Homer threatens to open a store of his own, and so does Pawikya of New Oraibi. The Hopi are certainly becoming commercially minded. [Homer ultimately did open his own trading post at Kikötcmovi, but Pawikya did not.]

When Ned heard the news, he remarked, "Homer spends too much of his time getting into girls." When I asked how Homer was so successful in his love affairs, in spite of his reputation for being "mean," the Hopi replied that Homer was rich.

Two dances are set for next Sunday. Oaqöl is to be given at Sitcumovi and Lakon at Shipaulovi. On the same weekend the Navaho are supposed to hold a Yebitchai.

During the past few days I have been particularly impressed by the great consideration Ida shows for Milton, her *imûyi*. By contrast, she does not hesitate to say that Edna, her ceremonial mother, is accused of having poisoned some of her husbands.

It is said that Cedric used to be sweet on Fern and that he was anxious for her to return from Chicago. [Fern was the stepdaughter of Panimptiwa, who once made much trouble for Ned [p. 72]. She had danced at the World's Fair in Chicago in 1933 and had had many lovers after she got back to Oraibi. Rumor has it that she once became pregnant by Charles and that he left the reservation in 1934 to avoid marrying her. She was the sister of Jacob's Clara and died more than two decades ago.] Despite her brother's difficulties with Fern's family, Ida is ambivalent in her feelings toward Fern. Ida used to go about with Edith, Dorothy, and Juanita, but as soon as they got married, her only age-mate without a husband was Fern.

Hopi age-grading is real but none too formal. It runs something like this: infancy, up to *katcina* initiation for both sexes; adolescence, up to the tribal initiation at Wuwutcim for boys and membership in female societies for girls; manhood and womanhood, only upon marriage. [O.O., p. 36, n. 19, gives more information on this subject.]

Ned commented that it had got so cold while he was sleeping last night in his field house that he hated to go out-of-doors, so he urinated in his washbasin; yet, melons are often sliced in washbasins.

Old Edna dropped in for lunch without an express invitation. Ida was disgusted but went on boiling beans. She made the operation take so long that Edna got tired of waiting and went elsewhere.

Ned thinks it was a great mistake for Cedric to have sold his sheep. He says, not without reason, that when his cash is gone, Cedric will have nothing while Nick will always have meat for his family and will get an income from the sale of wool and surplus lambs.

Despite his many complaints about his poor crops Ned now says that he got a good yield and that "he won't starve this winter." The Hopi tend to "cry" about their crops, like an "A" student who is always sure that he has flunked. Thus, in 1932 there were many tears over the state of the crops, but in 1933 everyone admitted that *last* year was wonderful, but *this* year. . . . I suppose that it is a part of Hopi psychology of humility. It would be considered vain (*qwivi*) to admit that one's crop was good before it was harvested. [The same habits were prevalent more than a quarter of a century later.]

Fri. Nov. 3. In the morning Tom reported that his brother Quincy was taking a bunch of Navaho to the Yebitchai at Low Mountain. I made arrangements to go along.

Sat. Nov. 4. At the Navaho Yebitchai.

Sun. Nov. 5. It was cold and bleak on the way back from the Yebitchai. Luckily, we met Ted driving to the Oaqöl at First Mesa, and he offered me a ride home after the dance. Saw Nestcili and his wife at the dance and asked Ted to speak to them in

Navaho, but he was too bashful and refused. On the way home, though, he talked on and on in Navaho.

The Oaqöl performance turned out to be almost a replica of the Second Mesa Lakon and showed many similarities with the Marau. At one point during a fierce and protracted struggle for a plaque the crowd drew back and out rolled two men with the plaque between them. Everyone else remained aloof, sort of a fair-play idea, until one man triumphantly won the badly damaged plaque.

At noon there was a long distance race for plaques and a money prize. Every man who finished made a gesture to the dancers or actually passed through their ranks. In this way the runners expressed their participation in the ceremony.

Back at Oraibi that night I was telling about the Yebitchai when someone asked if any Hopi had taken part. When I said that I hadn't noticed any, I was told that Walpi men sometimes participated. [Men from Oraibi often accuse the people of Walpi of being mixed with Navaho. Ordinarily, the Hopi observe but do not take part in the rites of other tribes. If an opportunity arises, they like to use these occasions for trading.]

Nevertheless, Kane said that he had once been in a Navaho ceremonial hogan and had been asked to spell a tired drummer. He had also shared in a midnight feast that was served by men.

Joe was quite sexy. He said that Ed, my *ikwa'a* because he is the husband of my *ikya'a*, Edith, had threatened to castrate me; and when I asked Louis what he had done on his return from Flagstaff, Joe broke in to say slyly that Louis had been *very busy* that night.

Mon. Nov. 6. Asked Ida if she had yet seen Fern, who had returned on Saturday, and Ida replied, "Let her come to see me if she wants to." Yet, some time back, when Ida had returned from Flagstaff, Fern had immediately called on her. Now Ida would not go to visit Fern after her long trip home from Chicago. Although she had not yet laid eyes on Fern, Ida assured me that Fern was now "probably like a Bahana" ("'White' person"). [Ida's coldness to Fern may have a number of explanations, but one should not overlook Ida's loyalty to Ned, her brother. On the other hand, Fern was the stepdaughter of Panimptiwa, who disliked the Sun clan and who, despite his own trip to Chicago, opposed Ned's friendly dealings with "Whites."]

Several people asked what Quincy was going to charge for taking me to the Yebitchai, saying that he would ask a steep price because he was "just like a Jew." Strange to hear this stereo-type from the lips of pagan Hopi who would not recognize a Jew if they saw one. I suppose they picked up the phrase together with other aspects of "White" culture. [Some Mexican Indians have similar stereotypes about Jews.]

In a discussion with Ida about Sandra, she repeated that the baby's mother was suffering from lightning sickness. She added that "White" doctors were no good in such cases. She also said that Amy from New Oraibi had given birth to one child at the hospital in Keam's Canyon. On her return she had told an-other New Oraibi woman who was pregnant that "White" doctors were no good. Sure enough, Amy had had her next child at home.

Tues. Nov. 7. At the Yebitchai the wife of Nestcili had a run-ning nose. She would wipe the discharge with her fingers, rub them on anything that happened to be handy, and go on eating or cooking as the case might be.

A letter recently received from Ed Kennard speaks of "brittle monogamy" among the Zuñi. The Hopi have it too. In fact, it may be that the basket-carrier notion, which is designed to prevent the unmarried from having affairs with the married, may be interpreted as a device for protecting brittle marriages. (This leads to further speculation about the differences of "White" and Hopi attitudes to sex. The Hopi recognize the value of all babies for maintaining the existence of their society. They know that they have high infant mortality, hence they regard illegiti-macy with mixed feelings. Bastardy is "bad" insofar as it violates one of their "laws" or customs, but it is "good" because it pro-duces a new life, without which their society might perish.)

Today Ida railed against Edna on a new count. She is ac-cused of having stolen and sold some of Betty's corn. Betty is said to have cried and carried on when she found out what her mother-in-law had done.

Quincy maintains that the Hopi believe that if smoke from a fire drifts particularly toward one man, it is a sign that he has eaten too many beans.

Dorothy, daughter of Ruth's sister, spent the night with Ruth while Ned was away.

Joe is helping his parents with their harvesting. He refers to the mother of Cedric as "half-man," presumably because she does some of her own farming. Yet, her husband is blind Kelnimptiwa, and her unmarried brother Charles does help her out. [Many Oraibi women know how to farm and may even grow some plants or assist their menfolk. They are said to be particularly good at removing drift-sand. Very rarely does a woman engage in primary farming.]

Cedric wanted to order some housebuilding tools, so he went to Hotevilla to get the proper address. A builder named Perry, probably anxious to have a monopoly, refused to give Cedric the address unless he paid a dollar. Cedric would not pay, and waited at Hotevilla for the return of another man from Bakavi until around one in the morning. The latter freely obliged Cedric with the address he wanted. When it was suggested that the man who had returned so late from Bakavi had been on a *dumaiya* call, Cedric replied without hesitating, "Probably." Apparently, the custom is widely practiced in all the Hopi towns.

Wed. Nov. 8. Ida admitted this morning that she had been wrong about Edna's supposed theft of corn from her daughter-in-law. It turned out that the corn in question had been planted and harvested by Edna's last husband. It was rightfully hers, and Betty had no grounds for complaint.

NOTE.—Forgot to mention that at the Yebitchai, Navaho from many sections discussed matters pertaining to the entire tribe. The Hopi seem never to have interpueblo discussions among commoners. Thus the Navaho develop a sense of tribe, whereas the Hopi think primarily in terms of villages and have almost no sense of tribe.

NOTE ON MATRILOCAL RESIDENCE.—This custom is linked to the concept that women only can own houses and a married man must perforce live in his wife's house. But why is house ownership entrusted only to women? Does it have any bearing on brittle monogamy? In cases of divorce young children remain with their mothers and can be better looked after if the women own their houses. Is there also an important feeling, in matrilocal societies, that a son-in-law is less apt to make trouble than a daughter-in-law? Is it true that the Hopi believe that girls have "meaner" temperaments than boys, in the sense that they retain anger longer than boys? (Check on these points.)

Sandra is getting worse. No medicine man has seen her for several days. Delia simply sits glum and hopeless. She holds the sick child in her lap and mournfully watches her growing weaker and weaker, but she does nothing about it.

Thurs. Nov. 9. Polingyauoma came to treat Sandra. He also treated Louis's Clara, whose leg was badly swollen as the result of a fall. Ned had found her on the ground and had carried her home.

Ruth and Edna, who belong to clans in the same phratry, washed their hair this morning and searched each other's heads for vermin. Allen was present, building a shelf for Ruth, and he worked on with studied indifference. He and his mother still insist that they are Yellow Fox, but Ned and Tawaqwaptiwa call them Coyote, saying that they merely prefer to be known by another *wuya* in their group of clans. [See p. 9.]

Ned and Sidney are peeved at one another. They had been going to do some work jointly, but each had waited for the other at a different place.

When Ned drove his wagon to New Oraibi, he obligingly took Mary along to do some trading, waited till she was through, and carried her bundles. Very neighborly!

Dennis had lunch with Ned, Ruth, and Allen. Despite the latter's presence Ruth spoke slightingly of Edna and called her a troublemaker. Ned grew angry and Ruth said that he was "mean," using the same word that Joe had used in describing children who "couldn't get over their 'anginess'" and had to be cured at Sowika. Ned and Dennis promptly retorted that it was *women* who could really get "mean" if they wanted to. [Compare p. 14.]

Went rabbit hunting with Allen in the late afternoon. He showed me a wall which he claimed had collapsed and killed the people working on it because they were witches. He could not say what they had previously done to be called witches. Allen went on to tell me two variants of a witchcraft tale that is reported in Voth.[1]

One version deals with a pretty girl who rejects the advances of all men. She is killed by witches, buried, and exhumed by wolves and coyotes. The witches revive the corpse and take turns raping the girl. This causes her to die again, and a female witch, wife of the dead girl's brother, tries to get her husband to use some paint which he recognizes as his sister's blood. Having been discovered the witches decide how each of them will die. The woman falls while repairing a drain spout, and the men tumble down kiva ladders with spindles that pierce some vital organ. In another version or, as Allen puts it, "in another case," the brother gets a Mastotovi ("Death" or "Skeleton Fly") from the Little War God and releases it in a kiva where the witches are about to rape his revived sister. The Mastotovi carries the girl right out from under her first attacker and restores her to her brother. (Allen's narratives supply motivation for reviving the dead girl, not found in Voth.) [For information about Mastotovi, see p. 217.]

Allen bagged two rabbits and threw them at the feet of Poliyestiwa, husband of his *ikya'a*. Poliyestiwa will give them to his wife, in conformity with Hopi custom. [Allen is supposed to show "hostility" toward any husband of anyone of his *ikya'as*. This carries out the theme of an *ikya'a*'s great love for the son of any of her clansmen (clan brothers). [See p. 17.]

The husband of an *ikya'a* is called *ikwa'a* ("my grand-father"), and stands out for having a major joking relationship with an *imûyi* ("grandson"), whom he often "threatens" to castrate or render impotent, to keep him away from an *ikya'a*.]

Ned was peeved when he heard that medicine men were slow in coming to treat Sandra. He said that they ought to be more diligent because they had to treat the sick "for their lives." He feels very strongly that medicine men are witches who escape death by helping others to live.

Ned borrowed a gun from Nelson in the latter's absence. Ned said that no permission was necessary because Nelson was his *imû'inangwa* ("male relative-in-law"). [Brothers-in-law are supposed to help one another.]

Fri. Nov. 10. Yesterday Ida went to sewing class in the church at New Oraibi. She admitted that she had been so excited that she hardly knew what she was doing. She went down with Fern, and now that the ice is broken, they will probably "go around together" again.

Clara's injured leg is worse, and Louis went to fetch two medicine men. Despite all friendship Kane did not ask after the health of his sister-in-law. Nor did Ruth visit her sick sister of whom she is very fond. These people do not inquire about one another's health even when a serious ailment is involved. [As late as 1959 Kane admitted that he seldom saw his own brothers at Oraibi and that he never asked about their health.]

Ned remarked of a young man who had died while his wedding rites were incomplete, "too bad he never had a good time with his wife." This looks as if cohabitation should not begin before the completion of a marriage ceremony. However, I am not certain about this point which requires further checking. [In cases of this sort a boy's family is expected to go through with the wedding rites because a woman *must* have a wedding outfit [see Fig. 11] in order to make a proper adjustment to life in the otherworld.][2]

Yesterday I had told Ned about a letter I had received from Fred Eggan, and today, while I was chopping wood, he came into the house, searched for the letter, and was reading it when I entered. Again I am impressed with the all-pervading curiosity and love of gossip of these people. Are they so aware of their own tendency to gossip about everything that what looks like bashfulness is really dread of publicity? For instance, a girl at sewing class was teased about being sure to get a gift at the Hotevilla Masau *katcina* dance because she was well known in the pueblo. To this she had replied that that was the very reason she would not go. "I don't want to get a present with all those people watching," she said.

Nanny came up from New Oraibi to invite Hahai'i to help plaster her *piki* house. Edna was very resentful and went down without any invitation. I wonder why she is so eager to work for Nanny? Is it pride? Desire for reward? Eagerness for the company of other women?

Sat. Nov. 11. This is the day of the Masau *katcina* dance at Hotevilla. Kane says it is the oldest of the Hopi *katcinas,* but Joe argues that Sivuikwiotaka is older. [In the late 1950s Ned said that the oldest *katcinas* were Eototo and Aholi; the Qöqöqlom; and various chief (*mong*) *katcinas*.] Sivuikwiotaka is very old everyone agrees, but most men refuse to guess if it is older than Masau. Its mask used to feature a hand with outstretched fingers, and it used to carry a cooking pot on the back which a "feminine" partner pretended to stir. This *katcina* has not been impersonated for over half a century. Kane says that Masau *katcina* should distribute agricultural products but that it is appearing so late in the year that it will have to give out cooked foods, primarily old-fashioned Hopi dishes which are no longer regularly prepared.

As we were about to leave for the Masau *katcina* dance at Hotevilla in Bert Frederick's car, he whispered that he wasn't sure whether Grace and Martin would come because they were always jealous of each other and always quarreling.

Met Nestcili at Benjamin's store in Hotevilla. Joe spoke

to him in Navaho on my behalf. I was glad that Joe did not show
the usual Hopi reticence, although lots of people were present.
(It is strange that many of the Tewa men on First Mesa speak
Hopi but few Hopi men talk Tewa. On the other hand, quite a
number of Hopi males speak Navaho, but the Navaho do not
talk Hopi.)

Ida noticed Margaret in the audience. She said that it
was not fitting for a Soyal *mana* to watch many dances and that
Margaret generally observes this rule. By contrast Anita, who
is also a Soyal *mana*, frequently goes to see dances.

In its outward structure the Masau *katcina* performance
is an exact duplicate of the Jemez (Hemis? Humis?) *katcina*
which is a Hotevilla favorite for Niman. If native theorists who regard the Masau as very old are correct, the Jemez would be an
imitation. Yet, I cannot avoid the hunch that it was Jemez which
introduced the manner of shaking gourd rattles at the start of a
figure, as well as the use of scrapers on gourd resonators.[3] (Regardless of which came first, the similarities of Masau and Jemez
are as striking as those between Lakon and Oaqöl. All in all,
the feeling persists that many of the repetitive ceremonial traits
may be carry-overs or borrowings from a few ancient, established rites. The problem is to determine what is original and
what has been borrowed.)

When Masau was first described as a funny *katcina*, I had
assumed it was a reference to the grotesque costume worn. The
dance, however, burlesques several Hopi rituals, especially
women's ceremonies, and there is a great deal of clowning. Many
of the foods handed out are so archaic as to bring a laugh, and
the manner of gift distribution is frequently funny. A favorite
trick is to have a *katcina* offer presents and then snatch them back
(a comic device that resembles the ritual feint); and another
"laugh-getter" is to have a *katcina* lure a spectator—often an *imûyi*
("grandson") or some other relative—into the plaza and make
him eat in public food which he does not particularly like. This
is the kind of thing that Ida's friend probably dreaded [p. 115].
[Masau *katcinas* still appear from time to time. A full-scale performance was given at Hotevilla in the winter of 1965; and at
Moenkopi, recently, four Masau *katcinas* appeared in lieu of
clowns during an afternoon rest period of an ordinary *katcina*
dance. The Masau impersonators raised howls of laughter by calling spectators into the plaza to eat a variety of strange, old-
fashioned foods. Masau *katcinas* may appear singly; in small

groups, as when they form part of a large number of mixed *katcinas;* or as a complete dance unit of about two dozen men.]

Kane pointed out the young Hotevilla woman who had asked for the dance and showed me her husband, who was the first *katcina* in the line. He also discussed some of the duties and responsibilities of dance sponsors, and it was he who first revealed the custom of having sponsors remain awake all night in order to relieve a Village chief of one of his difficult duties.

Kane then pointed out a Hopi man whose hair had been "bobbed." He explained that this had been done by the man's *ikya'as* as a way of showing their resentment when he married a "strange" woman.

Sun. Nov. 12. The first item for today ties right on to the last entry for yesterday. The Sun clan women are going to Bakavi where one of their *imûyis* is going to be married. They will help grind corn, bake *piki,* and make themselves useful. They will also, however, attack the bride when she appears. As Ida says, "We just 'hate' this girl for taking our *imûyi* away from us.[4] Ruth was also planning to go to Bakavi but was prevented from going by the unexpected arrival of some Navaho friends.

Leland from Mishongnovi on Second Mesa came in. He said that he would have gone into his village's Wuwutcim in 1931 but he had been forced to go to school. He told me that some of the First Mesa Hopi boys at Polacca had been jailed for getting drunk on vanilla extract, and he admitted that he had tried straight alcohol but didn't like it. [In the 1950s Leland was married and the father of several children. He lived at New Oraibi and worked at odd jobs. In 1957 he was rather badly injured in an automobile accident. Shortly after, he was killed while fighting forest fires in California.]

Yesterday Ned took George sheepherding with him. They cornered a rabbit, and Ned let George have the "honor" of catching and killing it. It is Ned's ambition to make a good herder of George, so he took him along again today. On these excursions he also teaches him many other Hopi ways. [By midcentury the custom of herding sheep began to die out as younger men began to show a marked preference for cash-paying jobs in town. Today only two or three of the older men at Old Oraibi continue to herd sheep.]

Martin said, in answer to a question, that he was not going to work on dam construction because he was too lazy. Then he

smiled and modified his reply by saying that he couldn't work
on another job because he had too much sheepherding to do. Yet,
other men herd far more, and on the way to the dance yesterday
we saw Lawrence setting out on horseback to herd for Martin,
his stepfather. The little chap managed to smile bravely as he
waved to those who were on the way to Hotevilla for a good
time.

NOTE ON RACIAL PSYCHOLOGY.—Kane remarked on the
fine crops that the Hotevilla people had raised in spite of their
complaints of last year; and another man told me that nearly
all of the Moenkopi families had had good yields. So the frequent talk of starving is a culture trait that is 99 percent mental
and scarcely borne out by the facts. With the cash that is being
earned from the government building of dams, public buildings, roads, and bridges, the Hopi are materially better off
than they have ever been; but the old fear of starvation persists. This leads me to think that there may be such a thing as
a Racial Mind or Racial Memory, in the special sense of ideas
that are handed down from generation to generation. We know,
from our own experience, that teen-aged youngsters in our
society and culture understand electricity far better than did
their forebearers when they were middle-aged. That is how
cultural progress is made. There would be no gain if everyone
had to start from scratch. We benefit from some of the physical
and psychological things that our ancestors acquired in their
lifetime. Culturally speaking, there is such a thing as "the in-
heritance of acquired characteristics." Now, if the Hopi had
experienced disastrous crop failures in the past (as we know
they did), they might well have instilled a fear of starvation in
their children, who could have transmitted it to their de-
scendants who might never have experienced actual starvation.
Here we have the contemporary Hopi perpetually concerned
over crop failure, anticipating the worst, and worrying over
lack of rain for no good reason as they have had excellent crops
for more than two successive years. [In 1955 there was actually
a great deal of rain. Thereupon the Hopi modified their tune
slightly and complained "it wasn't the right kind of rain." However, severe drought did prevail from 1956 to 1958. For lack of
pasturage Ned had to sell some of his lambs. He got fourteen
cents a pound.] I believe that any kind of violent fear or love
experienced by parents can be impressed upon their children

through cultural conditioning. There could thus arise a specific kind of Group or Racial Psychology, in the sense of a number of individual minds that had been culturally conditioned in the same way.

Ned reported that George was rapidly becoming a good horseback rider because a medicine man had rubbed something into his rectum for that purpose.

Don't overlook the notion that the curative function of the *katcinas* is emphasized by the fact that a father of the *katcinas* is usually a Badger, and that the Badgers have charge of the *katcinas* for half of each year. In Hopi belief there is a close connection between the Badger clan and medicine.

Several men say that Masau *katcinas* are sometimes privileged to speak, especially when they are directing communal work. [O.O., p. 66, adds detail to this topic.]

Kane is planning to go to his permanent, winter sheep camp, where he expects to stay till spring. He intends to come into Oraibi only for occasional visits. He generally comes to dance *katcina*, returning early on the next day. His whole life certainly centers on his sheep.

Cedric was asked what he had done about getting a steer from Albert as payment for damages done to his crops. Cedric replied that Albert had refused to give him a steer, and it was plain that he was ready to let the whole matter drop. Everyone condemns Albert's inefficiency and carelessness. Kane noted that the Hopi never cooperated in such matters because each man was "jealous" lest someone else get more out of the deal than he.

Mon. Nov. 13. Ned entertained and traded with some Navaho, and they gave him a blanket when they left. Then Bill exchanged some admittedly poor beads for a blanket which he plans to sell for ten or twelve dollars to "White" travelers at the railroad station in Winslow or Flagstaff. (He openly admitted that he would pose as the weaver of the blanket because he is sure that "White" travelers will be unable to tell a Hopi from a Navaho.) The Hopi usually get the better of a deal when they trade with the Navaho.

It is being said that Bill has had love affairs with Louis's Clara (before she married Louis); Barbara (George's mother); and Edith. There is even some talk that Bill may be "cutting out" Edith's husband. Strange that Bill has been "playing" so many women of the Masau'û clan. There is a lack of censure for sexual activity, and people with reputations for looseness are as commonly entertained as any others.

Homer has opened a gas station at Kikötcmovi and is taking business away from Tom because he gives credit and charges one cent less on a gallon of gasoline. He is now encouraged to open a complete trading post. When I suggested that he was too unpopular to do much business, Lee came to his defense. She thought that he "might have learned his lesson," and it seems obvious that the thrifty Hopi will trade with him if he gives bargains.

Tues. Nov. 14. Problems for future studies of Hopi culture: a complete listing and analysis of the Hopi pantheon; totemism; semantics and linguistics,· with reference to such key words as *katcina, wimi, wuya, na'töla*, and so forth; accurate land holdings by clans; and archaeology for whatever light it may shed on Hopi origins, relations with other tribes, and moot points of ethnology.

Last night Louise went officially to Dick's house to begin grinding corn as part of her Hopi wedding. Since her groom's father is Parrot, the Parrot women are his *ikya'as* and will stage a mud-fight. [See p. 17.] In anticipation of this event, Fern's mother (Parrot) called out for her clanswomen to prepare to do something awful to the Badgers, Dick's clan. The actual attack will be deferred until the arrival of Tcumana, one of Dick's *ikya'as* from Hotevilla, and the announcement, full of jokes and made by Fern's mother, jestingly blamed the forthcoming fight on Hotevilla.

The preliminary stages of a Hopi wedding seem to be of concern only to the women. Dick and his father go about their daily tasks with every appearance of unconcern, and even some of the women involved show little interest. It may well be that the rites are so long and drawn-out that no one but the bride can give full time to them.

Barbara is here from First Mesa, visiting her mother. I am interested to see if she will look in on George, her own son, while she is here.

Edith just returned from Bakavi where she took part in a wedding ceremony. She stayed with her divorced father, Jasper. She lunched with Ruth on her return.

There is a good deal of warm devotion between Kane and his wife, Jessie, but even here a clear distinction is made between husband's and wife's individuality and property. When Kane sold three sacks of wool, for example, he kept the proceeds from two and Jessie got the money for the third.

Ida calls her brother-in-law "older brother," but uses male relative-in-law for men married to clanswomen who are not her true sisters. Joe says this usage is correct.

While Martha was at Bakavi, her husband, Luke, was asked to dine by his mother and Louise; Delia and Hahai'i; Ruth and Ned; and Ida and me. Thus did his own (Greasewood) and his wife's (Sun) clans rally to look after his comfort.

Wed. Nov. 15. One of the difficulties inherent in the Hopi lack of communications was illustrated this morning when Ned went looking for horses that were already corralled at Sidney's house in New Oraibi.

Ruth went to see Barbara at their mother's house, but Barbara did not go to see George, presumably because he had left for school. Apparently Barbara no longer cares about her son. Once the child had been given to Ned and Ruth, he came to be regarded as theirs.

Ruth's brother-in-law from Winslow brought some venison to her mother, who made it into a stew, *sowingnukwivi* ("deer stew"). The Masau'ù clanswomen prepared various kinds of *piki* and invited several people to dine. When some of the guests brought presents, all the clanswomen, and even some of the un- related diners, expressed thanks. [Compare p. 51.] (Is this a token of solidarity?)

While we were eating, the usual round of jests went on except for one new note—a serious sexual interest between a man and the women of his father's clan, his *ikya'as*.

Cedric arrived in the afternoon with the $300 that Nick had paid for his flock of sheep. Ida asked him, I thought in jest, for five dollars. Ida later said that Cedric had offered to pay her if she would lure Fern to Kikötcmovi so that he could "speak to her." [Although there are numerous ways for Hopi lovers to meet, they sometimes employ panderers.]

Just learned that while Ned was being attacked by the Hopi who had returned from Chicago, Martin had taken an active part, although he had neither been to Chicago nor had he ever seen the display in question. Ned is accused of having sold sacred objects, and there is much talk of witchcraft. In de- fending himself poor Ned says, "I know that if I had really sold those things, I would get sick and die." He is greatly upset by the whole affair which preys on his mind. He fears that he may be driven to insanity or suicide. (This shows the great power of public opinion and of witchcraft accusations.) [The attack mentioned here concerns the episode discussed on p. 72.]

Ned is particularly eager not to lose Tawaqwaptiwa's trust in him. [Perhaps Ned was afraid of being forced out of the Soyal ceremony in which he played an important role. Ultimately, between 1940 and 1945, he was driven out.

Today, Ned and Martin are staunch allies.]

Tom came in tonight with a long tale about his business troubles. At one point he disclosed that the true father of his wife, Anita, and her brother Nick was Talahöyoma (Bear), older brother of Tawaqwaptiwa. [Some thought Talahöyoma might become Oraibi's chief. He had once been very active in the Soyal. This explains why Anita and her mother had been Soyal maidens.]

Thurs. Nov. 16. More on Hopi indifference to dirt and sanitation. While dining, hands and utensils are frequently wiped on garments or the soles of moccasins. Sheep are butchered, too, on any spot of ground and with any knife that happens to be handy.

Among the foods distributed by the Masau *katcinas,* or on display during the dance, were various kinds of cornmeal dumplings, as well as *hahalviki* (a kind of mush made from a cornmeal batter, cooked in a Dutch oven between alternate layers of hot stones, and covered with rabbit skin so that it may steam till ready); *nevenkwivi* (Hopi "spinach"); *lemoktuki* ("pop corn"); *kutuki* ("parched corn"); *dutci* (hard, roasted corn, often stuck on a greasewood stick for roasting, usually taken from the supply of the preceding year); *dutcip hoyani* (roast corn that has been stored for winter use); *kaû hoyani* (boiled corn, from last year's stock); and *tcilitpe* (roast chili, from the supply of the year before).

Ned's father today made reference to another ceremonial partnership—this time between the Momtcit and the Nakyawimi. There were also many parallels between Momtcit and Soyal procedures. From one point of view the Hopi have a richly varied set of ceremonies, but from another viewpoint their rites are strangely lacking in inventiveness. [Compare this idea with the pottery designs individually made by particular artists but conforming to a sort of tribal pattern.]

NOTE.—For a nonliterate people who must, of necessity, depend on their memories, the Hopi are by no means remarkable for the tenacity of their minds. Often they will remember what they regard as the essential parts of something, but will forget all the accompanying details. They do *not* have marvelous powers of memory and may even forget things pertaining to important ceremonies. Of course, one must not overlook the fact of cultural differences of emphasis. This leads them to remember many things that we regard as unimportant, and vice versa.

Ned felt lazy this morning and did not round up his horses until the forenoon was well spent.

While Duvenimptiwa, with Ned as interpreter, was being interviewed about Hopi life in the old days, a couple of men listened in. It was quite obvious that they were looking for trouble, and the interview was going badly. In this predicament Ned showed good sense or a knowledge of psychology. Instead of trying to hide our activities from the "spies," he opened everything up and pretended to consult them on difficult points, with the result that they soon lost interest and wandered off. Ned simply announced that they were jealous of the money he was earning.

Just as the interview was ending I heard the start of the mud-fight over Dick, with the Parrot clanswomen attacking and Badger females defending. All the men discreetly abstained. Puhumana and Juanita were the chief defenders, and Tcumana from Hotevilla was the principal attacker. There was quite a bit of roughness and horseplay. The women doused each other with water and mud and pelted one another with decayed melons, old corncobs, and whatever else came to hand. Throughout the scrimmage a running fire of mock recrimination and of banter was kept up. At last both sides grew tired, and the "fight" came to an end. Ruth then removed a wooden obstruction from the doorway of the Badger house, and the pueblo returned to normal.[5]

Fri. Nov. 17. As soon as possible I asked Ruth why it was she who had removed the barrier to the Badger house. She explained that her father had been a Badger and that his clanswomen were therefore *ikya'as* to her.

Early today Dick and Louise were formally married, Hopi style, by having their heads washed together in a single basin. Even at this stage of the rites the groom's *ikya'as* must continue to show resentment over their "loss." So, they pretend to jostle the bride aside and try to put their own heads into the washbasin.

Louise made the last of four successive visits to the east

edge of the mesa at dawn to pray to the rising sun. Now she must prepare *somiviki*, and tomorrow she must make *tcukuviki*, alternating these two foods for the duration of her stay at the home of her husband. She will then return permanently to her own (mother's) house as soon as her wedding garments are finished.

Fern told Ida that her stepfather, Panimptiwa, "had got after her" and had forbidden her to go to New Oraibi's sewing class with Ida. Ida claims that Jacob, the husband of Fern's sister Clara, had left her for a Sun clan woman at Hotevilla. That is one reason why Clara and her folks have been attacking Ned. (Again it becomes evident that the clan as well as the family or household is an important social unit. Ned is made to suffer for the supposed misdeeds of a Sun clanswoman.)

Ruth is very bitter over Clara's behavior because Clara has so often eaten with her. [Food-taking is very important in establishing friendships.]

Tom mentioned that Quincy had left for Gallup and Zuñi on business. The frequency of intertribal contacts is impressive.

Sat. Nov. 18.

RANDOM NOTES TO SUPPLEMENT INTERVIEWS.—Allen believes that women may be buried in ordinary clothes or in wedding costumes. If a dying woman has not handled her wedding garments, they could be used again for a daughter. He knows of no fixed pattern in this regard. He also says that those who are brother and sister merely because they have fathers in the same clan are not supposed to marry but sometimes do. Regarding the term for mother's mother's brother, Allen says it should be *ivava* ("older brother"); Ida, contradicting an earlier statement, says *itaha* ("maternal uncle"); and Ned says either one. All three agree that the sex of the speaker makes no difference. Allen says that a brother-in-law may so be called or may be spoken of as a brother. He says that it is optional and the one term is used as often as the other.

Raymond, at New Oraibi, owes a big bill to Hubbell, yet he was resentful when a paycheck for roadwork was applied against his debt. "Why should I work," he argues, "if Hubbell gets my money?" He completely disregards the fact that Hubbell gives him credit, and it is very likely that much resentment against the trader is unwarranted. Probably, the trader also gets blamed for such cases as that of a Navaho whose paycheck the government ordered Hubbell (by letter) to give to an aggrieved family with whose daughter the man in question had been caught sleeping.

A social bombshell exploded this morning. Ida said that Edna had accused Moe of making love to the wife of his brother Allen. Although Betty is far advanced in pregnancy, Allen says that he would leave her except that he has no place to go. It is true that he has no sister and that he fails to get along with his mother, but it is also a fact that he is the laziest man in Oraibi. It is hard to get at the truth of this situation because Edna is a gossipy troublemaker and Allen is seldom away from home. Then, too, he showed no unusual resentment toward his mother when she came to ask him to fetch some melons that Ned had set aside for her. As usual, he simply refused.

To test how seriously the Hopi take the use of kinship terms I purposely called Edna Ida's mother, since she is her ceremonial mother. Ida flared up and said resentfully, "I told you that I don't call her mother any more." [This incident and attitude are discussed in M. Titiev, "The Hopi Use of Kinship Terms for Expressing Sociocultural Values," *Anthropological Linguistics*, May, 1967.]

On a walk along the mesa's west edge, Allen pointed out some crude Spanish signatures, dated 1894; the alleged house of Matcito; the Sun shrine; and the place where impersonators of the real Masau'û dress up. The Hopi call this side of the mesa south, but it is sort of southwest. Allen also spoke of a deer picture at which men used to fire for target practice. [This rock fell down long ago.] He said such a deer figure still exists somewhere on the road to Hotevilla, but I have never seen it. [The bison painted on cave walls at Altamira, Spain, might have served a comparable purpose for Ice Age hunters. Target practice only, and not mimetic magic, seems to have interested the Hopi.]

Allen says that he has no idea where medicine men learn their craft. He guesses, since there is no curing society on Third Mesa, that each medicine man works independently, but he goes on to remind me that as "a common man" he wouldn't know of the "wonderful" things done by two-hearted medicine men.

According to Allen, a family says nothing whenever a girl rejects all suitors. "It's up to the girl to marry or not," he contends. (Good old Hopi individuality, but I still wonder why this theme is so very common in Hopi folklore.)

Tawaqwaptiwa reports that the Soyal *katcina* will appear

in eight days to usher in the open season for *katcinas*. [See chapter X, section E, for a detailed description.][6]

Ruth was alone since Ned and George had gone herding, so she came to lunch. Shortly after, Dorothy summoned her to eat with her (Ruth's) sister, Louis's Clara. Here is another instance of showing family and clan solidarity through the sharing of food.

Allen and Betty were seen chatting amiably, and Ida's report of a rift between them must be wrong. Ida, however, stuck to her story and insisted that Allen was going "to get after Moe" when he returned from dam work over the weekend. She then said that Edna was grinding corn at her house, and this led her to go into further detail regarding her reasons for rejecting Edna as a mother.

Once, when Edna had been entertaining Qöyavenka (Coyote, from Mishongnovi), Ida, then about twelve, and some other girls, curious to see this woman who had a tribal-wide reputation for looseness, peeked in. [Qöyavenka used to go from village to village as a prostitute, so it is said. She was supposed to accept "even Navahos"; and rumor has it that any coin could be used in payment because she didn't know one from another. All the women are said to have hated her, and all the men to have liked her.] Edna had been furious when she saw the girls looking in and had given them a severe tongue lashing, saying that their mothers were just as bad as Qöyavenka and she, and that all the girls would be even "crazier" when they grew up.

At another time Allen had brought some rabbits to Gladys, his now deceased sister, and Ida, who were grinding corn together. Edna had come in and taken a brace, saying that she would have a feast with a neighboring woman. The girls were suspicious and tracked her to the home of Panimptiwa, then her lover and for a time her husband. Again Edna was furious and bawled out the girls.

Ned gave an account of impersonations of the real Masau'û. They most often appear during communal harvests, or in the spring, and they may be accompanied by Maswik *katcinas*. [See O.O., pp. 184–87 and 139–41.] Masau'û actors dress in costumes that feature hoods covered with fresh rabbit blood, and they frighten people by pretending to rush at them with clubs, in the same manner in which the deity is supposed to make people die. They do many things by opposites, a confirmation of the idea that death is the reverse or opposite of life.

Ned also told me that on the occasion of Hahai'i's premature "death" and visit to the otherworld, it was Yokioma who had cured her by singing a discharming song from the Momtcit ceremony.[7] This society has no specific ailment or "whip" that it controls, but its members are supposed to know how to cure lonesomeness and grief. They may be called on to back up the ministrations of medicine men in cases where females are thought to be going *qövisti* [p. 14].

Ned rates the attachment of a Hopi to various relatives in this order: own family, family of mother's sister, own clan, own phratry, father's clan, ceremonial father's clan and phratry, "doctor" father's clan and phratry. He is uncertain whether own phratry ought to follow or precede father's clan.

Sun. Nov. 19. Asked Bert about war. He gave much information about the taking of scalps in former times,[8] and the rites for real warriors. Initiates had to sit at the north end of a kiva, with knees drawn up, for the better part of four days. A line made with cornmeal marked the limits of a "house" beyond which they were not supposed to go. When this ordeal was over two paths were drawn to the kiva ladder or exit. One was of *yalaha* ("specular iron") and *suta* ("red ocher") and went along the east side; the other was of cornmeal and went west. Neophytes were expected to know, without special instruction, that the Hopi way followed the cornmeal path leading out of the kiva along its west side. This was the path they were supposed to take.

The relation of *kaletakas* ("warriors") to one another and to the Momtcit rites is quite confusing. There are at least three kinds of *kaletakas*. There is the Village Kaletaka or War chief; then there are officers in each ceremony who play the parts of *kaletakas;* and then there are brave warriors who were not afraid to take scalps and who were also known as *kaletakas*. It may even be that the last group did not fight with bow and arrow like ordinary warriors but used only a club such as *kaletakas* carry in ceremonies. (This is reminiscent of Masau'û's method of causing death by a touch of his club. Moreover, the phratry which contains the Masau'û clan also has Kwan, Kokop, and Coyote, all of which are connected with war and death-dealing. Is there a major guiding principle that links together all the clans in each of the phratries? I do not think so.)

Edna dropped in on Ruth and Ned and invited herself to breakfast.

NOTE.—Hopi speech is often redundant. When a person approaches they say, "Are you arrived?" Answer, "I am arrived." Also, if a person comes in during a meal, he asks, "Are you eating?" Answer, "We are eating."

Yesterday Ned mentioned, and today the chief confirmed, the former existence of a kiva called Tcotcovi. It was already extinct and filled in during Tawaqwaptiwa's youth—around 1900. No one today knows much about it, but the chief thinks that it may have been built by the Bluebird or possibly the Spider clan and that it may once have housed the Momtcit ceremony before it moved to Pongovi.

In another connection the chief says that Oraibi was originally established by Matcito after a quarrel with his brother at Chimopovy, which was then situated on the plain and not atop Second Mesa. (Further evidence of a new pueblo being founded as a split from an old one.)

Tawaqwaptiwa told more about Masau'û impersonations. He said that the two men who had played the part for the last time at Oraibi were Kötiwa (Lizard-Snake) and Mokyatiwa (Rabbit). [Kötiwa was the older brother of Ned's grandfather Homikni, who was a famous medicine man.]

Tawaqwaptiwa then got going on the Soyal *katcina*. He says that the impersonator enters the village from Matcito's house, goes to Tawaovi to receive prayer offerings, and returns to his starting point. [In 1933] the chief figured the Soyal dates thus: Sunday, November 26, Soyal *katcina* appearance; sixteen days later the official Crier chief will announce the Soyal; next day the Soyal leaders will begin the rites, being joined after three days by the regular members; and the ceremony will culminate, as far as can be made out, on December 21. Strange how close they can come to the winter solstice although they get badly mixed up whenever they try to reckon other things.

The word *tcumona* came up for discussion. It is a kind of locoweed (Jimson or Jamestown) that is said to make human beings crazy. It is supposed to be related to ordinary locoweed but differs in having a white rather than a pinkish flower. The blossom is something like that of a squash or tulip. Mixed with water it is considered to be good medicine for fresh cuts.

NOTE ON HOPI MENTALITY.—These people are by no means stupid despite their lack of "facts." Yet, by our system of logic, they sometimes act in silly ways. Thus, the Hopi who had been in Chicago and who are accusing Ned of betraying his part in the Soyal admit that they first took the figure in question to be Luke. But Luke is short and slender, while Ned is tall and sturdy. The two men do not look at all alike by our standards. [Actually, the "Star priest" figure is made of plaster of Paris, tinted reddish brown. It is not made to resemble anyone in particular.] Furthermore, Ned's accusers are now saying that he is also playing the part of the *kaletaka* in the same Soyal group. Yet, Ned is not a warrior in any ceremony, and his detractors know it. This is certainly queer logic from our point of view.

Mon. Nov. 20. There was a call for all men to begin carding yarn for Louise's wedding garments. Some men have been working nights since Louise had her head washed, but today there was to be communal carding by all men who wished to participate. All workers were to have a feast, and Dick's mother, Puhumana, made the rounds of the town giving out individual invitations. Ruth went to help get the food ready, but Ned emphatically refused to go. That may be his way of getting even with the Parrot clan that has been attacking him. [The groom's father is Parrot.] Still, Ned said that he would card if he had the time.

Kane dropped in for a little while. He is using Bill's field house for the winter but is thinking of getting his brothers to help him put up a new camp in a more convenient location. He is planning to return next Saturday to join the feasting that takes place in anticipation of the Soyal *katcina*'s arrival. But he will not remain awake all night in the kiva because he has never gone through the Tribal Initiation (Wuwutcim) and is not a Soyal member.

Kane asked Ned to bob his hair. If it is long, it gets dirty too easily, and there is no one to wash it at his winter camp.

NOTE.—The Hopi emphasis on individuality extends even to dogs. Whenever Ned is asked if he plans to take his dogs when he is going somewhere, he says, "Well, it's up to them. They can come along if they wants to."

Yesterday Ruth's mother and Ned's old aunt had lunch with Ruth. They had eggs for sale and Ida bought some.

The chief affixed red *nakwakwosi* ("prayer feathers") to the heads of Bear *katcina* dolls because, he said, bear is from the north—but the color for north is yellow. Joe later explained that all men *katcinas* (in the sense of "he-men" or "warriors") have red prayer feathers. These include Bear, Tca'akwaina, He'ito, and Motcin.

While Ned was doing an errand at Kikötcmovi, Horace told him that Fred Johnson was spreading the rumor that we were making fortunes out of the Hopi material I was getting. (This makes me think of another trait of Hopi psychology that strikes me as peculiar. No matter how much they dislike a person, and no matter how untrustworthy they consider him to be, they feel that they must give full weight to any accusation he makes. Johnson is rather widely disliked because of his alleged share in burning sacred paraphernalia, yet any accusation he makes is taken seriously even by orthodox Hopi.)

Lee was quite talkative on the subject of witches. She said that she had felt something clammy touching her one night although nothing was visible when she made a light. When her parents learned about the event, they advised her to pay no attention and to do nothing about it. (This is the proper Hopi attitude toward witchery. It is reminiscent of their advice never to resist and not to worry. Worse will befall anyone who shows a violent reaction or who gets emotionally keyed up.)

Lee then repeated a story about having a lock of hair mysteriously snipped from her head while she was ill. She added that the same thing had once happened to Dell's mother. "So you see," she concluded, "there are witches everywhere." When I replied with some jest about Masau'û, she warned me not to get fresh about him. She went into a long tale about a group of young men who had disregarded the warnings of an oldster to stop bragging about what they would do if Masau'û were to appear. That night Masau'û appeared as a mysterious light, whereupon the young men fell all over each other, beat up the older man, and scattered. Nothing happened to them, but I was warned not to be careless in talking about Masau'û.

Other tales of the supernatural followed. Lee's father had once had his horses frightened by a mysterious white object; and at another time a little man had jumped on one of his horses and badly frightened it. There was also a story of a misadventure that had befallen Lee's brother Ted. "You know how nervy he is," she said, by way of introduction. Ted was returning from rabbit hunting one evening when he encountered a pale, white-faced figure and fell unconscious. He said nothing when he first got home, but a few days later he became seriously ill and reported his experience. Promptly, his parents diagnosed his ailment to have resulted from an encounter with Tihkuyi Wuhti, and shortly after, Ted recovered. Lee says that "White" people are wrong to call Indians superstitious, because such encounters actually happen. Lee professed not to know what Tihkuyi Wuhti meant, but Ned told me that it referred to a woman who was supposed to have died in childbirth near a place called Palatkwapi soon after the Hopi had come forth from the Underground. Because her baby had partially emerged, this woman is known, Ned says, as "Child-water Woman," or "Child-protruding Woman." He says that she also goes by the names of Tuwapong Wuhti or Tuwapongtumsi.[9]

Tues. Nov. 21. We left fairly early in Ned's wagon to fetch wood. We were going to take Edna as far as Hotevilla. In order to avoid gossip Ned had asked her to meet us well beyond the limits of the village. (Once before Ned had dropped Edna just before we reached the pueblo. It is likely Ned's name has been linked with hers, and once more does one sense the force of public opinion.)

On the way we passed Allen who had summoned Poling-yauoma to treat his wife. She was ill but not yet in labor. Edna repeated the accusations that she had leveled at Moe. Ned thought that Betty might have realized that Allen was sterile and had begun an affair with his brother in the hope of becoming pregnant. For all his threats Allen took no steps against Moe, possibly because he did not like to work and was glad to get whatever money Moe paid for his keep.

We arrived before lunch at the hogan of Nestcili, who was treating his sick wife in their sweathouse. Nestcili, who had learned to be a singer from his father-in-law, has been very busy of late. He travels about a good deal and is well paid for his services.

After eating, we went to load up. On the way Ned explained how he teaches George to be industrious and energetic when they are out herding. He does not allow him to dawdle at meals, and he warns him that he will never get a good wife if he is lazy.

I managed to turn the talk to salt-gathering, and Ned spoke of the ritual copulation that each member of an expedition is supposed to perform with a rock that represents the Salt goddess and is known as Öng Wuhti ("Salt Woman"). As is true of all sexual affairs, except in marriage, each man is expected to make some sort of payment for favors received, and everyone vows to leave some salt with the deity on the return trip. Many tales of misfortune are told about those who skimp or renege on their promised payments.[10]

From this the talk turned to matters of sex, and Ned verified practically all that had been said about the prevalence of *dumaiya*. He then went on to say that Ida disliked Allen because he was much given to calling on girls and women by night. She calls him a "sneaker" (that is, one who sneaks into houses, hoping for sex favors) and says that he is prone to go *dumaiya* whenever his wife spends a night in Hotevilla. (This is puzzling because the behavior of Allen on this score is no different from that of many other Hopi men.) Ned says Allen is greatly disliked at Hotevilla, and that is why Betty lives with him at Oraibi in defiance of matrilocal residence. [Yet, a few years later, Allen and Betty did take up residence in Hotevilla.]

Solimana of Old Oraibi is nicknamed Hu Wuhti ("Gasp Woman"), because one warm night she had been overheard breathing hard during intercourse outdoors with her husband. She is sometimes called by her nickname to her face, even though she is aware of its significance.

Ned admitted that he had sometimes had affairs with Navaho women. He claims to have been withdrawn from Squaw dances in order "to do a business." He believes this sort of thing to be a common procedure at Squaw dances. He said that the wife of Nestcili's brother-in-law had once invited him to possess her. She had taken a fancy to a string of beads that he was wearing and had put it between her thighs to signify what he could have in exchange, but he felt that the price was too high for "that business"; besides she was the wife of a Sand clansman and thus his "mother" because his own father was Sand.

Before retiring for the night, Ned went out to defecate. Later he said that the excreta had immediately been gobbled up by dogs. When I expressed disgust, he replied that it was all right and that it wouldn't hurt the dogs who were used to "that kind of food." Hopi dogs have similar habits, but in each tribe they are allowed to lick plates without restraint.

Wed. Nov. 22. While Ned was fetching the horses in the morning, the rest of us in the hogan washed up. On his return, Ned remarked on his unwashed condition but said, "Well, let it go." Our Navaho hosts wash much more frequently and thoroughly than Ned.

While Ned was out and before breakfast was ready, Nestcili regaled himself with a chunk of pressed, cold meat (pemmican?) from which he cut bites with a pocket knife. He offered some to me, saying in Hopi, "Kwangwa!" ("'Sweet!'" or "'Good!'") I felt duty bound to try some and found it vile stuff—full of tallow, smelly, and gritty.

Nestcili's mother-in-law, who lives in a nearby hogan, asked us, by messenger, to take coffee with her. (The Navaho mother-in-law taboo prevented her from entering the hogan where Nestcili was present.) We did not want to hurt her feelings, so we went over for some tortillas and coffee before returning for our regular breakfast. To their friends, the Navaho are just as liberal and gracious with food as are the Hopi. (Several Navaho were curious to know what I had eaten at Nestcili's. Like the Hopi they were pleased to find that I had eaten without fuss whatever had been served. The social significance of food is extremely great.)

On the way back to Oraibi Ned remarked that the winners of races such as those of the Snake and Flute ceremonies were likely to be lazy and indifferent farmers. Naturally, he cited Panimptiwa as an example. [Oddly enough, many years later, when he was befriending Panimptiwa, ostensibly for having cured him of rheumatism, Ned praised him as an excellent farmer who had taught him a great deal.]

At Oraibi the men finished carding for Louise's wedding outfit today, and they are now ready to begin spinning. Cedric said that the most diligent workers were Dick's uncles. Thus the pattern persists.

Since Ned and Ruth have moved right next door, every visitor, not just Ida, strains to overhear whatever is being said at Ned's. Similarly, if Ned leaves the house without disclosing his errand, visitors invariably ask where he is going. I have developed the habit of never divulging whatever information I may have. "Who told you that?" is forever being asked, and I have learned to give evasive replies.

Thurs. Nov. 23. Tawaqwaptiwa says that the Soyal *katcina* is supposed to appear on the last day of (immediately after?) the old Tribal Initiation (Wuwutcim) rites.

Anita recently got after Jacob's Clara for failing to keep clean her part of a passageway between the two houses. Clara made the usual comeback, "I'm not a Bahana." Then she went further. "If you want to clean up and be like a Bahana," she taunted Anita, "why don't you move to New Oraibi?" (Thus again is cleanliness linked to the "White" man's way of life. Over the years the Hopi have borrowed many things from the "Whites" but not their ideas of cleanliness.)

Luke came around with a story he claims to have heard from Sidney. They report that Byron Adams, a native missionary from First Mesa, and an unidentified "White" man are coming to take away part of each Hopi and Navaho flock because of the shortage of pasture. It is said that they will pay only $1.50 per head. Sidney worried about the rumor all night, and Ned was badly upset. There was a call at noon for all owners of sheep and cattle to attend a conference at Kikötcmovi. All the men are unhappy at what they regard as an unfair decree from Washington.

On Saturday the members of Tawaovi are supposed to fetch wood so that they may remain awake in comfort all night before the Soyal *katcina* comes.

MISCELLANEOUS NOTES.—Several women who have been grinding corn for one another worked for Mary today. They belong for the most part to Mary's phratry containing the Parrot and Rabbit-Tobacco clans.

Jests about eating horseflesh fall flat, because eating horsemeat is here taken for granted. Some Hopi also claim to have eaten dog.

Lee says that her parents warned her never to tickle a dog since it is not natural for a dog to laugh. They reported the case of a dog that laughed, only to die four days later. Other Hopi say that they know nothing of such beliefs.

Mules are worth $60 to $75; horses only $10 or $15 each. Mules are said to eat less and to be sturdier and longer-lived than horses.

Ida refuses to believe that any "White" people are poor. She puts down as nonsense whatever I say about the depression, beggars, breadlines, and starvation. "Indians are poor, but Bahanas are rich." That's her belief and she sticks to it—and so do all the other Hopi. They don't know when they are well-off. [This attitude has been observed elsewhere and seems to be standard among American aboriginal groups that are in contact with "Whites."]

One Sun Watcher is supposed to observe each sunrise for half the year [June to December solstices] from the Buffalo shrine called Atcamoli. [This shrine is near Jack's house, and it is said that his wife, who claims to be Oraibi's present chief, sometimes watches from there.] Another Sun Watcher is expected to observe each sunrise for the remaining six months from the real

Sun clan house and to announce the proper times for planting various crops.[11] One of the watchers is a Flute chief.

Many years ago, the Flute "priests" (leaders?) used to make offerings to the sun. Four days later, the male heads of the Sun clan would also make offerings to the sun. [Compare p. 52 and p. 360, n. 12.] All the offerings had to be finished before the Niman, the final *katcina* dance of the open season. They used to be deposited at Tawaki (Sun's house), a shrine on the eastern horizon that marked the point reached by the sun at the time of the summer solstice.

Is there any connection between the Sun clan and the Flute societies? Does the Sun clan own the Flute ceremonies at other Hopi pueblos? If so, did the Sun people reach Oraibi so late that some other clan was holding the Flute rites? [Do these rituals have some relationship to the summer solstice?]

In talking about the forthcoming Soyal rites Tom and Ned make it clear that the Soyal is the culmination of the Tribal Initiation (Wuwutcim) observances. Tawaqwaptiwa, Martin, Duvenimptiwa, Ned, Tom, Humiletstiwa, and Panimptiwa are among the Oraibi men who can be pretty well counted on to smoke all night before the coming of the Soyal *katcina*. Very likely they will be joined by some men from Moenkopi and others from Oraibi.

I forgot to mark down that the wife of Nestcili and her brother's young son, whom they are raising, are extremely skillful at cat's cradle. By themselves each can make a large variety of designs. Even small Navaho tots make many string figures. The Hopi are fair at cat's cradle, but the Navaho are much better.

Fri. Nov. 24. Ned left to let his sheep out this morning. His father will then take over the herding so that Ned can attend the meeting called for this afternoon at New Oraibi. Ned told me his plans but said nothing to Ruth, who asked *me* what Ned was going to do. Queer, to say the least, but that's the way things go between many couples, even when mates are on good terms.

Fletcher Corrigan tried to straighten Ned and me out on the program of stock reduction that was under discussion. Mr. Collier's chief purpose is to bring about erosion control which requires cutting down on the size of sheep herds to prevent over-grazing. (Herds grew too large during the depression because far fewer animals than usual could be sold for meat to packing houses.) The government will pay $1.50 for ewes and $2.00 for wethers. Any animal in good flesh, regardless of age, will be accepted. There is to be no compulsion on those who do not care to sell.

Corrigan's version puts the entire matter in a different light. It actually gives the Hopi a chance to rid their flocks of undesirable animals. Moreover, leaving the decision up to each individual conforms to native practice, and now most men plan to sell off some of their old sheep. [The subject of stock reduction was still a lively topic for debate in the 1950s and later. In an effort to control the sizes of herds the government issued grazing permits to each owner for a given number of livestock. Natives got around the system by buying up permits from those who had sold off all their animals and by failing to turn in the permits of those who had died. A few men whose herds were drastically reduced found that it was economically senseless to retain so small a flock that the annual profit was negligible. Such men tended to sell off their animals and to go entirely out of the herding business.]

Oscar gave me a different slant on the Masau *katcina*. He says that it came into being after a famine and that its main purpose is to teach people to eat everything. That is why, says Oscar, the Masau *katcinas* force some of the bystanders to eat foods that they do not like. Oscar claims to be learning a lot about old Hopi customs from his father. [It was Oscar who said in 1955 that *katcinas* were sometimes told to withhold presents from naughty children until the last moment. This has a disciplinary effect as the naughty child will begin to fear that he will not get any present.]

Sat. Nov. 25. Cedric and his wife, Juanita, are none too popular at Oraibi. It is said that they live so much with Puhumana because Juanita is too lazy to conduct her own household. There may be some truth to these charges.

Dan arrived from Chimopovy and announced that there was to be a Wuwutcim at Hotevilla tomorrow. It turned out that Dan was "lying" (joking). He has the reputation of being a great teaser. He insists that he had left Chimopovy to get away from the girls who were always chasing him because he was rich. [Compare p. 108.]

Dan is a phratry uncle to Louise. An older man in one's own clan-phratry is called *itaha* ("uncle") in practice, although in theory *ivava* ("older brother") is permissible. Louise does not like Dan and calls him a witch.

Kane is in Oraibi for the night but is planning to go back to herding tomorrow. He intends to return about once a week because, as he says, his family wants to see him, and he loves them. Kane does not like the site of his present camp partly because it is surrounded by *tcinti* hogans. He claims that the Navaho at Piñon are using a cemetery for their dead because *tcinti* hogans are taking up too much valuable space. While he was away, Kane had trapped two coyotes. His family had wished him good luck in coyote trapping, and he says that "it sure helped."

It was no surprise that Kane got from Martin an exaggerated account of the false, earlier version of the proposal regarding stock reduction. Nevertheless, when his family had expressed concern, Kane had quieted their fears and had expressed confidence that everything would turn out well. It is his sensible, calm, carefully reasoned attitude that marks Kane apart from his fellows. When he was given the correct story, he immediately grasped the point and decided to sell off some of his sheep. He also made the wise suggestion that it would have been sensible to have included the sale of goats in the scheme because they are usually herded with sheep but are of less value since they produce no wool. (However, it must not be overlooked that American dealers can market the meat of sheep or lambs far more readily than they can dispose of kids or goats.)

Ned remains troubled by the accusations of the Hopi who had been to Chicago. I went over the story with him again, carefully explaining that his enemies had seen only museum dummies, but just when I felt that he thoroughly understood the whole business, he remarked that his antagonists had failed in an attempt to photograph the display case because "the power of the figures" had been too strong. He did realize, though, that the talk of his opponents had done much to spread Soyal secrets among uninitiated people who had no right to know them.

At about nine in the evening Ned went into Tawaovi for the all-night vigil preceding the arrival of the Soyal *katcina*. He said something about Ruth's remaining awake till midnight as her way of participating in the ceremony, but she retired as soon as he had left.

Sun. Nov. 26. Men who stay up all night during rites are supposed to go about their usual duties on the following day, but they may go to bed earlier than usual.

Noted some potsherds near a sheep corral but suspected they were sacred and did not gather them. They proved to be remnants of jars that had once held snakes and were then deposited at a Snake shrine. From the size of the fragments each jar seems to have been about eighteen inches high. It was made of redware, smooth, and with no design except for a braided effect around the neck that might have stood for a snake. The body of the jar had apparently been pierced here and there to provide airholes so that the enclosed reptiles could breathe.

Moe and Allen pointed out a spot where a huge boulder had been dislodged in recent times. It had disturbed several graves of children and had even exposed a skull. No one molested it, but no one reburied it. (It becomes more and more apparent that the Hopi do fear the dead and will not voluntarily desecrate a grave. Pottery pertaining to the dead is never handled.)

Everyone at Oraibi is looking forward to the arrival of the Soyal *katcina* this afternoon. Stew and *pikami* are being served at most houses, and nearly all of the inhabitants have had their heads freshly washed in yucca suds. Although only one *katcina* will appear, this day counts as *tikive* ("dance day"), exactly the same as on the occasion of a group dance.

Around noon Martin went southwest of the village with a large bundle. Word is being passed that Martin is to impersonate the Soyal *katcina* for the first time and that Tawaqwaptiwa will receive him at Tawaovi and present him with prayer offerings.

It was about one in the afternoon when the Soyal *katcina* entered the village in costume. He acted like an old man recently wakened from sleep, and his coming indicated the start of the open *katcina* season. [A detailed account of this performance is given in chapter X, section E.] Several children, but no adults, came up from New Oraibi to witness the performance. There were no visitors from other villages even though the Soyal *katcina* does not appear there. For instance, Nelson, who takes part in Hotevilla rites, had never seen a Soyal *katcina* performance before. (The reasons why other Third Mesa pueblos have no Soyal *katcina* and why this performance fails to attract visitors are not known. Possibly, other villages lack the requisite paraphernalia, and the rites may be too short to warrant a visit to another town.)

All the Second Mesa villages have completed their Tribal Initiations (Wuwutcim), and Bakavi held its concluding Wuwutcim dance today. Perhaps this accounts for the absence of guests from Hotevilla or Bakavi at Oraibi's Soyal *katcina*. Nelson plans to take part in the Wuwutcim at Hotevilla.

Ned reported that all the expected participants in last night's vigil had been on hand except for his father. The old man, about seventy, had to herd today and did not feel equal to going without sleep. Even Ned was tired and grouchy all day. He went to bed around half-past four.

Frank Siemptiwa has not yet come to Oraibi, although some other Moenkopi men have arrived.

It was strange to hear the pagan Village crier announce a Sunday school meeting an hour or two after the performance of the Soyal *katcina*. Most of the women who usually attend went to Voth's church.

Joe came in after supper and got going on sex in great style. He described some of his own experiences when sneaking into houses. Once he had made love to a very young girl, thinking she might be virgin. He was surprised to find that "she already knew all about that business." Her parents had found out about this affair, but they did not want their daughter to marry Joe because he was an older man and came from Hotevilla. (Joe claims that he is now glad not to have married this girl because she is "mean" and stingy. Somehow, neither set of reasons seems very convincing.)

Joe's wife is soon to be confined. He intends to observe the forty-day period of continence prescribed and says that he will sleep at home in order to look after his other children. He also says that he will not go "visiting about" as do other men. [He did not keep his word.]

Mon. Nov. 27. There was much talk today of love affairs, and at one point Tawaqwaptiwa mentioned *ikya'as* whose favors he had enjoyed. He then asked, "How many 'aunts' have you got into?" And when I explained that such relationships were forbidden among us, he expressed sorrow and went on to say that he had found his ceremonial *ikya'as* (Sun clanswomen) the sweetest of all. (This clinches the idea of the sex motive that underlies the *ikya'a-imûyi* relationship. This is probably the reason, too, why an *imûyi* teases any man who is married to an *ikya'a*.) There were also stories of visits to houses of prostitution in various towns.

Worked extremely hard this afternoon on the Oraibi view of an incident described by Cushing.[12] It concerns an attempt on Lololoma's life; a declaration of war; and the appearance of an impersonator representing Pukonghoya ("The Little War god," the elder brother of twins). Joe's mother, Sinimka, played an important part. Later, Joe added a few details to what the chief had said, but in general he confirmed Tawaqwaptiwa's account of the event.

Joe also says that the rabbit-fur garment traditionally worn by a Masau *katcina* represents melon vines; and that the necklace of sheep horns stands for string beans. He backs up earlier statements made by Kane to the effect that the Sand clan "owns" racing; and that men do not like to race for their "aunts" because they would feel too deeply hurt if their *ikya'as* failed in public to show their love and gratitude. [The Hopi used to have all manner of races by civilians each of which was a good in itself.[13] [See chapter X, section K.] The custom of group racing has died out at Oraibi, but Ned, whose father was Sand, was thinking of reviving it "some day." In the end, he took no action.]

> NOTE.—The household group, although not a consciously defined unit by any means, is beginning to emerge quite definitely as being made up essentially of a woman, her married daughters, and their unmarried children. Even in 1906 many married daughters were forsaking their mothers' houses, so that the household has not been a fixed and stable unit at least since the turn of this century.

Rumors were circulating at New Oraibi that I was to be thrown out of Oraibi because of Ned's troubles. However, just today letters from the Field Museum at Chicago arrived. They completely absolved Ned and attributed the troublemaking display directly to Voth. That ought to clear the atmosphere.

Strange how the New Oraibi people profess an interest in keeping Old Oraibi's orthodoxy pure. Jim, who subscribes to the *Christian Science Monitor* and who has announced that he will judge for himself if Hopi ceremonies are evil, assured me that I could enter any ceremony I pleased because, he said, "They're not strict up there any more." Lee turned up her nose when she heard that Martin rather than Tawaqwaptiwa had played the part of the Soyal *katcina,* and Jim condemned the whole affair by saying accusingly, "They broke a tradition up there." Apparently, the nonorthodox feel that they can justify themselves by debasing their pagan fellows.

> NOTE ON MEDICINE MEN.—The great puzzle here is to learn who teaches medicine men their trade. It seems to be an individual matter, and those who wish to practice merely proclaim themselves to be "doctors" and then seek to establish reputations for cures. [There must be more to it somewhere, but it is hard to learn more on this topic.]

Tues. Nov. 28. Tawaqwaptiwa had entertained the gathering of men who had stayed awake in the kiva with a story after which Martin had put on the Soyal *katcina* mask and had begun to practice for the next day's performance. The men in the kiva teased and joked with him as he rehearsed.

Yesterday morning, following the all-night vigil at Tawaovi, Ned came to feed his "friends," meaning his *katcina* mask and other ceremonial objects. He made no prayer but simply deposited a little *pikami*, a pinch of bread, and a kernel of hominy in the cupboard where the things are stored. (All orthodox Hopi, but medicine men in particular, are supposed to feed sacred objects before they themselves eat.) [The rule is still in force, but it does not seem to be observed. All *katcinas* are commonly spoken of as "friends."]

Tawaqwaptiwa plans to haul wood to Tawaovi tomorrow in preparation for the forthcoming Soyal.

Wed. Nov. 29. It was so cold and rainy this morning that Ned hated to mount and go herding, but after stalling for a while he started out in reasonably good humor. Ida remarked that it was lucky their old father didn't have to herd on such a day, whereupon I teased her, saying that if she ever got married, her husband would carry on in place of her aged father. Ida took me seriously and answered that she knew I was right, but she didn't expect to wed because she was too "ashamed" to have a sweetheart.

All the women were excited at the prospect of a free Thanksgiving dinner at the school in Kikötcmovi. They went down in spite of the nasty weather for chicken sandwiches, coffee, and doughnuts. A great many New Oraibi women were present.

George had a part in the entertainment. He was an Indian, no less. His parents did not attend, and he spent the night at Kikötcmovi with Horace and his Sun clan wife, Jane. It is their son who loaned George his costume.

Edna spent the night with Ruth and Ned. For all her notorious love of men she objects to smoking. Nor will she taste lard which is, she says, made from spiders. Ned informed me in all seriousness that some "White" men ate spiders.

Ned explained that Martin had been chosen to be Soyal *katcina* because the chief wanted him to help out until Sam was old enough to take over. Before Tawaqwaptiwa, the part had been taken by Talaskwaptiwa (Sun). Talaskwaptiwa, as the husband of the Bear woman who had reared Tawaqwaptiwa and Bert, had once been an important figure at Oraibi. He had a great reputation for weaving and was much in demand for making wedding robes. When Talaskwaptiwa died, he was buried by Ned and Hahai'i, but Tawaqwaptiwa assisted in order to show his respect for the deceased. (On one occasion it was said that Talaskwaptiwa had been buried in his Al costume, but at another time informants claimed that he was a Wuwutcim man and not an Al man.)

Ned then went on with several details about burial practices and related items. Clothing, water, and *piki* are placed with a corpse for the soul's use. The grave is sealed with rocks. If a person had been two-hearted, coyotes might loosen the rocks to help the spirit begin its painful journey, one step a year, to Maski ("Death House" or the otherworld). Sometimes a bull snake, representing a witch, will emerge from a grave and crawl back into the village. If it should be killed, its soul would speed to Maski like that of a one-hearted person.

This brought Ned to the subject of snakes. He claims that the only reptile Snake dancers will not use freely is a *duwatcua* ("sand rattler"). He says that a dancer once swallowed one of these snakes, which killed him by boring through his body and emerging at the rectum. At Shipaulovi, however, a single sand rattler is said to be used for some particular aspect of worship during the rites.

Although Ned is not a member of the Snake society, he says that he would never kill a snake unless it struck at him and missed. There is no element of snake worship or totemism in his attitude as he describes it. He says only that he would not kill a snake because he "takes pity on it—just like a Boy Scout." [Compare p. 8.] He also mentions an idea that is part of the folklore of our own culture. He believes that a deadly snake guards the ruins of old villages.

On another subject Ned says that rites similar to those connected with the making of *piki* ovens, *dumas*, are observed for the quarrying of mealing stones, i.e., *metates* or *matas*. The leader of such a project is usually a woman who prays while her husband makes prayer feathers at the preceding Soyal and again when an expedition sets out. (Ned's mother, Hahai'i, often took charge of such projects.) The best time for getting mealing stones is between the month of March and the time when peach trees blossom. The Hopi believe that these stones are "cold" and would cause frost if gathered out of season. They may be installed, however, at any time.

Thurs. Nov. 30. Martha did not go to the program at the New Oraibi school yesterday because she had company. She was entertaining Tilly Tawahongka, of Kikötcmovi, whose father was a Sun clansman married to a Bow woman. Tilly is a Christian, but she has had one bastard and is about to bear another. At Oraibi Betty, wife of Alex; Mary, wife of Joe; Grace, wife of Martin; and Juanita, wife of Cedric, are all about to have babies in the order named. Betty is spreading the news that the child she had had last year had died because it had been bewitched by her mother-in-law, Edna. She insists that Kiacwaitiwa had made the discovery and that it had been confirmed by Polingyauoma.

In the course of the morning Ida passed Betty's house and found that the sun had been curtained out.[14] She thus knew that Betty's baby had been born, and since Betty had attended the school program last evening, it was obvious that she had given birth during the night. This proved to have been the case. Betty's child was a son. She had been attended by a New Oraibi woman of her husband's clan, Shalakmana (Coyote), former wife of Sidney. Edna was not called.

Only a woman who has given birth for the first time is expected to avoid sunlight for the full twenty days.

[If a birth takes place at home, all objects connected with the delivery are thrown on special rubbish heaps or scattered to the east. See Fig. 12.]

NOTE ON KATCINA DANCES.—When there are two fathers of the *katcinas*, as is generally the case of Niman dances, the men simply assist one another. The speech made at the end of a performance is supposed to be set and delivered verbatim, but memories sometimes slip. As a rule, a kind of unity develops in a group of dancers, even though they cannot hear each other's voices. They may all grow tired simultaneously or else the whole group may feel fresh.

Jim came to fetch me for Thanksgiving dinner. On the way down the mesa he pointed out a house that was supposed to have been haunted when he was a small boy. He also said (as others had before) that in the old days a Village chief was supposed to be the last to retire and the first to awake in his pueblo. He was expected to remain up well into each night and to receive a final report from the War chief who made the rounds after the populace was asleep. All authority was vested in the chief. His judgment on any issue was final. His decrees were enforced by the War chief who had the right to punish and, according to Jim, to kill anyone who was disobedient. (Thus a concept of the Hopi state is beginning to take shape. Apparently the Village chief is the principal officer, but the power behind his decrees is lodged in the War chief. More and more it looks as if the military societies once had definite police functions. As examples, we have members of the Kwan and Al societies guarding the town during the Wuwutcim or Tribal Initiations; the policing functions of the War chief; and the use of warriors to guard kivas during the performance of esoteric rites.)

The chief took into the kiva the four prayer sticks that the Soyal *katcina* had left four days ago.

Tom told an amusing tale of joking with an *imûyi*. The chap was young and did not take the jests gracefully. He showed anger and resentment, but Tom refused to quit because, he insisted, it was the Hopi way for an *ikwa'a* to tease an *imûyi*.

Ruth's parents went to Winslow to bring a load of watermelons to their daughter whose husband had recently given them some venison. Ruth didn't go along because George wouldn't let her. She admitted that he was sometimes "mean," but she went on to say that he was her only son and that she was afraid to whip him lest he sicken and die. As it happened, Joe soon invited Ruth and Ned to dine with him because he had some beef from a freshly butchered cow. George, however, refused to go along, so Ruth and Ned ate at home.

Ned gave me an account of how Flute and Snake races are started. It supports Bert on the subject. A *kaletaka* ("warrior") is supposed to motion with a lightning frame to the four cardinal points, and possibly up and down, after which, as soon as the sun appears on the horizon, spectators on the mesa top cry out. (Nowadays the *kaletaka* uses a bow with red horsehair. It resembles the standard of the Snake society.) The shouts are to notify the Cloud people, and as soon as the shouts are heard, the race is supposed to begin. [Compare p. 17.] The movements of the *kaletaka*, according to Bert, signify that he is acting like Sotukinangwa'a, the main sky god. When an effort was made to prompt Ned into saying the same thing of his own accord, it was unsuccessful. Yet, when Bert's interpretation was mentioned, Ned immediately said that the idea sounded good to him and was certainly correct, even though he had never thought of it that way. [Does Ned's failure to associate the role of the *kaletaka* at the start of a race with Sotukinangwa'a indicate the customary Hopi disinterest or inability to make the kind of conceptual tie-up or generalization that springs immediately to our minds, or does it mean only that Bert's interpretation is an individual matter and not a standard part of Hopi belief? This is the kind of problem that perplexes an ethnologist who is trying to get a systematic but reliable picture of Hopi culture.]

CHAPTER VI

Diary for December, 1933

[*December is a dangerous month because unseen evil spirits abound.*
The droll Qöqöqlom katcinas, in miscellaneous garb, perform
as the first katcina group dance of the year and also complete the
opening of the katcina season.

Hotevilla's men stage Wuwutcim (Tribal Initiation) dances and
other activities; while at Old Oraibi preparations are being made for
the great Soyal (Winter Solstice) observances. The climax of this
ceremony is timed to coincide with the sun's arrival at the southernmost
extreme of its apparent annual journey. It aims to induce the sun to
"turn the corner" and to begin traveling northward, in the opposite
direction, bringing longer and warmer days and making conditions
suitable for planting.

The Sun Watcher at Hotevilla has somehow lost track of a
full month. In spite of the cold, Hotevilla's inhabitants loyally insist
that it is only November.

There is much visiting; and people frequently stay up late,
listening to the tales of popular storytellers.]

Fri. Dec. 1.

NOTE.—The concept of a "pueblo spirit," as suggested by
some experienced ethnologists, seemed at first to be invalid.
However, in view of the disintegrative possibilities of this
pueblo, as one analyzes its social organization, there must be
something that does hold the inhabitants together. This intangible something, whether it be the force of public opinion,
social inertia, participation in communal activities, religious
cooperation, or cultural conservatism, may well be termed a
kind of "public" or "pueblo spirit." This *may* exist as an active
force, but I've never encountered it in tangible shape. Kinship,

in and of itself, and no matter how widely it is extended, does not seem to be enough to keep an entire pueblo together.

It was quite cold in the morning, so Ned very kindly loaned his overcoat for his father to wear while herding.

During this morning's interviewing it became clearer than ever that the Soyal is the culmination of the Wuwutcim (Tribal Initiation). The main Soyal officers also serve in the Wuwutcim; and the Soyal *katcina* appears when the Wuwutcim concludes.

Ned reports that a Palhik dance [See O.O., p. 125, *et passim.*] is to be held at Chimopovy in January, and that it is connected with the winter offerings of the Marau society.

Martin appeared at noon and was so friendly that Ned thought his antagonism was diminishing. (Martin is the stepson of Panimptiwa.) However, his face became clouded when reference was made to the Qöqöqlom *katcinas* who appear during the Soyal to open all the kivas and who sometimes indulge in obscene gestures. [See O.O., pp. 111, 214–15.] The question of obscenity came up again later in the day, and Ned once more insisted that such actions were "important" and expressed resentment at "White" interference.

Joe offered to have his mother tell him the whole story of the attack on Lololoma [p. 139]. He promised to get the details without revealing the cause of his interest to his mother. [There was very little help from this source.]

Puhumana seems to have tired of Juanita's and Cedric's long-drawn-out residence at her house. They suddenly began to clear and arrange their winter quarters, and today they moved into them for the first time this year. As had been predicted, Cedric and Juanita have indulged in an orgy of spending and have bought so many luxury items that half of the $300 is already spent. Everyone is condemning their lack of thrift, and it does look as though Cedric will soon have neither money nor sheep. [Perhaps it is too much to expect people who have never lived in a cash economy to save money.]

Oscar came in during the evening. He said that he was walking back to New Oraibi from Bakavi where he had gone "to hear good music." He announced that he was starved, and while some food was being made ready, Ned let him read the letter he had received from the Chicago Field Museum. Ned wants news of the letter to reach Panimptiwa in roundabout fashion. He does not intend to show it directly until he can use it like a trump card.

During the night Martha summoned Ned to help the pregnant Tilly who had developed violent pains. He responded promptly and good-naturedly. Ned has a strong sense of courtesy that manifests itself in his "not wanting to hurt their feelings." For instance, whenever he butchers a sheep at Nestcili's, he is embarrassed by the disposal of the blood. The Navaho value it highly for food, but Ned doesn't. In order "not to hurt their feelings" he never wastes it, but carefully goes through the motions of collecting it in a pan. He never gives it to his Navaho friends lest they suspect that he doesn't care for it, but as soon as he is out of sight, he feeds it to the dogs. Similarly, on the occasion when his mother-in-law served venison stew, he did not want to eat it because he believed it was bad for his illness; but he forced himself to partake because he "did not want to hurt the feelings" of his hostess.

Sat. Dec. 2.

NOTE.—It would be hard to understand today why the Hopi stress antelope so much. Why, for example, is the Antelope society so important among them? "The Hopi Journal of Alexander M. Stephen" [see n. 27, chapter II] makes it plain that antelopes and rabbits were once important game animals and sources of meat. Cultural conservatism may have retained the high regard which the Hopi once had for antelopes.

Ned's dogs barked at Nasiwaitiwa, the father of demented Ralph, reputedly mean and a witch. Nasiwaitiwa menaced them with a pole, whereupon one of them bit him. He threatens to poison them, and Ned makes no move to defend or protect them, saying only, "He might do it. He's mean that way." If the dogs were to be found dead tomorrow, Ned would bury them with some comment like, "That fellow sure is mean." (Ned's attitude seems to be rooted in the fear of witchcraft and is indicative of the Hopi reluctance to forestall any threatened move on the part of an enemy.)

Went to see the Wuwutcim at Hotevilla. Only a few Oraibis were present, and no one from New Oraibi. [For a description, see chapter X, section F.]

We went to the house of Siyesva. He was taking part in the ceremony, but his wife received us hospitably, although she was far advanced in pregnancy. Soon after our arrival Siyesva came in to arrange about his dance costume. His hair was loose, and he wore a blanket carelessly draped over his naked body that was clad only in G-string and moccasins. He showed no embarrassment at all. Siyesva wanted to borrow Ned's fox pelt, but it was moth-eaten and in such poor condition that Siyesva went out to dance without a "tail." Deficiencies of dress do not seem to mar the effectiveness of any ritual.

During the day we saw many parts of the public rites, and at night we heard some of the bawdy songs that are particularly composed to tease Marau and other women. Only a small number of Wuwutcim activities are still performed at Hotevilla. Tribal Initiation rites occur at Mishongnovi; at Chimopovy, sometimes in combination with Shipaulovi; and at Walpi-Sitcumovi (which are now said to have a single chief).

Ned was more than ever careless about urinating today. At one point he relieved himself at a convenient woodpile without interrupting a conversation that he was carrying on with Ruth and the wife of Siyesva.

Several Hotevilla men brought water to their households. As usual, all the feminine residents, all their clanswomen present, and, sometimes, unrelated women guests gave thanks.

Little children, boys especially, were running about naked, even though it is December and the wind is biting cold.

There was no ceremonial feasting today, despite the fact that an important set of rites was going on. Tonight the men will remain awake just as if the Soyal *katcina* were being expected, although it does not appear at Hotevilla. Feasting will nevertheless take place tomorrow.

Ruth showed a little more positiveness than usual. When Siyesva's pregnant wife went out to chop wood, Ruth, in recognition of her condition, asked me to do the chore for her. Ruth also made George share some candy with other children. Good for her!

Sun. Dec. 3. Tom surprised me this morning by saying that he and Ned were "mad" at one another. This was a puzzle until it came out that one of Tom's clansmen had just wedded in such fashion as to make Ned, by extension to his ceremonial clan, Tom's *ikwa'a*. They thus found themselves in a joking relationship and "mad" at each other. Similarly, Solimana, who is the groom's *ikya'a*, "accused" the bride of being a troublemaker and "warned" her never to appear at Oraibi.

Raymond came up with some *katcina* paintings and asked to be paid in clothing rather than money. He fears that Hubbell will take away, as part payment on debts, whatever cash he may earn. Raymond also brought word that many boys and young men from New Oraibi had gone to see a Zuñi hunting dance at the Santa Fe roundhouse in Winslow in preference to the Wuwutcim at Hotevilla. Old Hopi customs are certainly losing their appeal in Kikötcmovi. Regarding the latter, Ned broke in to say that except for a few of the chief's loyal followers, such as Sidney and Nick, who had moved below at marriage, all the other inhabitants of New Oraibi had left the parent village because of a quarrel with Tawaqwaptiwa.

Before dark I went with Ned to hobble his horses. He wanted to show me a rock on which Matcito was supposed to have tallied the enemies he had slain with just a tomahawk and no bows and arrows. Ned says that "the same tomahawk" is now carried by the *kaletaka* in the Soyal. Externally, the rock is unimpressive. On it are scratched a crudely executed bear's claw, a defaced sign of Masau'û, and a symbol thought to represent the Kokop clan. The rock shows two crudely parallel rows of little pits, each of which is supposed to stand for one slain enemy. It looks something like this:

o   o   o   o   o   o

o   o   o   o   o   o

There are seventy-five pits in the upper line and eighty in the lower. [This rock is still on view.] Ned was so reverent when contemplating the supposed evidence of Matcito's power as a warrior that I was led to a consideration of the Hopi feeling toward bravery in war. Surely, as *Forgotten Frontiers* brings out,[1] and as so many stories of the past attest, the Hopi were once no slouches when it came to fighting. If so, why the present psychological distaste for killing? Why do they pride themselves on being the Hopituh ("Peaceful People")? Why did they change from warriors to pacifists? Did they always fight against their will and primarily for defense, as they now say? Did they always dread the idea of killing, even when they had to slay enemies and did? Were the rites described by Ned's father always performed by warriors who had killed opponents? Was the scalp of a victim called a "child" as a means of mollifying him? Were those who bragged of killing always regarded as "different" and as having some sort of unusual power? Did they always attribute the actual slaying to some outside agency such as Kwatoko, Masau'û (clan symbol), or their *wuya?* If all these questions are to be answered in the affirmative, it may mean that even during their fighting days the Hopi killed under a sort of psychological protest. When the pressure was off and the necessity for killing had been removed, it could have resulted in a violent counter-reaction that is evidenced in the current dislike of killing.

On our way home Ned showed me a spring which had dried up when a Chimopovy medicine man had removed the little *palulokong* ("water serpent") that had been the source of the well's flow of water. [The Hopi believe that the ultimate source of each body of water is a water serpent (*palulokong*) that lives within it.][2]

Near the village the trail led past a corner formed by two large boulders. On the face of one rock had been carved the pictographs of a reed (*bakap*), gun, vulva, and coyote head [Fig. 13]. Ned said that these pictographs indicated that at this spot someone had detected a Bakap clansman having intercourse with a Coyote clanswoman. [One wonders how many pictographs actually are just as trivial as this one?]

Tawaqwaptiwa has a bad toothache. His jaw is badly swollen, but he has called no one to help him. He is just waiting patiently for the pain to go away and for the swelling to come down. Why on earth do these people hesitate so when it comes to summoning a medicine man? I wonder if they would act more promptly if there were a medicine man right in Oraibi, making unnecessary the long journeys for "doctors"? [Never got a satisfactory explanation of this reluctance. Instead of fearing them as witches, some folk even regard medicine men as good people who help the sick.]

Mon. Dec. 4. Walked over with Ned to see Betty and her baby. She was delivered only four days ago, but we found her up and about, washing dishes and preparing meals. She seems to look far better and healthier than she did after her first baby was born last year. Allen is at home, showing no signs of jealousy or resentment on the surface. Just the same, Ida insists that he is planning to leave Betty to Moe just as soon as he can find another wife with whom to live.

While working on the old census of Oraibi, it became more evident than ever that sexual relations often preceded a couple's marriage. Instances of such behavior apply to Dick, Joe, Cedric, and others.

Tawaqwaptiwa corrected earlier accounts of chiefs' markings. Wuwutcim, Singers, and Horns have the right eye coated, but Kwans coat the left eye. [This supports the hypothesis that death (Kwan) is the *opposite* of life.] Even when they are out of costume, members of the Kwan society are known as Masau'û's men. Their patron is the god of death, and they are not supposed to fear the dead. That is what marks them apart from their fellows in the Tribal Initiation.

The comic and bawdy songs that were sung during Hotevilla's Wuwutcim are being recalled and repeated at Oraibi. In this way they are widely enjoyed, and their implications provide grounds for much gossip. Generally speaking, mates who first learn of marital infidelities in this way are supposed to laugh them off. If they should take them seriously, however, they are supposed to defer action until the rites are completely over.

Tomorrow is the feast day for the official spinning of the cotton to be used for Louise's wedding robe. Many people have come to Oraibi for the event, and there were more Hotevilla women than had ever before been seen in the pueblo. Several sheep have been slaughtered, and nearly every woman in Oraibi is baking *piki*. There is an air of hustle and bustle and pleasant activity that is rarely evident at Oraibi. Cedric has butchered fourteen sheep. Ten were provided by him, the groom's brother-in-law, and four were supplied by Luke, the groom's half brother. (Rather than skip his turn, however, Cedric went herding next day and did not eat with the others.)

Tues. Dec. 5. More guests came from Hotevilla and Bakavi to join the festivities connected with Louise's wedding. Today's is probably the biggest event of the lengthy rites. The bride's father, Andrew, was "boss" of the spinning, and practically all of the men went into kivas to spin. When the time came, Andrew summoned them to feast on mutton stew and *piki*. Delia, who has taken her deceased mother's place as Louise's ceremonial mother, had charge of all *piki* baking. The crier summoned the women for their feast after the men had eaten. No ladies first among the Hopi. Hahai'i remarked that it was too bad that Ned had not helped with the wedding. The main days for carding and spinning happened to fall when it was his turn to herd. (However, had he been genuinely eager to participate, he might have hired someone to herd for him.)

Joe told me of a plant or drug that could be used as an aphrodisiac. For men a little is applied beneath the testes; and for women some is rubbed at or near the rectum.

Siyesva arrived with his wife and child. They stayed at Ruth's. He spoke much of death beliefs, confirming a great deal of what has been told and adding nothing new. He also said that his son Miller had been intended for twins but had been twisted into one. All the details about twins correspond exactly with what Ned says about himself.

While Siyesva was visiting, I heard Ned talking next door. He was telling the story of his premature journey to Maski to his wife's old uncle.

Raymond brought the picture of a *katcina* that I did not know. It is called Korowista. Instead of a dance kilt it has on a *manta* ("woman's dress"), with a petticoat underneath that shows at the bottom, arms, and shoulders. A woman's sash is draped across the shoulders and hangs down at the right side. Korowista wears men's moccasins and carries the customary gourd rattle in the right hand. [This *katcina* is supposed to be a farmer. It is interesting because of the bisexualism represented by its garments. There are many religious figures that indicate bisexualism. In addition, all male *katcinas* that wear skirts may be called Kwasaitaka.

Neither in 1933 nor in later years did native informants interpret or emphasize bisexualism, yet this topic may be worthy of greater study and may prove to be the Hopi counterpart of Chinese notions of Yang and Yin.

Perhaps, in the Hopi case, it is recognized that successful farming depends on the intermingling of both sexes.]

Wed. Dec. 6.

NOTE.—In respect to the great number of Hopi divorces, do not overlook the possibility of a connection with premarital license.

There is no wedding feast scheduled for today, but many women, especially those who are in-laws, are busy making folded (not rolled) *piki* for Louise.

Hahai'i's stove had been used in preparing yesterday's party, and in exchange she had been given a generous portion of mutton stew. She used it to entertain some of the overflow guests from Louise's feast. [Note the reciprocal and redistributional aspects.]

NOTE.—There seems little point in calling a group of reputed kinfolk a named lineage rather than a clan. After all, it is not very important whether we call a line of relatives a lineage or a clan since by definition a clan may consist of one

or several lineages. It is hard to see what is gained by following
Parsons's practice of combining several named lineages into an
unnamed clan.

To Ruth's amazement I reattached a spout to a teapot
with liquid solder. "You must be a *poaka* ['witch']," she said laughingly. There probably wouldn't have been any laughter if the
job had been done by a Hopi she didn't like. (Anything out of
the ordinary is attributed to witchery. Medicine men who
"extract," inventors of ceremonies, leaders of revolts, even chiefs
of villages are likely to be accused of witchcraft.) Yet, a "doctor"
may avoid the forfeit of his own life, the supposed penalty for
being a witch, by helping others to remain alive. That explains
why people feel that a medicine man *must* come to the aid of
the sick and why Ned resents slowness on the part of medicine
men who are slack in "doing their duties."

Siyesva's small son went to bed very late last night. These
people are extremely permissive in rearing their youngsters.
Ned and Siyesva tease each other a great deal because Ned's
wife is Siyesva's *ikya'a*.

The Hopi have none of our attitude to fresh air. For the
last two nights five adults and two children have slept in a little
room, without an open window. Apparently they learn early to
sleep without fresh air, as neonates are cradled and completely
covered with blankets for the first twenty days of their lives.
Those who survive seem never to feel a need for fresh air when
sleeping.

Nelson is an excellent weaver. He himself made all of
Delia's (his wife's) wedding outfit when they were married. Did
he do this because he chose to or because he could not get help
since he was marrying an Oraibi girl? (Probably the former.)
Still, Nelson has retained strong ties with Hotevilla.

Several Oraibi residents are planning to go to Zuñi for
Shalako, even though its timing conflicts with the Soyal.

Ned ordered lavish Christmas presents for George and a
doll for one of his little *ikya'as*.

Thurs. Dec. 7. Siyesva stayed up talking most of last night. Ned
says that he is "making himself for a public speaker," and that his
stories often differ from conventional Hopi forms.

There was much talk of bastardy and premarital sexual
experiences at Hotevilla. While virginity is known, it is certainly
not regarded highly.

Looms were carried out of kivas today and set up in the house of Puhumana. They will be used in the weaving of wedding garments for Louise and her baby.

Sponsorship for the Qöqöqlom *katcinas* that appear at the close of Soyal is supposed to rotate from kiva to kiva, somewhat in the same fashion as Niman sponsorship. Last year Tawaovi was the controlling kiva, and Poliyestiwa had charge. This year Duvenimptiwa is to be sponsor, and Hawiovi will be used. [Traditionally, various kiva groups are supposed to take annual turns in providing sponsors for certain ceremonies. Unfortunately, Oraibi's sequence was so badly disrupted by various schisms that in 1933–34 it could no longer be correctly recalled by informants.]

When a man speaks of "*his* house," he usually has reference to his natal home, the house of his mother—where he was born—not the house where he is residing with his wife. I am grateful to Fred Eggan who first called my attention to this fact. If the inmates of a natal household remain attached for life, it would explain why children of sisters are so close and why men and women are so keenly interested in their siblings' offspring. I believe that ties with natal household kin exert a potent force, yet the unit is neither overtly conscious nor stable.

Fri. Dec. 8. Tom and Ida attribute the paternity of Tilly's child to a Chimopovy man. Being eager to determine how such news gets about I asked a few questions, only to be told, "The people say. . . ." (Again, speakers are given credence, even when they have proved untrustworthy in the past.)

Ruth's old uncle Lomayauoma (Coyote) returned to Hotevilla this morning with a box of *piki* which Puhumana had given him for his help in making Louise's wedding clothes.

Paid a call on Bert and purposely asked if he were going to take part in the Soyal. Got a great reaction. He had been kicked out by Tawaqwaptiwa who was acting in keeping with an old legend. Matcito, who had founded Oraibi after quarreling with a brother at Chimopovy, had, like Tawaqwaptiwa, a Parrot wife. Even as more and more clans came to Oraibi, it was foretold that some day a schism would occur and that the chief at that time would gradually lose his following. His other surviving brothers have already contended with and left Tawaqwaptiwa, and now the chief and his wife are doing what they can to cast Bert aside as their legend dictates. Just the same Bert protests and admits that it was he who had called an informal council meeting [p. 62]. (Perhaps informants had refused to discuss this meeting because it put the chief in a bad light.)

Bert's comments closely back up the remarks made by Otto to the effect that Tawaqwaptiwa had been chosen chief after the death of Lololoma because his headstrong, obstinate character and quarrelsome disposition were best suited for the fulfillment of Matcito's prophecy.

The chief and Ned are going to fetch wood for the Tawaovi kiva in which the Soyal is to be held. They certainly are the most active men in town so far as the religious life of Oraibi is concerned.

Tawaqwaptiwa calls Martin his son, although he is really his wife's sister's son. Hence, Martin's selection to play the Soyal *katcina* is not out of the ordinary. [In 1965, as part of his support for Martin's claim to Oraibi's chieftainship, Ned (as well as Martin himself) joined New Oraibi's council. The residents of Old Oraibi interpreted this move as a sure indication of their disinterest in traditional ways.]

Sat. Dec. 9. Little Sandra continues to be ill and is growing weaker, yet no help has been summoned except for a brief visit by Polingyauoma. Nelson, the child's father, left for Hotevilla to take his regular turn at herding. Milton cried for his father whereupon one of his maternal aunts poured water on him. This was to stop him from being a crybaby, and to teach him not to be afraid to get wet. The Hopi express contempt for those who dislike getting wet.

NOTE.—Thoughts on the seeming indifference to illness and dying. There may be two factors at play here. One concerns witches who cause sickness and death and who attack those who grieve or worry. The other factor [possibly farfetched] may be that a good person is very well off in the other world. He will join former relatives and friends who had preceded him, and in time he will be joined by those who have remained on earth. Since every person is fated to go to Maski, why resist a summons to the other world? This attitude may help to explain Hopi fatalism when confronted with illness and death.

Edna is working on a *duma* ("*piki* stone"), which is intended for the chief's household.

Louis is having the roof of his house finished, and a host of people, including his New Oraibi brother-in-law Lucas, turned out to help. This may be an instance of the "pueblo spirit" in action. [See p. 146.] Louis's roof, the chief's *piki* stone, Louise's marriage, and so forth are not individual affairs, nor even family or clan matters. Instead, they are village concerns, with the whole pueblo taking an interest and providing help. Relatives may form the nucleus of those who give help, but many nonrelatives lend assistance. Louise's wedding is an excellent example of "pueblo spirit." Members of practically every Oraibi household, as well as many Hopi who live elsewhere, did all they could to make the affair a success.

NOTE.—Before Oraibi began to fall apart the "pueblo spirit" may have been still more active. The people, as a people, were always doing things for one another and for the chief. They harvested his crops as a sort of public duty. If a spring needed cleaning, it was not the chief who forced the issue. Customarily, some public-minded citizen was expected to note the situation and to arrange a work party for cleaning the spring. All able-bodied men, not otherwise occupied at the time, were rounded up and put to work. Others, moved by zest for the occasion, assumed the garb of disciplinary *katcinas* and acted as supervisors. Public opinion rather than the yucca whips they carried served to put a sting into their commands. [When dealing with other aspects of this subject, one should not overlook the powerful cohesive force of large-scale participation in major, calendrical rituals that serve to bind a society together.

Communal work parties, as well as the ceremonial calendar, are now virtually extinct.]

During appearances of the true Masau'û, a secret society, such as Lakon, names an official whose corn crop they will harvest. But is the work restricted to the society? No. The whole pueblo turns out and cheerfully does the appointed task. In "spinach"-gathering too, one society, Wuwutcim, forms the nucleus but the whole village takes part. Also, baked sweet corn, although individually produced, is for everyone. "Help yourself" is heard on all sides. Every *katcina* dance is an example of "pueblo spirit." Without public-minded citizens, willing to assume a certain modicum of hardship and work, there could be no dance. The very antagonism of each village toward the others may be interpreted as an expression of solidarity *within* each village, and "village solidarity" is only another way of saying "pueblo spirit."

All this, of course, seems to contradict the *potentially* disintegrative hypothesis, and yet, since no culture has *conscious* direction from the very moment of its inception, why shouldn't it show contradictions? Every society and its culture are in a state of balance between integrative and disintegrative forces, and as one or the other carries the day, you have harmony (euphoria) or disturbance (dysphoria). [Learning to identify and to measure or weigh, with precision, the strengths of these contrastive kinds of forces, and seeking to determine precisely how each ongoing society's patterns of culture succeed in achieving an equilibrium or balance between antagonistic and opposing sets of forces should be major objectives in any study of the dynamics of culture.] When pueblo unity prevails, the disintegrative tendencies are submerged, and at other times the opposite is true. Both archaeology and history prove that the full story of the Hopi is one of fluctuations between euphoria and dysphoria. So it follows that the concepts of a "pueblo spirit" and "a *potential* for disintegration" may both be correct and together may give a rounded picture of the actual nature of pueblo life.

Ned says that in the old days Moenkopi people used to bring their children to Oraibi for *katcina* initiations. When it was found that this interfered with schooling, the "White" authorities stopped the practice. Thereafter, Moenkopi youngsters were whipped and partially initiated in their home town, but they did not see the altars and the rest of the rites until they visited Oraibi after their schooling had ended.

In the midst of an evening interview Tawaqwaptiwa suddenly broke off to tell Ned that there was to be a Soyal initiation this year. In spite of his belief that he is fated to end Oraibi's ceremonialism, the chief still is making an effort to continue it after his death. Since the lapse of the Tribal Initiations that used to precede admission to the Soyal, Martin has been taken directly into the Soyal; and now Sam is to enter right into the Soyal. Ned, who put Sam into the *katcina* cult, will serve as his ceremonial father for the Soyal initiation.

More on bisexualism in rituals. Lucas says that a woman's wedding belt is often worn as part of a *katcina* costume. [He is right. It is believed that raindrops fall from the fringes of a wedding belt, and *katcinas* are supposed to bring rain.]

Otto went to Hotevilla to seek recruits for a new work project. A meeting was called out but no one showed up. Certainly, any able-bodied Hopi who is out of funds this year has no one but himself to blame.

Sun. Dec. 10. The dogs again acted viciously and chased Humiletstiwa. It was suggested to Ned that he kill the leader of the pack. He answered in typical Hopi fashion. "Well," he said, "It's up to them. If they want to kill one of our dogs, they might do it."

When a man awakens in the morning, he almost invariably begins to sing a *katcina* or other song. There is no regard for others in the room who may wish to sleep a little longer. The attitude seems to be that as soon as one sleeper gets up, it's time for all to arise. [Morning or *katcina* singing is no longer done.]

Tom, Kiacwaitiwa, and many other Hopi left by truck for the Zuñi Shalako. Most of them will trade with the Zuñi. They seem unconcerned at the possibility of missing the Soyal.

Ida started for some event at church today, but she found so many visitors from other mesas that she became bashful and did not enter.

Oscar called and mentioned a cousin who had run away from the Indian school in Albuquerque. Apparently, it is not uncommon for Hopi youngsters to detest boarding schools.

After a time Oscar asked if the old cripple was still crawling about. He was referring to Nakwavei'ima, Ned's maternal uncle. He then proceeded to say that while Nakwavei'ima's mother was carrying him, she had had a love affair with a man in ceremonial costume. As sexual relations are taboo for all participants in rites, the child was born badly crippled. "That's what these Hopi believe," concluded Oscar.

Frank Siemptiwa arrived for the Soyal, together with several other Moenkopi men. Ida and Ruth repeat their dislike of him in no uncertain terms.

Joe backs up the statement that there used to be a Hovahkop clan, but he says that it was taken over by Masau'û. On the other hand, he insists that Kokop is distinct, and that Yokioma was a Kokop.

Mon. Dec. 11. It is being said this morning that last night the doctor did call on Sandra and that she is somewhat better. Delia, Juanita, and Jessie are said to have been so weak as youngsters that they spent little or no time at nonreservation schools. Tom's baby is suffering from spells of fainting and vomiting. Like so many people among us, the Hopi are forever talking of ailments that are "just the same."

NOTE.—Whenever the Crier chief makes an official announcement of a ceremony, he is supposed to be addressing the Cloud People as well as the inhabitants of the pueblo. Voth has already published this fact. Nor should one overlook the invocation to the Cloud People that is made when sweet corn is being baked.[3]

Ned has begun to spin cotton in preparation for the making of prayer offerings during the Soyal.

While Ida was roasting some piñon nuts, a couple of "White" visitors dropped in for no more than five minutes. Ida became flustered and let the nuts burn. She explained later that she had been "ashamed" to look into the stove while strangers were present. If so casual a visit can cause "shame," no wonder such bashfulness is displayed at the Marau dance.

NOTE.—Here is one of the links that binds the present inhabitants of Oraibi to Tawaqwaptiwa and the pueblo. Cedric's mother, Qöyawaisi, was married to the chief's brother and is related to the Moenkopi chief, Frank Siemptiwa. These ties account for the large Pikyas contingent at Oraibi. (The bulk of the pueblo's present populace is the progeny of eight women.)

Tues. Dec. 12. Very early in the morning, before the sun was fully up, the Crier chief announced the forthcoming Soyal celebration[4] from the roof of the Kele ("Chicken-hawk") clan house. He spoke softly, as in prayer, thus emphasizing the fact that he was addressing the Cloud People rather than the townsfolk.

Otto's father is not a Christian, although Otto and his sister have been converted. This again brings out the individualism of various members of a single family.

Ned has several times mentioned the shabby, dirty appearance of the Little War Twins, who wipe running snot from their noses with the backs of their hands. Why are these gods so wretched in appearance? Why are Masau *katcina* females so shabbily dressed? Why does the Soyal *katcina* appear so decrepit? Is the unimpressive appearance of so many deities a sign of humility?

Practically every woman from Oraibi went to sewing class in the church at Kikötcmovi.

Frank Siemptiwa is staying with a Pikyas clanswoman. Ruth's old uncle is again staying with her.

Went to see Louise and her baby today. Louise had her hair done in two long braids at the sides of her head. This is the coiffure of a married woman. She was wearing an old *manta*. She and the baby appeared very well, and people said that it was no wonder since she did not have "lightning sickness" like Delia.

Jenny's ceremonial father is Ray Siemptiwa from New Oraibi. He has no sister, so his mother become Jenny's ceremonial mother. Jenny's sister Ada has Tom for a ceremonial father and Mary, Tom's clan sister, for a ceremonial mother. George's ceremonial father used to live at Oraibi but now resides in Moenkopi.

A Sun clanswoman from Shipaulovi is visiting Hahai'i. She recently turned Christian when two of her children died within five days of each other. (There is a close connection between religious conversion and death.) This bereaved mother was drawn to Christianity by the glowing picture of the afterlife in Heaven.

Wed. Dec. 13. Ruth went to see Betty's baby for the first time since it was born.

Ruth and Ida, who do not like Jacob's Clara, agree that she "pulled a fast one" on Jacob. According to them she returned pregnant from Prescott and accused Jacob of having fathered her child after he had "visited" her just once. Clara had the "White" authorities arrange the marriage, and Jacob was afraid to protest lest he be thrown in jail. He lived with Clara until two more children were born, after which he left her and married a Sun clanswoman at Hotevilla. (It is hard to tell whether there is some truth to the gossip, and whether the Clara-Jacob affair is typical.)

Conversation having turned to matters of sex, a good deal more was said on the subject. Ed was said to have been Ida's lover until Edith claimed him as the father of her child; and Cedric is supposed to have loved Fern but to have married Juanita when she "blamed her big belly" on him. By now I am convinced that premarital pregnancy is a customary prelude to marriage. In fact, "She had her big belly for so-and-so, but she picked the wrong man" has become so much a stock phrase that it can no longer be given much weight.

Thurs. Dec. 14. Joe took me to see the shrine of Talautumsi. It is singularly unimpressive. It is a stone cache, blocked with rocks except for an eight- to ten-inch opening in front near the top and roofed with small twigs and thatch and one prayer feather was suspended from the ceiling. [O.O., Pl. III b.] Through the opening may be seen a crudely made image of what looks like cottonwood, leaning against the back wall. The figure is about five or six inches across the body, perhaps ten inches long, and has arms and legs carved free. No other features and no sex traits are emphasized. Within the shrine she appears to be seated, facing east, and about a foot in front of her lies her "husband" (unnamed) face down. There is no carving visible on him. He looked like a solid cylinder of cottonwood, about two feet long and three inches around. A sprig of a plant, now badly withered, seems at one time to have been attached to what appears to be the back of his head.

Joe said that his mother-in-law and her husband, both from Moenkopi, were staying at his house and would remain until after his wife's delivery. Both the older people had been previously married and divorced.

A brother of the chief, James Sikwi, from New Oraibi, came in during the afternoon. He used to be a Christian while he was married to a Christian woman, but after divorcing her he forsook Christianity. [Around 1938 James Sikwi married Martha, whose first husband, Luke, had died in March, 1934. James died around 1951, and Martha vowed never to marry again because she had had such hard luck with her two husbands.]

Several Hopi visitors gathered in the house during the afternoon, and there was a great deal of loose talk. Ned, who had been doing his share of talking, suddenly observed that all of us were ka-hopi ("un-Hopi" or "improper"). On the contrary, talk about sex seems to be very much à la Hopi. Indeed, the older men present plainly state that the old custom of oveknaiya was little more than a sex party. [See O.O., pp. 31–32.]

Only Oraibi and Moenkopi men are taking part in the Soyal. Even non-Christians from Kikötcmovi fail to participate, mainly because all of them have openly quarreled with Tawaqwaptiwa who has charge of the rites. Those Oraibi people who are not actually engaged in the Soyal preliminaries are going about their customary duties in their usual fashion. On the surface one would not know that a major ritual was getting underway.

Fri. Dec. 15. Ed, carrying his small son David on his back, came in while Ida and Joe were present. If the gossip is true, it was a strange gathering. Ed is supposed to have been Ida's lover, and Joe was once the sweetheart of Ed's wife.

Early in the afternoon Ned called for Sam at Tawaqwaptiwa's house and escorted him into Tawaovi kiva for his Soyal initiation.

Dropped into the Powamu kiva to see how Louise's wedding robes were progressing. The smaller gown is finished, and the larger one nearly so. A Hotevilla man was completing the belt. Dick, who is no weaver, sat by. He helps out only by supplying wood to keep the kiva warm.

Joe took *piki* to Lily in New Oraibi on behalf of his wife who is of her clan. The fact that Lily's baby is almost certainly illegitimate makes no difference. Charles's mother also sent *piki*, and Delia is planning to send some because of a ceremonial connection.

Joe scoffs at the idea of courtship in terms of corngrinding by night. He regards the overt pattern as a rare and minor event.[5]

Toward sundown the Soyal men emerged from Tawaovi to smear war medicine on relatives and friends. Edith, who has no Soyal men in her immediate family, came to Ruth's house with David so that they might be smeared by Ned. Joe was summoned home by his wife so that he could be smeared. [The moist clay, prepared in the Soyal kiva as an important part of the rites, used to be regarded as a potent and extremely beneficial war medicine that made all recipients brave and healthy. This aspect of the Soyal ceremony lapsed around 1950.]

Soon after, the Soyal men took food into Tawaovi in order to have supper in the kiva. Participation is expressed by those outside the Soyal by their eating at the same time as those in the kiva.

A Moenkopi visitor had recently married a girl of the Sun clan. She had baked *piki* at the home of Hahai'i, then had gone to the house of Edna, her husband's *ikya'a*. Edna promptly "quarreled" with the bride and "drove her out," as an *ikya'a* of the groom should do. That done, she called the bride in and washed her head together with the groom's.

Ned came in briefly and bitterly commented on Tom's absence as they were shorthanded in the kiva. The Soyal *kaletaka* proudly announced that he would lead the men in dawn prayers to the sun tomorrow. At daybreak, women will bring special *piki*, and beans and gravy, prepared without salt or fat, to the chief's kiva, Tawaovi.

Sat. Dec. 16.

NOTE ON ANTHROPOMORPHISM IN RELIGION.—Is it true that the same ideals that a society holds on earth are always prevalent in the other world? Does any society have contradictory ethical standards for its afterlife? The ideals of every society are projected into the life after death, and so the otherworld becomes a continuation of this one.

When the oldest daughter of Tom and Anita died at Albuquerque, the authorities asked whether the body was to be shipped home. Since this was contrary to Hopi custom, the parents said *no*. This must not be interpreted to indicate indifference. Far from it. Anita is said to have grieved deeply, and one of the charges leveled at Christianized Hopi is that they take the death of a loved one with a smile.

Ida always speaks of Ruth as *imû'wi* ("female relative-in-law"), but she invariably uses the term for brother when speaking of Luke, her brother-in-law.

Joe reaffirms that a lover is always expected to pay something for every favor he receives from a mistress. Gifts may cost as much as three dollars. Unscrupulous women are reported to regard such payments as a source of extra money, and some lazy husbands are said deliberately to look the other way so that they may profit from a wife's "earnings." This custom may help to explain why rich men are said to have so much success in their love affairs. [It is still a Hopi convention that, aside from marital relations, a man should pay his partner for every favor that he receives.]

Allen's baby is soon to have its naming feast. In counting out the days that remain he uses the same terms that are applied to ceremonies or dances. Tomorrow would be *piktotokya;* then would come *totokya;* and *tikive* would be the day of the naming feast.

During the Soyal there has occurred one of those fortuitous events that strengthens a people's belief in the efficacy of their rites. There had been no precipitation for many days before the Soyal, but it rained on the first night of the ceremony and snowed two nights later. Hence, by bringing precipitation the Soyal is proving its worth.

Tom's absence is very badly felt. All in all, only a dozen or fifteen men are conducting the Soyal at Tawaovi.

Hahai'i was overheard while she was teaching her grandson Milton the proper kinship terms that he should use.

Charles said that he was in a hurry to get home because on this night watchers from the Soyal would order everyone to put out lights and go to bed. [I never heard again of night watchmen connected with the Soyal.]

Between kiva rites Ned came in. Ida deliberately teased him by offering salted foods that she knew were taboo to him. He beamed as he explained that he couldn't eat salt, and he magnified the discomfort all out of proportion. There is no question but that one effect of the food taboos is to swell the egos of those who observe them. The more "hardship" a man "suffers," the higher he rises in his own esteem.

Sun. Dec. 17. Early in the morning Ned came in to say that the Kaletaka nearly froze during dawn prayers. It certainly was cold to be going outdoors scantily clad.

Much more talk of sex, but learned nothing new except scandal and gossip that linked various villagers together.

NOTE.—Dr. Elsie Clews Parsons calls attention to the fact that words compounded with *siva* ("metal") must be post-Spanish because the Hopi did not use metal before the Spaniards came. This is correct, but it does not follow that *yoisiva* ("rain-metal") was transferred from stone knife to metal knife. In pre-Spanish times stone arrowheads were common, but after the introduction of metallic knives and guns they became scarce. The Hopi stopped making them but occasionally found them in the ground, especially after a rain, and so thought that they were the tips of lightning bolts. Thus the word *yoisiva* is certainly post-Spanish, but it does not follow that the Hopi beliefs associating lightning and arrowheads are necessarily post-Spanish.

When Louis's first wife, Kyacyamka, lay dying she is supposed to have revealed the names of many witches. For some unknown reason she named Mary, who is not related to her. She said that Mary was "always hanging around and grinning at her"; and that Mary sometimes appeared to her hanging head down and feet up. [Is this a reference to the god of death who does many things by opposites? For instance, the Maswik *katcinas* associated with him often act in reverse, and clowns sometimes enter a kiva head down. In many regards the world of the dead is a land of opposites.]

Just before she died, Kyacyamka also named as witches two Pikyas women, Joe's mother's mother and Cedric's maternal grandmother. It is interesting that words spoken in delirium by a dying woman are given credence as gospel truth and help to bolster beliefs in witchcraft.

Joe's naming shows a departure from the normal pattern.

(A child is named with reference to its father's clan by one of his father's clanswomen.) Joe's mother was unpopular with her female relatives-in-law, and Joe's father had quarreled on her behalf with his clanswomen. Accordingly, when Joe was born, his father gave him for naming to an unrelated Coyote woman.

Charles explains the birthmark on his face as the result of his mother's watching a Buffalo dance just before she was delivered. Buffalo dancers have blackened faces, and that is why the child was born with a dark birthmark.

Today is Suckahimu'u ("Once not anything"), the first of the final four days of the Soyal. All the women are preparing for the bustle of Piktotkya tomorrow when vast numbers of prayer offerings are made.

I asked Ned if it were warm enough in the kiva, and he answered that they had "plenty of wood and plenty of lice." It seems that old Qöyayeptiwa has become a snug refuge for swarms of vermin. Since he regularly sleeps in Tawaovi, the kiva has become infested. The Soyal men are planning to move him elsewhere after the ceremony and to delouse the kiva. Bert had twice found Qöyayeptiwa being eaten alive by vermin and had stripped and bathed the old man. He seems to need another treatment now.

Tom finally arrived from Zuñi. His wife and several members of the Soyal have grumbled about his absence. Without him the rites suffered from lack of an official Tobacco chief. Possibly, he had wanted to return earlier but had had to wait on the pleasure of some New Oraibi men who cared nothing about the Soyal.

Mon. Dec. 18. Dennis came in early for a snack and a smoke before going herding. He says that the start of the Wuwutcim begins the annual cycle of ceremonies and that the time is set by the Al ("Horn") chief who is the Sun Watcher for six months after the summer solstice. This official at Hotevilla somehow lost track of a month, so that Hotevilla's ceremonial cycle will be a month behind that of the other Hopi towns. There has been much bickering over the situation, and the men of Hotevilla stoutly defend their village's accuracy, although they know privately by observing the weather that they are wrong. (The mistake is unlikely to affect planting by farmers. It was said that they would recognize when it was time to plant and would go right ahead. The Sun Watcher would then have an announcement made to skip a month, and everything would proceed normally.) [This is what actually happened.]

Mention of Al led Dennis to speak of the burning of the Al paraphernalia, supposedly by Johnson [p. 130]. Dennis says that Johnson displayed the sacred objects for all to see. Orthodox Hopi were afraid to look lest they be stricken with the Al society's whip, but Christian Hopi looked freely. Dennis remarked sadly, "Now there are no real altars left." When he was asked what could be done about it, he made the customary reply. "If anyone wants to make new things," said Dennis, "it's up to him."

Dennis also told a long tale about the sorcery of Nelson, a Tewa policeman stationed at Second Mesa. The story involved the mixing of dyes in a bowl and taking it stealthily at midnight to the cemetery. There Nelson looks into the otherworld and converses with the dead. The purpose of all this Dennis claims not to know. Tom heard the recital and said that Tawaqwaptiwa had told the same tale to a group of men in Tawaovi.

The chief will not let Tom come late into the Soyal. He claims that he cannot be sure that Tom observed all the ceremonial taboos while he was at Zuñi. Tom is sorry to be missing the rites, but his regret is tempered by the fact that he did some good trading at the time of the Shalako. He plans to make prayer sticks with other "common" Soyal men in Hawiovi kiva. Ned, who is usually very friendly with Tom, is so angry that he refuses even to greet him.

NOTE.—There are several parallels between Christianity and Hopi beliefs. "Our Father, which art in Heaven" is understood by the Hopi to be a reference to the head chief of the Cloud People. "Give us this day our daily bread" is taken to be a prayer for crops and food. Thunderbolts are wielded by the sky deity, Sotukinangwu'u, as well as by God who "hath loosed the fiery lightning. . . ." And Masau'û, like the Lord, "giveth and taketh away."

Today is Piktotokya. As the name implies, much fresh *piki* is being baked. In the kivas the men are so busy making prayer sticks that they may forego lunch.

Ruth came to eat lunch, and Ida elaborated on the story of Nelson that Dennis had told. Ida adds that Nelson took his bowl of dyes to the grave of a woman who had died of witchcraft. This woman, who was pregnant, began to feel labor pains during a cornbake but insisted on being taken home for the delivery. Near the village they saw a light which soon faded out. This proved to be Masau'û, and the woman died in childbirth just outside her pueblo. In this way Dennis's story of strange actions at an anonymous grave has become converted into a "true story" with identified characters.

I purposely asked Ida if she were going to make *somiviki* and *qömi* for kiva distribution during the Powamu. She said, "No, I haven't any sweetheart."[6] As a matter of fact she is not to be blamed if she refuses to attend. She and Fern are the only unmarried young adult females at Oraibi, and they would be conspicuous sitting with little girls. If she does attend, she will go to Tawaovi because it belongs to her (Sun) clan. However, she was initiated into the *katcina* cult at Hawiovi.

Many families have been staying up late at night this month. There are numerous visitors, and people like to drop in to tell stories. [This custom persists. December is a favorite month for storytelling.] Narratives concerning the Little War Twins are favorites. (The Hopi believe that those who tell such stories out of season may be subject to snakebite. The concept of "out-of-season" is likened to activating a hibernating snake.)

[Sidney has long been a favorite storyteller at Oraibi, and Joe has more recently become popular.]

There was a great deal of activity in Tawaovi. Charles announced that he planned to dance as a Qöqöqlom *katcina* next Wednesday. It had been assumed that only Wuwutcim-Soyal men took part, but Charles says that all sacred paraphernalia will be removed from Hawiovi right after Soyal, so that all who volunteer may dance as Qöqöqlom. Ned is also planning to take part in this dance, and there will be at least eight or ten participants.

Tues. Dec. 19. Just after sunrise several messengers carrying *hihikwispi* ("objects-to-be-breathed-upon") arrived. One man, dressed in ordinary clothes and draped in a blanket, stopped outside the door and said, "Hov!" He then held forth a cornhusk containing corn, pollen, and honey for me to breathe on. Women are supposed to donate *piki*, but men give nothing. Other messengers followed the first, until I had breathed on six different *hihikwispi*. After all the villagers have breathed on the *hihikwispi* as sort of a collective prayer, they are closed and deposited at a shrine. [Note that these objects hold the collective breaths or "souls" of all the villagers. This communal aspect of the Soyal at Oraibi was dropped around 1950.]

Later, Hahai'i brought me a bundle of varicolored ears of corn, tied together with yucca fibers, to be given to the Soyal messengers when they called.[7] [These bundles are "blessed" overnight in the Soyal kiva and returned the next day. The corn should be used for seed the next spring.]

During an interval when Ned was out of the kiva, I offered him some piñon nuts. He refused them because seeds and nuts are additional food taboos for Soyal men. (Only Soyal men must abstain from nuts and seeds in addition to fat and salt. No reason for this was known. Sexual continence is required of Soyal members, as it is for participants in all rites.) [It is possible that since the Soyal is designed to make seeds grow in order to bring good crops, it is considered wrong for a Soyal man to destroy seeds by eating them.]

Today for the first time during the Soyal there is a real holiday spirit in the air. Everybody is on the go, and women are cleaning their houses and sweeping the streets. All the plazas are being tidied up and cleared of rubbish.

Soon after lunch everyone gathered in the plaza near Tawaovi to watch for the coming of the Mastop *katcinas*. [O.O., pp. 110–11.] They are a pair of ludicrous *katcinas*, who always emerge from Hawiovi. Should this kiva close, there would be no more Mastop impersonations at Oraibi. [Years later Ned contradicted this and told me that the Mastop *katcinas* came originally from the Kwan kiva. Then they switched to Hawiovi. More recently the Mastop *katcinas* have appeared from the Powamu kiva, with Ned, Panimptiwa, and one other man taking turns as impersonators. Appearances of the Mastop *katcina* were given up at Oraibi about two decades ago.]

After coming out of Hawiovi in civilian clothes, the two Mastop actors go to dress at a shrine northwest of the pueblo. (This is the direction of the Maski and is generally associated with the death god, Masau'û.) In costume they make a circuit and may enter the pueblo by any street they choose. This year the parts were played by Sidney and Humiletstiwa, and they arrived from the northwest. They rushed to the Soyal kiva, peered in, gesticulated in pantomime, and descended on all female spectators, regardless of age, pretending to copulate with them by placing their hands on their shoulders and jumping up and down. In spite of their antics they are taken seriously, and their mock copulation is an important fertility rite for all females. Hence, their simulated embraces are sought rather than avoided, as usually happens in the case of clowns. By arrangement the Soyal *mana,* in this case the chief's wife, accompanied by Betty, now emerged from her house and started for Tawaovi. The Mastop *katcinas* promptly seized her and pretended to copulate with her. (It may be that there was a time when only a few feminine officers were "fertilized" by the Mastop *katcinas* on behalf of all Hopi females. With the shrinkage of Oraibi's populace all females submit publicly to the embraces of the Mastops.)

There then emerged from Tawaovi four Soyal men. They wore *katcina* kilts, belts, fox-pelt tails at the back, anklets, and moccasins. Bunches of feathers were affixed to their heads, and their faces were painted white except for short stripes made with red ocher and specular iron. [Are these Pukongkûkû?] Each held a stick over the left shoulder from the end of which a cornhusk dangled on a string. In the right hand each carried a small tray heaped with cornmeal into which four prayer feathers had been set. They circled the kiva eight times, singing as they went, and then left for Lenva ("Flute Spring") where they deposited their sacred objects.[8] I noted that Ned and Sam, ceremonial father and son, were two of the four special Soyal men; and the Mastop impersonators were also a ceremonial father, Humiletstiwa, and his son Sidney. While the Soyal men were making the circuits, the Mastop *katcinas* sometimes retreated along a special cornmeal line to the southeast (the Hopi path of life, directly *opposite* to the road of death); and sometimes the Mastop *katcinas* fell in behind them and mimicked their actions. When the others had left, the Mastop *katcinas* entered the kiva, received sacred meal, emerged, and went "home."

Throughout most of the Mastop performance the bird whistle used in the Soyal rites could be plainly heard from Tawaovi. As a matter of fact, the Mastop impersonations are so directly linked to the Soyal that the actors do not emerge from Hawiovi until they get word from a Soyal man. [In retrospect, the Mastop *katcinas* may well be linked with Masau'û and the world of the dead. Their actions may be some enactment of the theme of life and death.]

Charles and Joe spoke of their eagerness to dance as *katcinas* now that the open season has come. They delight in dancing and do not regard it as drudgery.

At about nine at night singing and war whoops could be plainly heard from Tawaovi. They indicated that war medicine was again being brewed. About half an hour later Ned appeared to give me a second smearing with mud. He rubbed my back, chest, and bent elbows. To see if there was any directional significance, I purposely offered my right arm first. (He had started with my left last time.) Ned corrected me and insisted on doing the left elbow first, proving that it was no accident. [Since this was written, I have become aware of the dichotomy pointed out by Robert Hertz in *Death and the Right Hand* (translated by the Rodney Needhams) (Glencoe, Ill.: The Free Press, 1960). This topic needs further investigation among the Hopi.]

FURTHER NOTE ON GROUP PSYCHOLOGY [Compare p. 118].—By this term I mean only that a number of individual minds can be culturally conditioned to react in one way. This is really at the base of all patterns of culture. That is why a potter may dream up an "individual" design only to have it conform to the general pattern of the group. No conscious imitation need be involved. True, "a great man" may be an innovator and may deviate from established norms, and thus inaugurate a new approach that may later become a pattern. This would involve acceptance by a number of individuals, who could then transmit the new ideas by training youngsters. If the great man's innovations do not gain wide acceptance, they remain individual aberrations and do not become patterned. One must not forget that cultural conservatism or inertia makes it hard for a new idea to take effect on a mass of people.

Among the Hopi these reflections bear directly on the matter of *katcina* songs. For each dance new songs are supposed to be composed, but so closely do they adhere to established patterns that the accompanying gestures and dance steps are fixed for each *katcina* type and there is little trouble in learning new words and tunes. That is why the Qöqöqlom will take place some time tomorrow afternoon, but rehearsals may not be held much before noon. No one seems to worry about learning new songs. "They're used to it" is the way Bert sums it up. Yet, each composer feels that he is making up an original song.

It is the kind of group mind here discussed that accounts for "national character" or "racial psychology." Despite its intangible nature it is as "real" as any abstraction. It may be hard to select one individual who typifies the "group mind," but the main difficulty is the tendency to regard a "group mind" as one entity instead of a composite of individual minds, each subject to change.

It is often said that there is but a small difference between insanity and genius. Well, what is the difference? In each case there is an individual whose ideas and actions differ markedly from those of his group. The insane man cannot control his aberrations, can reduce them to no organized plan, and rarely manages to develop a following. The genius is more likely to be aware of what he does, to follow a systematic plan, and to get others to imitate him. He may be considered "crazy" or "queer," but if others follow his lead, he becomes a "great man."

Wed. Dec. 20. At five minutes of two this morning Ruth woke me for a head wash in yucca suds. The idea is to let the hair dry before going out-of-doors at dawn. Most villagers will do the same, but not quite so early.

Just as daylight showed, the Soyal men began to distribute special *pahos* ("prayer sticks") that they had made. These are made of long, slender willow twigs to which prayer feathers are attached. A donor pauses on one's threshold, cries "Hov!" and hands over one or more *pahos* with a set speech advising the recipient to pray for long life, happiness, and good crops. The whole custom is known as *kuivato,* the same word that is used for a morning prayer to the sun. Men run to the Buffalo (Antelope?) (*Tcupki*) shrine near Voth's church. There they insert their prayer sticks into the ground, pray, sprinkle meal toward the shrine and to the sun, and run home. In former times, according to Ned, men and boys ran naked except for G-strings, had their hair loose, carried bells, and shouted, "Wa-hoo!" as they ran. These things were now being done piecemeal. That is, one man might be naked, another might carry a bell, and so on.

Women and girls deposit their *pahos* in bunches close by Sowika. [This is a shrine dedicated to children.] Many wear wrapped leggings of white buckskin; and some, though long married, appear in wedding garments. Little girls who were born before the mother's nuptials were completed appear in tiny wedding garments. It was quite a sight to see the entire populace hurrying to deposit prayer sticks in the early dawn. A striking community feeling was aroused even in this badly split-up pueblo. [This custom for both sexes lapsed over twenty years ago.]

Louise and her baby appeared in their recently finished wedding finery. Louise will not go home until the new moon is to be seen, as it is dangerous for brides to end their nuptials this month. [December is a dangerous month because evil spirits may abound.] Along the way, two of Dick's *ikya'as* teased Louise for having "stolen" her wedding robes from them by marrying their "nephew."

This is the first morning since their rites began that the Soyal men have eaten at home. Their food taboos are lifted, but they will sleep in kivas for the four additional nights that they must abstain from sex.

Shortly after breakfast, practice for the Qöqöqlom dance began in Hawiovi. Around three in the afternoon the dancers made their public appearance. [See O.O., p. 111.] They wore a strange mixture of *katcina* and "White" garments, and they did a lot of clowning, but they went through the forms of a regular *katcina* dance. They have the serious purpose of opening all the kivas to allow group dances to be held for the balance of the open season. There were seven male and three "female" *katcinas*, and they lined up side by side in parallel rows with the "*manas*" in front of the men, instead of standing in two columns in single file. The males used masks that were repainted from last year's Niman. They had black backgrounds with blue eyes and designs. [About thirty years later, one of the men who had danced in Oraibi's Qöqöqlom performance of 1933 had completely forgotten the very existence of this *katcina*.]

As had been predicted only a few visitors came from New Oraibi to see the dance. [At one time the farming colony of Moenkopi used to stage an independent but simultaneous Qöqöqlom dance in keeping with the Oraibi performance. This custom prevailed in 1933 but was given up long ago.]

Kane showed up before bedtime. Charles is going to sponsor next year's Niman, and he has asked Kane to be the leader. Other officers have not yet been selected. Last year Kane was sponsor, and he speaks proudly of having been Village chief for a day while Tawaqwaptiwa "rested." [In the mid-1960s one of Kane's sons sponsored a Niman dance at Old Oraibi. The next day he learned that his father-in-law had been killed in an automobile accident near Keam's Canyon. Although the victim was far away and was not being buried in the traditional Hopi way, the dance sponsor somehow felt responsible and burst into tears. A sponsor replaces the Village chief on the day of his dance.]

The next Niman will impersonate "long hair *qwivi*." (Is this the same as long hair, Angya *katcina*?) [Years later informants maintained that Angya, which was performed, is not a *qwivi katcina*.] The dance is scheduled for sometime in August, and since Masahongva has resigned from the *katcina* chieftainship, the performance will be an ordinary dance, without the rites usually attendant on a full Niman celebration.[9] It is anticipated that more and more ceremonial features will be dropped as time goes on. [This prophecy was fulfilled long ago. What is called Niman nowadays is usually nothing but a "plain" dance.]

Thurs. Dec. 21. Although there was no official announcement, all the Soyal men left for the first of four days of rabbit hunting. They went informally, some on horseback and some on foot, a few with guns and others with throwing sticks. Participants came from the Marau, Hawiovi, and Tawaovi kivas, and the kills will be clubbed together by kiva units. [At one time the men of Moenkopi also hunted rabbits for four days after the Oraibi Soyal, but this custom has long been abandoned. Rabbit hunts by various groups, however, still take place from time to time.] In Hopi belief, rabbits once stood for small game and antelopes for big game. Both animals belonged to Tuwapong Wuhti.

Several pagan women are going below to New Oraibi to shop for Christmas presents. The point is that many children take part in Christmas programs at school and their parents like to give them presents. In order not to make other youngsters feel hurt, presents are given to all. So has the custom spread.

Dennis came in and was teased about Hotevilla's calendrical mistake. The Soyal is to begin there in four days. Dennis laughingly defends Hotevilla and accuses all the other pueblos of being out of step.

Fri. Dec. 22. Nelson told a long story about a Coyote that went on a visit to Maski. His story had all the familiar elements—two roads, Kwanitaka, a head wash in white or red yucca suds, naked people (witches) lined up by a fire, and sorcerers emerging from the flames as beetles or, according to Nelson, as spiders.

One instance of how "White" culture undermines the old Hopi way came out during the Soyal. Not even the most orthodox families kept their children out of school. Even on the day that the Qöqöqlom *katcinas* appeared in public, everyone went to school as usual. Thus do youngsters get out of touch with their own culture and move toward a new mode of life.

Ruth and Edith went shopping at New Oraibi. Tom treated them to a lunch of meat, bread, pie, and soda pop. When they told about it, they warned people not to say anything to Tom's wife lest she get jealous.

NOTE.—It is not hard to understand most of the repetitions so noticeable in Hopi ceremonies. Garments like *katcina* kilts are very difficult to make and are worn in all sorts of rites. [That the Snake men wear different kinds of kilts is another feature that helps set them apart.] Furthermore, what would happen if a Hopi attempted to invent a brand new ritual? The chances are that he could not imagine anything which had not been in his consciousness at one time or another. Most of the "newness" would be a recombination of elements already known to him. He would thus be likely to draw chiefly on established Hopi rites, with additional features taken from Christianity or the ceremonies of other tribes. Basically, his new ritual would be a reshuffling of familiar elements with some outside exotic traits mixed in. That may explain why so many Hopi rites bear the stamp of "sameness." If this be true, it remains likely that only a few ceremonies were "original" and that the others were modeled on them.

Two women from New Oraibi were accused of being witches. No one seems to know exactly whom they were supposed to have bewitched. Instead of making specific accusations attackers gave only the typical sweeping reply, "That's what the people are saying."

I asked Ruth to lunch by using her Hopi name. Ida intervened, pointing out that it would be improper to call Ruth anything but *imû'wi* ("female relative-in-law").

Sat. Dec. 23. Charles asked me to watch the rites connected with his official announcement of the Niman for next year. Joe accompanied me into Hawiovi kiva, and Charles and the others present invited us in as we started down the ladder, asked us to be seated, and offered us a smoke. Charles, naked to the waist, sat west of the fireplace, nearest the ladder. To his left, in order, sat Poliyestiwa and Humiletstiwa in full civilian dress. North of the fireplace there rested an Angya *katcina* mask, a small tray containing sacred cornmeal, two ears of black corn, and several prayer feathers. Just north of this there were two *katcina* leg rattles of turtle shell, two *ayas* ("gourd rattles"), and a kerosene lamp that provided the only light in the kiva. Near Charles there lay a bag of Hopi tobacco and several clay pipes.

Every newcomer who entered showed his intention of taking part in the dance by laying his rattles north of the fireplace and smoking informally. After a while Kane came in, put down his leg rattles, took off his shoes, loosened his hair, and sat down between Poliyestiwa and Humiletstiwa. Then Charles filled and lit a pipe, took a few puffs and handed it to his left. It thus went the rounds, and at each shift reciprocal terms of kinship were exchanged between recipient and giver.[10] At the end, the pipe was returned to Charles who smoked it to the very bottom.

After most of the men who were expected had arrived, Charles suddenly began to sing one of the songs that had been newly composed for the Niman of August, 1934. As the song was repeated many times it was not long before the others picked up a phrase or two, and pretty soon everybody was singing in unison. Thereupon, Charles made the first formal announcement of next year's Niman and named Kane to be leader of the male katcinas, Humiletstiwa to lead the "females," Poliyestiwa to be father of the katcinas, and Moe and Cedric to gather spruce.

Then the men painted and dressed but did not mask. There was an amazing lack of competition for good spots in the center when the men lined up to dance. When all were ready, Poliyestiwa started to sprinkle the lined-up men. When he reached Kane in the middle he paused; and Kane, as leader, shook his gourd rattle and the men began to sing and dance.

Apparently, the gestures and steps were dictated by the rhythm of the words and tune, for everyone danced and gestured without hesitation even though the song was new to them. [Compare a new waltz tune to which dancers in our society readily fit their movements.]

From Hawiovi the group went informally to Tawaovi where the dance was repeated. Poliyestiwa stayed behind and prayed. The Soyal men looked on, and their kaletaka served as sprinkler. Two Soyal manas came in, stood on the upraise near the ladder, and sprinkled meal toward the dancers. When the performance was over, the men went up the ladder. Charles paused, with his left hand on a rung at shoulder height, to repeat the formal announcement of the dance. Much the same procedure was followed at the Marau kiva, and afterward the group returned to Hawiovi and disbanded.

Sun. Dec. 24. Joe expanded on some of the details regarding last night's performance. The new song had been composed by Bert and taught to Charles. The outlines of a song conform to the type of katcina that is to be impersonated, but within the general pattern, which is fixed, a great deal of variation is possible, much like a rhyme scheme for a poem or the formula for a dance tune in our culture. There is no formal instruction for

katcina dancing, and youngsters acquire the art only from observation and informal practice.

The very last act of the Soyal is to take place today,
and Ned said it was funny to observe the greater zest with which
the men in Tawaovi sang the morning songs. It is as though they
were happy at the thought that the observances are so nearly over
and that they could soon resume normal lives with no ceremonial
taboos to observe.

Early in the afternoon the Soyal men painted up in
Tawaovi, then marched in G-strings to the house of the Soyal
mana, Talasnönsi. Here other Soyal women and interested females
splashed them with water dipped out of buckets that had been
lined up on the terrace of Talasnönsi's house. During the soaking
the men went into the house, seized the *somiviki,* melons and
other fruits that had been prepared, and threw them to the
crowd. They were liberally doused all the while, and the symbolism of water and crops was made perfectly clear.[11] [This episode
is plainly an acting out of the things for which the Soyal men had
long been praying. During the course of their rites they had
asked for rain and good crops for the whole populace. Now, while
they are being doused, they throw vegetable products to the
spectators. Thus do they enact the immediate fulfillment of
their prayers.]

On the way back to Tawaovi, after all the food had been
distributed, Ned carried his ceremonial son Sam pickaback. [Ned
was treating Sam like a young child, as is done in the Wuwutcim.]
After drying up, all the Soyal men feasted on the rabbits that they
had recently slain. The meat had been made into a stew by the
chief's wife for Tawaovi; Hahai'i, head woman of the Sun
clan, for her husband's kiva, Hawiovi; and Sikyaletsnim, wife
of the *Katcina* chief, for the Marau kiva.

NOTE.—Turtle meat is highly prized for its medicinal
value. (Is there any connection with the use of turtle-shell leg
rattles worn by *katcinas?*) [Later questions brought forth replies linking turtles and *katcinas* with water. It was also said
that turtles were pets of the *katcinas.*

Ned, who had seen and liked a turtle dance in a Rio
Grande pueblo, introduced a turtle *katcina* at Oraibi around
1940. A number of variations soon sprang up in different Hopi
pueblos.]

Mon. Dec. 25. Ida reported that she had had a bad dream last
night. Her dead brother Perry had appeared and had asked her

for his Soyal prayer stick. She thought that their father had made one for Perry, but she was not going to tell him about her dream.

Had a chance to review several recent events with Ned. He verifies that prayer sticks received by males at the end of the Soyal are placed at an Antelope shrine with prayers for good luck in hunting; whereas females put their prayer sticks down at Sowika with prayers for fertility. The Antelope shrine should be decorated with an antelope skull, but badger or any wild animal skull is acceptable. The present adornment is an old elk skull from a beast that Kane had shot long ago. Whatever is used must first be smoked over and sprinkled with cornmeal. Two of the major motives of the Soyal are unquestionably human fertility and hunting success. The latter suggests religious conservatism, since it emphasizes a culture trait that is now unimportant.

The Qöqöqlom *katcinas,* says Ned, learn only one song which they repeat at each of their stations. They carry bits of rabbit fur as prayers for success in the rabbit hunts that occur at the end of the Soyal. Some of the sex burlesque is "just like *oveknaiya.*"

Homer, the storekeeper at Kikötcmovi, was supposed to be Oraibi's Kwan chief, but he could not function since Horace, one of Hubbell's clerks, refused to carry out his rightful duties as Wuwutcim chief in the Tribal Initiation.

When I told Charles that I was surprised to see Masahongva, who had given up the *katcina* chieftainship, dancing in the Niman announcement by Hawiovi and in the Qöqöqlom, Charles replied gruffly, "Oh, he wants to turn Christian. He just dances to fool the people." So much for the harmony among participants in a rite. The concept of turning Christian, one must not forget, is not necessarily of recent origin, but may have its roots far back in the Spanish mission period. [Actually, the man in question never did turn Christian.]

Tues. Dec. 26. The hypothesis for the *potentially* disintegrative nature of Hopi society was strengthened today when Tawaqwaptiwa and Ned described bickering, factionalism, or splits at Moenkopi, Bakavi, and Hotevilla, to say nothing of Oraibi and Kikötcmovi.

The chief thinks that there may be a Patcava ritual in conjunction with Oraibi's forthcoming Powamu observances. Patcava was customarily held whenever neophytes had been taken into the Tribal Initiation. [See O.O., pp. 119, 120, 222–26.]

Sam's induction directly into the Soyal may be interpreted as a sort of Wuwutcim (Tribal Initiation). In that case a Patcava ceremony would be appropriate. The Powamu chief, who must make the ultimate decision, resides at Moenkopi. He is expected to come to Oraibi with several other Powamu men in a couple of weeks.

Ida admitted that she had heard of the possibility of a Patcava, and she thought it likely that she might be asked to serve as a Patcava maiden. She had played the part together with Fern and Juanita during Oraibi's last Patcava when Martin had entered the Soyal, but she claims she will not play the role again even if asked. It is hard to tell if she really means it or is merely protecting herself against the possibility of disappointment if she is not asked. The strongest reason she gives is unconvincing. She says that she does not care to observe the salt taboo. Other women, says Ida, refuse to participate in the Patcava because they do not want to become subject to the taboo on sex.

Louise is slated to go home tomorrow at daybreak. Today she bakes *pikami* and makes stew. Tomorrow she is supposed to make *somiviki* and *tcukuviki* at home and to send a huge portion to her mother-in-law, Puhumana, at whose house she was married. When Ned went to Puhumana's, he was careful not to eat anything because he had done no work on Louise's wedding outfit. Feasting is plainly an exchange or repayment for those who help make marriage garments.

Wed. Dec. 27. Before sunrise Louise went home as a bride. Puhumana led the way, carrying Louise's baby wrapped in a small wedding blanket, and she had some sort of a bundle in her hands. Then came two little girls, Euberta and Betty, Puhumana's granddaughters. Their presence might have been fortuitous rather than prescribed. Last came Louise, garbed in her large white wedding robe and wearing wrapped moccasins of soft white buckskin. In her outstretched arms she carried a smaller wedding garment, wrapped in a reed case. [See Fig. 11.] The groom takes no part in this procession but joins the bride at her home during the day. (In the event that a young man has been "trapped" into a wedding, or for any reason does not choose to live with the bride, he may allow the rites to proceed without interference but can achieve an automatic divorce by failing to show up at his wife's house.) [December is supposed to be a dangerous month during which brides do not go home. Yet, it is interesting to note, Louise went home before December had ended according to our calendar. Possibly it was over by the lunar calendar.]

Practically the entire village turned out to watch the wedding procession. Sikyaletsnim, Louise's mother, sat on her doorstep to await her daughter's arrival. Broadly speaking, the lengthy and elaborate nuptial rites are much more than the union of two individuals. They unite persons, families, clans, phratries, and, to some extent, entire villages.

Heard a long story that Hahai'i has been telling. It is also in the repertoire of Dan Nakwawaitiwa. It deals with a pretty girl at Chimopovy, who had many lovers and suitors. One of them was a married man and that, the people say, is "a shame." Presumably, there would have been no shame if the sweetheart had never been married. This girl became a Christian, possibly as a form of repentance. Many orthodox Hopi believe that some who are *ka-hopi* ("un-Hopi," "improper," "wrong") turn Christian in order "to get over it."

One night the girl was chatting with a couple of callers when they heard a voice followed by the barking of a dog. The callers got sticks and were surprised to find that the animal was a coyote. Somehow, it seemed to have a Hopi body but a coyote's face. They clubbed it and it ran away. Next day they followed the trail of blood and came upon a Hopi man called Dupeve (Sun). [Dupeve was Ned's clan uncle.]

Dupeve was sitting alone, sick and disconsolate. He had a lame hip, and his face was a ghastly yellow. He asked his assailants not to tell on him and gave them necklaces. They first accepted the gifts but soon realized their error and returned them. Had they acted correctly, Dupeve would have died at once.

As it was, Dupeve became very sick and even began to "smell." He asked a medicine man to help him, and the medicine man immediately recognized Dupeve as a witch. Dupeve's ailment caused sores to erupt on his fingers and toes; he applied to Sanaiso'yoko, who gave him relief. [Sanaiso'yoko is a giant, who was once fought by the Little War Twins, and is a terror to children. People with oozing sores on their fingers may seek a cure at his shrine. The correct procedure is to put down prayer feathers and hastily pray for help, and then hurry home before Sanaiso'yoko can overtake one. Sanaiso'yoko beliefs and stories are still current.]

The chief has several times said that his uncles had taught him not to brag of his ability to rule properly or to bring rain.

On the way to Oraibi from Kikötcmovi after dark, the moon clouded over. At one point I made out a couple of figures but found no one present when I reached the spot. I thought it queer but as I continued to walk, I heard a low moaning sound coming from a huge conduit pipe that was lying beside the road. I was startled and my "Hello" must have sounded strained. A couple of youngsters had hidden in the pipe and had tried to scare me.

Closer to Oraibi there was a bush with live sparks on it. It had been lighted a little earlier and was still glowing. Further along there was a second bush that had previously been set afire and still showed some glowing embers. The combination of mysterious figures, moaning sounds, and burning bushes would have given any Hopi reason to believe that he had had a real encounter with Masau'û.

Thurs. Dec. 28. Little Dorothy is sick. She inserted a finger into her throat to make herself vomit, but her mother, who was nearby, made no effort to help her; nor did her stepfather who went to New Oraibi to help Lucas with housebuilding. Such seeming indifference on the part of loved ones is simply amazing. Their fear of revealing worry or grief must be overpowering.

Community participation in Louise's wedding continues. Many women from Kikötcmovi and Oraibi helped her to make a big batch of *tcukuviki*. Those who are *ikya'a* to the groom are particularly helpful. It is their way of showing that their "resentment" of the bride has worn off.

There is more talk of the possibility of a Patcava. Again Ida says that she will not take part, even though it is customary for Patcava maidens to serve four times. Of course, this year's performers have not yet been selected, and even the occurrence of Patcava has not been officially decided.

During lunch Ida reported that a Moenkopi man, Robert Puhuyauoma, had brought word of intensified friction at Moenkopi. During Frank's absence the men of Upper Moenkopi, under Poli Payestiwa's leadership, are reported to have burned their *katcina* masks in a public fire. This is said to have shown their contempt for Hopi ways and to have symbolized their liberation from the control of the chief, who is supposed to "own" all the *katcinas*. The loyal faction, says Robert, far from showing anger, feels sorry for the rebels because "something awful might happen to them."

Late in the afternoon Sikyaletsnim held the last of Louise's wedding feasts—this time at the bride's permanent home. Quite a few people were present. Ruth was invited but, like Ned, she would not go because she had done no work. Ruth grows lazier day by day. She is now so sure of dining with me when Ned is away that she does not even trouble to light a cooking fire.

Hahai'i had been left motherless quite young, and her uncles had forced her to marry Duvenimptiwa. They wanted to get Hahai'i's care out of their own hands. They knew that Duvenimptiwa was a hard worker and a good weaver, capable of making his bride's wedding outfit; thus they overlooked the fact that Duvenimptiwa was considerably older than Hahai'i and arranged the match. In later years, when the wedding had long proved to be enduring, Hahai'i would sometimes tease her husband by recalling how she had been forced to marry him. Duvenimptiwa would grin and reply that he was more active and potent than most of his contemporaries and that he had outlasted many a younger man.

Tawaqwaptiwa had met Charles, his converted brother, in Tom's store at Kikötcmovi, and Charles had tried bitterly to convert him to Christianity. He claims to have remained calm and unmoved. Nor was he upset when he was told that Tom Mutcka had recently announced his conversion. Instead, he chuckled gleefully and adopted the attitude of "I told you so." He has repeatedly asserted that all the residents of New Oraibi would become Christian, and whenever one of them is converted, he gets the satisfaction of having made an accurate prediction.

As the chief was leaving, Tom came in. He said that news such as the alleged burning of *katcina* masks at Moenkopi used to distress him, but now he has adopted a cheerful "devil-may-care" attitude and does not allow himself to get upset. He praised the chief's self-restraint during the argument in his store, and he said that most of the bystanders had sided with Tawaqwaptiwa. In what was really a touching appeal, Tom begged that when I told my friends about Oraibi, I should make it clear that he was an old-fashioned Hopi and that he hoped to follow the old Hopi way until he died. [He did.]

Fri. Dec. 29. The chief claims that he is not grooming Sam to be *katcina* chief in place of Masahongva. He points out that the Powamu chief still has control over the *katcinas* for half the year. He adds that both officers act for him, so that even if the two of them "retired," control of the *katcinas* would simply revert to him, their rightful owner.

NOTE.—The main philosophical tenet of these people seems to be that life is the most important thing there is. Hence, they abstain from grief and worry as these may lead to witch attacks or illness and so to cutting life short. Much the same idea seems to underlie their unconcern on the surface when sickness or death strikes, as well as the brevity and simplicity of their mourning customs.

Small-town curiosity has again manifested itself. A Christmas parcel came for Delia, and it was not easy to restrain Ida from opening it. Then Ruth arrived and the battle was lost. Together the women opened Delia's parcel and examined its contents.

So customary is it to probe into the affairs of others that the conventional greeting is *"Um hakami'i?"* (" 'Where are you going?' "). The question is asked even if someone is merely going from one street to another within the pueblo. They may not use the greeting for a nonrelative or one whom they dislike, but in such a case they will try to get the information from someone who is likely to know the answer.

In the evening I called on the Corrigans. Someone asked about snakebites, and Mrs. Corrigan said that she had never heard of any Hopi or Navaho that had *died* of snakebite. She thinks that the medicine men of both tribes have sure remedies, and she cited cases of badly bitten Navaho and Hopi who had been cured.[12] As a rule, both the Corrigans are pretty bitter against the Hopi.

Sat. Dec. 30. No wonder the San Francisco peaks play so large a part in Hopi mythology. One must see them in winter to appreciate their appeal. They seem surprisingly close at hand, they are heavily blanketed with snow, and banks of clouds often appear to rest on them or to be lifting up from them. Nothing could be more "natural" than to think of these mountains as the home of snow and clouds, hence, of *katcinas*.

Bad teeth cause much suffering here. This is one ailment that "extraction" of poison arrows doesn't seem to help.

Tawaqwaptiwa says that in the old days the Qöqöqlom *katcinas* used to wear buckskin shirts and trousers and collars of rabbit fur. The wearing of miscellaneous American garments he regards as a recent innovation. It arose, probably, after buckskin became scarce.

While Tom was out of the Soyal, Tawaqwaptiwa had a hard time selecting a Tobacco chief, as none of the men present belonged to the correct clan, Rabbit-Tobacco. He was forced to select Jackson Lehongva (Lizard), son of Tom's father's brother. Not even Jackson's father belongs in the proper clan group for the office, but Jackson's father's sister-in-law is of the appropriate clan. This is a dreadfully farfetched example of substitution, but it shows the extent of the makeshifts to which the shorthanded Hopi sometimes are forced to resort.

There was much gossip about Louise's stinginess in hiding candy, and about Juanita's meanness in finding and eating some of it. Moreover, there are other indications that sister-in-law strife may already have begun. It is being said that while Louise was getting married at the home of Puhumana, Juanita gave her no help but continuously made sarcastic remarks about her.

The matter of keeping candy to one's self is not simple to understand. Ned is usually generous and has often shown his fondness for us. Yet, he bought nearly ten pounds of candy for himself at Christmas; and this evening he ate a few pieces while at work with Tawaqwaptiwa and me, but he offered none to either of us.

Sun. Dec. 31. Ned reported that some Hotevilla people are thinking of calling him to a council to discuss the Soyal display in the Field Museum in Chicago. Tawaqwaptiwa tells him not to go to any trouble to clear himself there. He says that they have no jurisdiction over an Oraibi man and that they are acting thus not because they are good Hopi but because they want to stir up trouble at Oraibi.

Two important points came out of recent interviews. There is an implied rather than an overt feeling of resemblance between the Palulokong ("Water-serpent") rites and the Powamu. Also, not every society should be called military simply because its members wear hawk feathers and Little War God markings. Judged by this test the Palulokong dance would be a war ceremony, but it is so completely a fertility rite that any other interpretation would be erroneous or misleading. Dr. Parsons at times picks out one or two aspects that are alike in two ceremonies and then assumes that the rituals are virtually identical. This is pseudoscience and debases anthropology in the minds of many people. [No Hopi village has given a Water-serpent dance in re-

cent years; but since the appropriate puppets and other proper-
ties remain, the dance cannot yet be called extinct.]

There is much sexual laxity at boarding schools, and three
Moenkopi girls are reported to have returned home pregnant.
One wonders if conditions were much different a generation ago.

Ned has observed that many "Whites" get drunk on New
Year's Eve. He says that the custom has spread to Moenkopi,
where the boys sometimes bribe Mexicans to buy liquor for them.
Ned and the chief have talked the situation over. They hope
that the custom will not reach Oraibi, and they have decided to
drive out the first offender if it does. [In spite of such fine words
and ideas, drunkenness is now rife at Oraibi. None of the offenders
has been driven out or forbidden to dance as a *katcina*. Possibly,
no action has been taken because some of the heaviest drinkers,
all of whom are returned veterans, are closely related to Tawaqwaptiwa. For example, one of Oraibi's worst drunkards—there are
about half a dozen in all—is the son of the late chief's adopted
daughter.

Whatever may be the case, the Hopi have no established
way of dealing with drunkenness.]

Neither Tawaqwaptiwa nor Ned can recount the Hopi
months in order. They know all the names in sequence, but some
discrepancy always seems to arise. No wonder Hotevilla (and
presumably other pueblos) can lose a month now and then. Part
of the difficulty may be due to the effort to fit thirteen lunar
months into two equal periods between the solstices. Most of the
trouble comes just before the winter solstice.

Services at church were called out, but no one came.
Accordingly, Suderman had a second announcement made. This
time, most of the women responded because, so it is being said,
they were curious to know what the second call meant. Several
New Oraibi folk, including recent converts, attended the services
in Voth's church on the mesa top.

CHAPTER VII

Diary for January, 1934

[*Because many dances take place, usually in heated kivas at night, January is regarded as a happy month. Sometimes, too, house repairs are made, and women make plaques, perhaps in conjunction with the forthcoming Powamu rites. A purely social dance, such as Buffalo, may be held outdoors. Several men are weaving* katcina *sashes on narrow looms.*

In advance of the Powamu, men secretly plant beans—some officers plant corn—in kivas that are kept superheated.

Very young children, not yet initiated into the katcina *cult, get special, close haircuts that they do not like. During the next moon, the principal features of the Powamu are scheduled to be held, and when the new moon is sighted, the happy month comes to a close.*]

Mon. Jan. 1. People say that the "White" New Year's Eve was celebrated last night with bell ringing.

There was a peculiar crackling sound as the wood burned in the stove this morning, and Ida said it was the voice of Masau'û, who is associated with fire as well as with death. She then changed it to the sound of So'yoko and made the comment that mothers sometimes take advantage of such sounds for frightening disobedient children. She claims that So'yoko is shown as black because he is supposed to be charred by the fire in which he lives. [For a So'yoko performance, see O.O., pp. 216–21.]

When Tawaqwaptiwa was asked outright if he wanted Sam to succeed him as Village chief, he replied in the affirmative, naming Sam or Martin as likely successors. He says that it isn't commonly known, but legends state that if the Bear succession fails, the Village chieftainship is to go to Parrot, Pikyas, and so forth. Since he named the clans in the order of the usual succession of Soyal officers, it may be assumed that he was only rationalizing the existing situation. It is most unlikely that any Bear clansman will succeed him as Village chief.

All the women are busy weaving plaques. There seems to be some connection with the coming Powamu.

There has been a change in the reputed basis of Panimptiwa's grudge against Ned. Now it is being said that not Sidney but a long dead brother once beat out Panimptiwa in rivalry for the affections of a woman, deceased many years ago. Others say that Sidney and Panimptiwa's brother were rivals.

Tom is no longer subject to harsh looks from Ned or Tawaqwaptiwa because he missed the Soyal. Thus, Tom's policy of smiling and not getting angry has paid off.

During interviews on the Split of 1906 the chief reiterated that each side insisted that there must be no killing.

Jack stopped in. This was unexpected because Panimptiwa is his wife's stepfather. He said that he had composed four Hote *katcina* songs which he had sung to the men of the Marau kiva. Some of the younger members had liked the songs, but the kiva chief was noncommittal. Jack's hopes of getting up a dance fell flat.

Tried to discover from Charles why no dances had been sponsored since the season had long been opened. Neither Jack nor Charles had any special reason to offer, but each man seems to be waiting for some other fellow to take the lead. [The shame of failure to get cooperation makes people reluctant to propose sponsorship of a dance. Many intangible factors are involved, and the assumption of responsibility for a dance is not as simple a matter as it appears on the surface.]

Jack states that his marriage to Margaret was a family affair, not a romantic attachment. While he was hauling freight, the mothers of the principals arranged for a wedding. Just the same this couple gets along very well. [They are still married and living happily together. They are the parents of many children.]

Charles walked to New Oraibi and back. He remarked on how tiring the last part of the upward climb was to racers, and then he added that he often stopped to rest on the mesa top when he returned from love adventures, especially if he were running away from some irate parent. He also said that night prowlers run the danger of being shot for burglars, and he spoke of a ghost that sometimes appears at the head of the trail. Its moaning is occasionally heard about the village.

A meeting to discuss the countercharges of the two cattle-owning brothers was held at Kikötcmovi, but nothing definite was decided. (The council had found for one brother, but the loser had simply refused to abide by its decision.)

Tues. Jan. 2. Ida says she is not mad at Fern, but they never seem to meet. She repeats that she will not dance Patcava, even if asked, but she expects Fern to take part. Ida refused Louise's invitation to accompany her to Kikötcmovi.

Bert claims that it was he who taught Voth to speak Hopi. He got seventy-five cents a day and his lunch for language lessons and chopping wood. [The Reverend Mr. Voth is one of the very few "White" men who ever learned to speak completely fluent Hopi.] He claims that Voth bought up lots of Hopi things and that he erected altars in various museums, in addition to having built and furnished an Indian room at the Grand Canyon.

Soyal prayer feathers are tied to the manes or tails of horses and mules, as well as being affixed to dogs, shrines, homes, kivas, and so forth. They are also put in fields and orchards. In every way the Soyal is the most inclusive of all Hopi ceremonies.

Last night Hahai'i, Ida, and Jenny called on Poliyestiwa, who told them a "true" story. It was about an Oraibi girl who was so *qwivi* ("vain" or "fussy") that she rejected all suitors. [This is a common motive in Hopi folklore.] One night Masau'û decided to call on her in the guise of the Chimopovy chief's son. He asked her to notify her parents and promised to fetch her as a bride in two days. She got some corn ready, and when Masau'û came again, he led her along a strange road to a kiva where his old uncle lived. The girl fixed food for them, but they merely sniffed it and declared themselves satisfied. Each night they took on the appearance of men, but in the daytime they looked like Masau'û. By night the room was hung with pretty garments such as bridal robes, but in the morning they appeared faded and smelly. The girl began to waste away, but in time she herself became a Masau'û and continued to live with her "husband" and his uncle. On the fourth day after the girl had left Oraibi, some of her people went to bring presents to her at Chimopovy, but the chief's son knew nothing about her. The people searched everywhere, but they never again saw the girl.

Today the women are making plaques to distribute as Powamu gifts to female *imûyis*. [This trait still persists.]

Charles says that the Angya *katcina* mask which was used for announcing the Niman dance [p. 175] was the property of the chief. [This is just coincidence. Any dancer's mask, representing any kind of *katcina*, might have been used.] The date of the performance, which Charles will have to set, will depend not on the sun but on the ripening of sweet corn.

Charles revealed that the men of a village, as a prank, often unhobble the horses of visitors, especially if they remain overnight after a dance. He then spoke of a tradition that all the Hopi will some day become Christian. He says that many youngsters do not even know their own clans, and he claims that he was full-grown before he understood clan and relationship ties. He is not surprised that clan incest sometimes occurs among people who marry into distant villages or off the reservation. As to the exchange of kinship terms that I heard in Hawiovi, Charles makes it plain that they are entirely individual.

Wed. Jan. 3. Tom reported a dream in which he was chasing wild horses, one of which turned into an angry snake. He interprets it to mean that Sam Pawikya will continue to make trouble for him about his store. In another dream Tom entered Kwan kiva. There he found a man named Kuwanventiwa, father of Juanita, and once married to Puhumana. Kuwanventiwa was dressed for dancing, and Tom saw him sprinkle cornmeal toward the kiva ladder from which a "White" man's doll was suspended on a piece of rope. To Tom this means that Kuwanventiwa is giving up Hopi ways in favor of the "Whites." He says that Kuwanventiwa used to be a medicine man and chief of the Kwan society. He resigned his office and was succeeded by his brother. Tom somehow links this dream with his own troubles and with the cattle-owning brothers, who are also of the Masau'û clan.

Charles claims that people often hear dancing at night and sometimes see fire in the old, abandoned Kwan kiva. Tom backs him up. There is an implicit connection in this item between Kwan and Masau'û.

Charles reports that there is to be a Buffalo dance on Second Mesa following a performance at Phoenix.

According to Charles, Hotevilla gave a Palulokong dance last year. There were also some other puppetlike dolls worked with strings. "Female" dolls were made to grind corn while a number of Köyemsi supplied music. The performance was staged by the men of Hawiovi kiva at Hotevilla. [Compare the performance that is described in chapter X, section L.]

Tawaqwaptiwa remarked that so far no one had volunteered to sponsor a *katcina* dance. (It is said, however, that Hotevilla is having a *katcina* dance tonight.) He expects one to be held when some Moenkopi men arrive for the Powamu. The chief does not think that Moenkopi will hold an independent Bean dance this year, although such a dance is usually given in each village.

Women who are making plaques claim that sunflower seeds make better dye if mixed with spring rather than rain water. That is why Hahai'i fetched a load of water from Lenva ("Flute Spring").

Thurs. Jan. 4. A little boy at New Oraibi was run over by a tractor. Hahai'i says that he is in bad shape, turning "rotten" and "smelling." My guess is that gangrene has set in. The boy's mother is a Christian but insists on using a native medicine man. The local "White" medical staff got angry when its offer of help was refused. The child is being treated by Tawaletstiwa, a "bone doctor" from Mishongnovi.

Charles says that when he had his *katcina* initiation, he was whipped by his father, Kelnimptiwa, who showed no favoritism. Afterwards, when he was full grown, someone put him into Powamu. He is thus eligible to act as a father of the *katcinas*. Ida was whipped by her brother Perry.

Delia and Nelson returned from Hotevilla this afternoon. They found it more pleasant and congenial there than at Oraibi, with lots more people taking part in the Soyal. They brought along Nelson's sister Harriet, a pretty girl who is suffering from a skin disease. The ailment is connected with Masau'û, and Harriet is being treated by Kuwanyamptiwa, a full younger brother of Yokioma.

> NOTE.—When taking account of Kuwannimptiwa's assumption of leadership and his chieftainship at Bakavi, remember that he is married to a Spider woman. (His wife is Qömamönim, niece of "Uncle Joe" Lomahongyoma who was a leader of the Conservative faction that broke away from Oraibi in 1906.)

For some reason the chief refuses to give information about the Puppet-doll shows. He calls them "secret" and will not discuss them. Likewise, neither Tawaqwaptiwa nor Ned will admit that they ever heard of a cone-shaped object used in the Soyal, even though Voth specifically describes it. They refuse to acknowledge that his word for this cone, *tokwi*, has any meaning in Hopi. [Many years later it turned out that the word should have been *tukwi*, which means "cliff."]

Fri. Jan. 5. Not much of note is going on here these days. Neither Oraibi nor Kikötcmovi has a dance scheduled, but Hotevilla's *katcina* season is supposed to be under way, and Bakavi is having a kiva dance tonight. A Buffalo dance is to be held at Mishongnovi this Sunday, and another has been announced for Chimopovy a week later. All Oraibi men say that they will not go to Second Mesa until after the Bean dance.

The women are still busy making plaques, but some of the younger females are grinding corn. There seems to be an underlying notion that those who receive plaques should give an equivalent amount of meal in exchange. There is mention of a custom whereby an *ikya'a* gives a small plaque to a female *imúyi* and then increases the size of the plaque year by year.

During the morning Ned went to the home of Betty for the treatment of a swollen knuckle. Betty's father, Qötcvuyauoma, is visiting with her and knows how to deal with such cases. He "snapped the finger back into place."

Charles says that two-hearted people often have bull snakes within them, and that sometimes these crawl into a sleeping baby without anyone's knowledge.

Tom has just heard that Dalton is coming to New Oraibi to engage a truck driver for E.C.W. (Emergency Conservation Work). He is the son of Tom's brother Seba and one of those with whom Tom is having difficulties. [This man was working as a cook at the New Oraibi school in 1955.] Tom fears Dalton but plans to be "nice" to him. No one can ever accuse Tom of being the first to act ugly in a quarrel.

Ruth and Ida complained that the missionaries gave better presents at Christmas to Navaho than to Hopi women. They were also complaining that the government gave more jobs to the men of other Hopi villages than to Oraibi men. [Complaints of these kinds are very typical of the Hopi.]

Tom traded a silver bracelet with a huge turquoise stone to Bill, who gave him a yearling steer in exchange.

Today there was some intervillage trading, when some women publicly exchanged beans for coffee.

This morning's interviewing was most exasperating. Neither Ned nor the chief has any conception of a hypothesis. Giving illustrations serves only to confuse them, because they discuss the illustration at great length and overlook the point that it is supposed to illustrate. If I say, "Ned, yesterday we talked about so and so, and today I'd like you to ask the chief such and such," they will launch into an elaborate discussion of yesterday's "so and so," and may not get around to talking about today's "such and such." Ned is very literal with trivia, but not when it comes to interpreting all that the chief has said. He often tries to put me off by saying that something is "secret" even when Tawaqwaptiwa has spoken about it freely. Ned is a worse offender than the chief in this regard. Apart from matters dealing with the sacred and secret Tawaqwaptiwa talks freely on every subject. He tries to think hard and to be helpful, but Ned was spoiled by the "Whites" of the 1932 party, including myself, and now, under the guise of frankness, he carefully edits whatever is said.

Today's work dealt with the seasons in the otherworld. Are they the same as on earth; or do their winter months correspond exactly to the earth's summer months? Nothing was clear. The upshot is that all ideas will have to be put on a theoretical basis.

Sat. Jan. 6. Louis and Harold are helping Kane build a permanent field house at his new sheep camp. Here is one set of brothers who pull together. [About twenty years later there was far less cooperation among these men.]

In some way Charles already knows that he is slated to become the ceremonial father of one of Jack's children when he comes of age to enter the *katcina* cult. Precisely when or how Charles got the information could not be determined.

During the last two days there has been much talk about the use of urine for medicine; and about the bawdy talk and behavior of the Yellow Qöqöqlom *katcinas*. [Ned, quite recently, spoke of drinking urine. He said that it was strong medicine.]

NOTE.—In discussing the occurrence of archaic and meaningless words in various Hopi rites, remember that many Christians use Latin or Greek words that they do not understand; that Jews pray partially in Arabic which means nothing to them; and that the ancient Semites sometimes used Sumerian as a ritual tongue. No more may be involved than religious conservatism. Sometimes, in matters of religion, the mysterious and unknown proves to be an attraction rather than a drawback.

Besides his cold George is also suffering from toothache. That is certainly one of the major ailments out here. Incidentally, from the thick, scabby, hidelike coating on his hands, it would appear that George has not washed them all winter.

The bells carried by the Maswik *katcinas* are Kwan bells. [The patron of the Kwan society is Masau'û with whom the Maswik *katcinas* are associated.

NOTE ON RITUAL FOOD TABOOS.—Avoidance of salt, meat, and fat during ceremonies points up Radcliffe-Brown's idea of the social value of food. Salt used to be hard to obtain and is associated with the Little War God. Meat, too, was so scarce in former times as to be regarded as a dainty. Note how sad Sitiyo felt because his bad luck in hunting deprived his sister and him of meat.[1] Fat is also a highly regarded delicacy. Ida treasures the strips of fat that have been trimmed from pork chops. The Hopi love to put as much fat as possible into soups and stews. Thus, salt, meat, and fat have high social value, and to deny one's self the pleasure of eating them is a form of body punishment that is very common in religion.

Cedric says that Louis is planning to sponsor an Angya *katcina* dance as soon as he is through working for Kane. Its base will be the Powamu (Hotcitcivi) kiva.

At last a Hopi became un-Hopi. A story is going the rounds that the Walpi husband of Tcuhongnim, who used to live at Oraibi, went jealous and severely beat his wife and a neighboring man who had tried to interfere. Both victims are in the hospital, and the man is supposed to be dying. Tcuhongnim is Otto's mother's sister, so when Otto learned that the agent at Keam's Canyon was not planning to bring charges, he wrote a letter to Washington, explaining the whole affair.

Nelson (Sand) went to help install doors and windows at the home of Louis (Sand).

The Katcina clan owns the name So'yokmana ("So'yok' girl"), a *katcina*.

Sun. Jan. 7. Joe has been busy weaving himself a *katcina* sash for use at Powamu. He had used parts of Bill's costume during the Niman announcement at Hawiovi.

During Oraibi's Soyal the members of the Powamu and Hawiovi kivas used the latter because there were not enough men to warrant the use of both. Later in the winter both groups moved jointly to the Powamu kiva. Non-Soyal men refrain from entering Hawiovi during the Soyal rites.

Cedric is beginning to weave a new *katcina* sash. The warps are first arranged horizontally, but are hung vertically on a narrow loom when weaving of the complicated design starts. It was bitter cold in the room where Cedric was working, but Juanita sat with their baby and made no fire. By her own admission she is too lazy to tidy up for the Sunday school meeting that will be held later today. (Juanita is one of the schoolgirls who wanted to stay in town and resented coming back to the reservation. She expresses her resentment by refusing to speak English, which she knows quite well. Thus, she answers all English questions in Hopi.)

Charles came in later. He had gone to Bakavi to see some night dances, but the kivas were overcrowded and rather than stay out in the cold he had returned to Oraibi. Quite casually Charles remarked that their mother's mother had died on New Year's Day. Cedric scarcely looked up from his weaving. The correct Hopi attitude seems to be that there is no use in lamenting the death of an old person. As Charles put it, "We couldn't help that."

Mon. Jan. 8.

NOTE.—If culture is a mechanism for sustaining group life, and religion is chiefly a buffer for taking up the shock of death, then the total culture pattern should be more firmly rooted than the religion. Also, if a rival explanation of death were to come along, it could be more readily accepted than a different mode of existence. If we take food and eating habits as a case in point, we find that they tend to persist far longer than religious convictions. [This is not the whole story because the Oraibi Hopi of late have borrowed and accepted more material than spiritual items. It is a complicated topic and requires the assembling of a great deal of specific detail.]

A night *katcina* dance in a kiva is scheduled for tomorrow in New Oraibi. Night dances are always held on *totokya*. This is because someone might ask for a plaza performance on the next day, which would be *tikive*.

Tues. Jan. 9. Mary's baby was born last night. It is her fourth daughter, and she has had no sons. [Her next child was a boy.] Joe is out herding and may not even know that the baby has arrived. His mother, Sinimka, will come from Hotevilla to help name the child.

Ida repeats that Sidney had won out over Panimptiwa in a love affair, and accuses Panimptiwa of having remained angry "just like a woman." In this connection, remember Ned's statement that he had once tried to make up his mind to die but had failed because he wasn't a female.

Dell is the true sister of Panimptiwa, but she long ago forgave Sidney. She and her husband, Herbert, are experienced show people. That is why they were invited to dance at Chicago, and they took Panimptiwa and some of his relatives along.

Martha expects to be the ceremonial mother of Juanita's daughter Betsy in a few years. She is already making a plaque for Betsy.

One of the Oraibi kivas is preparing to do an Eagle dance, and Ruth and Ida discussed the subject at lunch. When Perry, Ned's deceased brother, was young, he and Baldwin did an Eagle dance. Some time after, Perry was stricken with a sickness during which "he began to act like an eagle." His eyes fluttered, he scratched his head with a peculiar motion, and he flapped his arms like a bird. (It is not hard to see why the movements of some sick people should be interpreted as resembling those of a bird.) Once, when summoned by his mother to eat, he squatted down and began to hop toward his food. In alarm, one of his older brothers seized him and held him till he recovered. However, in response to questions, Ida answers that Perry did not die of "Eagle sickness" but of tuberculosis that he got from his wife, Sakwapa's daughter. This fairly modern statement Ida went on to amend with the remark that Perry's heart got "rotten" and "began to smell." [Compare p. 190.] Now it is being said that Baldwin, Perry's partner in the ill-fated Eagle dance, has a strange head ailment which makes him scratch his scalp "just like an eagle." [Actually, nothing untoward happened to Baldwin.] In view of these "facts" Luke refused to do the Eagle dance. Fern has issued a request for an Eagle dance, and her brothers, Martin and Sam, will probably take part, danger or no danger.

Ned, too, believes that the "power" of the eagle can get into a dancer and make him ill. He says it is like the Water-serpent and Puppet-doll dances. Their "power" sometimes gets into a manipulator who has to hang on firmly lest the apparatus pull itself out of his grasp.

A man from Kikötcmovi came up to borrow Hahai'i's rabbit skin blanket for use as a Masau *katcina*. Qwivi and two other types are also going to appear.

Kane plans to come in from herding in order to rehearse and take part in Oraibi's first night dance this season. Duvenimptiwa is preparing to appear as a Köyemsi.

Last year Charles had once dressed as a Kwikwilyuka *katcina*. This type is a mimic and imitates the voice and movements of anyone whom it wants to tease. Charles made up a song poking fun at the women, and it made such a hit that he was forced to repeat it several times in each kiva. [Kwikwilyuka is still highly popular and is occasionally impersonated nowadays.] Instead of repeating his success, as might well be the case with us, Charles now says that he won't participate at all this year, but he will probably take part in a different impersonation.

Kane was asked about the order of the months and seasons in the world of the dead. He claims not to know the calendar in the other world but says that he has been given to understand it is always summer, although the months correspond to those on earth. [The belief that it is always summer, although the months are named like those of this realm, suggests that at least some of the otherworld ceremonies must occur at a different season from those in this world. While this does not make as strong an argument for the theory of duality as would be the case if the otherworld summer months corresponded exactly with this world's winter months, the concept may still be correct. For instance, the winter offerings of Hopi societies are certainly meant to show the sympathy and cooperation of those on earth with corresponding summer ceremonies that are taking place in the world of the dead. Conversely, the spirits of the dead probably express their cooperation by doing something during the summer ceremonies of the living.]

Hahai'i has told Ida that even if Ida did give birth to a child, she would be unable to suckle it. The reason is that while she had worked in Flagstaff, she had often gone outdoors lightly clad. Consequently her breasts had "frozen" and could not produce milk. [Her mother also warned her that her breasts would grow very large if she allowed men to fondle them.

Regardless of the irrelevance of "frozen" breasts to infertility, Ida is childless after many years of marriage.]

Tom got some fresh beef, so he invited Cedric, his brother-in-law, and Juanita, Cedric's wife, to dine with him.[2]

Watched the night dances in New Oraibi's Rabbit-blanket Hill (Tavuptcomo) kiva. It had been built by the chief's brother James Sikwi. Each of Kikötcmovi's two kivas staged only two kinds of dances, and the whole show was over by eleven. Very few Oraibi men were among the spectators, perhaps because they were busy rehearsing for their own dance.

Wed. Jan. 10. Today is *totokya,* and everyone is busy preparing food. Ned returned from herding. He plans to learn a song today and will appear as a Köyemsi tonight. Martin is definitely slated to do an Eagle dance.

Bert is unwilling or unable to explain the calendar in the other world, but he insists that night *katcina* dances should begin (?) when the Marau and Snake societies make their winter offerings. It appears that winter offerings have more significance than had previously been supposed. They may show communion with the spirit world, or else they may pertain to the annual return of the *katcinas.* In years when a Snake dance is to be held, the Flutes make prayer sticks; and when Flute dances are to be given, the Snakes make prayer sticks.

NOTE.—Why should a people such as the Hopi, once regarded as daring, be so fear-ridden at present? The answer may lie in the catastrophes that struck them around 1780 when hunger and pestilence were so rife that Governor Anza judged the Hopi tribe to be "in the last stages of its extermination."[3] Such a date may have been the turning point in the shift of their personalities. They could well have been bold, independent, and courageous before 1780, and timid and fearful thereafter. Memory of the bad times could readily have been handed down from generation to generation and could have thus been worked into their "racial psychology." [See p. 118.]

At sundown went to Tawaovi, where the men were practicing the song to be used later on. After the rehearsal the chief took some honey into his mouth, thoroughly mixed it with saliva, and spurted four times into three masks and over assorted bits of dance equipment. The song, composed by Tawaqwaptiwa, will be sung by other members of Tawaovi, while the chief beats the drum. While they sing, Martin will do the Eagle dance, assisted by Humiletstiwa and Sam.

Following a pause there was an informal dress rehearsal, with Panimptiwa beating the drum to give the chief a rest. The singers carried gourd rattles but did not mask, and Martin and his helpers wore bells. Humiletstiwa and Sam carried long bunches of what looked like yucca. When this practice dance ended, everyone left the kiva for supper.

After supper Ned filled a gift sack with baked sweet corn that had been softened by boiling, candy, and dried apricots from a large supply that Sutton had sent him. The fruit was in danger of rotting, so Ned's generosity may have been tainted.

During the night's activities the men of Tawaovi acted as Köyemsi except for the Eagle dancers; Powamu kiva did the Hote *katcina;* and Marau kiva impersonated Ho'li. [For an account of these activities see chapter X, section G.]

Allen and Luke were the only adult men at Oraibi who did not dance. George refused to take part because, so it was said, he didn't want to give things away as the Köyemsi must do.

Wutaka ("old man") is a common term of direct address; and husbands often call their wives *sowuhti* ("old woman").

Thurs. Jan. 11. This morning Cedric and his children ate at his mother's house, but his wife did not. Similarly, Tom went to dine at his mother's house, but Anita did not go along. Ned frequently eats at his mother's house without Ruth. Clan ties which bind a man to his mother but not to his wife thus cut across family lines as we understand them. (This trait also underlines the great importance of natal household kin and serves to differentiate them from affinal relatives, including wives. Among the Hopi, as among us, neither a man nor a woman feels as close to his in-laws as he does to his natal kin.)

What with all the gossip about the sexual proclivities of Masau'û women, they seem to merit their lecherous nickname of "billy-goat clan." This leads to a reflection on clan groups. If one bunch gets a bad name, like the Masau'û clanswomen at Oraibi, some of their relatives may not want to be intimately associated with them and may prefer to be known by the name of another *wuya* in their group which bears no stigma. Possibly, this sort of thing might have led to the separation, for example, of Kokop from Masau'û. [Maybe Sakwapa, who is Coyote, is forcing a separation by calling herself Yellow Fox. See p. 9.]

Mary's baby is being tended by Joe's sister, not by his mother. The mother remained at Hotevilla to await the birth of a child to one of her other sons.

Fri. Jan. 12. New Oraibi is planning a Buffalo dance for the near future. They plan to use old songs, so that very little rehearsal will be needed.

Reports of *katcina* dances at Hotevilla are all wrong. Since they have lost a moon (month), they will not reach the *katcina* dancing season until very late in January.

Charles says that the Hopi no longer dance at Zuñi because on a recent occasion some Hopi performers violated *katcina* rules by flirting with spectators, nudging each other, and whispering when they should have been singing. Several of the Zuñi elders were so incensed that they ordered some of their men to dress as whipping *katcinas* and to thrash the offenders. Although the act was entirely justified, it severed the earlier friendly relations between the Hopi and the Zuñi.

Charles says that his mother often speaks with horror of the last famine experienced by the Hopi, and several others frequently refer to the same event in the same way. Although it occurred many decades ago, people still shudder to hear of it, and the idea is a vivid and ever-present source of fear. [Compare p. 118.]

Ned's uncle Talasve'ima, father of Otto, greatly upset Tawaqwaptiwa by objecting to Sam's induction into the Soyal without his having first passed through the Wuwutcim (Tribal Initiation). Strange how critical nonorthodox Hopi can be whenever a traditional procedure is varied by the orthodox. Rumor has it that after he had moved to Kikötcmovi around 1920, Talasve'ima had wanted to return to Oraibi. Tawaqwaptiwa had refused permission.

Sidney is said to be the only man who ever moved out of the pueblo (at marriage) and was later allowed to return.

The Marau kiva men began to practice for a night dance that is to be held when Siletstiwa makes prayer sticks for the Powamu. Siletstiwa is expected in a day or two from Moenkopi, and it is thought that he will announce the Powamu within thirty-six hours after his arrival.

Tom thinks that Tawaovi should also begin to hold rehearsals. He hints that a Movitkuna *katcina* might be impersonated. This type wears a kilt fashioned of yucca. [Ned impersonated this *katcina* in the 1930s. Since then it has not appeared at Oraibi.]

Tom spoke freely of the trouble at Oraibi in 1906. He affirms that the Snake dance was held in September that year, and he dates the second expulsion of Lomahongyoma at the time of the Wuwutcim in October–November, 1907. [See p. 14.] This faction left without a scrimmage to found Bakavi when members of the Kwan society threatened to drive them out of Oraibi.

Sat. Jan. 13. The chief wants to go to Chimopovy to see the Buffalo dance. Many Oraibi villagers are indignant because they feel that he ought to remain home to welcome Siletstiwa, who is expected momentarily. Nevertheless, Tawaqwaptiwa is going.

Siletstiwa, Siemptiwa, and other Moenkopi officials came to start Oraibi's Powamu. More Moenkopi men are expected within a few days.

Tawaqwaptiwa has returned from Chimopovy. He plans to lead Tawaovi in a *katcina* dance that has been set for the day after tomorrow. The type of *katcina* to be portrayed has not yet been decided.

Lomanimptiwa, once the head of Hawiovi kiva, a clan brother to New Oraibi's Fred Johnson, and father of the demented Ralph, is no longer called upon to be father of the *katcinas*. He is a Hopi skeptic, and skeptics are not acceptable. In addition, some women once tidied up the plaza and dumped the rubbish near his house. Lomanimptiwa got angry and threw some of the dirt back into the plaza. Since then he has been considered thoroughly objectionable. Tawaqwaptiwa does not like Lomanimptiwa, yet he has never driven him out of the pueblo. (Is this due to fear of witchcraft?)

Sun. Jan. 14. No entry.

Mon. Jan. 15. Navaho youngsters acquire an early taste for tobacco. Nestcili's adopted son, aged eight or nine, chews tobacco; and at Hubbell's the other day a Navaho woman rolled a cigarette for a little boy.

A young Navaho man and a girl of thirteen or fourteen stopped in at Oraibi. She had a tiny baby with her. It turned out that the couple had been married only last week, but the infant was about two months old. Oh well, the Hopi don't have a monopoly on this sort of thing.

Ned returned from herding. He announced that although he had missed the first practice at Tawaovi, it didn't matter because he planned to do a solo with four songs that he had composed. He had practiced the songs and their accompanying dances when herding.

While he had been looking after his flock, Ned had found a slain sheep. At first a coyote was suspected, but bird droppings nearby threw suspicion on an owl. Ned did not consider the possibility that a coyote might have killed the sheep and that an owl might later have pecked at some of the meat. Ned also found and brought in a horse belonging to Siyesva, who had been unable to locate it. This sort of behavior shows the extent to which the old hostility between Oraibi and Hotevilla has died down.

Amy, at New Oraibi, made some fresh *somiviki*. She still likes to eat Hopi foods, although she has long ago given up the Hopi religion.

A Hopi girl got pregnant while living off the reservation and came home to have her baby, planning to return to town afterwards. Had she lived on in the village she would probably have married. As it is, she preferred living in town to getting married. Thus does the lure of nonreservation life help to break the old culture to bits.

Tues. Jan. 16. Everyone at Oraibi is busy preparing for tonight's kiva dances.

Frank Siemptiwa says that there will be no Patcava this year.

Just before sundown a last rehearsal was held in each kiva. There is some reluctance for outsiders to sit as spectators in Tawaovi. Thus, Dennis who came from Hotevilla to see the dances is planning to watch at Powamu kiva; and Roland, from New Oraibi, intends to be a spectator but not at Tawaovi. He says that this kiva "is only for the priests"; but I wonder if Third Mesa people do not avoid the chief's kiva.

The men from Tawaovi dressed in my house before their first dance. [For details see chapter X, section G, Jan. 16, 1934.] This was followed by the Marau kiva group who impersonated Bear *katcinas,* and the Powamu unit which did a modified Navaho *katcina* dance.

Wed. Jan. 17. Ned, Qopilvuh, Tawaqwaptiwa, and Sam left to fetch wood for the forced growing of beans in conjunction with the Powamu. Siletstiwa announced the Powamu officially, but he did not decree a Patcava. The local people are deeply disappointed and think his decision rested on a shortage of available men. Siletstiwa has returned to Moenkopi but is expected in Oraibi again at some time prior to the Bean dance. [Siletstiwa continued to come from Moenkopi to lead the Oraibi Powamu throughout his life. When he died, around 1942, his brother Panimptiwa took his place. See p. 342.] The official beans (and corn) were planted today by the Powamu's leader, and now "common" men and boys are free to plant beans whenever they choose in the next few days. Thus, last night's kiva dancing sig-nalizes the end of the happy month. The month of the Soyal, December or Kya-muya, is dangerous; then January or Pa-muya is happy with colorful *katcina* dances. The month of the Powamu, February or Powa-muya, is very serious, probably because the forced growing of beans is mimetic magic for good crops next spring. To show how seriously this is taken we have but to note Ned's response when he was told that Moenkopi might not hold a Bean dance because the men wanted to save their time in the event of a Patcava. Ned replied that it was wrong. He felt that the Moenkopi men would *have* to have a Bean dance because they wanted good crops just as much as did the Oraibi folk.

Siyesva came to Oraibi to get the horse that Ned had caught for him. He says that a fight over a woman took place between two men at the time of the Buffalo dance at Chimopovy. He also spoke of a youngster who had robbed a store. The owner claimed that sixty dollars had been stolen, but the culprit's father offered to pay back only ten dollars. The local school superin-tendent thought that the lesser sum was fair, and that is how the matter will probably be adjusted.

Siyesva thinks that this year Hotevilla's Al kiva will spon-sor a Jemis *katcina* dance at Niman after which the Snake and Blue Flute (Sakwalenvi) kivas will take turns. He is of the opinion that Niman, Mastop, and Qöqöqlom are all sponsored by the same kiva each year and that responsibility for all three rotates to-gether. Actually, Hotevilla has no Mastop *katcinas.*

Siyesva knows of the calendar confusion but he remains loyal to Hotevilla's viewpoint. He feels that all the other Hopi pueblos are out of step. Siyesva expects the Hotevilla *katcina* dances to begin after the winter offerings of the Snake, Marau, Flute, and Lakon societies. The latter custom is observed, even though there is no Lakon at Hotevilla.

For Buffalo and Butterfly dances, which are unmasked and essentially secular, it is customary for the female partici-pants to select their male partners, usually from among their *imûyis.* The chosen young men or their families generally give lavish gifts to the *ikya'as* who select them. Rumor has it that one of Tom's daughters was going to be in New Oraibi's Buffalo dance, but someone else chose the partner she had in mind so she quit in a huff.

The Crier chief does not call out for Powamu. He calls out only for Soyal and Tribal Initiation. (He also announces the Niman and one or two other things.)

Thurs. Jan. 18.

NOTE.—There may be a psychological tie-up between clowning and military activity among the Hopi. Men who must be brave in war can do so only by acting contrary to usual practices. They must deliberately be unpeaceful, and they must violate the most dreaded of all Hopi precepts: "Thou shalt not kill." As Ned often phrases it, "Human life is worth something." Therefore, a warrior is in a real sense the *opposite* of a normal Hopi. Clowns also act contrary to Hopi convention, as when they are permitted to burlesque sacred rituals, or when they indulge in "backward" talk, saying the *opposite* of what they mean. Note, also, that the Kwan and Al groups in the Tribal Initiation seem to have military and police functions. Unlike ordinary Hopi, the Kwan are not supposed to fear death, and like their patron god, Masau'û, they do many things by *opposites*. So do the clowns. It was the Kwans who drove "Uncle Joe" Lomahongyoma out of Oraibi for the second time. There is an implication that they were functioning as a military or police society which acts as protector of the chief who is the prime symbol of their social unit. Possibly, with the abolishment of war the erstwhile military societies became clown groups. [All of this supports the idea that behavior by *opposites* may refer to what goes on in the world of the dead. One should not forget that the god of death is the patron of the Kwan society.]

According to Ned the responsibility for the first and last group *katcina* dance of each year, Qöqöqlom and Niman, formerly rotated together annually, but sponsorship of the Mastop *katcinas* did not. [Compare Siyesva's statement on p. 202.] Ned also says that nowadays no one particularly selects the sponsors for a Niman *katcina* dance. He says that Kane, who acted last year, and Charles, who is to officiate this year, had volunteered for the post. Tawaqwaptiwa is thought to be "resting" for two years but is expected to sponsor the Niman in 1935.

Allen is finally doing road construction work. [In 1955 he held the responsible position of dynamiter on a road crew. He had begun as a helper, but when his immediate supervisor had been discharged for drunkenness, Allen had been promoted. He now works steadily.] In view of the gossip spread by Edna, it is hard to understand how Allen can go to work tranquilly while Betty is at home and Moe is loafing around the house.

Chief Tawaqwaptiwa invited Fred Eggan and me to raise beans in Tawaovi. I arranged to plant with Ned.

It seems certain that the disturbances at Moenkopi and the lack of available men and time are the true reasons why Siletstiwa did not order a Patcava this year. However, the official excuse is that Ned had failed to provide a chicken-hawk (*kele*) garment, commonly called wings, for Sam. [Ceremonial fathers are supposed to make Wuwutcim garments for their sons.]

Fri. Jan. 19. Sidney has been picked by a young *ikya'a* to be her partner in the Buffalo dance next Sunday at Kikötcmovi. He went out today to kill a sheep for her.

Ned and I planted beans in Tawaovi with no ritual. We first took blankets to a sandy spot, dug into the damp soil underneath with our hands, loaded the blankets, and carried them, concealed, into the kiva. (Others who had fetched earth from the same place had left *nakwakwosi* ("prayer feathers"). We put moist earth about three-fourths of the way up in containers, implanted seed beans, and sprinkled sandy soil on top. We selected only beans of uniform color, discarding the pintos. Then we put our "plots" on the east banquette, where several other "crops" had already been left.

As we were carrying our loads of earth into the kiva, Ned kept showing concern because I was carrying a heavy burden and repeatedly asked if I were all right. This is only one of several occasions when I have suspected that Hopi solicitude for others was really a form of vanity, designed, in spite of their protestations of humility, to call attention to their hardihood. Yet, I doubt if any Hopi could, or would, run the last lap of a fast mile race on "nerve" alone. [Perhaps their "gameness" manifests itself in different ways, culturally determined, from ours.]

At last Ned came out with the long-anticipated news that the owl which is suspected of having killed a sheep is supposed to have been a witch in disguise. Ned has figured out that sheep are slain only when it is his father's turn to herd. This, he is convinced, proves that the witch is afraid to act when younger and more active men like himself or Sidney are on the job. Ned believes that the witch wants him and his family to start worrying which would make them more than ever susceptible to sickness and death.

Luke's failure to have danced recently is ascribed to illness. He is thought to have become "infected" from unwittingly having handled lightning-felled wood. This is a convenient and irrefutable explanation for any ailment that is not understood. [Actually, Luke was dying of tuberculosis. I am deeply convinced that anything which cannot be fitted into a society's knowledge of cause and effect, and is not subject to the society's control, is likely to be assigned to a supernatural cause.]

The long-continued winter dry spell is finally beginning to be felt. All the local cisterns on top of the mesa are drying out, and women will soon face the necessity of carrying water from distant springs.

Sat. Jan. 20. Ned claims to have told the chief that when, in keeping with the prophecy, it came his turn to abandon the old faith, he would not become antagonistic. Instead of opposing his fate he would accept it. [Yet, when the chief did put him out of the Soyal, Ned did not hide his pain.] The chief's reliance on the prophecy that foretells the loss of all his followers may be a subconscious reaction to the disintegrative tendencies of Hopi society. With regard to the latter, Hahai'i has revealed that all clans in the same phratry have warnings against each other. She specifically cited Bear versus Spider and Sun versus Eagle. Others have mentioned Patki versus Pikyas. Other Pueblo people seem to have more cohesion than the Hopi and a better-organized system of government, as witness caciques, governors, and tribal councils. These point to the existence of some sort of a state, which is very weak among the Hopi.

Children younger than the age of *katcina* initiation (below eight years, as a rule) are being subjected to close haircuts, with a tuft left at the front for girls. They look strange and even grotesque. Just what the purpose is, is unclear, but it's a good sanitary measure regardless of its motivation. Ned says that youngsters are led to acquiesce the more readily by being told that they will get gifts at Powamu if they submit. [This custom may somehow be connected with the idea of fresh growth, or of readying the fields for a new crop and the renewal of vegetal growth such as occurs each spring. The practice of cutting hair has been given up in the last few years.]

Tawaqwaptiwa (Oraibi chief), Siemptiwa (Moenkopi chief), and Siletstiwa (Powamu chief) planted corn as well as beans. [With the collapse of the Powamu, no one plants corn nowadays. However, most Oraibi men still plant beans.] The chief warns that the planted beans are not one's own. They are supposed to be for the *katcina* Eototo (who stands for the head of the Bear clan and is the Village and Soyal chief) and for the *katcina* Aholi (who represents the head man of the Pikyas clan and is the Oraibi chief's "lieutenant" and head of Moenkopi). [Martin impersonated Eototo from 1934 until the mid-1950s. Since then neither Aholi nor Eototo has been done.]

"Gone to see a Shalako dance" is an idiom for "having died." [The same idiom, with the same implication, continued to be used in later years. Informants could not explain how the phrase got its idiomatic meaning.]

Everyone agrees that the Hehea *katcina* is shown with a crooked mouth, which is supposed to have become distorted from excessive crying.

Today the winter offerings of the Snake society are being made at Hotevilla. The chief says that the rites last eight days. They are to be followed by the winter observances of the Lakon, Flute, and Marau societies. Night kiva dances are expected to begin when these rites are finished.

A preliminary observance, connected with tomorrow's Buffalo dance, is to be held at New Oraibi. Bert says that Shipaulovi and Mishongnovi will have Buffalo dances tonight and that one of the dance groups is expected to perform at New Oraibi. Teams from the two villages will alternate throughout the day and will "compete" at the final dance.

Charles spoke a little more about the doll dances that the chief has decided are "too secret" to be discussed. The dolls are worked by strings and generally represent one or another variety of Gnumamantu ("Corngrinding maidens"). [These dolls continue, on occasion, to appear at Hotevilla.] Apparently, the dolls may portray Shalakmana ("Shalako girl") or Palhikmana ("Water-drinking girl"). [See Fig. 19.] Charles thinks that the strings which work the dolls are concealed in little cuts or trenches which lead to a house (screen) behind which the manipulators can operate in secret. [Compare "Stephen's Hopi Journal," pp. 287–300.]

Charles says that the Navaho *katcina* song used by his kiva in the dance last night had been composed by Kelnimptiwa, his father. (Cedric, his brother, had suggested doing Navaho *katcina*.) Charles learned the song from Kelnimptiwa and taught it to his kiva mates.

Charles also said that on *totokya*, the day preceding the Buffalo dance, the singers and drummer go at sundown to a village's Buffalo shrine. Here a pair of costumed impersonators await and allow themselves to be led into the pueblo. This ritual is called *musairutwikwisa* ("leading in the buffaloes"). The costumed men are supposed to spend the night in the sponsoring kiva.

(At Third Mesa the Buffalo shrine is called Atcomali. Girl dancers are supposed to keep their flat prayer sticks here.)

A number of Oraibi men went to Kikötcmovi to see the all-night rehearsal and, perhaps, to partake of a feast. Joe and Calvin, each wrapped in a blanket, went down, and Joe commented that they were all set to go *dumaiya*. He is sleeping at Powamu kiva, not at home as he had said [p. 139], and he is doubtless engaging in sexual activities in spite of his pledge of continence during the forty days when marital relations are forbidden. Joe does not hesitate to talk freely of sex in front of Calvin, an adolescent boy. Boys of Calvin's age begin to sleep in kivas rather than at home, and this makes them free to have sex adventures.

At about nine-thirty Charles invited me to go to Kikötcmovi with him. He advised me to wrap a blanket around me and not to speak aloud lest I be recognized. Like Joe he is ready for a little excitement in the form of a *dumaiya* expedition. Along the way he remarked that Calvin had already had sexual experience. When I showed surprise because of his age, Charles said, "He's too young, ain't it?" Very likely Calvin is no exception.

When Charles again spoke of running away if caught with a sweetheart, he was purposely asked why he ran. "They may not shoot me," he answered, "but I don't want to marry yet. I just want to have a good time." He was then asked why fathers and uncles chased lovers. He replied, "Just to find out who it is. If they like a boy, they might want him to marry the girl, and if they don't like him, they'll lecture the girl and warn her not to have anything more to do with him."

A favorite dodge when running away, says Charles, is to run to the cemetery where pursuers rarely dare to follow. He waxes indignant over the growing custom of stringing wires for various purposes where they cannot be seen at night.

All along the way every man we met kept silent and drew his blanket more tightly about him. Why did everyone going to observe the night activities in the kiva at New Oraibi act as if he were going *dumaiya?*

At Tavuptcomo kiva in Kikötcmovi the hatch was jammed with men and boys who were peering in as best they could. Coin was drumming, and a great crowd of men were singing. Three men sat west of the fireplace, the customary position for officers, smoking and passing pipes. North of the fireplace, again in keeping with orthodox ceremonialism, were various bits of paraphernalia that would be used next day. Most of the New

Oraibi men, except the most dedicated Christians, were present, but no one had come from Second Mesa.

After a short time we started back for Oraibi. Joe and Calvin had preceded us. At the head of the path we found Calvin alone. Joe had apparently gone off to try his luck at *dumaiya*.

Sun. Jan. 21. When Ned went herding, he took along a piece of cottonwood. He intends to make a *katcina* doll for Louise. She is his ceremonial daughter, but he has never yet made her a doll.

Soon after breakfast there was a regular exodus of Oraibi villagers on their way below to New Oraibi to see the Buffalo dance. Men and women, including husbands and wives, do not go or sit together. It was warm and sunny, an ideal day for watching an outdoor performance.

Ned left word that our beans should be watered and turned so that the cold sides would get heated. Incidentally, no beans had been planted in the New Oraibi kiva.

The chief says that neither he nor his wife ever attends ceremonies at Kikötcmovi. They stay away purposely, in order to avoid arguments with troublemakers.

Called on Joe who was to accompany me below, but he was not quite ready. Mary, his recently confined wife, prepared a yucca solution, shampooed his hair, and ironed a clean headband for him to wear. She also shampooed her older children and her brother Bill.

The Mishongnovi outfit was performing in the plaza when we arrived. They were followed by teams from New Oraibi. [For a detailed account of this dance, see chapter X, section H.] There was a large crowd of observers, and there were numerous visitors from other villages.

One of the singers in the Mishongnovi group brought a sack of salt to Hahai'i. She is his *ikya'a*, and he had received her plaque at the Oaqöl of 1932.

There was a good deal of loose talk, despite the presence of youngsters. Several things that had seemed to be mere gossip were given verification. An amazing number of scandalous items have turned out to be true.

Mon. Jan. 22. Ruth claimed an elderly Navaho woman as a sister. The tie was tenuous to the extreme by our standards. The Navaho belonged to a Wood clan, and there was a Cedar *wuya* in Ruth's phratry. Hence the Navaho and she were "sisters."

The Second Mesa Buffalo dancers had come to Kikötcmovi on *totokya*. They are said to have returned home when they got word of Dupeve's death. This seems to contradict the notion that the Hopi are indifferent and cold to the passing of fellow tribesmen.

Went to look after our beans in Tawaovi and found the chief sitting in a tub of water and taking a bath. (He was taking advantage of the forced heat in the kiva.)

Tues. Jan. 23. Having heard that Luke was troubled with trachoma, I went to give him some Neo-Silvol. Found him bent over with pain. Polingyauoma, the medicine man from Bakavi, sat beside him. Polingyauoma may have resented my arrival with medicine because he soon walked out. I treated Luke, and also put drops in Louis's eyes, which were badly inflamed and caused him much pain.

Whenever Duvenimptiwa is away for the night, Ada likes to sleep with her grandmother Hahai'i. Through a clan connection Sandra is supposed to call Ada mother's sister, *ingû'û* ("my mother"); but Ada, who is a sophisticated schoolgirl, does not like to be called a mother.

Cedric, son of a Sand clansman, made the proper offerings for opening the racing season at the end of Powamu. [Since Cedric began to reside at Moenkopi, Ned, also the son of a Sand clansman, has assumed this responsibility at Oraibi; but the contemporary Hopi are disinterested in the old custom of running, and at Oraibi no races have been held in recent years.]

Ned said that there would be a *katcina* dance in Tawaovi tonight "to help the beans grow." First, the men rehearsed an Angya *katcina* song. Then they danced to its tune, informally in the absence of spectators. They loosened their hair, and most of them put on dance kilts, affixed turtle-shell rattles to the right calf, and carried *ayas* ("gourd rattles"); but they were unmasked and unpainted, barefooted, without prayer feathers or cedar collars, and had no one acting in the capacity of father of the *katcinas* as they moved from kiva to kiva. (It is on such occasions that unskilled youngsters may dance to gain experience without embarrassment.)

Sam was not feeling well and took no part in the last dance. The kivas were extremely hot and the outside night air was very cold, but the dancers made no effort to cover their naked bodies as they went about. The Angya *katcina* song to which they danced may be one of the cycle to be given at the Niman this summer, but there was no absolute verification.

Wed. Jan. 24. Fred Eggan arranged to work at Shipaulovi, on Second Mesa, where he will live with the chief.

There was more informal dancing at Tawaovi for the sake of the beans. This time a Qwivi song was used, from a dance given at Oraibi about three years ago. No other kivas were visited because Siletstiwa had put up a standard barring non-Powamu men from entering Powamu kiva. The esoteric formal Powamu rites began today.

Thurs. Jan. 25. There is a rumor that Edna will marry again. She is said to be planning to wed a Moenkopi man and to go there to live. Many Oraibi women go to Moenkopi if they marry a resident. (Such a practice contravenes the custom of matrilocal residence. Neither at present, nor in the census data of the turn of this century, is there any evidence of any man from Moenkopi living with a wife at Oraibi.) [It is still customary for girls who marry men from Moenkopi to go there to live.]

One topic for future research loomed up strongly after conversations with Fred Eggan. What, other than language, do the Hopi share with other Shoshoneans? What sort of culture did they have before they came to the Southwest and became predominantly agricultural?

Ned said that he used to live at Moenkopi with an *ikya'a* while he had a sweetheart there. [See *Sun Chief*, p. 198.] He came back to Oraibi when "all the good-looking girls" went off to school. He hated to see them go, but their departure saved him money. In those days Dennis used to be his "partner"—presumably in seeking sexual adventures.

Dennis and Ruth have mothers who are own sisters. He plans to dance at Hotevilla next Saturday. In the kivas of that village there are neither "White" lamps nor cast-iron stoves. Only an old-fashioned open fireplace, really a shallow pit, gives light and heat. [Around 1940 the Hotevilla kivas began to use such "White" items as stoves and lamps.]

There was another informal *katcina* dance in Tawaovi, but I did not see it.

The Crier chief arrived from Moenkopi.

Fri. Jan. 26. Ida claims that there is no truth to the rumor of Edna's remarriage. She says that the man in question was simply an old lover. He had paid her a *dumaiya* call whose significance some people had exaggerated.

Heard a long story about a man named Kyacyesva of the Pikyas clan. Long ago, Kyacyesva sold his wife's corpse for an automobile. [He was a wealthy man, a trader, and the first Hopi to own an automobile. His brother was Duveyauoma.] He never remarried, possibly because potential brides feared he might sell their bodies. Eventually, he fell ill. He wasted away and began to look like a skeleton, but in the same breath the narrator says that his body swelled up. At any rate, as Kyacyesva lay dying he is supposed to have heard the honking sound of automobile horns. That a great many years had elapsed between the alleged sale of his wife's corpse and his final illness did not keep the Hopi from interpreting his death as retribution for his misdeed.

Unexpectedly, I find the children unhappy and sensitive about their pre-Powamu haircuts. [I learned later that this was sometimes a punishment for stealing.] One child, whose head I rubbed casually, burst into tears and hid behind her mother. Milton not only objected but flatly refused to have his hair cut. Only very young children, like Sandra, submit without a fuss. No wonder youngsters have to be bribed with promises of gifts.

NOTE.—Tcowilawu is a *wuya* of the Badger clan as well as head of the *katcinas* who live at Kisiwu. This has reference to the Hopi belief that their *katcinas* are owned cooperatively by the Katcina and Badger clans.

In the evening there was another informal *katcina* dance at Tawaovi. Two He'ito songs were used. (During our first visit to the Hopi in the summer of 1932 we were taught a He'ito *katcina* song which Tawaqwaptiwa had composed. Since then our group has been linked at Oraibi with He'ito.) The usual membership of this kiva, swelled by some Moenkopi men, took part. Tom stepped out of line to sing a solo in falsetto at certain stages of the performance. Tom's part had been taught him by Tawaqwaptiwa who was supposed to have dreamed it. Despite what looked to me like variations from the customary *katcina* formula, the Moenkopi men easily fitted into the singing and dancing. Doubtless they could do so only because a pattern of some sort exists.

Sat. Jan. 27. One of the Hotevilla religious leaders needed eagle feathers, and the chief readily supplied him with some. Not only does such an episode throw light on the lack of antagonism between Oraibi and Hotevilla, but it also shows Tawaqwaptiwa's conviction that it is better to have a ceremony continued at Hotevilla than to have it die out altogether.

[In earlier days a number of men used to catch young eagles, feed them in captivity, then "send them home" by strangulation soon after Niman.[4] In 1955 Jack was the only man to keep an eagle at Oraibi. He delayed "sending it home" until after the departure of a "White" couple who were staying at his house. Conditions were better in 1964, for there were many captive eagles in various villages. For example, Tom had three at Oraibi, caught by the son of his brother-in-law Nick. The Hopi attributed the improvement to new laws designed to halt wanton depredation by Navahos. Hawks of various kinds may also be used. Sometimes, even if young birds are available, a pueblo may send no one to get them.]

NOTE.—There is a mythical bond between the Coyote clan and war. Coyote is in the same phratry with Kokop, an outstanding warrior clan. Coyote also makes stars and is thus related to Sotukinangwa'a, a sky and war deity, somewhat reminiscent of Zeus. This connection helps clarify the reason why Coyote women paint the *kaletaka* ("warrior") impersonators in the Marau dance.

Fred Eggan showed me Stephen's census of Oraibi clans. It surprised and gratified me to find that Stephen's data, gathered about fifty years earlier, tally quite well with mine. [See O.O., pp. 51–54.] The accuracy of my informants and the relative stability of Hopi clans are thus confirmed.

NOTE.—Since all the Hopi villages group some of their clans into larger (phratry) units, it looks as though this is an ancient trait. However, clans may be grouped on an individual or differently rationalized basis in each pueblo. If clan groups resulted from combination rather than segmentation and if ceremonial partnerships were the principal motives, then clans A and B might have joined to conduct A's ceremony in one town, whereas A and C might have combined for the same purpose in another pueblo.

There was a night dance at Hotevilla. Winter ceremonies were going on in the Snake and Antelope kivas. [Hotevilla's Antelope society lacked a kiva of its own and met in the Al kiva.] Men from those kivas, who were not members of the societies that were making winter offerings, made all their preparations for dancing in private houses. We went into Hawiovi, where we were privileged to see six sets of *katcina* dancers from all of Hotevilla's kivas. So often did performers carry bows that it strengthened the feeling that war and the hunt must once have been important aspects of Hopi culture. [Compare p. 148.] Only a few Oraibi and New Oraibi visitors were present, and there were no spectators from Bakavi because the people from there had teased Hotevilla so much about the calendrical mix-up that they were unwelcome.

Sun. Jan. 28. Mary's baby was named this morning. Only four women of its father's clan were present, but these did include Joe's mother. Of the four only two were from Oraibi. Joe and his family are none too popular with their fellow villagers. Some who went to the feast grumbled that there were so many children in the house that "they could not fill their bellies up."

Katcina initiates were whipped today at Bakavi.

Water is being hauled and sheep are being slaughtered in conjunction with Powamu's *totokya*.

Martin says that he was a good long-distance runner as a youth. He claims to have run about eighty miles once between early morning and late afternoon. (Fletcher Corrigan supported his statement. He had followed Martin by car.)

At dusk Fred Eggan and I were invited to see the Bean dance rehearsal at Tawaovi. When we entered the kiva, we were startled to learn that we were expected to dance as "female" *katcinas*. Tom was particularly urgent, and we felt flattered at being asked to participate. Needless to say, we were happy to accept the invitation; and we found the experience rewarding in every way. [This event is fully described in chapter X, section J.]

Luke and Martha showed a length of *humpawi* ("hair rope"). It is made of clippings taken from the heads of youngsters who had had haircuts at Powamu. All the hair is miscellaneously mixed and filled out with wool. The rope is used mainly for tying into two braids the hair of a newlywed woman. [It may also be used for putting up into "butterfly wings" the hair of an unmarried girl.] A bride whose household has no hair rope may borrow some at will. Before manila rope was known to the Hopi, a hair rope was used for all purposes.

Mon. Jan. 29. Preparations for feasting during the Powamu *totokya* continue.

There is no agreement on the date of the *katcina* initiation at Bakavi. Polingyauoma, the medicine man who lives at Bakavi, says that the event will take place tomorrow. He is here to treat Luke, who seems to be getting worse. While Luke is so sick, his father is herding in his stead.

Bert says that the Lakon society is making its winter offerings at Hotevilla. He claims that the women, on the fourth night of their observance, call on each kiva that has scheduled a *katcina* dance for a later time that night. Sometimes the Lakon women are accompanied by men who put on an Antelope dance at each kiva. (If Bert is correct, another link is established between the Lakon winter offerings and night *katcina* dances. There is also an implied bearing on the cult of the dead. If the winter offerings are in fact sympathetic rites done in conjunction with the otherworld, then the night dances might be a sort of reward during which the dead come as *katcinas* to gladden the hearts of the living.)

Ned instructed me to tie up our bean plants in the kiva so that they will not lean too far in any direction.

When Ned was a newlywed, he bungled the job of butchering a sheep for the first time. He was so ashamed that he left the carcass on the ground and ran away.

Tues. Jan. 30. Opinions continue to vary about the date of the *katcina* whippings at Bakavi, but most people agree that the event is to take place today. It turned out to be the correct day, but since all of the nine candidates were going into the *katcina* cult by way of Powamu, no one was whipped. [Only plain *katcina* initiates are whipped. Those who enter the *katcina* cult automatically, by way of being initiated into the Powamu society, are not whipped.] There is a possibility that modern parents, as well as children, are too sophisticated to have whippings. This would be particularly true of Bakavi, which is supposed to be the most progressive community on Third Mesa.

Checked several miscellaneous items with Ned. He claims not to know how snow is made, although Ida equates it with rain. There is a Kwasaitaka ("Dress-wearing man") *katcina* known in "Pueblo" [sic!] as Korosta (Korowista). As the name implies, this *katcina* is male but wears the *manta* ("dress") of a woman. Like a farmer, Korosta carries a bag of seeds, which he hands out to spectators. Recipients are supposed to plant them at appropriate times. The obvious link of bisexualism and fertility is impressive. Ned says only that this masculine *katcina* who wears a woman's skirt is "acting himself like a sissy" (*hova*, i.e., "homosexual" or "transvestite"). [Nevertheless, this bisexual figure may symbolize fertility rather than homosexuality. Apparently, any masculine *katcina* that wears female garb may be called Kwasaitaka. For comparative details, see p. 153. The Kwasaitaka *katcina* was supposed to have come from Zuñi. It has not been impersonated at Oraibi for the last twenty-five years or so.]

When pressed for more information on the general subject of sex, seeds, and fertility, Ned volunteered the statement that all manner of seeds (not only nuts) were forbidden to Soyal men because the Soyal maiden is supposed to be "hatching out" (fertilizing? giving birth to?) seeds just as a hen hatches eggs.[5] Therefore, the Soyal men (by a sort of sympathetic magic) must not break or destroy seeds by eating them, lest the Soyalmana's efforts fail. It seems as though the Hopi regard women as multiple rather than single personages, because they contain within them "seeds" from which children grow.

Also spoke to Ned about Natacka. He interprets it as a big So'yoko *katcina*. It used to appear in January at Oraibi, but Ned voluntarily said that on First and Second Mesas it might come in conjunction with the Powamu a month later. He did not think that at Oraibi it was associated either with the ordinary Powamu or the Patcava.

Ned knows that water-pouring after Niman takes place elsewhere, even though it is not done at Oraibi. He regards it as *qwivi*, a sign of vanity, suggesting that the Niman always brings rain. [Ned's reaction may show only village loyalty. If Oraibi poured water after the Niman, as it does when the Soyal ends, he probably would not have regarded the act as *qwivi*.]

When asked if the sacred stone [p. 68] was connected with the Schism of 1906, Ned replied that there was no direct connection. He did know, however, of another "wonderful" stone that was supposed to have been in Yokioma's possession. This stone Yokioma is said to have shown in Washington to the president of the United States. (Theodore Roosevelt?) It is reputed to have symbolic meaning and to depict the two paths lying before the Hopi. Either they could take the right path by decapitating witches or else they could travel along the road of the "Whites" that leads to Christianity.

There is a Buffalo dance scheduled at Hotevilla this week. Is there a link with the Lakon?

In speculating on why Hotevilla keeps up the Lakon winter offerings although it does not have a full Lakon ceremony, one is led to the conclusion that while it has lapsed among the living, it may be thought still to be going on among the dead. Hotevilla's chiefs may be showing their sympathy with the observances in the otherworld by making winter offerings on earth.

Wed. Jan. 31. According to Ned the Hopi never performed *katcina* dances by single clans. Particular clans may be custodians of certain masks or *katcinas*, but the Village chief is their real owner and the cult is pueblo-wide (tribe-wide).

Ruth's and Ida's mothers are reported once to have caught Nasiwaitiwa driving away the clouds.[6] He is supposed to have been standing on Oraibi rock at the time, while the women observed him from the plain beneath. As they watched, Nasiwaitiwa peered through his fists as children sometimes do when they "make a telescope." Then he waved his arms away from himself at first and afterward toward himself in a gesture of invitation. When he began, the clouds were thick and it looked like rain. Thereafter a dry wind sprang up, the clouds were dispersed, and no rain fell. The motions of Nasiwaitiwa were therefore interpreted to mean that he had driven off the clouds and rain and had invited a windstorm to come to Oraibi. He ran off when he noticed the women watching him. Now he is occasionally called Witch Nasiwaitiwa. He was not punished as a known witch because people feared he might do them additional harm. Nasiwaitiwa was bold enough to chase away those who molested him by saying, "I'm watching you all the time, and some day something is going to happen to you." (Fear of witches is a powerful force among the Hopi. It impels them to sit quietly and take whatever befalls.)

Many women are busy replastering their houses. This is also the season when, in the old days, kivas were repaired and redecorated. Like the haircuts given to children, these activities may bear reference to the concept of renewal that receives expression in the Powamu.

More on the use of puppetlike dolls. On Third Mesa there is a Shalakmana and a Palhikmana. They may appear during a Water-serpent dance, but they may also be shown independently. The dolls stand a foot or so high and are placed in grinding-stone bins in such fashion that they can be manipulated to look as if they were grinding sweet-corn meal (*tosi*). [Compare p. 206.] They are generally accompanied by Köyemsi, who may see that the meal is heaped on small plaques and distributed to spectators. The dolls can also be made to dance while the Köyemsi sing. [For a comparative account of a Puppet-doll performance at Hotevilla, see chapter X, section L.]

The maker of the dolls used at Third Mesa loaned them to a friend who had a dream about them. He thought that they were unhappy and had said it was because their maker had failed to name them. The manufacturer's four daughters died in quick succession soon after, and it was said that the dolls were feeding on them.

According to Ida, girls do not generally change their names through life, whereas boys do and use childish names, Katcina or Powamu names, and Wuwutcim or Tribal Initiation names, successively. Furthermore, says Ida, girls do not acquire new names when they are initiated into women's ceremonies. [Years later, other informants said that girls *did* get new names when they were initiated into ceremonies, but that they did not use them.]

Ida also confirmed that ceremonial parents are often chosen not on the eve of an observance but long before. Considerable variation exists and the whole matter is left to the true parents.

Kuwannimptiwa, the Bakavi chief, said that Hotevilla was planning a Buffalo dance soon, but he does not think it has anything to do with the Lakon winter offerings. Bakavi's Bean dance is to be held around midnight tomorrow. He comments acidly on Hotevilla's stubbornness in regard to its calendrical error.

Kuwannimptiwa explained that there had been no *katcina* initiates to be whipped at Bakavi this year because none of the men wanted to play the parts of whippers. (Usually, whipping is done by two Hu *katcinas,* who are accompanied by their "mother," Angwush-nasom-taka-Hahai'i.) No good reason for the reluctance to play these parts was given, but whipping is so contrary to usual Hopi practice that the men probably did not care to receive the lashes that the whipping *katcinas* give one another. [Years later it appeared more likely that the unwillingness of men to serve as whippers may have meant no more than a disinterest in Hopi ceremonies.] Ned regards ceremonial whipping as good for rheumatism and says that if asked he would gladly play the part of a whipper because it might give him good luck with his crops.

NOTE.—Mastotovi may refer to a greenish blue bottlefly which lays its eggs in dead animals or decaying matter of some sort. Possibly the idea of death giving rise to life may underlie the dual nature of Masau'û who is at once the god of death and a major vegetation diety. (Be careful in using this idea, but it may turn out to have important religious connotations.) [Sometimes, Mastotovi are linked to witches and other creatures of evil. It is often thought that their arrival may portend the coming of such calamities as the death of relatives. Mastotovi may be as large as horseflies and may buzz like bumblebees. They are generally regarded as pets (familiars?) of witches and, accordingly, as precursors of evil or creatures of bad omen.]

Last night Ida had a confused dream about Fred Eggan and *katcina* whipping. As she puts it, she was somehow thinking of Fred and yet not thinking of him. Perhaps that is how a nonliterate person phrases the idea of having something in the subconscious while it is absent from the conscious mind.

This evening Fred Eggan and I actually took part for the first time in the Bean dance rehearsal at Tawaovi. Our kiva was then visited by the men from Powamu kiva who did an Angya *katcina* dance.

Hardly had this group left when we got a visit from the Marau kiva. They used spruce that Harold had brought from Kisiwu, but our kiva planned to use ordinary spruce that was being gathered by a Moenkopi man. [Spruce from Kisiwu is almost always worn by Niman *katcinas*.]

On the way home Ned remarked that the Marau group had beaten our bunch completely. He said, "They flattened us like a pancake." Personally, Fred and I felt that the Tawaovi song was rather tuneless, but all we said aloud was that it was pitched a little too low for average masculine voices. Ned immediately shot back that had *he* been present instead of out herding when the song was introduced, *he* would have gotten the tune up. (Humility?)

We thought that our criticism was a private matter among ourselves, but Ned promptly broadcast what we had said. Why did he go out of his way to air our complaint?

NOTE.—The entire problem of kiva grouping and kiva loyalty calls for further study. It is possible that there was a time when each kiva group felt close-knit and apart from the others. If so, the more each kiva group drew together, the more would it tend to cut itself off from the rest of the village. Would this have any bearing on village fractionalism and disintegration?

CHAPTER VIII

Diary for February, 1934

[*In the popular mind this is a serious month. Bean and corn plants whose growth was forced in superheated kivas are "harvested" and distributed to various households. Women and uninitiated children are supposed to believe that the green plants grew entirely through the power of the Powamu, which terminates early in the month with a Bean dance. The Powamu is a complicated mixture of several themes, including the induction of youngsters into the* katcina *cult. Powamu initiates simultaneously enter the* katcina *cult without a whipping, and the boys have the added privilege of becoming eligible to serve as fathers of the* katcinas. *All those who go only into the* katcina *cult are whipped, and the boys are never eligible to become fathers of the* katcinas.

Another series of katcina *dances, held at night in heated kivas, begins. This post-Powamu series is called Anktioni ("Repeat"), because some of the dances repeat features of the Powamu rites. In addition, this is the time for So'yoko impersonations. So'yoko is a fierce-looking, bogey* katcina. *He threatens to carry off uninitiated children, and their parents plead for them and finally ransom them off with food.*

The racing season opens, and several kinds of footraces are held.

Women are busy collecting stones that are suitable, either for baking piki, a crisp, paper-thin cornmeal "bread," or else for conversion into milling stones (metates) for grinding corn into meal.]

Thurs. Feb. 1. Luke is frail and weak. He has been too sick to plant beans for himself. Andrew, his stepfather, and not Humiletstiwa, his own father, planted beans for him.

Drove to Bakavi with Fred Eggan and Bert to see some mixed *katcinas*. We wandered about the village, where we noted several clusters of old Soyal prayer sticks. This observation raised the question of precisely how a newly founded pueblo picks out and names its shrines. [Apparently, it is done just as arbitrarily and boldly as is the occasional manufacture of new or duplicate fetishes.]

Kuwannimptiwa, Bakavi's chief, sent for us, and we went into his kiva to dine on stew and *piki*. He proudly showed us a cast-iron stove and a glass window in the kiva. It is odd to see him so proud of cultural innovations, whereas in nearby Hotevilla the men are equally proud of the cultural conservatism of their kivas.

A long time elapsed before the *katcinas* came out. They performed out-of-doors by kiva units.

After rehearsing our own Bean dance at Oraibi, we danced at the other kivas and were later visited by them. The kiva fire went out during our absence, but as the sprouts were soon to be harvested, no one seemed to mind. [Not even the idea of an evil omen was mentioned.] Prior to the arrival of the other units Frank practiced the Aholi impersonation, and Martin did Eototo. This part is customarily played by the chief, but he is "resting" and allowing Martin to act in his stead. Neither Frank nor Martin wore masks as they practiced. Martin drew a cornmeal design [Fig. 14 a], Frank placed a long staff at the juncture of the center and base lines, moved it toward him in circular fashion, and thrice cried, "A-ho-li-i'i'i," making a long-drawn-out call that faded away at the end. [See pp. 205–6 for material on Eototo and Aholi impersonations.] (In this performance things go by threes instead of the usual ritual preference for four. For example, the masculine Bean dancers wore three-part symbols made of corn-husks [Fig. 14 b]. I could not determine the reason for this divergence from the general rule of four.)

Fri. Feb. 2. Ned woke Fred and me at half-past four in the morning and hustled us to Tawaovi to harvest our bean crops. It took but a few minutes to pull up the young plants, and the earth was dumped into a large hole that had been dug just west of the kiva. Two bunches of sprouts were left, to be wrapped with *katcina* dolls for the babies of Betty and Mary. A third bunch, north of the fireplace, was put down as payment for the *katcina* who was to deliver the presents. (Tom gave out the Tawaovi presents; Charles acted as messenger for the Powamu kiva; and Bill and Harold distributed gifts from Marau kiva. Each distributor is free to select whatever *katcina* style he fancies, and each names a successor from his own kiva to do the job next year.) The remaining sprouts were brought home while it was still moonlight. Uninitiated youngsters and women are supposed to think that the power of the Powamu ceremony had made fresh bean plants appear in the dead of winter.

The chief gave me some corn plants to bind with the presents of dolls and bean sprouts. At daybreak the chief, Crier chief, and Kaletaka took up their chiefs' sticks (*mongkohos*) and went to the east edge of the mesa to make a prayer to the rising sun. [The official Kaletaka was Talasvuyauoma, of Moenkopi. He belonged to the Real Coyote clan. The use of chiefs' sticks was given up years ago. As to morning prayers, the modern Hopi claim to be too lazy to perform them. They classify them with such ancient customs as running at daybreak or taking cold baths at dawn.]

When the chiefs got back, Frank and Martin painted, dressed, and masked as Aholi and Eototo, respectively. The rest of the morning was crowded with Powamu activities. [For particulars, see chapter X, section I.]

Ida prepared a stew of bean sprouts mixed with corn. She said that we had to eat it this noon or something would happen to us. From the house we went to a similar feast at Tawaovi. Only the chief's kiva has this special meal. Before it begins the crier climbs halfway up the kiva ladder and invites the Cloud People to share the feast.

The Bean dance started around two in the morning. We did not get to bed until well after five. [This dance is described in chapter X, section J.]

Sat. Feb. 3. We had slept only about three hours when Ida woke us with an invitation to dine at her mother's house. All about, youngsters were playing with new gourd rattles, *katcina* dolls, and other gifts that they had received earlier. There was a holiday spirit in the air such as I had noted at one point in the Soyal.

It was a lovely day, and Jim took us out in a car for a little casual shooting and sightseeing. He pointed out the ruins of a curved, communal pueblo, establishing that Third Mesa had been known long ago, probably during Pueblo III. (It may be asking too much, but it would certainly help if archaeologists could trace the contemporary Hopi back to their exact point of origin. If this were done, the culture of the homeland would provide an excellent point of departure for ethnographic studies.) The remains of the communal pueblo lay a few miles east of Hotevilla. A few miles west of this spot we saw other ruins at Hukovi, supposedly pertaining to "Mission" [?] Indians rather than to the Hopi. From there we went on to Aponivi where, it was said, "priests" (Jim did not know from which society) came and stripped naked before asking the dead to join in their ceremony.[1] Jim pointed out that Aponivi is supposed to lie in the direct line between Oraibi and Maski, the home of the dead. At another time a different informant repeated Jim's statement and added that no messenger from Marau went to Aponivi during the winter rites. He rationalized the point by saying that it was too cold for the messenger to strip, as custom demanded. [It is much more likely that it would be futile to ask the spirits of Marau members to attend winter offerings on earth, since that is the very time when the dead are supposed to be holding their main rites in the otherworld. See p. 196.]

One of the landmarks Jim pointed out is called Pivostcomo or Pitcomo ("Girl's Breast Mesa Point"). He also showed us the spot where a Coyote man, a maternal uncle of Allen, is supposed to have committed suicide by jumping off a mesa. Fred Johnson is said to have heaped rocks over the body. We were also shown a flat ledge with little pits in which ladders are supposed to have been set for an ancient ladder dance [Lamati]. From Jim's account I gather that the "ladders" were really poles, from which performers somehow swung out in space. It must have been a fearsome stunt as there is a sheer drop of several hundred feet at the spot. Jim believes that the Pima formerly lived here and that their village was destroyed while a "ladder" dance was once in progress.

Got back in time to see a *katcina* dance at Tavuptcomo kiva in New Oraibi. At least one *katcina* dance is supposed to be done at night after the close of Powamu. It is called Anktioni. No exact date seems to be set, yet Anktioni "is always done." (Its sponsor in former days was the Katcina chief.) On this occasion Kikötcmovi had four sets of dancers. They impersonated Köyemsi who sang while special performers did a Supai (Havasupai?) dance; Apache (?) *katcina;* Navaho *katcina,* with a side-dancer and one clown; and mixed *katcina.* In what was called the Apache unit, a director cried out strange words that the dancers took up. He moved his head with a nervous gesture, like a person afflicted with a twitching ailment. The part of the clown was played by a First Mesa Tewa whose wife lived at New Oraibi. His face was smeared a dirty white, his eyes were blackened, and he wore overalls, shoes, a blanket, and a "necklace" made up of half-a-dozen oranges on a string. He entered the kiva head first. There was nothing bawdy or obscene about his performance. He made fun of some of the dancers and bandied remarks with the father of the *katcinas*. Then one of his father's clanswomen (*ikya'as*) brought him a bucket of coffee and a heap of *piki*, which he consumed gluttonously.

> NOTE.—A thought on the Kwan "killing" of neophytes during the Tribal Initiation. The leader of the affair represents the god of death, so that when candidates are brought into his kiva, it is as if they were entering the home of the dead. When they emerge, they act (very likely) as if they had newly come back to life (as men—not boys) and as if they were emerging from the *sipapu*, the opening through which man came out on earth.

Sun. Feb. 4. Jim came up with his father and made arrangements to drive Tawaqwaptiwa, Fred Eggan, and me to Moenkopi. The chief showed no reluctance for going, even though he and Jim's father do not get along.

Joe is planning to do roadwork for much of this month, but he agreed to spend a week in Winslow with me when I leave Oraibi in March. As a former resident of Hotevilla he may speak more freely when we are off the reservation. [During 1955 Joe had a regular full-time job with a road crew. He did, however, manage to spend his weekends at home. Joe continued this kind of work, off and on, for a decade or so. Lately, road crews consist entirely of union men. Since he does not belong to a union, Joe cannot get work. He is very bitter about the whole situation.]

Like Ned, Joe does not know how snow is made.

(Stephen calls one clan Moth. He seems to use the term instead of Butterfly.)

> NOTE.—Regarding the use of kinship terms, it is important that in actual usage the Hopi call older male and female in one's own clan mother's brother and mother, respectively. Also, relatives whom we would regard as belonging to Ego's own lineage are called by descriptive kinship terms. The Hopi concept of clan most frequently refers to a person's matrilineal lineage plus the lineage of his mother's sister. Under ideal conditions of matrilocal residence [what later I have come to call unilocal, matrilocal residence], these relatives would all have been included in one's natal household and would actually have resided under a single roof.

Mon. Feb. 5. Jim drove us to Moenkopi as arranged. Along the way the chief showed us the mesas where he went to catch eagles and Tokonavi, home of *all* the *katcinas,* but more particularly of the Köyemsi. In fact, if questioned before entering a kiva the Köyemsi always say that they have arrived from Tokonavi. [The modern Hopi regard Tokonavi in purely secular terms, as a good place for gathering piñon nuts. Tokonavi is sometimes called "Navaho Mountain." In ancient times it was known as a home of the Cloud People, and probably had a connection with Shalako.]

Some Hopi statements do not conform to our ideas of logic. Tokonavi is the home of *all* the *katcinas,* but so is Kisiwu, and so are the San Francisco mountains. Hahai'i is the mother of *all* the *katcinas,* but so is He'e'e and several others. They also have more than one owner of *all* game animals and of *all* crops. Does this argue for a different system of logic or for an elaboration of the same idea that underlies kinship extensions whereby a person may have more than one mother, father, and so on? Might there have been successive adoptions of outside notions that became incorporated into the single scheme that is Hopi culture?

Tues. Feb. 6. We were fed and sheltered by Hettie at Moenkopi. After a time we walked about the village and then went into the kiva headed by Talasvuyauoma, Hettie's father. On our walk we saw a poolroom. It was much the same as a poolroom anywhere in the United States, but we were amazed to find it doing a flourishing business in a Hopi pueblo. It was a shock to see and hear loud swearing, emphatic gum-chewing, "balloon" pants, and a general "wise-guy" air of pseudosophistication. Now it is easy to believe statements charging the young men of Moenkopi with hanging about street corners in Flagstaff, drinking, and whoring.

In the kiva we were well received by Talasvuyauoma and by Frank Siemptiwa, who was here to dance as an ordinary *katcina.* No one objected to our presence while preparations for dancing were being made, and we noticed how much less seriously a rehearsal was taken at Moenkopi as compared to Oraibi. At the latter all practicing dancers stripped to the waist and went barefooted or wore moccasins, but in Moenkopi many men were fully clothed in "White" American style. Then again, while we had been getting ready for our Bean dance, Poliyestiwa had coached us to break away while face to face with our partners, but here there was no coaching, and many dancers turned their backs on their partners.

It was strange for persons like ourselves, brought up with the notion of sanctity that is associated with high office, to find Siemptiwa, the Moenkopi chief, and Siletstiwa, the Powamu leader, acting as ordinary dancers. Yet, a similar situation often prevails at Oraibi. Except in the given ceremonies which they lead, the Hopi chiefs got no preferential treatment. This relates not only to the excessive self-depreciation, humility, and individualism of this tribe, but also to the temporary nature of their "priests." The lack of a permanent priesthood makes all talk of a Hopi "theocracy" sound strange.

In order, at night, we saw the Powamu (Bean) dancers from Talasvuyauoma's kiva, another similar unit, and a group of Köyemsi who sang while some of their mates did a Laguna Corn dance. This called for a lively step, something like that done by Avatchoya or Motcapmonkwewa. The dancers have circular dots painted on their bodies and prance rapidly with both feet. They were followed by a group of Kwasaitaka, who wore Hopi skirts (*mantas*) and carried bags of seeds [compare p. 214], in addition to sticks with prayer feathers attached by strings. As a modern touch they had candy mixed with the seeds in their bags, and one performer chewed gum vigorously while he was dancing.

Several orthodox features found in Oraibi night dances were missing at Moenkopi. There was much less repartee between the father of the *katcinas* and the spokesmen of the various units that entered the kiva; and none of the unmarried girls gave gifts to the dancers.

Wed. Feb. 7. We estimated that the lower village at Moenkopi had about forty houses compactly set together. We then climbed to the upper village, which is inhabited by Poli Payestiwa's followers. Here the school is located, the houses are of better "White" construction, and there is less crowding. Moenkopi has a good irrigation water supply, the fields are very fertile, and the roads are constantly being improved. Many of the men own trucks, and there is far more dollar prosperity than at Oraibi. On the other hand, all the improvements tend to pull the people away from the old culture, so that, in spite of their nominal allegiance to Old Oraibi, they are almost as much weaned away from traditional practices as are the inhabitants of Kikötcmovi. (Even Siemptiwa has been struck by the parallel between Moenkopi and New Oraibi.) No wonder that so few of the younger element at Moenkopi are given ceremonial affiliations on the house census.

Their mode of life is so rapidly assuming a "White" appearance that their pueblo means little to them except as a tax- and rent-free place of residence.

Siemptiwa says that only some *katcina* masks had been destroyed at Moenkopi at the time of the Soyal. [See p. 187.] They were thrown into a ditch, he says, and not burned. Not all of Poli Payestiwa's faction has forsaken the old Hopi religion. Most of his followers belong to the "Horse" kiva, and during the Bean dance they gave a performance but remained aloof by failing to visit any of Moenkopi's other kivas.

Got home "just in time," as a clan race for women had been called out the night before. Two Soyalmanas, Masamösi, wife of Panimptiwa and sister of the chief's wife, and Talasnönsi, wife of Kelnimptiwa and mother of Anita, are in charge.

Thurs. Feb. 8. Early this morning Talasnönsi and Masamösi ran through the village. They had strings of sheep hooves and bells tied at the waist and made a series of announcements about the race to each kiva. Later in the day Talasnönsi, who is the head of the Pikyas clan, made up to represent Aholi, one of her *wuyas;* and Masamösi, who is Parrot and in the same phratry as Katcina, appeared as a Mastop *katcina*. Like the regular Mastops [pp. 169–70], she imitated copulation, and I was flattered when she acted thus with me (to the great joy of the spectators), because she is Panimptiwa's wife.

It was nearly noon when the participants went down the west edge of the mesa to a starting point near the spring. Men took part by dressing the women of their own clans, and no husband helped his wife. Masau'û clanswomen wore Kwan head-dresses with single horns [see Fig. 15]; but Ruth chose to impersonate the real Masau'û, although she carried no club. Edna, maintaining her claim to be Yellow Fox rather than Coyote, wore a fox pelt at the back and an elongated headdress that resembled the ear of a fox. Honanhoynim (Piqöc clan, in the same phratry as Bear), wife of Duveyauoma (Tom Jenkins), wore an old bear-skin, carried a bear claw in each hand, had red prayer feathers, and growled and threatened to claw people as she went along. The Sun clanswomen, Hahai'i, Martha, Ida, Jenny, and Ada, had on either old-fashioned Hopi dresses or parts of *katcina* costumes. Each, however, had a large sun-shield affixed to her back. The Tep ("Greasewood") women did not wear distinctive costumes, but each one carried a sprig of greasewood. Women of the Parrot clan wore bright garb bedecked with brilliant plumage.

Allen's Betty was an exception. She dressed as a Hemis *katcina* girl. Runners for the Rabbit clan had their faces whitened and wore tall headdresses shaped like rabbit ears and painted black and white. Some of them even had black whiskers painted on. Little Rabbit girls made a big hit when they came out of the kiva by dropping to the ground and hopping for a few places in bunny fashion.

All in all there was a surprisingly good turnout. The chief's wife did not run, but she had a few daubs of paint on her face, went out with the racers, and walked back by a path parallel to theirs. All this showed her sympathy with the race. Grace and Juanita were too heavy with child to run, but they, too, participated just enough to show that their hearts were with the runners. The racers lined up near the spring, listened to a speech from the leaders, and started off at a good clip. Coming up the mesa trail at the finish was too much for most of them, so they walked up the steep grade. Winning was much less important to them than it is to us. Clansmen among the spectators snatched costume accessories from the racers, who washed up, changed clothes, and then entered kivas for feasts provided by their clansmen. It was an excellent example of clan solidarity cutting across marriage and postmarital residence ties. The Sun women did not care to eat in Tawaovi with the Parrot folk, Panimptiwa's female in-laws, and therefore dined at Hahai'i's house. When the festivities had ended, the two sponsors officially announced the termination of their responsibility and turned future races over to the men.

NOTE.—When interpreting racing don't overlook the practical importance of running in ancient times before horses and burros were known. War, too, formerly demanded fleetness of foot. Realistic factors probably underlay the original stress on running and were later rationalized into the current belief that racing is mimetic magic for quickly bringing rain and crops.[2]

NOTE.—Planting and harvesting along clan lines may have been due in the past to the danger of sudden raids, which meant certain death if a man were caught out by himself. Perhaps that is why whenever a man returns home from the fields or from gathering wood, killing a sheep, and so forth, all the womenfolk present greet him with thanks. [See pp. 47, 51, and 121.] Possibly the custom implies the survival of ancient danger connected with any trip away from one's home and village. (This is a risky interpretation and should not be pressed too hard.) [There may also be a connection with matrilocal and unilocal residence.]

There was much talk about the women who had raced earlier today. Men whose female relatives were judged to have been nicely dressed were highly pleased.

Heard quite a story of a racing incident that was supposed to have occurred many years ago. At that time Ned and Ruth had had a young baby living. In a race for wives' clans Ned had dressed as Masau'û, club and all. Soon after, the baby fell ill, and it was decided that the "power" of Masau'û had got into it. The child broke out with sores called *masna'pala*. A Hotevilla medicine man, Kuwanyamptiwa (a Kokop, which is one of the clans that has Masau'û for a *wuya*), is supposed to have cleared up the sores; but the "poison" entered the baby's "heart" and it died. Ruth, who is now childless and unlikely to have another baby, is willing to dress as Masau'û, but she will not carry the kind of club with which the deity is supposed to touch those who are about to die. [See p. 39.]

It was reported that there had been a night kiva dance at Hotevilla in conjunction with the winter services of the Lakon society. The women are said to have danced first, followed by a set of Antelope dancers who carried a real antelope head. (There is some sort of a bond between Lakon and hunting rites, just as there are similar links in the Soyal and Al ("Horn") observances, The Al is "owned" by the Bow clan, and an Al man watches the sun from the Buffalo shrine. The Al seems to refer to horned animals and seems to be more closely connected to hunting than to war.)

Daisy supposedly danced in the Lakon, just before giving birth in the kiva. If the story is true, having a baby was just another event in the daily round for her.

Fri. Feb. 9. Ned went herding.

There was much talk of racing, and the remark was made that Harold (Sand) would probably sponsor the first race for men. The food that had been contributed to each clan group by its male members was discussed in detail, and Ruth charged Dennis with being stingy because he was in Oraibi but had failed to contribute anything to his clan's (Masau'û) feast.

Jim was asked the meaning of the symbol [Fig. 14 c] which is on a rock beside the road to Hotevilla. He said it was a friend-ship sign (signifying a handclasp), which someone had placed

above the mark of an arrow. Jim says that the whole idea refers
to the trouble in 1906. The arrow stands for the strife between
Oraibi and Hotevilla; but around 1910 or 1911 the residents of
the two pueblos made friends, and that is why the friendship
symbol is placed above the arrow.

Ned says that in the old days many Supai Indians used to
live near Hotevilla. In his youth they used to come to Third Mesa
to trade piñon wood for food. Other Hopi contacts with the Supai
occurred during expeditions for salt.

Ned is of the opinion that Anktioni (post-Powamu "Repeat"
dances) is in the charge of the Parrot-Katcina phratry—"just like
Niman." He believes it is always announced by Köyemsi impersonators at the special Kwan house. Ned did not know for sure
why the Köyemsi used the Kwan house, but he has noticed that
Köyemsi often appear in stories pertaining to the home of the
dead.

Charles wants to appear as a Kwikwilyuka *katcina*, but
his kiva mates object. [Contrast his statement on p. 196.] They
argue that they have so few members that they cannot spare
one for a solo. They prefer to have everyone impersonate whatever *katcina* type their kiva selects.

Tom arrived with the news that Walpi is going to have
a Water-serpent dance tomorrow. If informants are correct, it
means Palulokong at Walpi, Yellow Qöqöqlom and Bean dances
at Chimopovy, two Buffalo dances, and a (Choctaw?) Comanche
dance at Hotevilla, all will be held on the same day. Oraibi residents agree that the Water-serpent dance is incomplete and im-
properly performed at Walpi.

Sat. Feb. 10. Ned took several of us by wagon to Hotevilla to see
a Buffalo-Comanche dance. It was cold and raw, but there was
a good turnout of people from Oraibi and Kikötcmovi. Some of the
songs, Ned says, had pointed references to the dispute over dates.
The Hotevilla folk still insisted that they were right, and they
even poked fun at Oraibi. Native informants identified the practice as song-tying. "Hotevilla song-tied Oraibi," they said.

At one stage of the dance, while a man and his young
son were performing, a Bear clanswoman, *ikya'a* to the little boy,
jumped between him and the young *ikya'a* who was dancing as
his partner. In this way the older woman was expressing jealousy
and love. She was dragged away by another *ikya'a*, who was also
the grandmother of the little boy's partner. No one seemed to
know (or care about) the capacity in which she was acting.

The so-called Choctaw dance is another illustration of the theory that ritual elements are traded back and forth even within a single culture. Choctaw is supposedly a war dance, yet it is clearly no more than a variant of a Buffalo dance. The main differences were that the girl dancers carried arrows instead of prayer sticks, wore lots of buckskin, and had no sun-shields. The men were dressed in a sort of pseudo-Plains costume, with pants consisting of two single leggings, and beaded moccasins. Their faces were painted black on one side and red on the other, and they carried revolvers. Yet, the steps and gestures of the dance were virtually indistinguishable from a Buffalo dance, although some parts were more rapidly paced.

As at Oraibi, during the late afternoon the cluster of singers began to appear in ever more fantastic dress. One Hotevilla singer came out in blackface like a Negro, and another had a frying pan tied to his belt. Also, one group of singers and dancers would appear before a previous unit had finished, thus providing something like a "battle of music."

In one of the late dances a group appeared with two boys who wore nothing but G-strings. Their bodies were smeared with white clay, and they wore grotesque masks. They were supposed to represent Navaho clowns. The Choctaw unit now showed up in fanciful costumes and a mock battle ensued, with dummy bayonets and spears being brandished and blank cartridges fired. There was much snatching at genitals and tilting of buttocks. (When, later, this was described to bashful Ida, who had left early for Oraibi, she was very much put out to have missed the fun. Yet, she is "ashamed" to see a Marau dance, which I find much more decorous. I suppose there is no accounting for morals any more than for tastes.)

Sun. Feb. 11. Fred Eggan happened to mention the peyote cult to Ned. Even though the idea of consuming any strong drug is foreign to the Hopi, Ned expressed the opinion that peyote must contain a powerful spirit. On this basis the peyote cult "sounded good" to him. This is a striking example of tolerance of a belief that must be distasteful to a Hopi but seems to express goodwill toward others. On the other side of the coin, however, we find a belief that any Hopi who married a Zuñi would turn into a mule at death. Likewise, in Hopi dances, Zuñi impersonators walk with a clumsy limp and wear grotesque masks that feature a crooked mouth and face. The Hopi also do their best to make the Navaho appear ridiculous, and when Nick danced as an Apache at New

Oraibi, he jerked with a spasmodic movement reminiscent of Saint Vitus's dance. By such devices the Hopi, in their dances, express their sense of superiority over other tribes. (This demonstrates how dances can serve to express aggression, and how they may be used as outlets for tensions.)

Ned was asked some direct questions about the Al society and what its name and the idea of horns implied. He was by no means sure of all the relationships involved, but he did know that the Al *na'atsi* ("religious standard"), usually placed across the ladder of a kiva when a secret rite is in progress, was a spreading antler or horn taken from an animal such as an elk. In the Wuwutcim (Tribal Initiation) Al is linked to the hunting, especially of horned animals. Kwan, through its relation to Masau'û, appears to be more definitely warlike; Tao seems to be agricultural; and Wuwutcim is primarily a fertility cult, but it combines features of the other three. Moreover, war and hunt have much in common because they both stress bravery, daring, hardiness, the skillful use of weapons, luck, and the dealing of death.

Ned also referred to the fact that in the old days the Kwan society had to "baptize" a new Village chief and a new Crier chief. [Later information made it seem likely that the Kwan society once used to baptize nearly all of Oraibi's leaders or chiefs.] Again, note the high place attributed to the official Crier. Members of the Kwan society are consistently referred to as guardians or watchers for the chief. This undoubtedly smacks of former warrior functions. [See p. 203.]

Another point that requires further checking is Anktioni. It seems that this should be announced initially by a member of the Katcina clan group after which other night kiva dances may be requested by anyone else. Sometimes, too, this Anktioni is said to be like the Niman. This leads to two possibilities. In the first place, Anktioni is about six months removed from the Niman—adding a point to the repetition of features in the corresponding months of the summer and winter calendrical cycles. [This implies that the timing of Anktioni on earth corresponds with the Niman in the world of the dead.] In the second place, Anktioni marks either the assumption of *katcina* control by the Katcina clan group after the six months of Badger control have ended, as climaxed by the Powamu ceremony, or else (if the Niman idea is correct) it marks the cessation of Badger clan control of the *katcinas*. (In either case Anktioni coincides with the end of Badger control of the *katcinas* for half the year, and the Katcina clan's assumption of control for the other half of the year.) Thus, the Katcina clan group takes charge of the *katcinas* for the six months between Anktioni and Niman on earth. After the *katcinas* have been "locked up" at the end of Niman, the Badger group becomes the nominal head during the closed period, through the start of the night-dance season, and up to Anktioni.

The Bakavi chief's son, who was recently married in Bahana ("'White' man") fashion, is now having a Hopi wedding. His wife has begun to grind corn at his house in Bakavi. [This combination of marriages has become increasingly common and may be linked to a desire for official documents and legal proof of a wedding.

Marau winter offerings are being made at Hotevilla. When completed, the women will give night dances in the kivas. Possibly there will be a *katcina* dance when they finish.

Several men chatted informally. Now and then one woman or another was described as a former sweetheart or mistress, and a good sprinkling of these were *ikya'as* to their lovers. There were also a number of references to men who had moved temporarily to other villages in order to be near sweethearts.

Mon. Feb. 12.

NOTE.—Parsons is probably right when she postulates that the *katcina* cult is a later cult with the Hopi than with the Zuñi. The large number of foreign names, the confusion in ideology, the duplication of mothers and other relatives, the generally uncertain grasp that the average native has of *katcina* origins, all point to an introduction of the cult here with the Hopi after some other religious details had already been worked out. Perhaps the Hopi brought with them to their present villages from their original homeland a warrior-hunting culture and a religion which emphasized these two features. Then, as they adopted an agricultural mode of existence, fertility and agricultural elements were introduced, becoming more and more important as war and the hunt faded out, until we get the present insistence that *all* ceremonies are for rain and crops—even Buffalo dances or the rites of the long-extinct Warriors' society (Momtcit). In some way, the *katcina* cult may have come to be grafted onto the original religious pattern and gradually interwoven with it.

Both because of its primary emphasis on agriculture and because of its control of *katcinas,* the Powamu seems to be a later ceremony than the Wuwutcim (Tribal Initiation) and the Soyal. The Soyal *katcina* (though considered older) is very likely a later addition to the Soyal which, as a central ceremony, was called upon to incorporate one of the key Hopi notions (as the *katcina* cult came to be considered). Hence the Soyal itself took on some aspects of "*katcina*-ism"; but a study of the Soyal and Qöqöqlom *katcina* rites proves that in ideology they are not actually *katcinas*, such as the usual ones who return after the winter offerings. Then, too, there is no Kaletaka ("Warrior") in the Powamu, but there is a Kaletaka in the Soyal, Flute, and Snake rites. Thus, *purely* agricultural ceremonies and *katcinas* should be considered as later than war and hunting rituals.

Arranged to measure Charles's cornfield this morning. On the way he told of an occasion when Cedric had caught some Navahos watering their flock at a well that Cedric and his brothers had dug for their own use. When he had remonstrated, the Navahos had simply hit him on the head with a bucket and given him a good beating. Cedric did nothing more about it, but the Navahos quit using the well. Cedric is also the one who had failed to follow up his threats when Albert's cattle had damaged his crops. What a capacity he has for taking a beating lying down!

We had chicken, unexpectedly, for dinner, and Ida gave a long explanation. Sam Jenkin's dog had killed several chickens, some of which belonged to Hahai'i. All the women owners were sad, cried, and demanded payment, which Sam refused. They then threatened to kill his dog, whereupon Sam proclaimed that if they did, they would have to pay him because that was the "White" man's way. "If you kill a man's beast," said Sam, "you must pay him for it." This display of "logic" frightened the women, and they sadly retired. Although they continued to complain, they did nothing further. However, someone did kill Sam's dog, whereupon *he* did nothing.

A Shipaulovi girl had assumed that she was wanted in marriage after a single "visit" by a man from Chimopovy. The girl came to his house and began to grind corn like a bride. This angered the man and he told the girl to go home. There was a quarrel and a compromise was reached. His relatives refused to make her a full wedding outfit, but they did promise to make her a dress.

Some of the older women are busy fetching suitable stones for making grinding stones. In general, this time of year seems comparable to our spring housecleaning season. Children get haircuts, women plaster houses, new grinding stones are made, and kivas are freshened up. (Another possibility—is this the Hopi New Year's season that Voth mentions?)

Practically every cultivated field has a little wash running through it. This can be dammed beyond the limits of the field. Many trenches are deliberately and artificially cut, so that present Hopi farming methods are to some extent based on the principles described as "flood-water farming" by Kirk Bryan.[3] Also, Ned claims that many farms used to be situated in places where the Oraibi wash now runs. Furthermore, as insurance against scant and irregular rainfall, the Hopi like to scatter their farms as much as possible and to plant early and late at different stages of the agricultural year.

Tues. Feb. 13. Drove in Bert's car to Mishongnovi, where the Mishongnovi and Shipaulovi chiefs were having a conclave. Almost the first thing we noticed at Second Mesa were Soyal *pahos* ("prayer sticks"), which Martin said belonged to Shipaulovi. They were about a month old.

The Shipaulovi chief, Frank Masakwaptiwa, who had formerly been married to Ned's deceased sister, had consented to have Fred Eggan live in his pueblo, provided that he stay with Frank's niece Elsie, sister of Joe Sikyakuku and Hale. [Hale operates a general store at Mishongnovi. His brother Joe Sikyakuku is the Village chief of Shipaulovi and head of the Snake society. He used to run a curio shop in Winslow, but now is said to reside permanently at Shipaulovi.]

It seems that Anktioni is being delayed at Oraibi because so many men are working on the roads.

Wed. Feb. 14. Frank and Qopilvuh left early for Moenkopi. They plan to return in time for the Niman. After they left, the chief gave some details about Moenkopi. He says that Poli Payestiwa (p. 181), leader of the modernized faction that opposes Frank Siemptiwa, is not yet a Christian "but will become one some day." [Actually, he was never converted to Christianity.] The chief continued to talk about Moenkopi's troubles. Once he had been given some cornmeal by a Moenkopi youngster named Ernest who had thus asked the chief to sponsor his entrance to Oraibi's Soyal. Another Moenkopi youth had also sought admission to the Soyal, but since his ceremonial father is on Poli's side, he will have to get a sponsor other than Tawaqwaptiwa. Harold, from

Old Oraibi, has also expressed a desire to go into the Soyal next year. With Sam that will make three new initiates, possibly four. The plan is to call a meeting soon at which wool will be spun for the making of *kele* ("chicken-hawk") garments. At the same time songs for next summer's Angya ("Long-haired") *katcina* dance will be rehearsed. (The Angya *katcina* has been chosen for impersonation at the Niman dance next summer.) With so many candidates planning to join the Soyal, the chief feels certain that a Patcava ceremony will follow the Powamu of 1935. He says that many Moenkopi men are planning to come to Oraibi in order to take part.

The chief agreed to draw the old layout of clan lands, and, indeed, he wants a copy for himself.

Went to see Bert, and he told the following legend: when Oraibi was to be ended, there would come a catastrophic destruction which would wipe out all the Hopi and all knowledge of their present culture. Following this, there would be a cultural rebirth, with the Hopi being forced to start from nothing. Gradually, they would acquire arts and crafts and redevelop their total culture.

Nestcili and his wife dropped in during the afternoon. While they were in the house, Ruth searched their wagon. She was greatly peeved when she found that they had brought no meat.

Martha said that Ada did not know the identity of her father. Instead, she referred to Frank Masakwaptiwa as Jenny's (her older sister's) father. Martha cautioned me not to tell Ada that her real mother (Martha's sister) was dead. She regretted that schoolteachers sometimes disclosed this kind of information to children. [By 1958, however, when Frank Masakwaptiwa had died, Jenny and Ada knew who both their parents had been.]

Ida was "ashamed" to clean the stove in the presence of two boys from New Oraibi.

Another example of how dietary habits stick. Lee had prepared a good "White" American meal for supper—veal, potatoes, squash, cauliflower, cake, and tea; but she wouldn't eat it because she had asked her mother, Sivenka, to make *patupsuki*, a special Hopi dish of beans and hominy, eaten with onions. [Formerly, hominy was made by boiling corn with ashes. Soda is used nowadays.] Her preference for this dish was all the more noticeable as she is a good cook in the "White" American style. [Oddly enough, Lee had earlier refused to eat *somiviki*, a traditional Hopi food, calling it "that stuff."] Actually, she was delayed in getting to her mother's in New Oraibi, but on hearing that there was *patupsuki,* the sophisticated and much acculturated Oscar hurried to his grandmother's to eat. This dish, never seen at Old Oraibi, is said to be a delicacy that is hard to make properly. Although she is Christian, Lee's mother is an expert at preparing *patupsuki.* Hahai'i is said to know how to fix it, but Martha spoiled a batch when she tried it.

Bakavi and Oraibi are to have Anktioni tonight.

Thurs. Feb. 15. In the morning Ida got talking about *qövisti* ("willful suicide"). She claimed not to know how to go *qövisti,* although she admitted that sometimes she got very angry. She explained that the difference depended on sulking and maintaining a sullen silence. Delia, Jenny, and Ada are supposed to have the capacity for going *qövisti.* However, Luke has no patience with this sort of behavior, and when Ada tried it, he made her snap out of it by spanking her. Delia is said sometimes to go *qövisti* temporarily, even though she is a married woman.

The kinship terms that Sandra uses for her mother's mother's parents are *iqöqa* and *ivava* ("my older sister" and "my older brother," respectively), but modern sophistication makes the younger Hopi feel that it is wrong for a very young child so to address great-grandparents. Hahai'i has agreed that Sandra should be taught to call her *iso'o* ("my grandmother"). In the same vein Jenny and Ada object to being called mothers.

Ida opines that Jenny, like herself, is too "ashamed" to have a sweetheart, but she thinks that Florine will soon have sex experience. [In later years Ida was married and Jenny was briefly married, long enough to have a son named Roderick. Florine was married for a time to Charles. She works as a waitress in Flagstaff.]

NOTE.—A point worth remembering: The Hopi seem not to have been as stationary and isolated as some North American tribes, notably those in California. Trips to the Salt Canyon from Oraibi paved the way to diffusion from the Plateau and possibly the Plains; and Second Mesa expeditions to Salt Lake provided easy access to Zuñi and the eastern pueblos. Then, too, there were numerous intertribal trading expeditions. Thus, we might expect Hopi culture to have assimilated "foreign" traits in historic times, and perhaps earlier.

Ida mentioned Jackson Pongyayesva, of Hotevilla. She said that he would not do for a lover because she didn't like him;

he had no sense of shame and paid no attention to what people said about him; and, besides, he was her brother. In explaining the relationship she pointed out that Jackson's name referred to sand, because his ceremonial father was a Sand clansman. Since Ida's true father was also of the Sand clan, she and Jackson were sister and brother.

> NOTE.—There is no mechanism to curb Jackson's wrongdoing. If he pays no heed to what people say, he may be considered evil, but the only thing done about it is to say still worse things about him. Thus talk, and more talk, is the only punitive method employed, and if anyone is brazen enough to disregard talk, he can get away with anything. Despite his bad reputation, Jackson has no trouble in securing mistresses. Perfectly commonplace here is the opinion that so-and-so is malicious and nobody likes him, yet women readily accept him as a lover. [Is it a matter of wealth and ability to pay? Perhaps. See p. 108.]

Fri. Feb. 16. Martha and Ida looked at a picture of my sister-in-law and asked who it was. "Mû'wi" ("'Sister-in-law'"), I replied without using any possessive prefix. "Itamû'wi?" ("'*Our* sister-in-law?'") asked Martha. "No," I answered carelessly, "*my* sister-in-law." "All right," said both Hopi women, "if you're stingy and want to keep her for yourself, then you can't call Ruth your sister-in-law." Deliberately, I persisted. "Well," I said, "she's not my wife. She's my brother's wife, and you never adopted *him*." Whereupon Ida replied, "Well, that's just the same. She's *our* sister-in-law just the same."⁴

Thus does the custom of kinship extension among the Hopi come out clearly. Having adopted me, they apply the whole kinship system to my family, considering my brother as their brother, and my sister-in-law as their sister-in-law. Note, too, the emphasis and significance of kin term use. Martha and Ida were peeved at me when they thought I was withholding a relative from them, and they threatened to even the score by withholding a similar relative from me. This verifies the observation of Margaret's verbal attack during the mud-fight over Dick, at the time of his wedding, when she had "refused" to be called sister-in-law. [When this was first written in 1934, kinship terms were treated primarily as markers of relationships. Today I am convinced that the use of such terms may also have other purposes. The Hopi often use kin terms to express such high sociocultural values as great esteem.]

Apart from the definite plots assigned to clans that "owned" ceremonies, every clan, as such, cultivated "free" land assigned to it by the chief. Even such land was held on a somewhat religious basis as the chief expected commoners to "pay" for the use of their land by hauling wood to the Soyal kiva, doing odd jobs for the Soyal *manas*, and taking part in *katcina* dances, especially, the Niman. [With the collapse of Oraibi's ceremonies, land use has become entirely secular.]

Today's interviews on land also served to clarify and corroborate the important differences between actual, living clans and so-called extinct clans that were mere names or *wuyas*. In addition, individual men, if they were "good citizens," were awarded land, and they helped to raise the chief's crops, hauled his wood, or wove his wife's garments. Theoretically, the chief owned all the land pertaining to his village, and men worked it only at his pleasure. Here then is the sting behind the chief's decrees. If people disobeyed or displeased him, the chief could, at least in theory, deprive them of land or assign them to distant or unfavorable plots. Actually, he very rarely ousted owners from traditionally held farms, as there are several instances of men who had continued to cultivate good land in defiance of the chief's wishes. Whether or not the threat worked, the chief's right to withdraw land provided a theoretical club for enforcing his commands.

Also, since those who forsake Hopi ceremonies are supposed to quit their lands, there is a basis for the violent dissensions between Old and New Oraibi. This affords a contrast to the present-day friendliness between Old Oraibi and Hotevilla. For one thing, Hotevilla is keeping up the rituals while New Oraibi is not; and for another, the farmers of Hotevilla are using lands that were previously unassigned. When they left Oraibi in 1906, they gave up their old farms, whereas the New Oraibi folk continued to use their traditional plots. Thus the people of Kikötcmovi daily show their defiance of the Old Oraibi chief, who hates them partly because he is utterly impotent to stop them from farming land which, in theory, belongs to him.

They say that Harold of the Sand clan, which owns racing, is to call for a men's race by clans tomorrow; but nothing official has yet been heard. There is also no word about Anktioni as yet.

Bill said that on Second Mesa the So'yoko rotates together with the Niman. That is, the same kiva group that is responsible for the Niman is supposed to put on a So'yoko performance in the same year. This was later verified, at least for Shipaulovi and Mishongnovi.

Sat. Feb. 17. As there was no call for a race today, Ned looked after his horses and then we went to see the So'yoko at Shipaulovi on Second Mesa. On the way Ned disclosed that the rumor of a race had been started by Edna. He said that she was a renowned spreader of tales and that she did not hesitate to make up stories when it pleased her. Yet, in spite of his clear recognition of her propensity for lying, Ned accepts verbatim the truth of such statements as her account of having witnessed her son Moe having intercourse with his sister-in-law. [Compare p. 130.]

Frank, the Shipaulovi chief with whom Fred Eggan was staying, told Ned a long story of dissension at Shipaulovi. Frank said that at the time of Oraibi's Split in 1906 he had tended to laugh at the spectacle of an old village being divided against itself until it finally broke in two; but now, he confessed, Shipaulovi seemed to have reached the same point. Disagreements and arguments were dividing the little pueblo into two factions. While commenting on this, Frank said that the trouble extended even to today's So'yoko, which was going to take place at Mishongnovi, not at Shipaulovi. Arguments have broken out in the kiva that is sponsoring this year's Niman, hence the So'yoko was also affected. The men had appealed to Frank, but like a good Hopi he had replied, "It's up to them." He told us he was "waiting to see what they would do," a phrase that Ned has used hundreds of times in similar situations. Frank went on to tell Ned that in the event of further disputes, he, like Tawaqwaptiwa, would put an end to Niman rotation and would take unto himself the ownership of the *katcinas* and the annual sponsorship of an unofficial Niman. [Despite its chief's forebodings in 1933, Shipaulovi never came to an open schism.]

Before the whole So'yoko group appeared, just before noon, a So'yok' girl, bearing a long crook and carrying-basket (*hoapu*), came four times to announce that she would soon arrive with her mates. These comprised two Natackas, one We'e'e, eight or ten Köyemsi, and two Masau *katcinas*. [See O.O., pp. 220–21.] Each little girl in the village had been instructed to grind sweet-corn meal (*tosi*), and each small boy to trap mice and other small fauna. The Köyemsi would bargain with parents, who ransomed their offspring with generous supplies of foodstuffs to save them from being carried off by the fierce So'yokos or Natackas. Sometimes, a little boy would be stripped naked, doused with cold water, and made to run for his life in a mock race with a bogey *katcina*. Sometimes, too, a little girl would fail to show fear but would challenge a Natacka to compete in a game of hopscotch. It was ludicrous to see fierce masked figures seriously playing childish games. Since every house containing uninitiated children was visited, the *katcina* impersonators collected a huge amount of food.

I noted particularly that parents or other relatives who defended a boy always said that he was a good hunter—not necessarily a good farmer. The youngster was always said to have just killed a deer, and when his mice and birds were rejected by the Köyemsi, they always called violently for meat, especially deer meat. Thus does this ceremony, too, emphasize the importance of the hunt in Hopi religious and social life. Even rites whose overt purpose is to bring rain, crops, and good health may have hunting success as a covert motive. [Horned or antlered animals appear to be most desired. See p. 178.]

Everyone insists that wind and cold always accompany the So'yoko rites. There seems to be a relationship with calendrical logic or with clowns who are supposed to bring wind. In both cases the impersonators are thought to be mischief-makers, and perhaps the idea of bringing cold and wind, which are *not* wanted by the Hopi, is connected with the aspect of wrongdoing. One Hopi rationalization runs counter to this suggestion. It explains the behavior of "contrary" performers as designed to get the opposite of their usual objectives, which amounts to getting good results from the native point of view. It would not do to admit that any ceremony had a harmful purpose, yet clowns and So'yoko *katcinas* generally bring wind. They are not believed to be beyond sin, as some ethnologists have suggested, but are supposed to get good results through doing things by *opposites*. [In later years the close connection of clowns and the dead has become clearer than ever. Since death is the opposite of life, the clowns act in contrary fashion, and since death means the cessation of life, their behavior has evil connotations.

Most supernaturals bring warmth and rain, but clowns and other representatives of the otherworld of the dead bring the *opposite*, namely, cold and wind.]

Cecil, a married nephew of Ned, was home for the week-end. His fellow villagers had refused to allow him to enter the Wuwutcim because, according to Ned, they were afraid that he would disclose its secrets to "Whites." Cecil has, admittedly, had stories of Hopi life published in several periodicals.

While we were on Second Mesa, a Shipaulovi So'yok' *mana* ("girl") appeared to say that "she" was coming back with lots of companions in four days. "She" suggested that little girls should begin to grind sweet corn and that little boys should start hunting.

Ned and I went to Fred Eggan's house and had supper with him. Ned beat a small drum while he was singing some *katcina* songs. More plainly than ever before did I come to realize the difference between Hopi timing and rhythm and ours. Again and again did the drum beat on steadily regardless of voice accentuations. Thus, the song beat does not correspond to the drum beat. Furthermore, at one point Ned danced and drummed as he sang, and in one section while the drum beat double time—i.e., two strokes of the drum to one stamp of the foot—the accents of the song were different from either. Thus, to some extent but not, in all likelihood, with the elaboration of the Northwest Pacific Coast tribes, was there a complicated triple rhythmic pattern. More commonly the Hopi foot and drum beats go together, and only the timing of the song differs.

At one of the dances in Kikötcmovi, Ned and others recognized the type of a *katcina*, before it had come into the kiva, by the song it was using as it approached. [Several children could do it in 1933.] There is, undoubtedly, a fixed rhythmic pattern for each type of *katcina* song. For instance, all Bean dance songs open with "Ah'ha ha, He'-e-e"; and conclude with "Ah'ha ha, He'-e-e'-e-e," repeated. Rhythmic pauses seem to occur variably, but verse and chorus appear to be clearly marked to the Hopi ear, and sometimes to ours, especially in cases where the verse has meaningful words while the chorus consists only of nonsense syllables. (In such cases, do we distinguish verse from chorus on the basis of rhythmic pattern or on the score of vocabulary?) [The Hopi dislike having a great many meaningful words in a song.] Accordingly, it is not always easy for a "White" to tell verse from chorus. Words and syllables are freely borrowed from one song or another, and the same phrases occur time after time, perhaps in a somewhat different order or with an original touch here and there.

Ned spoke about his deceased sister, Duwamönim, who had been married to Frank Masakwaptiwa. Duwamönim had already been married at Oraibi but had refused to go to Hotevilla with her husband when he joined the Hostiles in 1906. Frank met Duwamönim at Oraibi. He, too, had been previously wed. Despite the fact that he was a chief, he had been "cut out" at Shipaulovi and divorced. In violation of the rule of matrilocal residence Duwamönim went to Shipaulovi to live and bore Frank two daughters, Jenny and Ada. Frank managed to spend a fair amount of time at Oraibi and even developed some fields there. He is anxious to have them conserved for his daughters.

Later in the day Frank came in and called Ned outside for a private chat. Ned afterward revealed that Frank had offered him a female bedfellow if he wished to spend the night on Second Mesa. The woman was Frank's niece who always did as he told her. Ned had refused the offer on the grounds that "the lady might not like" him.

Fred Eggan said that Frank had once asked him point-blank whether he would mind if he (Frank) sometimes brought in a woman to spend the night wtih him. Of course Fred replied in the negative, but it is highly doubtful that Frank, and especially any woman he might desire, would have nerve enough to indulge in sex in the presence of a "White" man. Even Frank's outright request is more than one would have expected from a cautious Hopi.

Thus did one day's visit to Second Mesa go far to confirm the Oraibi material concerning intravillage feuds and loose sexual conduct.

Fred also said that in the few days of work at Shipaulovi he had already got some marked divergences from Oraibi ceremonial practices. Apparently, the Marau and Lakon winter offerings at Shipaulovi come *after* Powamu, and ordinary night *katcina* dances do *not* occur in January. On the other hand, Anktioni seems to come soon after Powamu as it does ordinarily at Oraibi. It may be that rechecking will show that there has been a misstatement somewhere. However, it would not be surprising if some variations were to be found between Second and Third Mesa customs. It would take comprehensive studies of all the villages to disclose what was universal for all of them—and thus, presumably, basic for the whole tribe.

Somehow Ned got going on Monteczuma and spoke of his cleverness and of his ability as a prophet. Monteczuma is supposed to have emerged with the Hopi from the Underworld through the original *sipapu* and is thought to have known how to speak all languages. From Bert, who is believed to have heard the tale in Mexico or New Mexico, Ned had learned that in a contest with Christ Monteczuma was credited with having been the victor. He is also credited with having composed all the traditional songs used in the Hopi ceremonies. In the light of such statements one must hesitate long before accepting myths as "history," no matter how "dimly remembered."

Sun. Feb. 18. This morning Harold made the rounds as racing *mongwi* ("chief") to announce that he was sponsoring a men's race by clans. [For details see chapter X, section K.] When the race was over, the women of each clan brought food to the male participants, but it was evenly divided among all the members of each kiva.

Mon. Feb. 19. Tawaqwaptiwa has a bad toothache and a swollen jaw.

Worked with Ned on the making of salt expeditions. Got some excellent material and uncovered many links with other aspects of Hopi culture.[5]

Grace was delivered last night of a boy, although Kiacwaitiwa had announced that she was bearing twins. No one seems to know or care about what is supposed to have happened to the other child. I doubt whether this baby will be regarded as a converted twin, as no twisting ceremony [see p. 153] was performed. Kiacwaitiwa also explained why the baby was born later than it had been expected. He said that the child had several times changed its mind about being born at all because of the frequent dissensions between Grace and her husband. When it did decide to be born, it came late.

Ruth's sister Lucy is here from Walpi for an extended visit. She is pregnant and wants to be confined at Oraibi. "She always comes home to have her babies," it was said. This shows the strong link between a mother and her daughters, as well as between sisters and other natal kin. It represents the pull of the natal household, even on one who is living in another village.

Ruth is busy making a new *metate*. She is being helped by Edna and Qöyawai'isi.

Martin expects Oraibi soon to hold a men's race for the clans of their wives. He says that Anktioni will take place on Saturday night and that Cedric will ask for it. He claims to have heard singing and drumming practice, but he is not positive about the date. Later on, he expects the women to run for their husbands' clans.

Ned told a funny story about the last time he impersonated Natacka in an Oraibi So'yoko ritual. He had not tried on the mask at rehearsals, and when the ceremony began, he was horrified to discover in his mask a spider of a variety that he believed to be poisonous. In this type of *katcina* the wearer's whole head fits into the large bill of the mask. Whenever the spider had approached his face, Ned had exhaled violently, forcing it to scurry back to a distant corner. He kept this up at intervals until he got a chance to unmask.

Tues. Feb. 20. Cedric said that he did plan to call for Anktioni Saturday and that Charles would serve as sponsor of a race the next day. Cedric claims not to know what men will announce Anktioni. Whoever they are, they will appear as Köyemsi and will speak in jesting (clown), backward or reverse [opposite] fashion, ordering tiny girls to fix *somiviki* and men to prepare stew. It seems that on this occasion it is customary for unmarried girls to pass out *somiviki* to the dancers.

Hahai'i and a number of women from Old and New Oraibi left today for Bakavi to help in the wedding rites of the chief's son. The principal idea is to make a show of mutual help and cooperation regardless of clan affiliations. (Is the overriding of clan ties due to the fact that a chief is supposed to be the father of all his people?)

Heard a badly jumbled story about the sick daughter of Roland at Kikötcmovi. Somehow, somewhere, and at sometime, this girl is supposed to have "thrown away" her baby. Yet, her illness does not seem to be attributed to this deed. Instead, she is sick because she was badly treated by her Tewa mother-in-law during a lengthy visit to Hano. She had crying spells and is supposed to have visited the graveyard at night because she wanted to die. She carried on, according to Ida, "just like *qövisti.*" Now she is unable to move, eat, or talk (paralyzed?) and has been removed to the hospital at Keam's Canyon.

It was cold, cloudy, and windy all day, and Ida remarked that this kind of weather always comes when someone is being married. (Most Hopi weddings take place in the fall or winter when men are free of farming duties.) Some people guessed, however, that the sky was overcast because the clouds wanted to come to see the new *mû'wi* ("female affine").

Ruth, Louis's wife, and Nawisoa, all women of the Masau'û clan, carried huge bundles of washing to the laundry at New Oraibi, and they all came back pretty well tired out. The difficulty of carrying water here, now that the cisterns on the mesa top have dried out, seems to be the prime motive for the use of the New Oraibi laundry. [Nowadays, there is a regular laundromat at New Oraibi.]

In the evening Charles arrived to say that on Sunday he was going to be chief of a men's race for all female relatives by marriage, including wives. Those who had several *mû'wis* ("female affines") could take their pick. He explained that he had been suffering from a stomach ailment and had gone for relief to Edna, who seems to have the special ability to treat stomach disorders. However, she was probably entertaining someone privately, because she made Charles wait for a long time when he rapped on her door, and then refused to let him in. On another occasion, when Charles had hurt his foot, he had gone for treatment to the blind Powamu chief, Qötcvuyauoma, who has a good reputation as a bone "doctor."

It was cold in the house so Charles took a blanket. He wrapped it about him and said jokingly, "All right, let's go some place," meaning *dumaiya*. He then spoke of the recent exodus of women to Bakavi and ventured the opinion that the Bakavi men "would sure have a good time" while the Oraibi women (and others) were present.

Wed. Feb. 21. William came up from New Oraibi. He is making an agricultural survey for Mr. Hammond, but he admits that he has no accurate knowledge of acreage under cultivation or of land values. He either guesses at these items or leaves them blank on his charts. Hence, his "statistics" are worthless, and no proper conclusions can be drawn from his data.

It is now claimed positively that Roland's daughter, the wife of Leo Crane, is *qövisti*. She is acknowledged to be very ill and will probably die. Ruth got the news from Roland's wife while she was laundering at New Oraibi.

Martin returned from a trip to Flagstaff with Bert. He brought the news that a Navaho had been arrested in town and jailed for stealing. He went on to add that all the Navaho were thieves. This is reminiscent of a long indictment that Kane had once made. He had said, among other things, that all of the Navaho, including Nestcili, were accustomed to stealing pairs of horses or cattle and secreting them until several offspring had been born. They would then kill and eat the mother and sometimes her mate. Calves or foals would, of course, be branded with the thief's mark and added to his herd.

No one will make a firm commitment on the date of Anktioni or on the time and manner of the preliminary rehearsals. Tonight, maybe, maybe tomorrow, is all that is said.

Cedric asked Sidney to dance with the Powamu kiva group as they were very short of men. Sidney came up from New Oraibi for a practice session and found that none was being held. Thereupon he got angry and may or may not take part on Saturday night.

Martin regards Edna as a complete medicine woman. He said that she certainly was a regular "doctor" and not merely a stomach specialist. She had once cured him of sore eyes by the simple expedient of bathing them with clean water.

Joe also knew that Edna was a medicine woman. He said that she had been taught the art by her father, a Bow clansman who had gone insane.

As I was passing Tom's store at Kikötcmovi two little girls, the one six or seven and the other nine or ten, shouted something at me. I thought I had caught the word *dumaiya*, so I stopped short and asked, "What did you say?" The older girl hung her head and remained silent, but the younger one chirped up. "She wants you to *dumaiya* with her," she said. Later, to test the reactions of adults, I told of this incident separately to Joe and to Ida. In each case the only response was a hearty laugh.

Thurs. Feb. 22. Soon after breakfast Tawaqwaptiwa called out that women could come to trade corn for lard or potatoes with Jackson Lehongva, who had just come from Moenkopi.

Martha often calls on her brother Ned to chop wood for her while her husband Luke is sick. Ned always responds and is quite good-natured about it.

> NOTE.—The phrase "we're all alike" is sometimes used to describe the psychological unity of mankind. Insofar as this is true, it seems to depend on certain physiological and physical processes that must go on if the brain is to function, for the "mind" cannot exist without the body and brain. Among all peoples a sharp blow registers pain; hunger and thirst arouse discomfort; sexual activity is gratifying; and so on. It stands to reason that if all humans have basic similarities in some physiological processes, they may very well have similar psychological reactions associated with them. This is the way in which we are all psychologically alike.

Well, at last it has come. There is damning criticism of the new Hopi agent at Keam's Canyon. Even if the agent were a combination of Matcito (a Hopi culture hero), Sotukinangwa'a (a sky god), and Masau'û (god of life and death), he wouldn't be in office ninety days before the Hopi would be down on him with a vengeance. Today the chief commented on hearing that the new agent was no good; that he was just as bad as Mr. Miller, who had preceded him; and that he was too much influenced by Mr. Hubbell. So much for that!

A group of five San Domingo Indians arrived for trading.

They came in a truck with a white trader. He is said to have cleaned out Hubbell's stock of *katcina* dolls and has thus, of course, aroused Hopi resentment, although it means more business for doll-makers. The strangers stayed at Bert's store in Old Oraibi and sang through much of the night. Several of the Hopi commented that these Indians seemed never to tire of singing.

The Anktioni date still hangs fire. Ned said that Tawaqwaptiwa had decided to have Tawaovi kiva use an old song that would require but little practice if the men got only short notice. No rehearsal was held tonight even though the dance is unofficially said to be scheduled for Saturday, the day after tomorrow.

During an interview on the gathering of salt, Ned, with his customary prefatory apology, translated the name Clitoris Spring. George, who was sitting by, burst into laughter on hearing the word. It is surprising that at the age of nine or so George was perfectly familiar with a part of the female reproductive system that is unknown to many adults among us.

Fri. Feb. 23. Although there was a sprinkle of rain yesterday, with the prospect of more to come, there has not been a sufficient fall to fill the cisterns on the mesa top. Accordingly, Ned is planning today to haul water from a well at New Oraibi.

> NOTE.—Because of the potentially disintegrative nature of Hopi, and perhaps Pueblo, social structure, it may not be necessary to postulate an attack by enemies to account for each movement from place to place. Third Mesa history abundantly proves the point. This may be more certain of the Hopi than of other Pueblo tribes, which may have better centralized governments and less disintegrative tendencies. Certainly, the Hopi lack a political sense and the type of political structure that might counterbalance disintegrative forces.

At about half past five in the evening the Köyemsi finally appeared to announce Anktioni. The parts were played by Cedric and Allen. It was drizzling steadily at the time, but the people showed great excitement and hurried out in the rain to watch the antics of the Köyemsi clowns. All the onlookers appeared to be very much thrilled despite the fact that most of the activities were known in advance. One can well imagine the effect produced in the old days when strict secrecy was enforced and when the greater part of the population was genuinely surprised by the sudden appearance of the Köyemsi. The elements of secrecy and surprise are excellent dramatic devices and must have had thrilling effects on the observers. The sense of the dramatic that these people possess is greatly marked and should not be overlooked when interpretations are made. Note, in this connection, the great care taken during night kiva dances to prevent any group from performing twice in succession in any one chamber, and, at the same time, the arrangement of the schedule so that each unit opens and closes its evening's activities in its home kiva. Note, too, how the movements of the warlike Snake dancers dramatize their differences from the gentle Antelope men in the joint Snake-Antelope dance.

To return to the Köyemsi who announced Anktioni, they appeared with dramatic suddenness on the roof of the Kele ("Chicken-hawk") house, jumping about and making their bells jingle and jangle while they babbled the words of their announcement. Then they rushed down to street level and ran pell-mell through the streets to Tawaovi, where a crowd had gathered to watch them enter. Immediately after making an announcement inside they emerged, doubled back to the dance plaza, ran down what I have named Bakwa Avenue, and so reached the Marau kiva. Here they again made their announcement, hurried out, and ran to the Powamu kiva where they finished and disrobed.

Ida was wild with delight because she had been the first to notice the Köyemsi on the Kele roof. She hurried to notify Louise across the way, who snatched up her baby, Ann, and with her mother dashed into the rain to Tawaovi.

Rehearsals were held in the evening in each of the three participating kivas, Tawaovi, Marau, and Powamu. In Tawaovi the chief drummed while the other men sang a Navaho song in pseudo-Navaho (falsetto) style. On the main floor of the kiva Sam, Lawrence, and George were rehearsing the dance steps of the Navaho *katcina*. Each was barefoot, stripped to the belt, and had a string of bells about the waist. Each dancer carried two large eagle plumes, tied together, in either hand, and with these he gestured as he jogged up and down with his feet alternating. Only Sam knew the proper rhythm and the correct gestures; Lawrence was fair; and George was completely at sea. He was so busy watching the others that he was forever late in following the beat. The experienced men called out directions and corrected errors. During a period of rest Tom informed me that they were teaching the youngsters, and that next year they would be all right. At the public show tomorrow night the singers will dress as Navaho men, and the three youthful dancers will be clad as Navaho women. Thus, for the third time this winter, the men of Tawaovi are taking an easy way out by giving a performance which requires strenuous practice only from a few soloists, while the rest of the group plays the part of singers. [In 1933–34, in addition to the Navaho dance, the men of Tawaovi did Eagle and Apache. In each case there is only a small number of soloists, who dance while the rest of the membership merely clusters about a drummer and sings an accompaniment.

This type of dance has become increasingly common. It is most convenient for men who live or work off the reservation. They can participate as singers with little or no rehearsal.]

When the practice had ended, Ned and Poliyestiwa took pinches of ashes from the fireplace and performed discharming movements rather perfunctorily.

In contrast to Tawaovi's selection of an easy way out, Cedric had wanted the Powamu outfit to do the Angya ("Long-haired") *katcina*. He was overruled by the other men who felt that the hair arrangement, particularly, required too much trouble. [For an Angya *katcina* dance that was given at Oraibi on Saturday, July 9, 1966, Dave laid out about sixty dollars for wigs. Other dancers borrowed them at a fixed rate. Dave expected to get back his investment within a few years.]

Sam reported, with much laughter, that old Qöyayeptiwa had nearly fallen from the kiva ladder at Tawaovi. Ned had caught him just in time. Everyone is beginning to consider the old fellow a nuisance (he is in his nineties), and his situation helps me to understand why an unproductive old man may, in some societies, be put to death or abandoned. Qöyayeptiwa is just dragging out his days, and in some respects it would be a merciful act to end his life. Even Bert, who in the past has shown much kindness to the old man, is now disgusted with him because of his vermin-ridden state. However, Bert takes no stronger measures than to lock the door of his store whenever he goes out. This is to keep the old man from warming himself at Bert's fire and leaving lice behind.

An Oraibi youngster is accused of having stolen some tobacco from the chief and of having pilfered a dollar from Poliyestiwa. There seems to be no intention of punishing the alleged culprit, although his guilt is fairly obvious. As far as can be surmised, failure to punish a suspected evildoer is an old Hopi trait. This boy does not attend school on the pretext that his eyes are bad.

NOTE.—Where matrilocal residence is strictly observed, a married daughter remains in her mother's house. Thus, from a child's point of view, its household mates comprise its siblings, its parents, its mother's sisters with their spouses and offspring, its mother's unmarried brothers, and, in some cases, its mother's mother and her sisters, together with their spouses. Except for men who have married in, this unit corresponds to that segment of a lineage or clan which Ned so often singles out for special emphasis as "his people." From the Hopi point of view people whose mothers were sisters are close relatives.

Sat. Feb. 24. Early in the morning Louise invited Ida to go on an errand with her to New Oraibi. Ida hurried to get through her chores, but her mother pointed out that many preparations were necessary for tonight's dance and forbade her to go. Ida swallowed her disappointment and obeyed her mother.

Last night it drizzled and rained pretty steadily, and this morning there was a nice blanket of soft, wet snow that melted quite readily. Fog kept the moisture from evaporating too quickly, and the precipitation helped to put the ground in good condition for planting. Yet, it is unlikely that any Hopi will admit to getting a good break. Ned kept saying during yesterday's drizzle that everything would be all right if only the rain were a *little* heavier.

Ed passed by, and I wished his kiva good luck in tonight's dancing. Ned overheard me and began to kid Ed, saying that Tawaovi would put it all over the Marau kiva to which Ed belongs. This exchange seems to be a survival of the old days when kiva rivalries ran high and remarks like Ned's carried a real sting.

Throughout most of the day Ned was busy with preparations for the dance. He was much concerned about George's costume, and he made a special trip to New Oraibi to borrow some article that George was to wear. He made favorable comments on George's showing at last night's rehearsal, and he bragged about George's outdoing his partners. Like fathers everywhere Ned cannot see straight where his own son is concerned.

Ned replied, in answer to a question about Martin's failure to participate, that he "often acted that way." (Martin had not taken part when Tawaovi had put on an Apache dance.) At the same time, it must not be overlooked that Ned is always ready to jibe at Panimptiwa's crowd.

Fred Eggan has noted that while Shipaulovi does perform some independent rituals, it is tied in with Chimopovy for the Wuwutcim (Tribal Initiation) and Soyal ceremonies. He also said that up until recently it was considered bad form for Shipaulovi people, especially men, to intermarry with Mishongnovi folk.

According to Eggan, both Shipaulovi and Chimopovy had So'yoko performances today. This did not seem right because we had heard the preliminary announcement at Shipaulovi which set their date for last Wednesday. Fred explained that this was the original plan but that something had come up. The So'yok' *mana* ("girl") had appeared alone on Wednesday to say that the bogies had been delayed and would come four days later. This brought it to Sunday, but as Anktioni was scheduled for that day, the So'yoko performance was finally given today, Saturday, February 24, 1934. The Shipaulovi So'yoko differed only in a few minor points from the rites that we had seen at Mishongnovi.

Among the spectators who were seated in Tawaovi for the Anktioni dances was James Sikwi. Although this brother of Tawaqwaptiwa is known to have been a Christian, he showed no shyness in taking a place. Later, several uncomplimentary remarks were made about his behavior, but nothing was said to his face. The dances were highly entertaining and generally well performed. [For a detailed description, see chapter X, section G.]

Sun. Feb. 25. Everyone had feasts after last night's dancing. Cedric and his daughters ate at his mother's house, but his wife was not with them. Perhaps, natal household and clan ties are integrative in a large sense, that is, in going beyond the limits of the nuclear family; but they exert a disintegrative effect on the limited family, since clan and natal household bonds cut across nuclear family lines. (This is due to exogamy, which forces a man to marry outside his natal household and clan.)

In the forenoon Charles ran through the village in an incomplete Kwan costume. He announced a men's race for female in-laws, as he had said he would. However, instead of having a man select only one affine for whose clan he would run, it was agreed to let each participant wear the emblems of all his female relatives by marriage. In this way no woman would be neglected—another example of the nice Hopi sense of courtesy.

This race was very much like the last one, and the men again ran as clan units. As before, the Pikyas clansmen won. A jest is going the rounds about the Sun clan because Ned and I were last in the previous race. It is being said that we were running for the Hotevilla sun, an obvious reference to the fact that Hotevilla has fallen a month behind the other Hopi villages. Not bad at all.

Went below to watch Anktioni at New Oraibi. They too had had an announcement by Köyemsi, and their unmarried girls also made *somiviki* to give the dancers.

New Oraibi's Anktioni dances were primarily conventional. One group of performers, impersonating Qwivi *katcinas*, carried wooden blue-painted triangles and spruce in hand. The triangles represented the head scratchers used by novices in ceremonies.

Another group did a mixed *katcina* dance that included a Tcaveyo carrying a saw, Hote, Bear, and Holi. The third unit was all Hote, and the fourth was Angya. The latter were of a type called *ka-totci* ("without moccasins"). They were said to be a Zuñi variant. The dancers were barefooted and had sprigs of spruce bound at their ankles. They were accompanied by a "female" called Takucmana and a Hehea *katcina*. Hehea carried a small mealing stone (*metate*), and Takucmana kneeled and pretended to grind corn, keeping time with the rhythm of the dance. Actually, some ground corn had been prepared in advance. The meal, made of white sweet corn and known as *tosi*, is put on a little tray (*pota*) and left with the father of the *katcinas*, who distributes it to the spectators.

Mon. Feb. 26. Ned and Tawaqwaptiwa had a long discussion today. When it was over, they announced that there would soon be another Anktioni set of dances to be sponsored by Andrew for the Marau kiva. They do not expect any more races, however, even though Charles had left the sponsorship open for anyone who might care to assume it. Everyone laments the degeneracy of the modern Hopi and contrasts it with the virility of former times. [Actually, this seems to be another aspect of man's increasing reliance on culture and his persistent efforts to cut down on the use of human muscular energy.[6] New Oraibi, even in 1934, held no races at all, and around 1950 Old Oraibi gave up running as it took more and more to "White" culture.]

George and Lawrence did much better on Saturday night than they had done at rehearsal. Ned thought that it was "because the power of the *katcinas* had got into them." He did not mention the fact that while they were dressing, the chief had given them a pep talk. He had told them that unless they danced better, they would not make a hit with the girls and that they were lucky to belong to Tawaovi because its men always made the best marriages.

Lee told of a Winnebago baby a day or two old that is supposed to have spoken. It had predicted the end of the world, and had then died. Lee also claimed to know of a similar event that had concerned a Navaho infant.

Tues. Feb. 27. Sam, young as he is, talked much of sex. He says that Edna's present lover is Kuwanvenyoma, an old uncle of George. This man is nicknamed Luwa ("Vulva") and is sometimes so called to his face. Charles agrees with Sam and says that the nickname had reference to something Kuwanvenyoma had once done in a dance. Everyone is said to know that he is Edna's lover. Sam then named several of Charles's own mistresses.

Charles pointed out a Powamu prayer stick that he had deposited during the recent observances. It was made with a thick clay "brick" as a base, and from it there protrude several wooden *pahos* ("prayer sticks"), a wooden crook, and a small netted wheel.[7] Siletstiwa, the Powamu chief, made four of these, Charles says. One was taken to the north by Joe, another to the west by Charles, a third to the south by Moe, and the fourth to the east by Lewis. Lewis lives in Hotevilla, but he came to Oraibi to participate in the Powamu. The ceremony is very popular with Pikyas men.

The men of Powamu kiva keep up a friendly, club spirit. Today they fixed a lunch of eggs, bread, and other foods and enjoyed a sort of picnic. Sam joined them and said that he had slept in the Powamu kiva for the last few nights even though, officially, he belongs to Tawaovi. Through family ties he is bound to Tawaovi, but he goes about with the Powamu bunch because Tawaovi is generally deserted by young people, except when rites are in progress.

After lunch we went out to the fields. Along the way Charles pointed out a rock, called Yapontca, that is supposed to house a spirit. Boys used to throw stones at the rock until a little dirt or dust was dislodged. They would then cry out, "Yapontca is after you," and all would run away. [Yapontca is a wind spirit, connected with whirlwinds. He was probably worshipped by witches who sought to do harm to mankind. He was supposed to wear old, tattered and torn garments, and to have a red *nakwakwosi* ("prayer feather") affixed to his tangled hair.]

Luke's throat is swollen badly and he is much alarmed. He called for Kiacwaitiwa hurriedly because there was a dance scheduled for Hotevilla tomorrow, and he was afraid that Kiacwaitiwa would be too busy to come. As it was, Kiacwaitiwa arrived promptly and gave Luke some medicine. Luke felt much improved thereafter.

Sam came to say that old Qöyayeptiwa may be dying. He is suffering from a stoppage of the bladder and cannot urinate.

Wed. Feb. 28. Another incident shows the Hopi tendency to take lickings lying down. Charles remarked that he suffered from corns and bunions. He explained that at school he had been issued shoes that were too tight for him, but he had worn them without making a complaint. [Compare Kane's experience, p. 36.]

Sam says that Nakwave'ima, crippled brother of Qöyayeptiwa, was telling some of the men and boys at Tawaovi that Duvenimptiwa is still potent and occasionally enjoys sexual relations with his wife.

Tom spoke of the Navaho *katcina* dance which his group did the other night. He said that the Old Oraibi men were not ashamed of their obscene actions, as they gave the people a good time, but he was told that at New Oraibi their dancers were too ashamed to act in such fashion. (New Oraibi is far more acculturated than Old, and has many "White" residents. The ancient pueblo has none.)

Tom is much less mystic than Ned in regard to the recent performance of the boy soloists. His explanation is couched in terms of any dramatic performance. Without an audience the boys were lethargic; with an audience, says Tom, they were stimulated into outdoing themselves.

Hopi concepts of dramatics and showmanship lead to a possible interpretation of Hopi, and perhaps Pueblo, clowning in terms of stagecraft. Clowning may have to be divided into two parts. The first, dealing with the simple desire to arouse laughter, leads to buffoonery of all kinds. This may be entirely independent of or only slightly connected with serious ritual. Into such a category would fall the antics of a clown who dangled by one foot from a kiva ladder at Kikötcmovi; or the exaggerated swaying of the buttocks with which one man danced at Oraibi; or the lifting of his dance kilt by another man who thus exposed his

G-string; and a host of other activities. From the natives two sorts of explanations may be obtained for this kind of buffoonery depending, perhaps, on the temperaments of the informants. Men, like Ned and the chief, who make frantic efforts to justify everything in their religion take a defensive attitude. They explain this kind of clowning by reciting a formula. Such doings, they say, "are worth something. They (the buffoons) are doing it for rain, and for our crops, and for long life." On the other hand, Tom and most of the younger men who are less concerned with defending their faith admit that such antics are designed merely to amuse the spectators. If clowning were really fundamental, it would probably be more universally performed. It's strange that clowns should be said to have ritual value, yet clowns appear only in public performance and *never* in the secret kiva rites from which nonparticipants are rigidly excluded and which have far weightier implications than any public exhibits. Clowning occurs only during the least important part of serious rites, or in connection with ordinary *katcina* dances, which are among the least important ceremonies put on by the Hopi. Apart from the extinct Paiyatamu, no group of clowns at Oraibi appears to have had sacred altars and an esoteric procedure of its own. The only other secret ceremonial to which clowning is attached is the Niman ("Homegoing") *katcina* dance, and here the clowning may occur by analogy with other *katcina* dances. Thus, so far as Hopi clowning goes, scholars tend to overemphasize its ritualistic value and to neglect the dramatic element of sheer comedy for the sake of provoking laughter.

Turning now to the second category of clowning behavior, we come to something that cannot be explained away as mere comics—namely, the license to burlesque serious religious performances, including such things as imitating and mocking the steps and gestures of *katcina* dancers. Even here there may be a dramatic element in the form of comic relief. Prayers are serious; the thoughts of the onlookers should be weighty and devout; and religious performances generate tension and heaviness which burlesque tends to relieve. (This is dangerous reasoning, and such an analysis should be thought out more fully before a commitment is made.) Just why clowns should be permitted to mock aspects of serious religion, instead of being asked to limit themselves to straight comedy, is hard to say. There is a bare possibility that mocking is used because it is an easy and almost infallible way of arousing laughter. Defensive minds might have wrapped the cloak of sanctity about this aspect of clowning technique by such devices as calling clowns "fathers" of the *katcinas*. It is also possible that calling them fathers links the clowns with forebears, ancestors, and the dead.

[With the passage of the years, I have more and more come to hold the belief that clowns are often equated with the dead; and that much of the mockery arousing laughter stems from the notion that since death is the opposite of life, those who represent the dead, as do clowns, should also do and say the *opposite* of what is normally expected. This is a surefire way of arousing laughter; but in such cases the factor of amusement is entirely secondary, whereas the primary purpose is to behave like the dead—that is, to do things *opposite* to the way they are done by the living.]

Little Lawrence came in to report that Qöyayeptiwa had taken a turn for the worse. Thereupon Ned and Tawaqwaptiwa left immediately to carry the old man out of Tawaovi, as it is bad to have a man die in a kiva. "It might bring cold," said Ned. Accordingly, they brought Qöyayeptiwa to the Sun clan house of Ned's mother and bedded him down with considerable trepidation because of his vermin.

When the chief returned, he reported that he had urged Hahai'i not to feel sorry over the old man's impending death because he was so very old and feeble. Our talk then centered on the death of Talaskwaptiwa, many years ago. In the last moments Hahai'i had offered him food, and he had refused it, saying that he had just eaten a meal prepared by his deceased wife. People interpreted this to mean that Talaskwaptiwa's deceased wife was happy because her spouse was rejoining her. Much the same was said of his other relatives.

During the last few days Ida has been singing snatches of Eagle songs. Her mother "got after" her and made her stop, because she was unhappily reminded of her late son Perry whose illness and death were attributed to Eagle power. (Who said that the Hopi were indifferent to the death of relatives? Note also that the *katcina* cult's leadership was turned over to Masahongva by his brother who was still grieving over the death of a son.)

CHAPTER IX

Diary for March, 1934

[*More Anktioni* katcina *dances are being held in kivas at night, some-times while various societies are making their winter offerings. Hote-villa has scheduled, during its series, a Puppet-doll dance that bears a resemblance to a Water-serpent dance and repeats some features of the Powamu ceremony.*

Children of both sexes, but boys in particular, make wooden or stone tops and spin them by whipping.

Women are still busy gathering stones, for particular purposes.

At Old Oraibi, a large number of men and boys cheerfully co-operate on a community project to clean out a muddied horse pond.

Rehearsals are held for the Niman katcina *dance which is to be given at Old Oraibi this summer.*

There is a widespread measles epidemic among young children.]

Thurs. Mar. 1. Hahai'i decided to move into *the* real Sun clan house which had lately been fixed up. It belongs to Ida. [This house [Fig. 20, #26] is occasionally occupied by Sandra (Sun) and her family from Chimopovy whenever they visit Oraibi. They usually come for dances.] Hahai'i had often talked of moving but had put it off all winter. The presence of Qöyayeptiwa and his lice had forced her into making a decision to move.

Hotevilla is celebrating Powamu today. They must know by the weather that they have fallen a month behind in their calendrical count, yet they loyally refuse to admit it.

Ned's mother came in several times with bulletins on Qöyayeptiwa's condition. At one point Ned sent her back with instructions to have his brother Sidney sit the old man up "in order to help his breath escape." Ned thought that the change of posture might speed the old man's demise, and he saw no point in letting him suffer so that he might live a few minutes longer.

At any rate, Qöyayeptiwa died unaided around four in the after-noon. Hahai'i hurriedly fetched yucca for washing his head, and Ned and Sidney at once began to prepare the body for burial. Ned made Sidney, who had never done more than assist at a funeral, take charge. Knowing the Hopi distaste for observances at these events, I did not even offer to go along. Compared to Sidney, Ned shows no fear of the dead, yet he is supposed to suffer pains in the back because he has buried many corpses. After their old uncle was interred, Ned and Sidney took purifying baths, *masnave hompi*, in juniper, and now Sidney will have to make prayer sticks and prepare a "lunch" for the use of the dead man's soul. [Burial customs have undergone several modifications of late, but purifying baths in juniper or cedar are still taken.]

Afterward, Ned gave some of the details of the burial. A grave was dug about six feet deep. Then a groove was tunneled out at right angles, and it was into this groove that the corpse was placed, facing east. The opening was stuffed with blankets and weighted with stones. Then the whole thing was filled in.

In the evening, went to see Anktioni at Chimopovy. At first Ned was going along, but then he decided it would be "indecent" to watch a dance on a day when he had taken part in a burial. The Winter Marau was going on (note the different time from the Hotevilla rites), and their kiva would be closed to the public and not visited by the *katcina* dancers.

At about 10:30 P.M. we entered the Wuwutcim kiva and did not emerge until nearly 4:00 A.M. There were interminable waits between dances. Angya, Ho'e, Hehea, and Tcakwainiwa *katcinas* were performed. On their final appearance, the men who had done Ho'e returned as Köyemsi and put on the game of red and black corn which had been done at New Oraibi. [At the out-set four ears of black or purple corn are laid out alternately with four ears of red corn. A single space in the center is left vacant. In order to win, a player must move the ears one space at a time until all the ears of the same color are side by side. Clowns usually invite unmarried female spectators to play the game for prizes.] Only two unmarried girls were present in the kiva, so married women, too, were called on to try their luck. Before playing, each female made a short prayer with a pinch of corn-meal taken from the father of the *katcinas*.

Fri. Mar. 2. Ned is by no means sure that he will participate in the forthcoming Anktioni at Oraibi, as he is still afraid that it might be "indecent." He is leaving the actual decision up to the chief.

Tawaqwaptiwa has just received a letter from some outfit in St. Louis that wants Hopi representation in a National Folk Festival. Both Ned and Tawaqwaptiwa were much disturbed lest the dancers who had been to the World's Fair at Chicago should again grab all the profits; yet, when the chief ran over the list of prospective participants, he included the name of Panimptiwa, who had been to Chicago. [As it happened, the St. Louis project never materialized.]

Ned's father, Duvenimptiwa, was much upset when he told the story of his near expulsion from Oraibi and his flight to Zuñi. As Ned put it, the old man "took a pity on himself." Oddly enough, regardless of what he felt deep down, Duvenimptiwa never expressed sorrow over leaving his wife and children, but he did lament the fact that he had been forced to abandon his ripe sweet corn before it had been baked. (This episode occurred soon after the Schism of 1906. Duvenimptiwa's family outlook and his own personal philosophy were ultraconservative, but he did not want to go with the Hostiles to Hotevilla.[1] Instead, he had gone to Zuñi until things had calmed down at Oraibi, and when he returned to his natal village, he was allowed to live there without molestation.)

Ever since Luke's illness became critical, he has been a target for Christian visitors. They are using the story of newly born babies who predicted the end of the world to support Biblical references to the Day of Doom. It is odd how they seem to sense that a dying person might be more receptive to proselytizing. [This supports the theory that religion sometimes "negates" the effects of death. People turn most to religion in the atmosphere of death.]

Sat. Mar. 3. Bert says that people fear Ralph because he is crazy and talks bad. Whenever anyone offends him, he says that he is thinking up something evil for the offender and that something is going to happen pretty soon to those who displease him. [Compare the behavior of Nasiwaitiwa, p. 216.] Yet, he is allowed in the community.

Ned hired Calvin to clear weeds out of his melon patch for him.

Around noon Jack came to borrow some *katcina* equipment from Ned. He is going to be one of the Köyemsi to announce the second Anktioni that is scheduled for tomorrow night. The announcement will probably be made early tomorrow morning. Jack first admitted that he was getting ready for the part, but a minute later he said that "maybe" he would be one of the Köyemsi.

Ned is going to participate in Sunday's Anktioni. Once more the adult members of Tawaovi will serve as singers, probably in Köyemsi costumes, while George, Lawrence, and Sam will again do the dancing. A type of corn dance has been chosen for them to perform. The youngsters are busy practicing, but the singers have not yet had a rehearsal. While the boys are learning the routine of their dance, the chief beats the drum and one or two men sing. Sounds of practice can also be heard from the other kivas, even though the official announcement has not yet been made.

NOTE ON MOTOR HABITS.—Practically everyone who vehemently denies Group Mind theories will nevertheless admit the existence of different sets of motor habits among various societies. If this doesn't argue for Group Mind, in my sense of the term, how else can it be explained? What is wrong with thinking of Group Mind as a group of individual minds all of which have been culturally conditioned to react in patterned ways to certain stimuli?

MORE ON CLOWNS.—With respect to whipping, may it not be that the actions of clowns, although they have come to be sanctioned, are nevertheless felt (vaguely, of course, because of the coating of sanctity) to be ka-hopi ("un-Hopi" or "improper")? Hence, among the Hopi whipping is a common feature for all the clown groups except the Köyemsi. Then the same attitude of defending all ritual procedures is applied to the whipping, which comes to be "explained" by the customary formula of rain, crops, health, and long life. [Compare pp. 244–45 ff.]

For instance, it seems certain that "copulation" performed by clowns was from the beginning a surefire way of arousing laughter. This is what it invariably does even nowadays when the rain-crops-health formula is tagged onto such actions.

Ned received a letter from Marjorie Pierce, the sixteen-year-old daughter of Ruth's sister Barbara. Ned and Ruth once took care of Marjorie, and Ned is fond of telling how he had abstained from scolding her, even though she had once used up too many matches when starting a fire. Now Marjorie is at school in Albuquerque but is very sad. The poor child writes that she wishes she had never been born. Ned's reaction is quite praiseworthy—even though he did say, in passing, that he might "put her to a good use," by having her help his wife with housework. He wrote Marjorie a prompt reply, called her his daughter, promised to send her *piki* and parched corn, and did what he could to cheer up the despondent child.

Apropos of food sent to nonreservation schools. Food from home is the particular request of practically all boarding students. All of them hunger for the foods customarily eaten by their tribe. Ida says that her family used to send her *piki*, parched corn, and fried bread. She says that the Pimas loved *piki* so much that they pounced on any crumb that a Hopi might drop on the ground. (Besides expressing tribal superiority, this little anecdote also makes it appear likely that the Hopi students did not share their food packages with their schoolmates. Maybe it was not the custom for anyone to do so.) [Note how deeply ingrained food habits become. Small wonder that such customs are slow to change.]

Ned went to the kiva in the evening for practice. He returned with the news that the plans for Tawaovi's participation had been changed and that the members were going to be Koyala clowns instead of Köyemsi. The older men would still serve as singers, and the same youngsters were going to dance. The reason for the change stemmed from the fact that the chief had composed three new Köyemsi songs but had forgotten them. (Whether the Koyala songs were new or old is not known.) There may have been good reason for Tawaqwaptiwa's lapse of memory. Oscar had called on him in the course of the afternoon and had confused him with a long report of meetings in Flagstaff during which many of Mr. Collier's ideas had been discussed. For some inexplicable reason the government seemed much concerned with the improvement of the steps on the edge of the mesa, where the path from New Oraibi culminates. Oscar had tried to arouse the chief's civic pride in the hope that he might order the steps to be fixed. Since the area lies east of the pueblo, where newborn children are introduced to the sun and where other solar rites take place, the chief wants nothing in this vicinity to be tampered with. All this, coming only a few hours before rehearsal, so upset him that the songs he had newly composed escaped his mind.

Sun. Mar. 4. At sunrise two Köyemsi announced the second Anktioni from the Kele clan-house roof. The parts were taken by Andrew and Harold. They acted much the same as did their predecessors. [See pp. 247 ff.]

Bert talked about a number of things. He says that the colors used by *katcinas* all stand for different kinds of corn and that no *katcina* is associated with the Wuwutcim (Tribal Initiation) or the Marau rites. Hehea's mouth grew crooked from making faces at Hasokata, Bert said, and he also added a fine point omitted in the chief's story.[2] As Bert tells it, the *katcinas*, in trying to rattle Hasokata, "kicked his ass."

Bert also says that Yahoya was the brother of Matcito and the Village chief at Chimopovy. [Yahoya is reputed to have been a miracle worker, who could always bring rain. Some farmers are still believed to use his "magic songs."] Yahoya objected to Matcito's attentions to his wife, and this it was that led to Matcito's departure from Chimopovy and the founding of Oraibi. However, the chief and Ned contradict this portion of Bert's version. They say only that Yahoya was a Sun clansman from whom the late Qöyayeptiwa had inherited his "magic songs." Ned says that Qöyayeptiwa had offered to teach these songs to him, but he had refused because he preferred to be "a common man."

The special Sun clan ceremony [p. 52] is interesting because it provides one clue to the expansion of Hopi rites. The Sun clan has no major ceremony that it controls and is, consequently, considered to be a common (hence relatively unimportant) clan. Along comes Talaskwaptiwa, exalted from the ranks of the commoners by virtue of his marriage to Chief Lololoma's sister, and he starts a special Sun clan rite which he turns over to Ned. Were Ned of a different temperament, he would doubtless have expanded the ceremony by introducing, consciously or otherwise, features from the Soyal and other rituals with which he was familiar. [In spite of his diffidence, Ned constantly prayed to the Sun, which he regarded as the main god and father of all the Hopi.]

The new ceremony would probably have necessitated additional participants, and if Sun and its related clans could not furnish them, there would have been a call for help from men married to Sun clanswomen. Thus, in time, a new tribal rite might have been added to the already elaborate ceremonial calendar, and the new observances would have been owned by one (Sun) clan but performed by men of various clans, as is the case with all

Hopi rituals. This is probably the manner of growth of the Hopi schedule of ceremonies.

> NOTE.—Psychological explanations cannot be entirely disregarded when analyzing anthropological or sociological data. As long as one deals with people, their behavior cannot be properly judged if a scientist refuses to take into account psychological findings. One might as well ask a physicist to refrain from using mathematics; or a physician to abstain from learning biology.

In the afternoon a drum was heard beating to announce the appearance of the Koyala clowns who were going to fetch a Hu ("Whipper") *katcina*. Tawaqwaptiwa was the drummer, and he led into the plaza three little boys. The chief wore a Koyala headdress with black and white, horizontally striped horns. His face was whitened and his eyes and mouth were blackened, but he wore ordinary clothing and used his normal voice. The boys were naked except for little G-strings. They, too, wore Koyala (striped) headdresses, and their bodies were painted horizontally with alternate light and dark stripes. Their faces were whitened, but eyes and chin were blackened. They did a short song and dance after which they sprinkled cornmeal and made little speeches of invocation to the chiefs of the four directions, inviting the Hu *katcina* to come to Oraibi. Then the boys again clustered about the drummer and sang a new tune. "Girls, girls, come here, come here," went the words. "We lust (*chova*, "sex relations") for you, we lust for you." At the conclusion the three youthful Koyalas began to jump toward the spectators with exaggerated motions of the buttocks in and out. They singled out *ikya'as* ("father's clanswomen") from their real or ceremonial fathers' clans. They chased their *ikya'as*, especially the younger ones, and worked their buttocks as if they were copulating. Sometimes the girls scattered and the clowns chased them. [Contrast the behavior of females during the Mastop rites, p. 169.] From time to time the boys returned to the drummer, licking their lips and saying, "Sweet, very sweet."

While everyone was watching the antics of the Koyala, Sam, in the costume of a Hu *katcina*, ran into the *katcina* shrine over which a blanket had been draped. Then, when the clowns asked him to appear, a cowbell was heard issuing from the shrine, and suddenly out came Sam in Hu costume. (He was clothed as a different type of Hu from the one who whips *katcina* initiates during the Powamu ceremony.) He carried a yucca whip in each hand and charged at the Koyalas with a short but rapid shuffling step, raising and lowering his arms alternately. He came up to the clowns who drew back with alarm that was not entirely feigned. They hid behind the drummer and threw cornmeal toward the *katcina* from little sacks that were tied about their throats. (It should not be overlooked that all clowns are regarded as fathers of the *katcinas*, one of whose functions is to sprinkle *katcinas* with cornmeal.) Every now and then the Hu would threaten or strike a clown, and many a hearty "Anai!" ("Ouch!") was interspersed with the singing. At last all the performers went into the Tawaovi kiva, and the afternoon show was over.

Immediately, *ikya'as* of all sorts began to bustle about, bringing food for their *imûyis*. Old Kuwanmönim brought edibles to Ned, although he is not scheduled to perform until tonight. He went through the motions of mock copulation with her while Ruth, his wife, pretended to be jealous. [Kuwanmönim, who died years ago, was wife to Poliyestiwa, and the mother of Louis, Kane, and Harold. Poliyestiwa was their stepfather, and their real father was Panimptiwa. As a Sand clanswoman she was *ikya'a* to Ned.]

Thus did three little boys, all about eleven or younger, make public displays of sex. Ned, of course, would explain everything away by saying that they did it for rain, crops, long life, and good health. Incidentally, George, aged nine, already sleeps in the kiva whenever he pleases and is thus groomed in the art of *dumaiya*, so that at adolescence he will lose no time in getting started on his sex career.

Much "cutting out" by kiva mates may be due, in part, to the fact that they are more cognizant of each other's comings and goings. They would be sure to know when a man was to spend a night at his sheep or field camp and could then make a *dumaiya* call on his wife.

Several men from Kikötcmovi are planning to participate in tonight's dancing. None of these outsiders will join the chief's outfit at Tawaovi. Martin's youngsters and some of the Moenkopi men are the only irregulars who sometimes join the Tawaovi unit. (Virtually every non-Oraibi resident of any Third Mesa town has personally quarreled with Tawaqwaptiwa.)

In Tawaovi the men dressed for the dance. All the singers just smeared their bodies with horizontal stripes of white clay, letting the natural brown of their skins show in between. There were four clown dancers. A little fellow, a younger son of

Martin by his first wife, who had been too bashful to join in the afternoon performance, was taking part in the kiva dance at night. The boys, too, smeared themselves with white stripes. During a brief rehearsal they practiced how to elude Sam, the Hu *katcina*, who would try to whip them. Their plan was, in conjunction with the singers, to get him to face the wrong way while they escaped up the kiva ladder. The frustrated *katcina* would then beat the ladder in disgust. George was to be first, and his scheme was to bring the *katcina* to me for candy. While Sam pretended to be looking the candy over, George would escape.

The night songs contained pointed references to love for one's "aunts", i.e., father's clanswomen (*ikya'as*). These were specifically mentioned by name, but the singers taunted the Koyala dancers by saying that they did not know their *real* fathers' clanswomen because their mothers had been unfaithful. At this the dancing clowns fell to the ground and feigned sorrow because they had just learned that they were bastards.

Before the actual performance began, the entire group left the kiva for a few minutes. When the spectators had assembled within, the chief called down the hatch to say that he was a clown and not a *katcina*. He talked in his normal voice. The singers followed him down the ladder, sang a song about a cat, and scratched and meowed at each other in pairs, every set giving an imitation of a cat fight. Then the young dancers came down one at a time, each one calling the next in order by some impromptu nickname such as "Vulva-seeker." All this, of course, brought howls of laughter from the audience. [One of the most noticeable aspects of culture change is the absence of local entertainment at Old Oraibi.] Some of the youngsters had stage fright and forgot their lines, but the older men quickly prompted them.

When all had climbed into the kiva, the Koyala dancers sang of their love for particular "aunts," the singers taunted them with bastardy, the boys howled in mock anguish, and all "aunts" quickly distributed much food to their "nephews." Then the Hu *katcina* appeared, and every dancer and singer pulled a little ruse that allowed him to escape. Ned didn't do so well. He bumped into the kiva stove, lost his headgear, and knocked loose the second rung of the ladder, so that the show had to be held up while it was repaired.

As usual, the Tawaovi performance was spirited but impromptu, and it was by no means as elaborate as the observances of the other kiva groups. Martin did not participate. The Marau bunch did a Jemez *katcina* dance with ten males and three "females." It was very pretty.

The third group put on Angya *katcina*. This was so good that it got three encores.[3]

When the Koyala group returned to Tawaovi, they went through their previous routine except that all who made their escapes hid among the feminine spectators on the upraised level. This time the Hu *katcina* gave everyone a stroke or two with his whip before he got away.

After the second Koyala performance at Tawaovi the evening's entertainment was over.

Mon. Mar. 5. Luke is in pretty bad shape. He hasn't had a bowel movement for weeks and weeks. In front of his wife, Martha, he described graphically how constipated he is and how he only passes wind when he tries to evacuate. He is now properly scared and has at last made arrangements to have a nurse take him to the Agency hospital at Keam's Canyon at the same time that Louis goes for further eye treatments. Previously, Luke had delayed going because of lonesomeness. His mother, Sikyaletsnim, had offered to go with him, but he prefers Louis's presence.

Martha was all upset and cried when Luke left for the hospital. During his absence she is going to stay with Hahai'i, her mother. She says that she hates to go into her own house because it makes her sad to think of Luke's being away. (Once again, who says the Hopi are indifferent to the illness and death of loved ones?)

> NOTE.—Anktioni is one word and means "Repeat." This bears out what the chief had once said about Anktioni being a repeat of the Powamu Bean dance.

Joe mentioned quite casually that his three youngest daughters were ill with measles. In response to questions he said that no doctor of any kind had been called. He guessed that the children had measles because several cases had been reported at New Oraibi. When asked why he didn't call a doctor, he shrugged and said, "I don't know." [All three of the girls recovered.]

Ned got talking about the St. Louis trip. He does not expect to go, for he thinks that the chief will take only those whom he customarily takes to Tucson. Actually, Ned is badly disappointed, as he is most eager to go; but he speaks loyally of staying home and attending to his work, even though his face betrays his hurt and sorrow.

Tues. Mar. 6. Ida now says that Kiacwaitiwa had predicted Grace was to bear twins but that he had twisted them into one. She gives a practical reason for such actions. Women don't want to have twins because they are so troublesome to look after. (Apparently, there had been no twisting procedure, and it may be that Ida is all wrong; but her description tallies with the usual account of the process.)

Tawaqwaptiwa spoke of an occasion in the past when Lorenzo Hubbell had asked the men of New Oraibi to perform a Butterfly dance. Because he was rich, he supplied lavish feasts. People from Old Oraibi, thinking it would be nice to participate (and hoping to horn in on the good things), joined in but found that they were distinctly not wanted. The New Oraibi residents tried to stint them on the food. "Since then," says Ned blandly, "we don't like Mr. Hubbell." In the same breath he explains that he knows that Hubbell meant well and that he did not encourage the dancers from Kikötcmovi to act as they did. Still, Ned feels that if Hubbell hadn't asked for a dance, the people of Old Oraibi would not have been insulted. (Amazing logic!)

Ruth and Edith went to New Oraibi this morning to help with the wedding of Homer's (storekeeper's) brother whose Hano bride has been grinding corn at their house. As Ruth started down, Ida called out, "That girl is no good. She doesn't know how to grind corn." This is the conventional behavior of an *ikya'a* when her *imûyi* is being married. Ida is the groom's *ikya'a*. Sidney is also planning to play a large part in the wedding because Homer's father helped a great deal when Sidney's stepson was married.

Louise brought food to Ned for his clowning. She is Tep ("Greasewood") clan, and so, too, is Ned's ceremonial father. Hence she is Ned's ceremonial *ikya'a* and is supposed to feed him whenever he serves as a clown. At the same time, Ned is Louise's own ceremonial father. Hence, at the last Powamu, he made a doll for his "daughter." Thus do double relationships sometimes impose two sets of behavior patterns on the same people.

Ned says that during ritual smoking the Hopi term for partner is used in addressing a brother-in-law. *Imû'inangwa* ("male relative-in-law") is not used.

At Hubbell's trading post a Hopi was teasing a Mexican

clerk for being unfriendly to the Hopi. (Lorenzo Hubbell was himself a Mexican.) Ned remarked that the Spanish people were not at fault for the old-time attacks. Instead, he put the blame on Hopi witches who had invited the Spaniards to come and kill their people. [In many tales the Hopi ascribe enemy attacks to invitations from witches among themselves.] Then Ned went on to say that that's the way the Hopi are, in spite of the fact their name means peaceful. They are forever harming each other through witchery. They are jealous of each other, says Ned, and dissension is rife in every village. This is quite a contradiction of the idea that every pueblo is a social unit marked by integration and an ideal which has all the individuals pulling together for their mutual welfare.

NOTE.—The fact of roadwork interfering with dances leads to the idea that ceremonialism doubtlessly took up so much time in the past that there must have been a tendency for some of the rites to lapse. The ladder dance, Lamati, the Market dance, and others are examples of rituals that lapsed in ancient times. Unquestionably, the overelaborate ceremonial calendar must have given the men so little time for practical matters that some ceremonies had to be abandoned.

Wed. Mar. 7. Ida arrived with the startling news that Luke was back. It seems that he had been hospitalized in Winslow. He complained that the hospital was out of medicine, that he got no treatment of any kind, and that he was simply left all alone in a room. Some Hopi visitors heard his complaints, talked it over with the hospital officials, and got their consent to bring Luke back to Oraibi. He is staying at his mother's house. Poor Luke! Ida says that the doctor diagnosed his case as tuberculosis, and he is not expected to live very long.

Ruth and Edith again went down to New Oraibi to help in the wedding preparations of their *imûyi*. Hahai'i and other female helpers from Old Oraibi are planning to spend the night at Kikötcmovi.

NOTE.—There may well be a tie between some clown functions, such as whipping, and certain *katcina* activities. Among the Hopi, Tcaveyo, Masau'û, and other *katcinas* may play disciplinary, enforcement, or police roles that include the whipping of offenders.

Ruth kept nagging at Martin for his failure to dance with Tawaovi, which is shorthanded. She openly accused him of laziness.

There is to be a Puppet-doll, Corngrinding dance at Hotevilla soon. Martin says that such a performance is often given in conjunction with Anktioni, as is the Water-serpent dance. It is hard to understand why Tawaqwaptiwa makes such an issue of trying to keep the doll performance secret, and at the same time he is willing to go into great detail concerning the Water-serpent observances.

Martha says that her sick husband, Luke, several times heard someone trying the knob of the door to their house. He was very badly frightened, as he suspected that it might be Masau'û, coming to fetch him to the land of the dead. When Martha heard Luke speak thus, she, too, became badly scared.

Martin came by later and asked how Luke was. When he heard Martha's tale, he said that he had been planning to call on Luke, but now that Luke was so near death, he was afraid to visit him. Jay Kuwanheptiwa, an Antelope medicine man from Second Mesa, went to see Luke yesterday. So, too, did Kiacwaitiwa, the medicine man from Hotevilla, although he himself is sick.

Martha and Ida told of a strange incident that shows how prized are relationship terms and behavior. When Grace had had her baby last year, her mother had asked Hahai'i to help. Grace, being a Chimopovy woman living at Oraibi in violation of matrilocal residence, has no close relatives in Oraibi. Accordingly, Hahai'i and Martha did what they could to help Grace, who through a previous marriage had once been a female relative-in-law (*imû'wi*) to the Sun clan. This aroused the resentment of Martin's mother (Parrot), who feared that the Sun clan would continue to call Grace *imû'wi*, whereas this was now the privilege of the Parrot clan. She had made such a fuss that this year the Sun clanswomen are pointedly keeping aloof from naming-day preparations for Grace's new baby. Thus, it is clearly brought out that although some duties toward an *imû'wi* are arduous, still an *imû'wi* is a very desirable relative.

This evening Ruth, Edith, and Hahai'i returned from the wedding preparations in New Oraibi. They brought word that several Chimopovy women had arrived and had staged a dandy mud-fight. They even went so far, in keeping with the practices of other Hopi towns, as to visit a kiva and douse with mud Duveyauoma, a man of the same clan as the groom. Everyone pronounced the wedding to have been a great success.

Thurs. Mar. 8. Martha has been staying at the home of her mother-in-law, Sikyaletsnim, since Luke went there on his return from the hospital. Still, she doesn't feel at ease there because Andrew, Luke's stepfather, has only recently cut out Luke's own father, Humiletstiwa. She senses that Andrew resents the presence of Luke and herself, exactly as might be the case with a stepfather among us.

Fri. Mar. 9. Jim came up from New Oraibi. He is having his uncle Bert make him a bracelet. Jim and Oscar have remained more friendly with Bert than with his brother Tawaqwaptiwa.

When a little dusty wind blew up, Jim said that the old-time Hopi used to believe that crossing one's fingers would make a twister turn aside. He went on to say that this was a fact and that he believed it, quite in contrast to his usually superior attitude toward native Hopi beliefs. [Another way that boys sometimes divert a twister is to throw stones into its center. This is considered to be dangerous, inasmuch as the spirit of a whirlwind is supposed to understand the Hopi language and may retaliate by sending sickness to the stone throwers.]

Nothing much going on today. With so many women at the wedding in Kikötcmovi the pueblo seemed deserted. Only the chief remains busy in his kiva, making up songs and holding rehearsals for the anticipated trip to St. Louis.

For the first time Ned came out with a dig at the chief. The chief had asked him to speak to Ida about dancing at St. Louis. Then the chief had changed his mind and had invited Florine to join the party, without even waiting for Ida to be approached. Ned admitted that this "didn't sound good" to him.

Sat. Mar. 10. All the children are manufacturing wooden or stone tops and are making them spin by whipping them. Small girls as well as boys are equally interested. [Little boys were still whipping tops in the 1950s.]

Saw Betty crying loudly while soaking wet. Sam explained that she had been naughty and that her grandmother Masamösi had doused her. This does seem to be a common Hopi form of punishment. [Conventional punishments continue to include dousing with water and subjecting to smoke. In addition, nowadays, unruly children are sometimes slapped and even strapped.]

Sun. Mar. 11 to Tues. Mar. 13. At Winslow, Arizona, with Joe.

The following informal items have been gleaned at Winslow or deal with things that happened while we were out of the pueblo.

On our way into town we passed a group of Old Oraibi women walking barefooted across country in the open sun. We recognized Hahai'i, Edna, and Qöyawaisi. They were gathering accessories for the making of *metates,* an activity presently wide-spread in Hopiland, and Humiletstiwa had gone to meet them with a couple of burros on which their loads were to be packed.

Joe says that in the old days menstruating women simply wore any old piece of cloth to absorb the discharge and that some of them wore no pads at all. Whenever they sat down for any length of time, they were likely to stain the ground. The Hopi have an amazing indifference to menstrual blood, which so many primitive groups consider to be terribly dangerous.

Andrew, who happened to be in Winslow, rode back with us in Quincys' truck, and soon he began a song, linking Quincy with a woman named Lucy. Quincy retaliated by singing of Andrew's relations with two other women. Thereupon Andrew became uneasy and protested, saying that they ought not mention these matters in my presence.

Dick teased Ida for having an Apache sweetheart. She retorted that she would have nothing to do with any man, and also that her mother had told her when she went off to school to have nothing to do with boys of other tribes whose language she could not talk. Louise got after her husband to make him stop teasing Ida.

NOTE.—Although Bill takes meals with his sister Mary, he sleeps, as a rule, inside his store. This makes it easier for him to go *dumaiya* whenever he likes.

Wed. Mar. 14. Ned isn't feeling well again, but he was able to take his regular turn at herding today. I wonder if he really has gonorrhea.

Kelnimptiwa called out for trading this morning. A whole host of women scurried over, but very little actual trading was done. Many of them just welcome an opportunity to get together.

There is some talk of a Palulokong ("Water-serpent") dance at Hotevilla, but there is nothing certain about it.

Hahai'i is busy preparing food in return for the gifts received by a Sun clan girl who took part in the Buffalo dance at

Kikötcmovi some time ago. The girl was the partner of an *imûyi* named Paul, who had brought her a load of wood. Paul is *imûyi* to all the women of the Sun clan. Hence they are getting together to repay his gift to one of them. (Is this an example of food exchange?)

A heavy haze is hanging over all the low places. It is variously explained. Some give a purely physical explanation and say that it merely indicates the approach of rain. Others claim that the haze is longing for a woman. Bert has no explanation at all. Ned says it represents the haze of witches who are being burned in the other world.

During the recent Koyala performance at Tawaovi, Parrot clanswomen acted as *ikya'as* to all of Martin's children, even to those he had had by his first wife. Parrot females are women of Martin's clan and so function as *ikya'as* to all of his offspring.

Also, Hahai'i calls all Masau'û clanswomen *ikya'as* because they are women of her husband's father's clan. Nawisoa, who is Masau'û, gave a beautiful plaque to one of the racers who ran for her clan.

(It is confirmed that the Hopi word for prayer is *nawakna*. Literally this means want or desire. This is somewhat blunter than our word, but the underlying idea of wanting something is much the same.)

A Paiute from Utah came into town to trade buckskin for saddle blankets. He aroused much curiosity, and a great crowd flocked about his car. He spoke good English and was fat, dirty, and jolly. A New Oraibi couple, complete strangers, are going to put him up for the night. He will probably leave a gift for them when he departs.

Tom came in last night. He thinks that Hotevilla will have a Puppet-doll dance next Wednesday. Neither he nor Joe has ever seen one. Tom believes that the dolls will be Shalako and Palhik. [See Fig. 19.] This checks with what others have said and jibes with the traditional performance of Anktioni. Tom thinks that no more *katcina* dances will be held at Oraibi until the Niman because of roadwork and because of the chief's preoccupation with the invitation to St. Louis.

Tom also believes that Tawaqwaptiwa is planning to take to St. Louis all his wife's kinfolk, including Panimptiwa and his crowd, who were at Chicago. This explains why Ned is left out of consideration. Apparently, when the chief said that he didn't want the Oraibi people who had danced at Chicago to go to St. Louis, he had meant only the four participants from New Oraibi.

Thurs. Mar. 15. At last there is detailed confirmation for one version of Panimptiwa's grudge against members of the Sun clan. It seems that Shalakmana, present wife of Ned's older brother Sidney, had been living with Kuwanletcioma of the Badger clan, brother of Panimptiwa and of Dell from New Oraibi. At the time in question Sidney was a widower, and he had "cut out" Kuwanletcioma and married Shalakmana. For this, Panimptiwa has never forgiven Sidney or his Sun clan, although Dell has long since gotten over her resentment.

Ruth spent last night, while Ned was away at his sheep camp, with her maternal niece Edith. Ruth's sister Lucy gave birth to a girl yesterday. It was a large baby, but Lucy is said to have had an easy delivery.

The Paiute who spent the night at Kikötcmovi left a bracelet for his hostess. He now regards her husband as a "contact man" and plans to send him buckskins for trading. The making of friends and trading partners by Hopi with Paiute, Zuñi, Navaho, Havasupai, and so on is a well-established practice. If, as seems likely, it was also an ancient custom, it would account for the diffusion of Plateau and even Plains traits to the Pueblos.

Old Kuwanmönim dropped in around lunchtime. She insisted that she would take nothing but plain bread and black coffee and explained that she ate nothing but traditional Hopi foods. Apparently, she has forgotten, if she ever knew, that "store" bread and coffee were both "foreign" to the ancient Hopi. She has been used to these foods since childhood and finds them agreeable to her Hopi palate. Strange how youthful food habits persist.

NOTE.—When talking about witches, don't forget to stress the part played by "doctors" in keeping these ideas alive. It's a very convenient loophole for their failures, all of which they blame on powerful witches. Hence it is to the advantage of medicine men to keep alive notions of illness brought about through witchery.

Louis's Clara is reported to be pregnant again. If so, her baby will find itself at birth to be an uncle or aunt (by our system) to a boy of about five and a girl of three. Uncles or aunts younger than one's self are no uncommon phenomenon here.

The extended kinship system, which disregards generation lines, invariably provides a person with youthful relatives who are terminologically older than himself (as baby grandparents, for example). Such an occurrence is not regarded as unusual when it happens in the immediate family.

Luke is emaciated. His one medicine is cod liver oil, and Louise, his sister, regularly takes his temperature with a thermometer that was somehow acquired. Luke refused an offer of canned milk and cereal because he doesn't like anything but ordinary Hopi foods. He claims that at the hospital fresh milk loosened his bowels and made him feel worse than ever.

Ned got home from herding and chatted before bedtime. He said that sometimes, when he thought of it, he felt sorry for poor "White" people who had neither land nor homes and thus starved or "tramped" on occasion, even though they were willing and anxious to work. On the other hand, a Hopi who starved had no one to blame but himself.

Fri. Mar. 16. Kelnimptiwa called out in the forenoon for women and girls to go to the house of Solimana for a general corngrinding in anticipation of her granddaughter's (Mary's) forthcoming wedding. Mary is a Bakavi girl, and her engagement was announced by her pregnancy. The father is a boy from New Oraibi, and the baby has already been born. This case brought forth gossip about another Bakavi girl who was said to have married a boy she didn't really like because she found herself pregnant by him.

Speaking of Bakavi, last night two youngsters, Sam and Lawrence, talked knowingly about sex and sweethearts. Sam then flatly asked why I didn't call on a certain Bakavi woman who was hungry for money and willing to take on all comers.

Yesterday Jenny stayed home from school with a fever, but no "doctor" was called. Today George is down with a headache but is being left to himself. Why will not these people call in medical help, even of their own sort, when there is no question of their love for their children?

Tom reported that tomorrow Charles is going to call the men to spin and practice Niman *katcina* songs in his kiva. The custom of having men hold spinning or weaving bees, or of having women grind together for weddings, certainly crosscuts clan and family lines, and is a more important village-wide activity than appears on the surface. It is especially valuable for unmarried but nubile girls, who thus get a chance to show their diligence and skill. It also helps them to get reciprocal aid when their own marriages take place. Whenever females grind corn, they smear meal on their faces, supposedly as a cosmetic device, but also to show, especially if they are single, that they are not lazy.

Strange about old Duvenimptiwa. He begrudges every moment spent on interviews because it keeps him from his weaving. Even when he brings in wool or cotton and spins as he talks, he still feels put out, although it would take him hours and hours of weaving to earn what is paid to him. The urge to do traditional Hopi tasks makes him resent my persistence in seeking information.

Sat. Mar. 17. Soon after sunrise Charles went through the streets. As he went he called out, in a voice only slightly raised, for all the men to come to Hawiovi to spend the day. Hawiovi is being used because this is the kiva that will sponsor the Niman in the coming summer. Ned did not go, preferring to be interviewed. In fact, Ned says that he may not report at all for dancing in the Niman because he may decide to "rest" this year.

Louis called on his way to attend the spinning session. He says that tomorrow all the men will gather to clean out the local horse pond which is so muddy that the horses won't drink from it. Ned doubted if any disciplinary *katcinas* would come to supervise the work because horses would be used in the work, and *katcina* costumes might frighten them. Harold is to be *mongwi* ("chief") of the project and Village chief for the day.

Qöyawaisi told a story of her youth. She was a member of the Lakon and Oaqöl societies, but she had never wanted to join the Marau. [These are the three feminine secret societies at Oraibi. Women were generally free, if they wished, to join any one or all three. A handful of sacred cornmeal, given to a member, was all that was necessary for getting a sponsor.] One day her sister called her, saying that she was wanted at the Marau kiva. She, in all innocence, started to go down, but her grandmother yelled to her when she was halfway down the ladder, so she climbed back up, with several Marau members in pursuit. If one of these had caught her she would automatically have been initiated as a trespasser,[4] with her captor serving as her ceremonial mother. As it was, Qöyawaisi escaped, but in recompense for her near intrusion her mother provided a feast for the Marau society.

Charles revealed that only two songs had been rehearsed at the day's spinning; and that only ten or eleven men had showed up. One of the songs was that used in announcing the Niman [pp. 175 ff.]; and the second had just been composed by the chief. All the participants were fed by Tom and his wife, Anita, who is also Charles's sister. Several women helped Anita fix *somiviki* for the men in the kiva. Had a stew been provided, the practice would have lasted into the afternoon; but when *somiviki* is served, rehearsals end at noon. Sometimes the songs are gone over again in the evening.

Sun. Mar. 18. Kelnimptiwa cried out this morning on behalf of Harold, notifying all men and boys to report for the task of clearing out the befouled horse pond. There was a good response, with practically all able-bodied men taking part. The size of the turnout and the cooperation that prevailed were amazing. For example, Jack, though he was suffering from a sprained back, took part in the work; and so did several men who seldom participate in other village activities. No fewer than twenty-three grown men and boys showed up for volunteer work. This was *positively* the greatest example of community enterprise that I've ever seen. There was no time wasted in talk. Those who had horses hitched them up to shovel-shaped scrapers, and the others either filled the scrapers up or tipped them over at the edge of the pond where dirt was being dumped. Thirteen pairs of horses were employed, eleven scraping and two loosening the dirt with plowlike devices. The chief did hand labor with pick and mattock, and Bert and Lomanimptiwa also worked by hand. Except for a brief period of rest called by Harold, the group worked steadily from about one to half-past four. Everyone remained in excellent spirits, and there was constant jesting and teasing.

In addition to the Old Oraibi turnout there were three volunteers from Kikötcmovi. One was Hubbell's clerk Horace, who happened to be visiting Poliyestiwa when he learned of the work and decided to stay on; another was Sidney, Ned's brother, who has retained many ties with Old Oraibi; and the third was James Sikwi, Tawaqwaptiwa's brother. James came up specifically to lend a hand when he found out what was going on.

No wonder that the cleaning of springs was regarded as a semifestive affair in the old days and that it was important enough to be called out by the official Tca'akmongwi ("Crier chief"). What with the spirit of good fellowship and cooperation and what with the prospect of the women and girls soon to come with food, it must have been sort of a holiday despite the labor involved. [The Hopi have a knack of combining pleasure with communal work.] The response and cooperation make the idea of "pueblo spirit" and unity stand out as a much stronger factor in the past than can be guessed in the present-day situation. [See pp. 146 and 157.]

The tendency to laugh at mishaps was noteworthy. If the harness on a man's team broke, if a boy fell while trying to lift a load, or if any untoward thing occurred, it was the signal for loud hoots, catcalls, and wisecracks. This may be tied up with the timidity that these people overtly display. Perhaps the wisecracks give sanctioned release to covert (suppressed) aggressiveness. Yet, when some real trouble develops, there is no stinting of help. For example, just as the work was ending and after Tawaqwaptiwa had announced that he would sponsor further work next week, a team ran wild. Promptly, half a dozen men grasped at reins and harness and helped each other to untangle chains and to soothe the horses.

Fred Eggan said that he had seen several interesting things at Mishongnovi, including a kiva dedication with *sipapu* rites during which he and the Hopi onlookers had to turn their backs. Also, at Mishongnovi, he saw Kokopele, the flute-playing, humpbacked *katcina*.[5] He reported that the details of Tawaqwaptiwa's account were essentially correct. The dancers wore false penises of long gourds, painted red, and did a hectic "business" with female spectators. They also ran *ñötiwa* with bunches of blossoms.

Fred has found that in some villages the Soyal is not always an outgrowth of the Wuwutcim branch of the Tribal Initiation. Sometimes the Soyal is automatically entrusted to members of the Al division; and sometimes, to Tao. Oraibi emphasizes the Wuwutcim branch, but other Hopi pueblos may stress Al or Tao. In such cases the Village chief who controls the Soyal would be an Al or Tao man instead of a Wuwutcim. The importance of the Kwans also gets different recognition than at Oraibi. When the Village chief of Mishongnovi died, for instance, his Soyal (?) *tiponi* ("official fetish") was buried with him at his request; and the Kwan chief was forced to fashion a new one.

Sex is as truly bawdy on Second Mesa as it is here. Frank Masakwaptiwa, in addition to indulging freely with many partners, is reported to have lived in Hopi incest for a year with a related clan sister. Thereafter, she had returned to her husband. Ned was able to name three men with whom the woman had lived for varying periods of time, coming back to her husband after each affair. Is this to be considered as monogamy?

Not only do all the Hopi villages appear to be divided against themselves, but also the Taos villages. While Fred was at Fort Defiance, he had met a Taos Indian who had reported much internal strife at Taos and had expressed the opinion that his pueblo was the worst of all. Thus, *potential* disintegration is a characteristic feature of Pueblo life. This leads to the following questions: Why don't more pueblos fall apart? Why didn't they split up more frequently in times past? How far back into the past does the disintegrative tendency go? Is it, as has been suggested, a relatively new phenomenon resulting from disagreement about the reception of "White" culture; or is it an older trait, as Eggan is inclined to believe, whereby tensions and aggressions once directed against outside enemies came, with peace, to be turned inward within a given settlement? [At present, the *potential* for disintegration, as well as the constant bickering that is so typical of all Pueblo Indians, seems to be directly linked to crowded conditions and lack of space. In a pueblo everyone knows what everyone else is doing, and privacy is virtually impossible. Such an atmosphere may help to explain why the Pueblos cherish secrecy so much; and why accusations of all kinds, including witchcraft, are so common.]

Mon. Mar. 19. Rode out to measure Cedric's fields. He depends mainly on one large farm, but his brother Charles has several small plots in various locations. Cedric claims to get more from his one field than Charles does from all his scattered plots combined.

At Solimana's request Robert Talas fetched a load of wood to be used in the coming nuptials of Solimana's granddaughter.

NOTE.—When interpreting religion from the point of view of its being a sociocultural force, don't neglect the fact that almost universally religion deals not only with death but also with procreation. Through its control of sex (marriage) a society seeks to sustain its life as a group and thus perpetuates itself from one generation to another.

Ida looked at a picture on page 415 of a copy of the *National Geographic Magazine* for October, 1933. It showed some Persian women examining an airplane. Ida noted the concealed faces and said, "*Dumaiya!*" To an objection that they were women and not men she retorted, "Well, that's all right. Some women do it just the same as men."

Tues. Mar. 20. Joe confirms the *chimona* story of the toothed vulva, in much the same detail as published by Stephen.[6] [Chimona is one form of locoweed (Jimson). It is sometimes used by medicine men.]

Joe too says that a Village chief ought to be the last one in a pueblo to go to bed at night.

Joe also spoke about the quarrel between the chief and Bert. He favored me with a long harangue. According to him, the trouble started when Bert, who was ill, confessed to Kiacwaitiwa that Tawaqwaptiwa's behavior was worrying him. Bert felt that the chief was paying too much attention to the contentions at Moenkopi, whereas by tradition he was *never* supposed to be bothered with people's grievances. (The idea that subjects were not supposed to trouble a chief with their problems was well known to Tawaqwaptiwa.) When Joe was asked to whom, in ancient times, a Hopi with a grievance could properly turn in the hope of getting help or redress, Joe replied, "No one, I guess, in the old days." (Joe may have been wrong. It is likely that the Village Kaletaka ["Warrior chief"] heard and possibly even settled disputes.)

Bert leveled another indictment against his brother, namely, he failed to smoke Hopi tobacco and even poked fun at those who did since he was a habitual user of American tobacco. Thus Bert felt that the chief was going too far off the old Hopi path and that was why he had quarreled with him. Thereupon, Tawaqwaptiwa had promptly put him out of the Soyal.

The granddaughter of Solimana went below to New Oraibi this evening to begin grinding corn for her wedding. Her baby was included in the little bridal procession. The load of wood mentioned yesterday was brought not by Robert but by his brother, who is married to a Tep ("Greasewood") woman. Both Solimana and her granddaughter are Tep.

Hahai'i remarks bitterly that the people "just hate us." As she tells it, people come to feasts and profess friendliness to the Sun clan, "but they hate us just the same."

Wed. Mar. 21.

NOTE.—The relationship of *ikya'a* and *imûyi*, which is so sexual at bottom, makes it appear as if at some time in the past the Hopi did *not* object to the marriage of a man with his father's sister's daughter (*ikya'a*). Obviously, the business of

pretending to copulate with Salt Woman and naming an *ikya'a*
as one's partner; of shooting an arrow into a shrine while calling out the name of an *ikya'a;* and of simulating copulation
with *ikya'as* when a man acts as a clown, all point to an association which at some time in the past was undoubtedly
popular and proper even though it is now officially taboo. On
the other side, a male probably never married his mother's
brother's daughter, nor was a girl customarily wed to her father's
sister's son. (Check this through carefully. Even if cross-cousin
marriage appears as a possibility in the past, be careful of such
arguments. Use them warily, especially if they don't seem to
lead anywhere even after the facts and probabilities have
been established.)[7]

NOTE.—In a primitive community, religion is a *practical*
matter and an outstanding factor in the culture of the group.
It is one of the mechanisms for sustaining the continuation of a
society. Thus, ethics, as we understand the term, may not be
important. Nor do primitive societies concern themselves with
the religious beliefs of others. To them a religious system is like
a type of food production. Just because the Hopi herd and farm
is no reason for them to expect everybody else to herd and
farm. No more can the Hopi see why they should force their
beliefs on others; nor why other religions should be judged in-
adequate; nor why all the peoples of the world should sub-
scribe to a single faith. That is why primitive religions appear
to be so "tolerant." Is there any primitive religion that tries to
make converts? My guess is that this sort of thing comes in
with sophisticated and, perhaps, consciously wrought religions
and is a late factor in world history.

The so-called measles epidemic rages on and is worse
than ever. This morning Kuwanmönim walked sadly by, with
tears in her eyes. Later, it was explained that she was grieving
because her son's (Kane's) second youngest boy, Arlen, had just
died. Kiacwaitiwa said that the "measles" had got *inside* the
child and so caused its death. Kiacwaitiwa reports that three in-
fants have died at Hotevilla and that he could do nothing to save
them. Kane had been herding when Arlen fell ill, and his wife
took the baby to her mother at New Oraibi last Sunday. The
"White" field matron, Miss Cunningham, came to examine the
child and suggested having it taken to the Keam's Canyon hospital. When its mother refused, Miss Cunningham rode to Kane's

sheep camp with the news; but he, too, refused to have the
child taken to a hospital. Poor Kuwanmönim had wept bitterly
as she told the tale to Hahai'i.

Baby Ann is all broken out, Sandra is sick, and Milton
is ill. Hahai'i says that Milton became sick because he was
frightened by the whirlwind that appeared during a windstorm
the other day. Ned would probably have said, "The power of
that whirlwind got into him."

Thurs. Mar. 22. Some or all the children in every household are
ill with fever and "measles," but as usual, no medicine men have
been called by anyone.

As several of us were strolling about the mesa in order to
take a few miscellaneous pictures, Hahai'i appeared crying and
sobbing. She begged Charles to run for Duvenimptiwa, which
immediately suggested that Luke was dying. Solimana joined
Hahai'i, and they sobbed and wept in unison until Duvenimptiwa
appeared, whereupon they returned to the village.

The notion that the weeping concerned Luke was somewhat abated when his father, Humiletstiwa, was seen driving his
burros to Lenangva. However, it turned out that Luke had died
and that Humiletstiwa was going to bury him. The grief-stricken
father was merely hastening to get an essential chore done before
he started on his sad task. Then it was recalled that Louise had
been seen scurrying from the house with baby Ann on her back,
sick though the child was. Evidently Louise was taking Ann to
the house of her grandmother Puhumana, so that she wouldn't
be in the presence of death. Later, the whole family took refuge
at Puhumana's.

As soon as Luke's passing was definitely ascertained,
Charles said that he was going home as he didn't want to see
the burial.

A few minutes later Tom and Ned came to call. We were
all sitting around rather glumly when Ned protested that it wasn't
right for us to show sorrow. Similarly, when Ida arrived to carry
out her usual duties, her eyes were dry and she was chipper and
smiling, even though she is extremely fond of Martha and had
liked Luke very much. More surprising still was the fact that Ada
was with her and was smiling and happy, without a sign of having
wept. These people certainly condition themselves to shake off
grief, and thus, ostensibly, they make a show of not mourning
their dead.

NOTE.—Let us assume that in former times the two most important village-wide ceremonies at Oraibi, aside from the *katcina* cult, were the Wuwutcim-Soyal that the Bear clan had owned; and the Momtcit that had belonged to the Spider clan. The Soyal had at one time emphasized hunting [see O.O., p. 144, and fn. 19] and the Momtcit had stressed war. As these two activities lost their prominence in Hopi culture, the Soyal succeeded in transforming itself into a primarily agricultural ceremony; but the Momtcit, after the "Whites" had brought Indian warfare to a close, could do nothing but become extinct. As a result, the Spider owners of the Momtcit would have become much more resentful of the culture changes introduced or backed by the "Whites" than the Bear leaders of the Soyal. In other words, the Spider clan would have become more hostile to "White" influence than Bear clanspeople. Possibly, this helps to explain why the Spider clan developed into Hostiles, while their phratry-mates, the Bear, became Friendlies when Old Oraibi split in 1906.

This hypothesis should be carefully and cautiously thought through.

Fri. Mar. 23. Last day of residence at Old Oraibi. Went to Kikötcmovi for supper at Lee's and arranged to have her brother drive me to tonight's Puppet-doll dance at Hotevilla.

Ned and George came along. Sat in Hawiovi kiva to watch the series of Anktioni night dances. The first set of dancers impersonated the Taos Snow *katcina;* and the second and third groups appeared as mixed *katcinas,* including in their performance one song and dance that Ned said usually went with the Palulokong ("Water-serpent") rites. Even the words dealt with the water-serpent. Throughout the evening there seemed to be a sort of Water-serpent dance routine, although the main feature, done by the fourth set to appear, was a Puppet-doll dance and not a Water-serpent performance. [An account of this Puppet-doll dance is given in chapter X, section L.]

Earlier in the day, Hahai'i and He'e'e impersonators had appeared in Hotevilla with a large following of assorted *katcinas.* They had made a circuit of the pueblo, wandered about the streets, and disappeared into their respective kivas. [This feature, *qöqöntinumya,* is a standard part of the Powamu observances. In fact, a detailed analysis of the Puppet-doll rites reveals many resemblances, such as the forced sprouting of corn in superheated kivas, which is done in all three ceremonies. In effect, the Puppet-doll dance seems to be a substitute for the Water-serpent dance which, as a traditional feature in the Anktioni series, used to repeat many aspects of the Powamu. This is an important point to remember.]

Sat. Mar. 24. Was driven into Winslow and boarded a Santa Fe train for home.

Got home without incident, but full of remembrances of a memorable residence at Old Oraibi.

CHAPTER X

Some Rites, Dances, and Other Activities

[*This chapter consists of a number of items, taken from the diary, that were judged to be too long and too important to be left as journal entries. They are summarized in the diary under their proper dates, and these dates have been retained for purposes of identification. The items are:*

A. *Ann's Naming Rites*
B. *A Marau Dance at Chimopovy [Shongopavi]*
C. *Hano's Ya-ya'a Dance*
D. *A Lakon Performance at Chimopovy*
E. *The Soyal Katcina Comes to Oraibi*
F. *Observations on a Wuwutcim Performance at Hotevilla*
G. *Two Sets of Night Dances at Old Oraibi*
H. *New Oraibi Stages a Buffalo Dance*
I. *Closing Powamu Activities at Oraibi*
J. *Dancing in a Bean Dance at Oraibi*
K. *Men's Footrace by Clans at Oraibi*
L. *A Puppet-doll Dance at Hotevilla*]

A. Ann's Naming Rites[1]

Sept. 10, 1933 [p. 45]. At a quarter to four this morning I was awakened by Andrew, the stepfather of Louise, in order to help name her baby Ann. Today, the twentieth day after its birth, is the naming day.

When I arrived, all the men and several of the women visitors were still asleep, but the mother, paternal grandmother, Puhumana, and two "paternal aunts" (*ikya'as*), actually the father's clanswomen, were awake. One of the latter was preparing a

284

soapweed (dried yucca root) solution. When it was ready, Pu-humana, who had chief charge of the ceremony, washed Louise's head. Next, two "aunts" soaped her head thoroughly after which her hair was rinsed. Then, the baby was taken from its cradle by one of the "aunts." The grandmother and "aunts," one after the other, washed the child's head; and then I was invited to do the same.

The grandmother next prepared an ordinary soap bath in a hard porcelain pan and bathed the baby thoroughly from head to foot. It was then wrapped in warm blankets, and the grand-mother smeared its little face with cornmeal and put cornmeal smears on its breast and back. The child, which had cried very little, was now allowed to rest, although it did not fall asleep.

The strands of dried yucca fiber used for the washing were thrown on a small tray containing other refuse covered with sand. Then the woman in charge took a small brush and with it removed the last of the ceremonial cornmeal lines from each of the four walls and from a beam in the ceiling. These lines are for keeping track of the first twenty days till the baby is named. One line is removed all around every four days at which times the mother and child receive head washes. These lines are said to make a ceremonial "house" in which the child spends the first twenty days of its life.

As the grandmother removed the last line, she caught the meal in her hand and put it on the refuse tray. Then she took two live glowing embers from the fire, which has burned con-tinuously for twenty days, and put them on the tray. After this ritual she went out alone to dump the tray and its contents on a special maternity rubbish heap. [See Fig. 12.]

When she returned, one "paternal aunt" handed her the child and the naming began. The grandmother took three ears of corn, two of which had been placed by the child's side soon after the birth to act as its "mother" and "grandmother." These lie beside the baby throughout the twenty-day period. The third ear was brought in by one of the "aunts." All three ears had been washed in soapweed suds even before the baby and the mother had been washed. [Each ceremonial ear of corn must be full of kernels to the very tip and must not be defective in any way.]

The three ears are touched to the child's breast and waved rhythmically away and back again as the namer recites a special formula wishing the child health and happiness. Then a name is given, and the baby is passed on to the next person concerned. The grandmother and two "aunts" gave the child Hopi names, and then it was handed to me. I recited in English approximately what the other's had said in Hopi. "Now I am going to speak to you. I wish you long life and happiness, without sickness, till the time when you go to sleep (die), a very old lady. Now I am going to give you a name. I want you to be called Ann as long as you live."

When I had finished, everyone present said, "*Askwali*" (the woman's word for "thank you"). Then a third "aunt" gave the child a name, and the ceremony was over for the time being. The mother sat down to nurse the child, and all the women repeated the child's names, commented on them, and said that the child was a little butterfly because it had been born on the day of a Butterfly dance.

Just before dawn the grandmother in charge wrapped the baby warmly, put it on her back, and tucked it in with her shawl so that it was snugly carried. [See Fig. 22.] The mother picked up the corn-ear "mothers" and a tray of cornmeal, and in single file we walked out to the east edge of the mesa. Just as the very first light appeared, we each took a handful of cornmeal, breathed on it, made a silent prayer to the sun to give the child long life and happiness, and then threw the meal toward the sun. The grandmother also repeated all the names the child had received and gave the baby two long sucking kisses.

On the way back Louise said that on presenting her firstborn child to the sun, a mother is supposed to wear her white wedding garment while the baby has on a tiny duplicate of a wedding robe. Unfortunately, this was impossible for Louise because she has not yet had a Hopi wedding. She expects to go through the ceremony this winter.

Back in the house four big bowls of mutton stew (*nukwivi*) had been spread out on the floor, together with a pudding (*pikami*) made of sweetened cornmeal mixed with wheat and baked or steamed overnight, chili peppers, bread, and coffee. (Pikami would be delicious were it not for the usual sand.)

About twelve or fifteen people ate first, and almost as soon as one had finished, another would come in. To avoid any show of favoritism the maternal grandmother of the baby had gone to every house in the pueblo inviting all the people to come and eat.

B. A Marau Dance at Chimopovy [Shongopavi][2]

Sept. 23, 1933 [p. 58]. Arrived at Chimopovy during an intermission of the Marau dance. Later, several other men came from Third Mesa.

Bert repeated the notion that most women were ashamed to witness the Marau because of the kilts worn by some of the female performers. Use of kilts explains why this dance is popularly known as "Knee-high." Actually, there is no bold display of sex and no salacious touch of any kind. [Compare p. 53.] [At Hotevilla, as at Chimopovy, most women like to join Marau and dislike the Oaqöl.][3]

When the dancers appeared, there were about twenty-five, of all ages. Each went barefooted and wore an old-fashioned Hopi dress (*manta*) and a long red and white, ceremonial mantle (*atü'ü*), draped across the shoulders and fastened below the throat. Between the dress and the mantle, or under the *manta*, in the fashion of a petticoat, many of the performers had on silk shawls or other garments. Each woman had cornmeal daubed on her face, and in each hand she carried a flat board, about eighteen inches long and some six inches wide. These boards were painted in various designs, but generally had a human face (Muyingwa's [?]) and cloud or rain symbols in the middle.[4] Each board had corn painted at the bottom and a corn tassel fastened to the back. The boards, or prayer sticks, were held out in front of the body, one in each hand, and were waved rhythmically up and down, from a point just below the knee up to a point above the head. As they sang, the women bent their heads, and when they lifted their boards high, the tassels waved above them like a field of corn blown by the wind.

A shrine, somewhat like a small Dutch oven, had been erected in the Women's Plaza, which is not the same performance place used by masculine dancers. Nearby there had been buried in the ground, or mother earth, a number of sacred objects, including some that were later to be used in the Powamu ceremony. At Chimopovy, as far as could be told, the Bluebird clan, which is in the Spider phratry, owns the Marau; and the Katcina clan, which is in the same phratry as Parrot, owns the Powamu. At Oraibi, the phratry containing Lizard owns the Marau, and the Badger clan owns the Powamu. (There may be a linkage in the minds of the Oraibi Hopi between the Badger clan and the Marau and Powamu rites.)

The Marau performers came out of their kiva in single file and proceeded toward the shrine. A few yards behind them marched the female leader who was followed, a little later, by a dancer dressed as a *kaletaka* ("warrior"), who wore a short masculine dance kilt and a fox pelt attached to her wrist. She also had a little bell of the clapper type tied below the right knee. Between knees and thighs she was painted with intersecting straight black

lines in the fashion of a ticktacktoe game. (On her back she sometimes wears a sun-shield.) The ordinary dancers lined up to form
a nearly closed circle; and as soon as the leader and *kaletaka*
took up positions at one end of the line, they all began to sing,
bow from the hips, and wave their painted boards. As they
sang, the women moved sideways counterclockwise, gradually
closing the gap to make a full circle. The *kaletaka* moved backward instead of sideways and waved her fox pelt, instead of a
painted board, up and down. Before the song began each of two
regular performers placed a woven plaque, heaped with sweet-
corn meal cakes (*qömi*), bread, or peaches, on the ground in the
center of the ring.

After a few minutes of singing, two more *kaletakas*, without bells, entered the plaza. Each had a bow and two arrows,
and one carried a bundle of rushes or green vegetation. She
threw the bundle forward, toward the dancers, and then she and
her partner shot at it. (This is a fertility rite. The bundle stands
for crops, and the arrow-shooting signifies lightning, which means,
of course, rain.) After the arrows had been fired, they were
picked up, the bundle was tossed ahead, and the whole procedure
was repeated until the dancing women were reached. Thereupon
the bundle was thrown into the center, and the arrows were shot
into the ring. After that the two *kaletakas* entered the circle,
picked up the plaques of food, bowed to each other, and scattered the food in all directions. Men and boys crowded around
the dance group and scrambled for everything tossed near them.
[The significance of these actions seems to be that the ceremony
is capable of producing an unlimited supply of good things for
the Hopi. All the male spectators rush eagerly to get whatever
is thrown, regardless of its material value.]

When nothing was left, the pair of *kaletakas* tossed their
bundle of vegetation back toward the kiva by stages, shot at it,
and retraced their earlier route. Shortly after their departure the
song concluded, and the performers unwound their circle with
the leader going first, followed by the "dancing *kaletaka*." Two
of the dancers picked up the empty plaques and then retrieved the
bundle of vegetation and the arrows that were left by the
"special *kaletakas*."

The songs used by the women are shorter than those of
men *katcina* dancers, and their dance steps are less strenuous
and complicated. Correspondingly, the waits between performances are longer. The part of the "dancing *kaletaka*" was played
by one woman for most of the day, but another woman substi-

tuted for her at the conclusion. A different pair of Marau women acted as "shooting *kaletakas*" at each appearance of the society. Whenever they had trouble in shooting or aiming the arrows, the male spectators would shout derisively. (In the Flute dance, too, and at other serious performances by women participants, the men watching do not hesitate to hoot or to make fun of the female performers.)

At the concluding dance the masculine chief of the Marau came out with medicinal water with which he asperged the circle of dancers from within. He then poured out the remaining liquid at the shrine. (There was no distribution of sacred cornmeal or prayer feathers such as male dancers customarily receive.)

A number of women dancers, while still in costume, were seen to hurry home between songs in order to attend to the wants of diners or to nurse children. What with the women's need of continuing their usual tasks, it is no wonder that their ceremonies appear secondary to those of the men. (One albino woman took part in the Marau dance, but her participation aroused no comment.)

C. Hano's Ya-ya'a Dance[5]

Sept. 24, 1933 [p. 59]. Went to see a Ya-ya'a dance at Hano. We had hardly arrived when we were invited to eat by a Walpi man whose wife was Tewa. They had just acquired a new daughter-in-law, and our hostess was busy grinding corn while we ate.

When the dance began, only youngsters were performing, with one or two exceptions. They were, however, later joined by adults. A drummer sat in the center of the plaza, surrounded by about twenty singers some of whom carried gourd rattles. About them, holding hands to form a large circle, were the dancers. These were of both sexes and various ages. The men and boys wore nondescript clothing, but the girls wore wrapped leggings and attached moccasins of white buckskin, Hopi dresses (*mantas*), and either small ceremonial mantles (*atûhöyas*) or silk shawls draped across their shoulders. To her hair each female had affixed a prayer feather, and several wore over the forehead a fringe of hair. These resembled the horsehair fringes worn by girl performers in Butterfly dances, but in this case they were made of real Hopi hair. The dancers moved clockwise with a sideways motion. Every now and then, apparently at will, some of the dancers broke in and out of the ring while others danced in position continuously. Except for a lunch intermission at noon, the dancing went on without a break from forenoon to sunset. (This affords a contrast to Hopi *katcina* and other public dances in which periods of action alternate with periods of rest from daybreak to sunset.) One drummer performed almost without pause, only giving up his instrument for a little while before lunch and again just before the end of the ceremony.

The dance line was supposed to alternate boys with girls, but there was a shortage of males, with the result that at some points the ring of performers had girls side by side. During the dance the hands were lifted and lowered in time to the music. Suddenly, from the direction of the kiva, loud singing and rattling were heard, and soon a woman with a baby on her back entered the plaza. She was clad in the same style as the girl dancers except that she was barefooted. She carried a plaque that contained cornmeal and one ear of corn. She made a path, as she went, by sprinkling cornmeal on the ground. Along this path came two men. Directly behind her was a dancer who had a white, pear-shaped gourd rattle, which he shook as he sang. He was the Ya-ya. Fastened to the top of his head was a bunch of parrot feathers; across his naked torso ran a red bandoleer; and at the hips he wore a *katcina* kilt (*vitcuna*). About his ankles he wore beaded anklets, but his feet were bare. His face, body, arms, legs, and feet were painted yellow, sometimes in streaks and sometimes solidly. In his right hand he carried the aforementioned pear-shaped rattle, and in his left, an object [Fig. 16 B], which is supposed to be fashioned from a single piece of wood. This was painted yellow, but later performers who enacted Ya-ya used similar objects painted black or, possibly, dark green. These objects stood for the colors and things associated with the cardinal points of the compass. For instance, yellow represented the north and stood for yellow clouds, yellow corn, and so forth.[6]

Occasionally, a Ya-ya shouted or sang very loudly, and motioned with his special gadget toward the dancer who followed behind him as if to keep him off or at a distance. This dancer made a grotesque figure. He was clad in fringed red moccasins; full-length leggings either of buckskin or of cloth woven in open network fashion; a short kilt, featuring the colors green and black, and corn symbols; a belt of dentalium shells, set so closely together that they tinkled as he moved; a shirt, usually of "White American" make; large pieces of buckskin over his shoulders and back, much like those worn by side-dancers in Navaho *katcina* impersonations by the Hopi; and a bow in a buckskin case that protruded at the rear, something like a tail. This performer wore a particularly grotesque headdress. He had on a conical mask, covered with two *katcina* sashes sewn together but leaving an open tip. To this there were fastened prayer feathers and an ear of corn. The facial part of the mask was separate from the rest but attached to it. It was made either of light board or heavy cardboard, slightly oval in shape, and the design gave it a sort of bovine or horselike expression. The eyes were carved to appear large and bulging; below them there was painted sometimes a terraced cloud design, and sometimes a pattern of big, flat teeth; and at the bottom there were drawn a number of varicolored arcs. [See Fig. 16 A.] This portion of the mask was worn at a slight angle, giving the whole a whimsical tilt. Horsehair, dyed red, hung in strands from the mask face; and imitations of horns protruded from the sides.

The dancer who is so garbed is called Sumaikoli. He carries in his right hand a large bow, which he uses somewhat like a cane. About his right wrist there is bound the wing of a crow; in his left hand he carries a wooden crook to the rounded tip of which a prayer feather is attached [Fig. 16 C]; and from his left wrist there dangles a *katcina* fox pelt. [Generally speaking, each Sumaikoli is supposed to be the ceremonial son of the Ya-ya who precedes him. Different pairs of men play these parts throughout the day.]

Each woman makes a cornmeal path for a pair of special performers and leads them from a kiva toward the cluster of singers and the circle of dancers. Thereupon, the head of the entire ceremony, who is among the singers, comes forward and sprinkles sacred cornmeal on the special performers and in the direction of the singers and dancers. The members of the dance circle stop their activities, although some of them continue to beat time with their hands or feet; and they separate or widen out in an arc to permit the special performers to enter.

Each Ya-ya, singing as he goes, and his Sumaikoli dance four times around the drummer and his cluster of singers. The Ya-ya's song continues, even though it differs from the tune being sung by the chorus around the drummer. Neither lets up until the special performers start back for their kiva. At this, the circle of dancers resumes its activities. On the way back, a Ya-ya shakes his rattle and shouts, "Ya-hai-HAI," or "E-ah-E! E-ah-E!" As if in reply, the Sumaikoli, who is now dancing with a sideways, mincing motion, tilts his head and utters a muffled "Woof!" Occasionally, a Sumaikoli pauses to do a kind of deep-knee bend two or three times, and once in a while one of them rushes forward as if to charge his Ya-ya. Sometimes, too, a Sumaikoli prances sideways for a few steps in imitation of a shying horse. All in all, each impersonator gives a spirited and continuously active performance.

Throughout the day seven different men and women played the parts of the special performers. Some of the women were accompanied by babies or young children, but others were not. There were also many variations of dress and action. One Sumaikoli used a canelike rod with feathers affixed instead of a bow. Another wore a beautiful blanket featuring corn and cloud designs in place of buckskin sheets. Some of the specialists stopped to do a solo dance to the accompaniment of the chorus and drummer; and in one instance a Ya-ya gave his rattle to his Sumaikoli, who shook it as he did a solo dance.

At noon a halt was called for lunch. All the singers and the group of dancers ate with the drummer in one house; but all who had played special parts dined in the kiva. After a rest period the entire performance went on as before and lasted till sunset.

Several onlookers said that Ya-ya medicine men sometimes rushed out in the afternoon, shouted madly at one and all, and were horsewhipped by women. Nothing of the sort took place during this performance.

At the last dance of the day all the Sumaikoli actors came out together, headed by the male and female leaders of the dance. They circled the chorus of singers four times, then stopped while cornmeal and feathers were distributed to each of the Sumaikoli by the leaders. During this time many men and women, including most of the singers, sprinkled the specialists with sacred meal. Some of the singers were clad in street clothes and carried ears of corn in place of gourd rattles, but they sang the concluding song in the same fashion as the others. The Sumaikoli wore their costumes and performed their antics to the very end. Thereafter, they returned to the usual resting place of *katcinas* from Hano, where they unmasked and changed to civilian clothes.

In the circle of dancers there were several Hopi from Walpi. One of these dancers and two of the singers were Hopi men who had married Tewa women.

D. A Lakon Performance at Chimopovy[7]

Oct. 29, 1933 [p. 100]. The Lakon dance at Chimopovy was very unimpressive and tedious. There were only five performances, with exceedingly long waits between. All the Oraibi folk say that it usually goes that way on the other mesas. They claim that when the Oraibi women used to perform the Lakon, they made more frequent appearances and had shorter intermissions. (Is this really true or is it merely a matter of village loyalty?)

The performance began with a long, single file of dancers entering the plaza from the kiva which is just east of the square which they use. All the women of the Lakon society wore the usual ceremonial mantle (*atûʾû*), and most of them had on wrapped leggings and attached moccasins of white buckskin. Their leader carried two feathers and corn in addition to a plaque, but the others carried plaques only. The dancers formed a semicircle in the plaza near the shrine. There was no asperging nor was there any other ritual before the singing began. Each woman motioned up and down with her plaque in time to the song as in the Marau. Plaques were held with the convex side toward the performers, and there were a few sideways gestures. The dancers did not move counterclockwise as they do in the Marau, but remained in place and simply moved down and up as they sang.

A few minutes later a masculine officer and two Lakon *manas* ("maidens") entered the plaza from the kiva. His face was daubed yellow, and his torso was naked. He wore a *katcina* kilt at the hips. The Lakon maids were wrapped in elaborate ceremonial blankets, like those worn by Oaqöl performers, with corn designs [Fig. 14 d] at the lower borders. They, too, had yellow faces with a black line across the lower jaw. On their heads these women had a mass of feathers at the right and a single blue horn at the left. Bert interprets these objects as sex symbols and connects them with reproduction. He claims that the feathers really stand for flowers [blossoms?] and symbolize females, whereas the horn represents a phallus.

Each of the two Lakon *manas* had a large bundle tied on her back and carried two ears of varicolored corn. To each cob a differently colored feather was attached, but there were no sharp points or darts. The male chief who accompanied them had a plaque full of sacred pollen (cornmeal?) with which he sprinkled a long line across the path of the Lakon girls and two short lines at right angles, to give them a road. Then, in the customary counterclockwise sequence, the maidens tossed forward their yellow, bluish, red, and white befeathered ears of corn. The chief placed them on the path in their proper places and moved ahead a few yards, where all the proceedings were repeated. At the fourth stage the Lakon maidens reached the ring of dancers, whereupon they entered the circle and their male companion withdrew to the kiva.

Thereupon the *manas* unslung from their backs the heavy bundles that they had been carrying. (These had been fastened under the arms and had been carried without the benefit of a tumpline.) At this point all the masculine spectators began to crowd against the dance group, making peculiar clucking calls that sounded like "Oyk, oyk, oyk." Each Lakon girl removed an article from her pack, faced the other, waved rhythmically from within the circle twice or thrice, marched past her partner, and repeated the maneuvers several times before tossing the object to the crowd. The *manas* threw everything hard, whether or not it was fragile, and took no heed of direction. [Again, as in the Marau [p. 288] the underlying symbolism seems to suggest that the Lakon ceremony is so powerful that it can produce an unlimited number of good things. Hence, it doesn't matter if some expensive items get smashed.] The men scrambled furiously for everything thrown. When the girls had nothing left, they returned to the kiva; after their departure, the song concluded, and the ordinary Lakon women went back to the kiva in single file.

On the surface the main interest in the Lakon performance appears to lie in the distribution of gifts. None of the bystanders seemed to pay the slightest attention to the songs, and the singers were readily jostled. For their part they continued chanting, trying, in spite of the noise and confusion all about them, to render their songs properly.

Among the items that were thrown to the crowd were plaques, woven peach trays, sacks of Bull Durham tobacco, bags of salt, boxes of kitchen matches, Hershey chocolate bars, lollipops, bread, soda crackers, tin baking plates, pie plates, "China" dishes, Cracker Jack, and bars of soap. Everything was the object of a greedy and often noisy scramble, and each thing was fought for and its possession disputed unless some man was lucky enough to make a clean catch. When a large box of matches opened in the air, dozens of men dropped to the ground and scrambled for each individual match. Despite the ferocity of the competition there were no fights or real quarrels among the men, and feelings of good-natured fun and fair play prevailed. No matter how many hands fastened on an object, it became the undisputed property of whoever managed to wrest it from the others. The good spirits that were maintained were all the more remarkable since some of the competitors had their clothes torn and their faces scratched or bruised in the scrimmages.

No careful observer could fail to see the similarity of this dance to the Marau. The dress of the ordinary participants who formed a ring; their semicircular position; the singing, bowing, and waving of plaques or prayer boards; the later arrival of two distinctively garbed special performers; the manner of their approach by stages; the throwing out of gifts from within the ring of dancers; the scramble by masculine onlookers; and the method of departure, all were the same except for some minor differences of detail.

At the final Lakon appearance all the women had meal on their faces. The male chief deposited prayer sticks at the shrine, asperged in all directions, poured the remaining water into the shrine, and finally tossed the plaque that had held the sacred pollen, together with another plaque, far out over the housetops.

After the concluding public performance all the participating women entered their kiva. Many took babies or young children down into the kiva for initiation, blessing, or cure. (Joe says the youngsters are brought down to be "purified.") Soon the women and their male chief mounted to the top of the kiva to distribute whatever gifts had been left over. Some *ikya'as*, instead of randomly tossing away presents, especially the plaques that they had carried in the dance, handed them to favored *imûyis*. (Ned says Oraibi women always give their plaques to "nephews.")

E. The Soyal Katcina Comes to Oraibi

Nov. 26, 1933 [p. 138]. Everyone seems to have anticipated the coming of the Soyal *katcina* this afternoon. Mutton stew and *pikami* were eaten in many houses, and most people had had their heads washed in yucca suds. Although only a single *katcina* is scheduled to appear, and then only for a few minutes, the day is considered a regular feast and dance day (*tikive*).

At about noon Martin left his house with a bundle and went to the west. Later, word spread that he had been chosen to enact the Soyal *katcina*, and Tawaqwaptiwa was planning to greet him and to present him with prayer feathers for deposit. (At Oraibi, in the years just prior to 1933, Chief Tawaqwaptiwa had always enacted the Soyal *katcina*. His selection of Martin to play the role might have been his way of announcing to the populace that he had selected Martin to be his successor in office.) [Martin continued to enact the Soyal *katcina* at Oraibi until it lapsed around 1953. In later years, Martin frequently alluded to this episode in support of his claim to the Village chieftainship following the death of Tawaqwaptiwa. See pp. 344–45.]

At about one o'clock the Soyal *katcina* appeared on the trail leading into the east end of the village. He was dressed in openwork, full-length stockings, *katcina* dance kilt, fox-pelt "tail" at the back, red moccasins with bead strips attached, and a yellowish brown shirt of coarse weave, almost like a burlap sack. The shirt had black and some greenish designs at the cuffs and back, but it was old and torn in one place. The designs were frayed or tattered, and it was difficult to make them out. Two sacks, which looked like white sugar bags turned inside out, were fastened together with an opening in the center through which the performer's head passed, so that one sack rested on his chest and the other on his back. About the throat, at the base of his mask, the Soyal *katcina* wore a thin fox pelt. The mask was a simple affair of bluish green, with slits for the eyes, and a red line running around the lower border. It was made to give a circular appearance. At the crown there was a ball-shaped tuft, about five inches in diameter, bound with strands of reddish string or dyed horsehair. From this there projected two large feathers.

About the impersonator's right calf there was bound a turtle-shell rattle, such as *katcinas* usually wear; and a string of "sleigh" bells, which could be heard but scarcely seen, was tied around the left leg. Hanks of blue black yarn were fastened just below each knee. In his right hand the performer carried a clay-whitened gourd rattle, and in his left, he held a fairly large white sack of cornmeal, together with four large prayer sticks topped by red-tinted feathers.

As he approached the dance plaza, the Soyal *katcina* walked slowly and unevenly, like an old man laboriously picking his way. Once in the plaza he paused and did a "dance," that is, he imitated the customary stamping motion of *katcinas* like a feeble old man attempting to keep up with young and vigorous performers. (During this part of his act the Soyal *katcina* does not sing. Instead, he occasionally exhales loudly in gasping fashion, as if to suggest that at his age he is short of breath and lacks the wind to sing while dancing. In addition to age, he affects great weariness to imply that he has been locked up asleep for the last six months [during the closed *katcina* season].[8] When he does sing, he is expected to use a low voice, partly because he is supposed to be old, feeble, and sleepy; and partly, as Tawaqwaptiwa pointed out, because his words are secret and must not be overheard.)

After dancing in stumbling fashion at the plaza for a few minutes, including one clumsily executed about-face, the Soyal *katcina* proceeded to Tawaovi kiva. By prearrangement, old Qöyayeptiwa issued forth just as the *katcina* was arriving. The crowd laughed heartily to see a real ancient walking somewhat in the fashion being enacted by the young impersonator of the Soyal *katcina*. Qöyayeptiwa said to the *katcina*, "*Pai pitu?*" ("'Have you arrived?'") and then went back into the kiva. A few moments later he emerged again and went off somewhere on his own business.

Meantime, the Soyal *katcina* stopped north of Tawaovi and again performed his halting dance. Then he picked his way, stumbling along, to the south of the kiva, where he deposited his four prayer sticks in upright fashion. This done, he groped his way to the east side of Tawaovi and sprinkled meal, taken from his sack, from the kiva ladder to the outer edges of the chamber in the usual ritual order, north, west, south, and east. He repeated the circuit and ended by throwing meal down the hatchway. (This signified that he was opening the kiva for use by other *katcinas* who might come to Oraibi from any direction. His actions thus symbolized the opening of the *katcina* season.)

When he had finished, the Soyal *katcina* clambered down from the hatch and stood a few feet from the kiva, facing its southeastern edge. Thereupon Tawaqwaptiwa came out, carrying a little tray that contained a heap of cornmeal and some (four?) prayer feathers with breath lines of twisted Hopi cotton thread. The chief relieved the Soyal *katcina* of his gourd rattle and the sack of cornmeal and stooped to unfasten his turtle-shell leg-rattle. Then Tawaqwaptiwa gave Martin the prayer feathers and a handful of cornmeal. After that he sprinkled a path toward the southeast, the direction of the Hopi path of life. When the chief reentered Tawaovi, the Soyal *katcina* stumbled off eastward to the end of the street, turned south to the dance plaza, west at the next corner, and so back to the shrine known as Matcito's house. Sixteen days after this performance the start of the Soyal observances is officially announced.

F. Observations on a Wuwutcim Performance at Hotevilla[9]

Dec. 2, 1933 [p. 148]. Somewhat before noon Ned, Ruth, George, and I went with Martin to see the Wuwutcim at Hotevilla. At about half-past twelve we heard some Kwan men going the rounds from house to house, collecting cornmeal. Such women as were not ready at the time hurriedly prepared the requisite meal and ran to give it to the Kwans. Four men in costume were carrying trays on which each housewife was supposed to heap a saucerful of meal. The Kwans were dressed in *katcina* kilts and sashes, were naked in the upper body, had a bell suspended from each wrist, and wore a cluster of *nakwakwosi* ("prayer feathers") tied in the hair. They walked rapidly, jangling their bells as they went. Men, especially, kept out of their way, as any one they catch must be initiated for trespass. Males must join the Kwan society, and females must enter Marau. The Kwans are said to be perpetually shorthanded since the average Hopi fears to join their society because their rites bring them into contact with death.[10] They are set apart from the other Tribal Initiation societies and are said to be chiefs in the Soyal because they are regarded as defenders of the Village chief and guardians of the Soyal ceremony. They are marked in what Ned calls "chiefs' markings," which consists of a semilunar smear of heavy, white clay on the left eye and lid. A line of white dots, each about the size of a five-cent piece, runs around the right shoulder, arm, and leg.[11] Everyone questioned professed not to know what the Kwan men did with the cornmeal that they collected.

After an intermission of about two hours dancing began. First out were the men of Sakwalenvi, the kiva that houses the Soyal. (At Oraibi, too, the kiva in which the Soyal was held used to play the leading part in the Wuwutcim observances. This kiva is also known as Chief kiva. In Oraibi this title pertained to Tawaovi, formerly Pongovi; and at Hotevilla it is given to Sakwalenvi, as it was in Oraibi before the Split of 1906.) The Sakwalenvi group was headed by two leaders. As these two emerged, they picked up the prayer sticks that had been put south of their kiva hatch. The prayer sticks had been set in a white, wooden hemisphere with holes punched into it to face the four directions. (Ned claimed that this was the regular *na'atsi* ["ceremonial standard"] of the Blue Flute society.)[12]

The dancers faced each other in two parallel rows. Their leaders wore Al costumes and simply pranced up and down in steady fashion regardless of the rhythm of the song that the others were singing. The regular dancers lined up side by side and moved with short, sidelong steps. They crossed arms and locked their fingers (imbricated them) in one another's hands. Their Al leaders wore headdresses that featured wide, white horns that protruded upward, over their heads.[13] [These headdresses

are made from gourds at each initiation by a ceremonial father
for his ceremonial son.] Like the Kwans, the Al men wore chiefs'
markings, but on the opposite sides of their bodies. They also
had on large white buckskin sheets, wrapped about the torso,
and they wore a turtle-shell rattle on the back of each calf. These
were marked with four white circles each. The Al men also carried
wooden *mongkohos* ("chiefs' sticks"). They came out first and
were followed by the society heads who carried in their right
hands the prayer sticks that they had removed from the hatchway
of their kiva, and who held their left hands imbricated. The ordinary Wuwutcim members appeared last, clad in *katcina* kilts
and sashes, fox-pelt "tails," red moccasins, and beaded anklets.
Each had bound to his head a cluster of feathers beneath which
two corn husks were attached; and each had bound against his
forehead a blue green paper star, made by the intersection of
eight lines. (The stars stand for Hopi "spinach" and other forms
of vegetation.) Each of the ordinary dancers had a naked torso,
wore a red bandoleer across his chest, and had a silver bow guard
around the left wrist. The dancers tended to close the ends of their
lines, giving a horseshoe effect, and the last man in each of the
parallel lines wore a small ceremonial mantle (*atûhöya*), draped
across the shoulders. [Note the resemblance to the circular lines
formed by the women's societies; and the element of bisexualism,
since the *atûhöya* is a feminine garment.] Bringing up the rear
were two more Al men, who are supposed to be initiates from
the year preceding. They faced directly forward, at right angles
to the other performers who stood side by side. Within the "horseshoe" formed by the dancers marched a drummer, who carried
his own instrument and sang with the others [Fig. 17]. He occasionally did an about-face in the course of the dancing. He wore,
in addition to the standard Wuwutcim costume, a heavy plush
shirt, dark blue or black in color, with one or two streamers of
gay ribbon across his chest. Behind him came the official Crier
chief, wearing a shield with a fringe of red dyed horsehair depict-
ing the sun's rays; but this is not a true Sun-shield. [It is supposed to be one of those worn on the backs of dancing *kaletakas*
in the Marau ceremony.] He kept time with the drummer, and
they faced about in unison. In his right hand he carried a white,
disklike rattle, such as Antelope men use in the Snake dance. This,
some informants say, is supposed to announce that a Snake dance
is to be given within a few months. Were it the year for his village
to perform a Flute dance, some say, the Crier chief would have
carried a flute. Perhaps, as has been suggested, the Tca'akmongwi

("Crier chief") once played a greater part in announcing rituals. (Note the conceptual ties of the Sun, as shown by the wearing of a solar symbol, with the Snake-Antelope and Flute rites. Also, the interlocking of these observances with the Soyal and other performances is evident, since all other rituals are scheduled during the Soyal. Finally, it is also to be noted that in deference to their high ranking in the Soyal, the Wuwutcim men from Sakwalenvi are the first to emerge and are the only ones to be escorted by Als and to have with them the Crier chief, an important Soyal official. Oddly enough, as far as the Wuwutcim considered by itself is concerned, it is Hawiovi which is the most important kiva. This is the unit with which the Wuwutcim chief personally dances.)[14]

The dancers from Sakwalenvi preceded the other two groups, the Tcu and the Hawiovi, on a circuit of the pueblo. Their path is said to delimit the boundary of the Village chief's jurisdiction, but they do not literally cover the limits of the entire pueblo. After Sakwalenvi had been dancing publicly for about ten or fifteen minutes, the Tcu ("Rattlesnake") kiva group came forth. Their leaders also took the sacred objects or standards at the south end of their kiva, and they, too, formed two lines. No Al men accompanied them. All these dancers locked hands, and they enclosed their drummer in the center. Their circle was closed at the rear by two men wearing ceremonial mantles (atûhöyas), and a similar garment was worn by one of their leaders. (No fixed rule seems to apply to the number of men who wear atûhöyas.) In general, the Tcu dancers followed the same route as their predecessors.

Last to emerge was the Hawiovi unit. Their costumes and lineups exactly duplicated those of the Tcu.

Sakwalenvi, which had gotten started well ahead of the other units, was the first to complete its circuit and return to its kiva. The men seesawed back and forth beside their chamber until their final song was finished. The escort of Al men sprinkled meal toward the place of the standards on the kiva hatch, then went back to their own kiva. As each outfit ended its circuit and started to enter its chamber, one man would pause by the ladder. He would muffle his voice by putting a hand over his mouth, would make a joke about the Marau society, then would say something complimentary about the Wuwutcim before entering the kiva.

A short while after all three units had finished their performances, the Sakwalenvi dancers came forth again to duplicate their earlier circuit. This time they lacked an Al escort. The Crier chief, in kilt and heavy plush shirt, with an abalone shell at his chest and a Sun symbol at his back, but without an Antelope rattle, danced beside their leader and not between their lines with the drummer. A much shorter circuit was followed than was earlier the case, and when the other units came out, they, too, followed the abbreviated course. Not long after the public dances had ended, the Al men went from kiva to kiva, sweeping each one clean.

All the dancers now prepared to eat in their kivas, with each man fetching a share of the food. Siyesva came to his house for his portion. He was again naked except for a G-string, and he had a blanket wrapped about his body. Without a word he snatched an herb from a tray and chewed it while his wife fetched *piki* and a pot of stew. Thereupon, before leaving the house he spat the contents of his mouth toward each of the four directions. This, it was explained, was the discharming rite performed by all members of the Wuwutcim society. It is supposed to prevent "twisting" ailments.

NOTE.—The Wuwutcim ceremony has many military features. According to Voth, the Squash clan, whose phratry "owns" the Wuwutcim at Hotevilla, was one of the leading military groups in the last fight of the Hopi from Oraibi against the Navaho.[15]

Around eight o'clock in the evening, about an hour after supper, there came out of Tcu kiva a small knot of singers, clustered about a drummer. In a somewhat informal manner, but reminiscent of the way they had danced earlier, the men moved to the plaza where they "marked time" while they sang a *nikuc* ("bawdy," "naughty," or "evil") song that they had just learned. Its purpose was to tease the women of the Marau society. (Theoretically, the teasing is supposed only to provoke the societies to do their very best, but this "theory" may be forgotten.) There was no disturbance during the singing, other than laughter at some of the sallies. There was no pouring of water or anything of the sort. The bystanders must be allowed to hear what is being sung.

While we awaited the emergence of the next group, a solitary Kwan man was observed going to the main spring of the pueblo. He returned shortly, and there was no explanation of his trip.

About half an hour later one of the other groups came

into the plaza in Buffalo dance formation. Two men in front carried bows and arrows and danced with high, prancing steps. They were followed by two "girl" partners, who moved with the shuffling or waddling motion characteristic of feminine dancers. Behind them followed a chorus of singers, crowded around a drummer. Those who were dressed as males wore burlesques of Buffalo dance costumes, and each performer had a ring of corn husks suspended between the eyes and over the bridge of the nose, thus achieving a grotesque but comic effect, slightly suggestive of the Masau *katcina*. The "women" wore shabby *mantas* ("Hopi dresses") or disreputable "store" dresses. Each carried corn husks in "her" hands, in place of the customary sprigs of spruce. On entering the plaza the Buffalo dance routine began, males and "females" giving excellent comic imitations of the movements of the sex they were portraying. They kept perfect time, as if they were doing a serious dance, but the barbed sallies of the singers kept the crowd laughing throughout the performance.

We did not wait for the third group, as it was getting very late and there was no assurance that the third unit would appear at all. Early the next morning, so it was said, more bawdy songs would be sung; and this time the women who were being teased would be permitted to retaliate by pouring water, urine, or filth of any sort on their tormenters.

The songs were typical of bawdy songs anywhere. There was the linkage of girls with sweethearts and of wives with lovers. No hesitation was shown in the use of actual names, but in some cases indirect allusions were made in place of direct accusations. For example, in one song a husband was said to have caught his wife, whose name was given, with an unnamed bear in her arms. The latter was an obvious pun referring to a Bear clan lover. In addition to sallies dealing with specific cases, there were some jests of a general nature, as when the singers poked fun at recently returned schoolgirls, who were said to be limping or lame because all of them had just been deflowered. Hereupon the Wuwutcim men had all burlesqued walking with painful, halting steps, as if in imitation of the distressed and despoiled former virgins.

In addition, there were the usual quips that are conventional among us. One woman's vulva was said to be so small that entrance could be effected more easily, it was suggested, with the aid of a knife. The private parts of another female, taunted the Wuwutcim men, were shaped like a tobacco pouch.

A third was so hairy in the pubes that her lover was advised to use a comb. Then the singers suddenly adopted a righteous tone and offered a reward of twenty-five cents to anyone who caught and ousted a sneaker (i.e., a clandestine lover who is going *dumaiya*) from any home at all. So it went, with bawdy badinage being freely poured out in the presence of men, women, and children. Such uninhibited quipping affords a marked contrast to the pained bashfulness of the "knee-high" dancers in the Marau. In this connection, informants said that if a Marau performer failed to conform to the standards of beauty held by Hopi men, she was very likely to be made the butt of pointed remarks at Wuwutcim time.

Another thing that struck a "White" observer as strange was the actual naming of reputed lovers. Despite their relatively loose behavior, the Hopi are much given to sexual jealousy. In fact, on the way to the dance I had suggested that Ruth might be more comfortable if she rode with the driver, Martin, in the enclosed cab of the pickup truck, while all the men rode in the open in back. Ruth had refused to sit beside Martin, whispering that Grace might get jealous. However, when we returned in the dark, Ruth did not hesitate to ride with Martin since there was little chance of her being observed. (This fear of public observation ties in with Ned's care to meet Edna outside Oraibi's limits.) [Once again it seems that Hopi shame and bashfulness stem from a dread of publicity rather than from distaste for wrongdoing. See p. 84.]

In view of the prevalence of jealousy, the open teasing of husbands and wives that went on at the Wuwutcim was particularly noteworthy. It seems inevitable that some spouses would first learn at this time about hitherto unsuspected infidelities on the parts of their mates. (All informants agreed that it was bad form to show anger at the time, but revelations of this kind may lead to future quarrels or divorces.)

Neither during the formal dances nor in the evening's teasing did I observe any Wuwutcim men wearing false vulvae made of watermelon and horsehair or any phallic devices, such as are sometimes said to be featured by Wuwutcim men. Whether the absence of these features was of a routine nature or the direct result of "White" complaints could not be determined.

The real initiation garments made for Wuwutcim men are supposed to be worn only during the initiatory dances. They are then supposed to be converted to *katcina* G-strings and to be worn as parts of *katcina* dance costumes.

G. Two Sets of Night Dances at Old Oraibi

Jan. 10, 1934 [p. 197]. Toward sundown Ned took me into Tawaovi kiva, where I found the members busily practicing a new song, composed by the chief, which was to be used later that night. The singers were planning to appear in Köyemsi costume, with the chief as drummer, while Martin, as principal actor, Humiletstiwa, and Sam were to perform an Eagle dance.

After a period of singing there was a rest, followed by an informal dress rehearsal. Panimptiwa took over the drumming to spell the chief. At this time Tawaqwaptiwa took some honey and, mixing it with saliva in his mouth, spurted it into the neck openings of the three masks that were going to be used by the Eagle dancers. He made four spurts into each mask, then spewed what was left in his mouth at random, directing the liquid here and there in the general direction of various items of dance paraphernalia that were scattered about the kiva.

During the second part of the rehearsal the singers shook gourd rattles, the three Eagle dancers wore strings of small bells, and Humiletstiwa and Sam carried in each hand what looked like long bunches of yucca.

After supper the men painted up and dressed. The same atmosphere prevailed as on a show night anywhere. Men smeared one another's backs with *suta* ("red ocher"), helped their fellows to adjust masks, assisted in tying shawls about the hips in place of *katcina* kilts, and so forth. All those who were enacting Köyemsi had their gift bags slung across the body. The chief, as drummer, wore a Köyemsi outfit; but the three Eagle dancers wore kilts. Martin, who was going to be *the* eagle, wore a *katcina* kilt, had a fox-pelt tail at the rear, and carried eagle wings. The chief daubed Martin's body and arms at intervals with big dots of sticky, white clay, and when dabs of white cotton were stuck on the clay spots, a downy-breasted effect was achieved whenever he squatted and extended his arms. Humiletstiwa and Sam, who were to dance as Martin's assistants, put on special, elaborate kilts but wore none of Martin's accessories. When everyone was about ready, Tawaqwaptiwa hurried out of the kiva and soon returned with a bundle of long eagle plumes. He tossed them informally north of the fireplace, and each Köyemsi picked one up with no apparent reverence. During the performance every singer held an eagle plume in his left hand and a gourd rattle in his right. (No special significance should be read into the chief's action. He simply remembered that he had some long eagle feathers, and he thought it would look nice if the men used them.) [Köyemsi usually carry eagle or buzzard plumes.]

At the last moment Joe came dashing down the ladder and began to dress hurriedly as a Köyemsi. As far as could be gathered, he had not learned the new song, but he knew the rhythmic pattern of Eagle songs and could therefore hum and rattle in time. In a short while, as the chief later reported, Joe learned the words and tune, and before the evening's rounds came to an end, he was singing right along with the others.

Chief Tawaqwaptiwa was the last to dress. As soon as he was ready, the dance paraphernalia that were not going to be used were hidden away behind the stone benches, and the men picked up their masks and carried them to the house of Poliyestiwa, where they were to put the finishing touches on their costumes, don their masks, and emerge as *katcinas.*

The idea appears to be that it is unseemly for spectators to observe *katcina* performers in the act of masking. (This helps preserve the notion that a masked dancer is a spiritual being.) To prevent the possibility of surprise in the event that a spectator should enter the kiva too soon, no one masks in the ceremonial chamber. Moreover, all *katcinas,* or masked performers, are supposed to enter a village from their mythical homes. Hence, dancers always complete their costuming in a house or at a shrine in order to give the effect of coming into a pueblo or kiva as if they were genuine spirits coming from afar.

Hardly had the men left the kiva for Poliyestiwa's house than women and children began to file down the ladder as spectators. Most of those who chose to watch the evening's performances at Tawaovi were directly related to members of that kiva.

The seating arrangement, customarily the same at all kiva functions, had women and uninitiated children on the upraise behind the ladder; the father of the *katcinas* near the southwest corner of the fireplace, at the juncture of the upraised section and the lower level; men and boys on the stone banquette along the east and north walls; and unmarried girls at the west side. (Banquettes look solid, but their sides consist of sliding slabs of stone behind which, as in cupboards, secret objects can be stored.) All persons, except those who are connected with Masau'û, must enter a kiva to the right (east) of the ladder and depart from the left (west). Since they dance on the lower floor, they file past the unmarried females just before they leave. It is at this time that the girls hand food and other gifts to the performers; and encores follow if someone guides the first man in a line around the ladder and back to the main (lower) level.

Very quickly after the spectators had assembled, a drum was heard approaching the kiva. Soon, in Köyemsi costume, there appeared at the hatch the chief, as drummer, and Panimptiwa, as leader. In muffled and disguised voices they entered into conversation with Kelnimptiwa, father of the *katcinas*. When he had repeatedly urged them to enter the kiva, they accepted his invitation. First down the ladder was the drummer, who began to beat his instrument immediately as he moved backward to the north. Each of the Köyemsi who followed him promptly fell into rhythm, and they also backed up northward. When all the singers had clustered about the drummer and had sung a preliminary verse, Sam came down, followed by Martin and then by Humiletstiwa at fixed intervals. Martin postured like a bird, lifting his "wings," hopping about, making pecking motions, and uttering eagle calls. After the dance, Sam, Martin, and Humiletstiwa, in that order, jumped onto the raised section and dashed up the ladder. Soon after, the Köyemsi concluded their song and went about informally distributing gifts.

When the Köyemsi started to withdraw, Masamösi led the first man *around* the ladder, thus calling for an encore. The singers resumed their former places, and at the appropriate time the Eagle dancers returned and repeated their performance. This time they were allowed to leave, and after their departure the Powamu kiva unit arrived. They were dressed as Hote *katcinas*, and their identification was correctly made by a small boy. The Powamu kiva's dance was so well done that Masamösi insisted on two encores. She then allowed everyone but Cedric to depart. Him she led, carrying his drum, into the center of the main floor, whereupon he sang an impromptu song teasing his father, blind Kelnimptiwa, for always "calling out" for the "ladies." This got a big laugh. Kelnimptiwa exchanged some bantering remarks with Cedric, and when they were over, Cedric left.

Almost at once the Marau unit entered. They did a Ho'li *katcina* dance, and once more did a young boy make a correct advance identification. Bill was the drummer, and again Masamösi called for two encores after which she detained Bill by himself. He got lots of laughs by talking backward, that is, by saying the *opposite* of what he meant.

When he withdrew, the Tawaovi men reappeared, repeated their first performance, and so rounded out the evening's entertainment. Just before going out Martin crouched by the ladder, and several women rubbed their hands on him, then motioned to themselves to indicate that they were absorbing some of the eagle's power.

One interesting sidelight occurred during the performances. A little girl of eight or nine, who had been seated on the upraise, had to urinate. She did not leave the kiva but, with the help of her mother, raised her skirt and passed water right on the platform among the women and children and in full sight of all the assemblage. There was some laughter, but no one seemed to regard the event as unseemly or unsanitary.

Jan. 16, 1934 [p. 201]. Tonight the men used my house while preparing for a dance. Someone brought a bowl of white clay (*duma*); and Ruth produced an old pot covered with soot. As the dancers dressed and painted up, the theatrical nature of a *katcina* dance was made strikingly evident. It was in every way absolutely like backstage before a show. An audience was entering the kiva, makeup was being put on behind the equivalent of closed doors, the performers were eager to surprise and please the spectators, pieces of jewelry, strings of beads, and parts of costumes were strewn about or were freely loaned to those who needed them. There was even a mirror in front of which the dancers applied makeup.

In dressing for dancing the bulk of the men first stripped off their civilian clothes. Then they put on G-strings and coated the entire body with a thin wash of white clay. When this had dried, the performers put on large G-strings. These consisted of pieces of cloth, four or five feet long and between one and two feet wide. They were affixed to the body somewhat like an apron, parts of which hung front and back while the sides were left bare. Moccasins of various kinds were worn, and headdresses varied from paper cones to flat headpieces. Sam and Lawrence even wore big Plains-like feather coronets. However, most of the men had on impermanent, conical headdresses which were fastened by strings under the chin. All faces were blackened with soot and flecked on the nose, cheeks, and forehead with white clay.

All in all, the costumes were pretty much mixed, but the overall effect was supposed to be that of Navaho-Apache warriors, and the words of the song were in Navaho. The composer was Frank, who is fluent in Navaho.

Unlike the others Ned dressed in the costume of a Qwivi *katcina*, but instead of the usual *katcina* kilt he wore a plain cloth in the fashion of a short skirt. He had "sleigh" bells bound about the calves of both legs, instead of the customary turtle-shell rattle on the right leg only, and he wore a variant of a Köyemsi mask in place of the conventional mask of a Qwivi *katcina*. Being a Köyemsi, at least in part, he had the right to talk in a strange voice, and that was the purpose of his getup.

When all were ready, the chief took up his drum and a final dress rehearsal was held in the house before the group proceeded to Tawaovi. Ned was the first to go into the kiva, and he did his solo act before the others entered.

When the group's performance was over, Masamösi asked for an encore in the customary fashion, and after the encore the Tawaovi men left and the Marau group came in. On the previous occasion the Powamu unit had followed Tawaovi, but this time Marau came next. This sort of variation has a double purpose. It makes identification harder; and it is good showmanship to mix up the order of group appearances. In all cases, though, the home kiva opens and closes each night of dancing in its own chamber.

The Marau men were dressed to impersonate Bear *katcinas*, and they growled fiercely before they started to sing and dance. They put on so spirited a dance that they had to give three encores. When they had finished, the Powamu unit filed in and did Navaho *katcinas*, but they had neither a drummer nor a side-dancer.

Nevertheless, the Navaho *katcinas* were so effective that they were asked to perform two encores. When the lineup of dancers made it hard for the spectators on the upraise to see clearly, Talasnönsi slipped down from the upraise and deliberately moved some of the performers into a different formation. At first they pretended to balk and hold back, but after a token resistance they stood where Talasnönsi had placed them. No one spoke a word, but it was clear that night dances are quite informal and must be completely agreeable to the onlookers.

As soon as the men of Powamu kiva had departed, Tawaovi's Navaho-Apache war dancers returned for their final performance. As they danced, Masamösi and Hahai'i got so excited that they suddenly began to jump up and down in time to the music. After a while, Masamösi got so worked up that she leaped from the spectators' platform and lined up with the dancers. Thereupon, her daughter Fern joined her. At this stage the men were ranged in two rows, facing each other. Fern pushed her mother into the row opposite her, and together they kept time by jumping up and down. They continued thus until the dance came to a close. At the end of the dance the *katcinas* were asked to give an encore, and Masamösi and Fern calmed down and sat among the women observers.

This done, Ned entered and did a fairly funny solo, imitating a Navaho song and dance. Ruth's voice rose above the rest, shouting encouragement and praise at her husband. Ned's performance was well received, and he, too, had to give an encore.

H. New Oraibi Stages a Buffalo Dance

Jan. 21, 1934 [p. 208]. I waited for Joe while his wife, Mary, crushed some dried yucca fibers, made soapsuds, and washed his hair. She then shampooed their children's hair and sent for her bachelor brother Bill so that she might wash his hair, too. Then Mary combed Joe's hair and tied it in a big bun at the back. She also ironed Joe's *banda* ("headband"), so that it looked fresh and neat. All this she did cheerfully, although she herself was to stay home to look after her baby.

When we got down to Kikötcmovi, an outfit from Mishongnovi was performing in the plaza. The main dancers were men, but they wore what looked like Oaqöl (feminine) blankets. In contrast, their girl partners had male dance kilts wrapped around their shoulders. (Note the elements of bisexualism in ceremonial dress.) The girls carried huge Sun-shields at the back, wore anklets and armbands, and carried a Buffalo prayer stick in each hand. The men were dressed in fancy, orange yellow leggings, had yarn tied about the knees, and wore flashy, American-style shirts of gaudy colors. Their faces were blackened around a whitened mouth; each had a woman's wedding belt tucked in at the rear of the belt, in the fashion that *katcinas* wear fox-pelt "tails," and each had a string of metallic bells, without clappers, about his waist. Beads and shell necklaces were much in evidence among performers of either sex. In their right hands the male dancers carried gourd rattles, and in their left, they held long lightning (?) sticks of black and white to each end of which a prayer feather was attached.

A drummer, in daily garb, beat time for the dancers. He was surrounded by a cluster of singers who were also uncostumed, except for a dab here and there of red, white, or black face paint. Leading the singers and drummer were three or four men in assorted or makeshift costumes. Two of them carried bows with which they gesticulated; and one, who acted as a kind of clown or grotesque, had on a ragged outfit that featured a sheep pelt, a boot hung on his body, and a sheepskin cap on his head.

At one phase of the dance the two male soloists and their feminine partners did a short takeoff on the Oaqöl, with the clownish figure giving a comic imitation of a female singing, after which the dancing men threw a few gifts to the crowd. Later, there was a brief burlesque of the Marau after which the men ran ñötiwa. At this time the grotesque pretended to fall on his back and waved aloft his gifts, a package of soda crackers and a hunk of raw meat, until someone approached and took them from him.

When the Mishongnovi performers withdrew, a set of New Oraibi dancers entered the plaza. They were differently costumed. The women wore Hopi dresses and male dance kilts over the shoulders (again, bisexualism). The men wore small, feminine ceremonial robes (atûhöyas), openwork leggings (knitted), and a woman's belt at the back (more bisexualism). Their upper bodies were naked but were marked with white zigzag lines [Fig. 14 e]. The New Oraibi male dancers carried animal antlers covered with cotton in the left hand and gourd rattles in the right. Each had a single cowbell fixed to the waist. Both the Second and Third Mesa groups danced in sets of four, with two men and two girl partners. All the males wore headdresses that looked like blackened skins covered with white dots. The headdresses concealed the top and the back of the head but left the face exposed. [These are not considered to be masks. Only katcina performers wear masks.]

The New Oraibi singers, like those from Mishongnovi, gathered about a drummer. Most of them were in daily dress and wore shirt, overalls, shoes, and socks; but several had on miscellaneous belts, feathers, and other ornaments; and some carried bows and arrows [Fig. 18].

The New Oraibi Buffalo dancers used no standards, unlike the Mishongnovi performers who had several standards. One featured a fox pelt; others, arrays of feathers; and so on. Those who took major parts and did the actual dancing appeared only once. After they got out of costume, they either looked on or joined the singers.

Two of the Buffalo impersonators put on a vigorous and spirited performance, including some excellent pantomime. At one phase of the dance they knelt in front of their girl partners who pretended to club them about the head with their prayer sticks. The "buffalos" then fell to the ground and dragged themselves along as if they were badly wounded. Sidney, one of the performers, got a laugh by putting his hand to his head and examining it to see if he were bleeding. When their pantomime was finished, the "buffalos" jumped up and continued their dance.

The older girls and the best male dancers appeared late in the day. The last set was really excellent and introduced several steps that were very pretty. At the time this group came into the plaza, the singers appeared with additional fragments of costume. [Note the Hopi sense of drama, whereby the best dancers, like old-fashioned vaudeville headliners, appear late.]

When the day's dancing was over, the singers escorted the last performers to the kiva. Here they left the girls. The singers returned to the plaza for a brief act with the male dancers only. That done, the singers again escorted the "buffalos" out of the plaza. This time the men ran off to the shrine from which they had been brought the day before. At this shrine they deposited the prayer sticks that the girls had carried in the dance.

I. Closing Powamu Activities at Oraibi

Feb. 2, 1934 [pp. 221 ff.]. At some time late at night a big hole was dug in the ground a few paces west of Tawaovi. Ned woke us at about half-past four in the morning, before daybreak, and we hastened to the kiva to harvest our crops of beans. It was a simple operation to pull up the sprouts from the soil, and the dirt was dumped into the aforementioned hole. Back in the kiva, bunches of sprouts were left to be wrapped around gifts of *katcina* dolls for the recently born babies of Louise and Betty. An additional handful of sprouts was left north of the fireplace as a reward for the *katcina* impersonator who was going to distribute presents for all the members of Tawaovi. The remaining sprouts were taken home. Women and uninitiated children are supposed to believe that the young plants were brought to the village in winter by supernatural means, that is, through the agency of the Powamu ceremony's power.

When daylight appeared, Tawaqwaptiwa, the Crier chief, and the official (Soyal) Kaletaka or "Warrior" took up their *mongkohos* ("chiefs' sticks"). Martin sprinkled a meal path for them and out of Tawaovi they went to the eastern edge of the mesa to make a morning prayer (*kuivato*) to the Sun. The warrior led the way, followed by the crier and the chief in that order. When they got back to the kiva, Frank and Martin dressed and painted up for the parts of Aholi and Eototo, respectively. [See

p. 220.] Tawaqwaptiwa gave Martin, who was about to impersonate Eototo for the first time, some final instructions. [It must
have been a trying moment both for the chief, who was retiring,
and for Martin, who was entering on a new set of duties.]

Shortly after daybreak Angwucnasomtaka ("Raven-wings-
bound-up") was heard singing "her" song. The *katcina* appeared
at the eastern edge of the mesa, moving slowly forward and
constantly singing in a low voice as "she" went. According to
tradition, Angwucnasomtaka is supposed to have just come from
"her" wedding. After visiting Oraibi "she" is sent back to her
home in the San Francisco mountains. (Joe was playing the part
for the second year, as he had been chosen by Siletstiwa in 1933.
The old mask, which is supposed to be used, is too small for Joe,
so he painted a new one. We had seen it in the Powamu kiva during our visit there last Thursday. Joe plans to enact Angwucnasomtaka four times before retiring.)

Soon Aholi and Eototo began making the rounds of the
village, performing the actions that they had recently rehearsed
in Tawaovi. The lines, drawn with sacred cornmeal, represent the
pueblo and its houses, and the motions with the staff symbolize
the inclusion of all the village lands as pertaining to the chief.
On this day, Martin drew the cornmeal lines, then poured water
from a netted gourd (*mongwikuru*). (This probably signified rain
falling on the pueblo's lands.) When Eototo and Aholi reached
Powamu kiva, they made four cornmeal lines from each of the
cardinal points toward the kiva's hatch. At the end of each line
they leaned over, threw a pinch of meal down into the chamber,
and poured down a little water. [These actions sanction *katcina*
performances.] Martin (Eototo) always acted first, and Frank
Siemptiwa (Aholi) followed. From Powamu kiva they again made
the rounds of the village, smearing cornmeal lines on certain
houses. (The Hopi explanation of this custom could not be ascertained. It may be that the *katcinas* were marking, and thus blessing or protecting, the homes that contained clan or ceremonial
fetishes.)

While this was going on Angwucnasomtaka gradually
reached Powamu kiva and stopped east of the entrance hatch.
"She" waited there until Siletstiwa came forth and gave "her"
some sacred cornmeal and prayer sticks. After this, others followed suit, whereupon the *katcina* left for "her" shrine. (Joe said
that he had dressed for the part of Angwucnasomtaka before daybreak, at a distant shrine east of Oraibi. He did not say where he
went at the conclusion of the rites at Powamu kiva. Joe is a mem-

ber of the Powamu ceremony and of the Patki clan, one of whose men traditionally plays the part of Angwucnasomtaka. This *katcina* is probably one of the ancients or *wuyas* of the Patki clan, which is closely affiliated with all the Powamu observances.)

By now it was broad daylight, and we went to Tawaovi kiva to eat. Several women, including the wife of the chief, brought food to the kiva. They did not enter, and Poliyestiwa climbed the ladder to receive what they had brought. Four loads, in all, were brought. Each consisted of four flat trays containing sheets of unfolded, ordinary-looking *piki;* four small plaques with *wotaka* ("gravy");[16] and four small pottery dishes filled with beans. Poliyestiwa set all the food out in a square north of the fireplace. At this point Tom, who had been chosen to distribute the Tawaovi presents, began to dress as a male Navaho *katcina*. (The choice of impersonation is left entirely to the man who has been selected to serve as messenger for his kiva. In 1933 Ned had acted in this capacity and had named Tom to succeed him.) Before the feasting started the Crier chief climbed the ladder till he was about halfway out of the hatch and issued an invitation for the Cloud People to come and eat. Only Tawaovi feasts in this way and at this time. Each man must start with "gravy," as is also done at Soyal. This is said to symbolize rivers and ponds. After eating in Tawaovi we went home and found Ida preparing a stew of bean and corn sprouts. She said that we had to eat this or something would happen to us. We ate a little and took the surplus to Tawaovi. Our kiva mates did the same, and we combined everything into a joint feast.

Only one discordant note was struck. Mary had asked her brother Bill's (Marau) kiva to appear as Köyemsi in the afternoon, but his mates balked. They rightly claimed that they had acted Köyemsi for two years in succession and that it was now up to some other group to perform. However, Bill could not ask another unit to act; and since none of the other outfits were requested to appear, no performance was held. Thus, again, are intrakiva loyalties balanced by extrakiva jealousy.

J. Dancing in a Bean Dance at Oraibi

Feb. 2, 1934 [p. 221]. One evening, about six days before the Bean dance, Fred Eggan and I were called to watch a *katcina* dance practice in Tawaovi. When we got there, we were told that we were expected to dance as "women" in the forthcoming Bean dance. Tom was particularly insistent that we take such parts. We found the men rehearsing a new song that the chief had composed for the occasion. After a time everyone but we two stood up and danced without prior instruction regarding the "steps." (This confirms the opinion that there is a fixed rhythmic pattern that varies from type to type, and each new song of a given variety must fit into that pattern. [Compare p. 176.] The men seem to have absorbed the requisite motions that accompany each prestructured song from the time they were youngsters. By carefully watching at rehearsals children learn how each dance goes. For example, all Angya *katcina* performances begin with the stamping of the right foot for several measures. Then, one after the other, each man in the line makes a half-turn. When these half-turns have been completed, each man in succession, starting with the first, makes a full right-about turn. During these maneuvers a steady stamping with the right foot never ceases. Only after the leader, who stands in the exact center of the line [where the best singers are clustered], has finished his complete turn and signaled to the others by shaking his gourd rattle, does group singing and dancing begin. This routine is so invariable that no one calls attention to it even when new Angya *katcina* songs are being rehearsed for the first time.

Along the same lines, each dance of the Qwivi *katcinas* includes a part during which the performers take four steps forward, pause, then take four steps backward. Throughout this phase everyone shakes his gourd rattle continuously and stamps steadily with the right foot. Again, near the close of a Qwivi dance the *katcinas*, rattling without a break, move forward four steps, pause, take four more steps forward, and so conclude. Thus, every type of *katcina* song seems to have at least a fixed opening and close. It may be that some rhythmic freedom is allowed a composer in the middle portions of a tune, but of this there is no certainty. Even if this is the case, the fixity of the start and finish show that a composer's individuality is not given free play. There are certain patterns that he must observe, just as is the case among us, where a waltz can be written only in three-fourths time. [One is here reminded of the likelihood that potters and weavers are also expected to conform to some aspects of tribal patterns even when they execute seemingly original, individual designs.

Thus does the impress of a group's way of doing things on an individual's behavior again become apparent. Moreover, the way in which each person absorbs the patterns of his group seems to lend further support to my interpretation of "group mind." [Compare pp. 171–72.] Every man on a dance team reacts in the same way to the clues contained in the pattern. Apparently, he absorbs the whole thing with as little conscious effort as one makes in learning to speak his native tongue.]

During the rehearsal the dancers were, as usual, barefooted. Some tied their shirts about their waists so that the upper part of the body was bare. Apparently the lineups of male and "female" dancers were still fluid. However, the routine of the dance was evident. Men and "women" lined up side by side, about five feet apart, in parallel rows facing each other. As the song progressed the two lines moved sideways to the right or north. Then, those who headed each line came together and clasped hands, imbricating their fingers, the "women" using their right hands and the men the left. Each "couple" took four steps forward toward the south, between the lines of their fellow dancers. As the song continued, they retraced their steps, northward, paused, and danced southward together again for four paces. Then they broke, and each partner rejoined the end of the line appropriate to the sex he was portraying. That done, another "pair" joined hands at the north, and the whole procedure was repeated at a fast tempo until the song ended.[17]

After the rehearsal of the Bean dance was finished, the men practiced an Angya *katcina* song and dance. In all probability this will be a part of the Niman performance in the forthcoming summer.

We asked Ned to give us the words of the song so that we could write them down and memorize them. To our surprise we found that although he had appeared to have been singing lustily with the rest, he knew less than half of the words and was by no means sure of the tune. This gives additional point to the notion that there is a fixed rhythmic pattern for each type of song. As long as a man knows the pattern, precise details of content are of little moment. Most of the words that Ned did know consisted of nonsense syllables, showing that stress and rhythm are more important than meaning. [Once again it should be noted that the Hopi actually dislike a song that is too full of meaningful words.]

At another rehearsal the next night Tom's father, Lomavuyauoma, who lives in Kikötcmovi, was present and readily danced as a "woman." Tom was busy making moccasins for one of his daughters who is at school, so he did not appear at practice. The second of the two Bean dance songs was learned, and it was decided that when Ned got back from wood-gathering, a visit would be paid to Marau kiva. (The Powamu kiva was closed to outsiders because secret rites were in progress.)

The second song is much like the first with regard to melody, start, and finish. In the middle portion, though, it varies rhythmically from the first. Thus, where the first song has a slow section for four successive steps, the second slows down only for one step. Even though Lomavuyauoma had arrived late and had not heard the song, he danced without losing his stride.

After each of the two songs had been rehearsed in Tawaovi, we prepared to visit the Marau kiva. Those dancing as males dressed in *katcina* kilts, but the ones impersonating women remained in their customary rehearsal togs. Informal as Tawaovi's visit was to be (no outside spectators were expected to be present), some efforts were made to make a good appearance. We performed only the first song and dance.

Before we went down the ladder of the Marau kiva, Poliyestiwa, a member of our group, muffled his voice and exchanged a little Köyemsi-like banter with the Marau man who was serving as father of the *katcinas*. Then we entered and did our dance. Afterward, the men of the Marau kiva asked me how our beans were coming along in Tawaovi. Although ours were probably a little higher than theirs, I said that they were about equal. This tickled the Marau men because, as they were quick to point out, they had planted four days later than we had. They also said that they had more "gardens" than we. This I contradicted because we actually had six or seven more "plots." It was amusing to find kiva loyalty so strong and to see how *qwivi* ("vain") they were, despite the outward distaste for boasting.

In due time we received a return visit from the Marau men, who did an Angya *katcina* dance. This group had spruce from the *katcina* shrine at Kisiwu. It had been gathered by Harold and had been brought to them by Moenkopi visitors. The men outnumbered the "women," possibly because of the need for gourd rattles (carried only by male performers) to keep the rhythm going. On the night of the actual Bean dance they achieved a better balance of males to "females" by the use of dancers from other pueblos.

Afterward, Ned said that the Marau group had beaten our bunch completely. "They flattened us out like a pancake" was the way Ned expressed it.

On the night of February first we rehearsed again in Tawaovi. This time we were informed that we were going to visit the other kivas in order to show them our second song. Like the others who were taking female parts we stripped to the waist. The rhythm of the dance was so fast and the approved mode of singing so "continuous" that the effect was like a long-drawn-out humming with the words indistinctly pronounced even by those who knew them perfectly. Of course, we came in for a riding from the members of the other kivas, but from our own point of view we did pretty well.

When we got back to Tawaovi, we found that the forced fire in the stove had gone out, but as the beans were to be harvested early tomorrow morning, no one seemed to mind.

Soon after our return we were again visited by the Marau men who sang us their second song as they danced. They were followed by a contingent from the Powamu kiva who were using Hawiovi while their regular kiva was housing the secret Powamu observances.

Just before our visitors arrived Martin and Frank Siemptiwa practiced the Eototo and Aholi impersonations that they are going to do as part of the Powamu. Eototo's mask is all white and Aholi's is tall and conical.[18] The impersonators did not mask at this rehearsal. The chief and some of the older men occasionally prompted Martin, but Frank, who has had much experience in his part, required no prompting.

The next night, February 2, 1934, was the night of the Bean dance in which Eggan and I were participating.[19] We were worried about our costumes, but the chief assured us that he would see we were supplied with whatever was necessary. He then asked if we would mind being whipped as part of the rites, and we replied that we had no intention of backing out, no matter what was involved. (I later came to the conclusion that the whipping was felt to be necessary since we had never been initiated into the *katcina* cult, an initiation that is accompanied by whipping.)

In the course of the evening the chief, Hahai'i, and Ida brought our costumes. We tried them on, then went to Tawaovi for our final rehearsals. In the kiva we found several new performers. Four or five men had come in from Moenkopi. They had practiced and were now ready to swell our ranks by dancing with us. We were delighted at the addition because it meant that we would have to go southward, down the middle, less often. We sang and danced to each of our two tunes several times and then sat around and waited for the Powamu chief, Siletstiwa, to summon us for action.

All the participants were supposed to remain awake during the night, but the taboo on sleeping was not enforced. George was the only one who actually lay down, but nearly everyone dozed or nodded, and Tom and two or three others fell sound asleep as they sat. (According to Joe, Tom always falls asleep during all-night vigils.) A Navaho had been given permission to sleep in the kiva this night, and he stretched out on the raised platform be-hind the ladder and snored lustily, utterly indifferent to the noise and excitement of the Bean dance.

Ned and several other men asked Tawaqwaptiwa to trim their hair. The newly arrived Moenkopi residents shaped and painted the symbolic ornaments that they were going to wear later. Those who planned to dance as men made three-leafed flower designs of cornhusks; but those who were acting as women painted blossom symbols on circles of cardboard.

Starting at about midnight Siletstiwa came three successive times to announce that the moment had come—first, for painting up; second, for getting into costume; and finally, for dancing. [He is said to tell time by the stars.] As he made each announcement he stood on the upraise, holding the ladder and facing north. His stance was reminiscent of Charles's when he announced the Niman dance [p. 176]. Siletstiwa's announcements were delivered in a very low voice. They seemed to be formal rather than prac-tical, as all paints had been prepared long in advance and making up and dressing went on simultaneously.

After the second announcement had been made, Fred and I left the kiva and went home to get into our costumes. On re-turning to Tawaovi we found our mates nearly dressed. Under the guidance of Joe Qopilvuh we smeared our faces, hands, and arms with a *duma* ("white clay") solution. Then we picked up the twigs of spruce that we were to carry, and we were ready. We had been warned that we would be expected to pass out gifts, so we put up three bags apiece of peanuts and crackers, one for each kiva where we were to dance. Ned and the other Hopi car-ried boiled sweet corn and had it ready for distribution.

It was after one o'clock in the morning when Siletstiwa announced that it was time for the dancing to start. We each took a handful of sacred cornmeal from a tray near the north banquette, filed out of the kiva, and assembled in the dark behind the chief's house. The dancers who were to perform as men were fully clad, but they carried their turtle-shell leg rattles so that no one would hear them clanking. Behind Tawaqwaptiwa's house each of us breathed on his cornmeal and tossed it upward in the four cardinal directions. Then Tom produced a long yucca whip and tapped every man lightly four times on a bare, extended arm. Apparently this was not enough to satisfy the chief, for he seized the whip, brushed Tom aside, and gave each of us two swift, hard slashes. Then Martin took the whip, gave the chief two severe cuts, and after he had made a discharming motion, ran off somewhere to deposit the whip. [This whipping is given to dancers only in conjunction with the Bean dance and applies to all groups except the men of the Powamu kiva, who are never whipped. Most men say that the whipping should be light. The fact that everyone in our unit was whipped had the effect of demonstrating that there was no discrimination.]

When Martin returned, we clustered about him and ran through our first song, singing the chorus twice over and the entire tune once. While this was going on, spectators were filing into Tawaovi. It was now close to two o'clock in the morning.

As we started to enter the kiva in single file, Poliyestiwa stood on the hatch, and in a muffled voice, shouted remarks down to Kelnimptiwa, father of the *katcinas*. We learned later that he had made wisecracks about each dancer as he was climbing down the ladder. Of Tom, who is quite stout, he said, "This one got his big belly (became pregnant) at Sherman before coming home from school." Of Fred and me he said that we had bad ears, meaning that we understood only a little Hopi. In the same spirit, when Charles later appeared with the Powamu group and was carrying a stick, Charles said of himself that he was a cow girl (divorcée or widow) who couldn't get a husband, so used a stick instead.

One or two of the "women" dancers from other kivas were made up as Negroes. All the units were swelled by the addition of Moenkopi men, as well as two dancers from Second Mesa villages. All newcomers just picked up the tunes and rhythms and did the best they could without further ado. [Bean dance *katcinas*, regardless of costume, are never masked. This is to enable youngsters, who are watching the first dance since their recent *katcina* initiations, to see for themselves that the performers are actually human beings, impersonating supernatural characters.]

Our group had ten or eleven male performers and nine or ten "women." It was by far the largest of the three participating units. When we had finished at Tawaovi, we walked over to the Powamu kiva. Poliyestiwa again made caustic remarks about each performer. Here we were asperged by the Powamu chief, Siletstiwa, and sprinkled with sacred cornmeal. As soon as we began to sing and dance, Siletstiwa withdrew to the northwest corner of the kiva, where he sat with his face to the wall. He remained thus absorbed in prayer throughout the night, interrupting his vigil only when a new group of dancers had to be asperged.

In this small kiva there was only one light and a crowded mass of spectators. The dancing figures completely filled the floor space of the lower level and, with their waving spruce boughs, caused a fantastic pattern of flickering shadows to alternate with streaks of light on the kiva walls. The heat of the kiva, the pack of onlookers, the play of light and shadow, and the strong beat of our song and dance had a marked effect. Here, and here only, did I strongly feel the hypnotic effect that is supposed to be a part of primitive dancing. Actually, one did lose himself in the rhythm, aided, in my opinion, by the shifting combinations of light and dark. These were especially noticeable as we moved sideways, northward to the head of the line. At first the light was wavering and unsteady, thanks to the bobbing shadows caused by the spruce boughs that we carried in our hands. Then, as we prepared to take hands with our partners, we were in almost total darkness, but when we went down the middle, we found ourselves in a steady, white light. (Fred Eggan agreed with me when we talked over our reactions. He, too, felt that the performance in Powamu kiva had produced a peculiar, hypnotic sensation. This contrasted with our reactions in the other kivas, where we felt nothing strange.)

One surprise, amounting to a shock, awaited us during the actual dancing. When it came time to start down the center and we reached out to take the hands of our male partners, we found them slipping us packets of *somiviki* or other gifts that they had acquired. Those who take masculine parts must carry gourd rattles in the right hand and keep the left free for clasping their partners. It is thus left to the "women," who do not need to shake rattles in rhythm, to carry their partners' gifts in the left hand, together with their spruce boughs.

As we left each kiva and filed past the unmarried girls on the west bench, they gave each of us some packets of *somiviki* or simliar items. Once we got outside, a blanket was spread into which we tossed our gifts. Probably, a few of the men occasionally failed to unload; and it was at such times that they palmed things off on their "feminine" partners. Quite a little *qömi* was mixed in with the *somiviki*, but it was of no special size or shape and had no courtship significance.

Apparently, the different dance groups often play tricks on one another as they go from kiva to kiva. It is also standard procedure for outfits to jest and exchange uncomplimentary re-

marks whenever they pass each other. Along similar lines, one
of our bunch saw a man from another kiva conceal some gifts
that he evidently intended to hand out at a later time. As soon as
he was out of sight, the Tawaovi group pounced on the package
and shared its contents among themselves. This was considered to
be a great joke.

After we had finished our first song at our last stopping
place, the Marau kiva, we gathered around Martin and went
through our second song. Then we danced to it in the Powamu
kiva, went on to the Marau kiva, and ended up at Tawaovi.
Thus, we began and ended in our home kiva in accordance with
Hopi custom. This closed out the evening's dancing, and as soon
as the spectators had left, we began to disrobe. The chief invited
all the dancers who were going to their homes to wash up to
return to Tawaovi in order to feast on the good things that had
been collected. He also asked if he could come to my house to
clean up, as he was afraid to go home lest Betty, who had not
yet been initiated into the *katcina* cult, should recognize him.
(In former times, of course, uninitiated children were never allowed to see a Bean dance with unmasked *katcinas*, but the old
pattern is sometimes violated nowadays. It is strange that Betty is
not permitted to see a Bean dance, yet she has twice viewed the
Soyal exercises in preparation for taking the part of a Soyal
mana.)

After we had washed up, we returned to Tawaovi where
we feasted on a veritable mountain of *qömi* and *somiviki* that had
been heaped just north of the fireplace. It was nearly half-past
five in the morning when we finally got to bed.

K. Men's Footrace by Clans at Oraibi

Feb. 18, 1934 [pp. 242 ff.]. Harold appeared this morning in the
capacity of a racing chief to announce a clan race by men. I did
not expect to take part, but Qöyawaisi, a Soyal *mana* and therefore an important personage, called out that I had to run for
the Sun clan. Since I was out of shape, I agreed, as Ned had advised, to run only the short course, which was customarily taken
by women, old men, and small children. The other men, of course,
planned to run a much longer route, from the foot of the mesa
around Kikötcmovi and back up the mesa to Oraibi.

Just before noon I went into Tawaovi with Ned. He helped
me dress in a *katcina* kilt and sash, tied a bunch of bright feathers
atop my head, and attached a large cardboard Sun-shield to my

back. My upper body was left bare, but Ned painted a big white star with white clay (*duma*) on my chest and a crescent moon on my back [Fig. 14 f]. He then asked me to crook my arms at the elbows, whereupon he ran a generous amount of white clay across my upper and lower arms at once. Meantime, the chief was assisting Calvin and Lawrence who were to run for the Bear clan with him. Each participant featured something symbolic of his clan, even though the devices used might be unofficial and chosen according to whim.

In due time Harold came down the kiva ladder to make the final announcement that it was time for the race to start. As he spoke, he faced north and rested his hand on a rung of the ladder about shoulder-high. (This is the conventional position taken whenever an official announcement is made.)

North of the fireplace, as was customary, was a tray of sacred cornmeal. Here too had been put the racing balls, one for each clan. Martin's was made of piñon sap (*sani*),[20] but the others were fashioned from sandstone. All were about two inches across, squarish, with the edges rounded off. The racers were barefooted, but some had bits of cloth tied about the big toe of one or both feet.

We left the kiva by clans, each led by its head or principal man. Thus, the chief preceded Calvin and Lawrence, and Ned took precedence over me. Each leader took a kicking ball and a handful of meal from the tray, and all of us proceeded to the starting line near Flute Spring (Lenangva), west of the village. When we got to the starting point, cornmeal paths were sprinkled, and the balls were placed on them.

Soon the other kiva groups arrived. When all the runners were lined up, Harold made the usual speech for these occasions, urging the racers to run with happy hearts so that good things would accrue to all. As soon as he was through, one man from each clan got his toes under the ball used by his group and "kicked" it forward, as far as he could, with a pendulum motion. [Actually, there is no real kicking.] Meantime, others of his clan ran ahead. One approached the ball as soon as it had landed and propelled it forward again, while the others ran on ahead once more.

In spite of the pauses for "kicking" the race went at a far faster pace than I had anticipated. It was remarkable to see how the runners, barefooted though they were, plunged into cactus or thorny bushes without the slightest hesitation. Those who had no partners in the race made only one or two token "kicks," then picked up their stones and carried them as they ran. Clans which had multiple representatives continued to run and "kick" all the way.

The short cut came out on the main highway between Kikötcmovi and Oraibi, only a few hundred yards below the pueblo. We rested at the juncture while we awaited the racers who were making the full circuit.

It was not long before the leading runners appeared and even the last man was only fifty or sixty yards behind. Little Lawrence, to my utter amazement, was out ahead of the pack, puffing up the hill in great style. As he had done no "kicking," his feat was discounted by the others, especially by Sam, who accused him of having taken shortcuts. In spite of everything it was some stunt for a kid of about nine to have run barefooted about three and one-half to four miles and to have finished in the lead, despite a mile-long steep upgrade at the finish.

Close behind came the men of the Pikyas clan. They were the official winners, having "kicked" and run all the way. They just beat out a team of young men from the Badger clan.

Those of us who had taken the shortcut waited until all the leading groups had passed to avoid giving the false impression that we had run all the way. We then fell in with the stragglers and jogged along to the finish line at the east edge of the pueblo. Here the women, children, and male nonparticipants greeted the runners with thanks. Some of the women helped themselves to assorted portions of the paraphernalia that had been worn or carried by their clanmates.

A few of the men inserted their fingers into their throats and forced themselves to vomit. (This is a standard Hopi rite of purification.) None of the younger participants did this.

Thereafter each clan group went to the kiva of its headman. Inside the kiva, while the racers were changing clothes and cleaning up, every detail of the race was fully discussed, and everyone manifested great interest in each and every incident touched upon. As soon as Ned had gotten into street dress, he said that he was going out to the edge of the mesa "to purify" himself, meaning "to induce vomiting."

In a short time women began to arrive at the kiva entrance, bringing liberal quantities of food for their clansmen. The lavish profusion, far more than we could eat, again reminded me of the conspicuous waste of food that is found on the Trobriand Islands. [Compare p. 63.] We got lots of stew, beans of all kinds, *piki*, fresh bread, fried bread, doughnuts, and coffee. There was enough food spread out to satisfy three times our membership. I had asked Ida to buy a dozen oranges as my gift to the kiva, but she insisted on paying for them out of her own pocket. (On those occasions it is not fitting for a man to provide food. Everything is supposed to be supplied by a man's clanswomen.)

Before we started to eat Ned took several pinches of food from various dishes and offered them to the *katcina* house in the center of the north wall of the kiva. Then the food was divided into equal portions. Each man ate all he could and carried the rest home. Although the food was contributed by each participant's clanswomen and although each gift was announced as being for the benefit of a particular clan, all the items were put together and everything was shared by all. In this way kiva loyalty and solidarity were maintained, despite the fact that the race and its food rewards were supposed to be for particular clans. (Consciously or otherwise the Hopi have developed various mechanisms to break up clan alignments and to prevent allowing clan solidarity to outweigh loyalty to the social whole.)

L. A Puppet-doll Dance at Hotevilla[21]

Mar. 23, 1934 [p. 282]. Ned, George, and I went to observe a set of night kiva dances that were part of the Hotevilla Anktioni cycle. We went into Hawiovi kiva and saw performances of the Taos Snow *katcina* and two sets of mixed *katcinas*. One of these, so Ned later revealed, had a song and dance that pertained to the Water-serpent (Palulokong) dance. The words made direct references to Palulokong. Indeed, throughout Hotevilla's Anktioni there ran a Water-serpent motive, even though the main feature was to be a Puppet-doll dance and not a Water-serpent dance. [See p. 282.]

It was the fourth group that put on the Puppet-doll dance. At the beginning some mixed *katcinas* arrived with Hahai'i and He'e'e. He'e'e carried a gourd of water, and offered a drink first to the fire tender and then to the man serving as father of the *katcinas*. In each case He'e'e held the gourd and so tipped it that the drinker was doused about the head and face. Thereupon, He'e'e gave each man several cakes of *somiviki*.

The *katcinas* who are allowed to speak then ordered the kiva fire to be covered. While several male spectators held blankets over the fire so that the light was effectively cut off, other performers entered and in the darkness, along the north wall of the kiva, they set up a screen that had been brought down in sections. Two puppet dolls were put in position, next to the screen, and at each corner there was placed a small spruce. The figure of a sandpiper appeared at the top of the screen; and a number of clay cones from which corn sprouts protruded were set out in front.

With the other performers a number of flute players and singers, who shook dentalium shell rattles, had entered the darkened kiva. In the dark they began to sing and play. I'm sure that they used Flute dance songs. This probably comprises a prayer for rain, as the clay cones are supposed to represent a field of corn. Throughout this part of the performance the various *katcinas* made their characteristic calls, so that a mad cacophony resulted. At last all the Flute men retired behind the screen (puppet-doll house), so that when the fire was uncovered, they were no longer to be seen, although their piping was sometimes heard. Only two Hehea impersonators, one crouched at each corner of the screen, were left in plain view. [See Fig. 19.][22]

One *katcina* dressed as the sky god, Sotukinangwa'a, and carrying a whizzer (bull-roarer) and a lightning frame, was also behind the screen. However, he was visible from the shoulders up because, from time to time, he stood up to shoot lightning over —but not directly at—the cornfield. Also, at irregular intervals, the sandpiper was made to "skate" across the top of the screen.

The dolls, probably one Shalako and one Palhik maiden, were about two feet high. They stood upright in open spaces, like doorways, one on each side of a figure of Muyingwa, the main god of germination. As the dolls were made to move their arms up and down, in time to the rhythm of the song, they actually appeared to be dancing like women.

When the first song had concluded, the dolls were bent over small *metates* in such fashion that as they moved their arms exactly as before, in time to a second tune, they seemed to be grinding corn. When this was finished, in each doll's right hand was placed a tiny broom with which "she" pretended to sweep meal onto a little plaque. Thereupon, the father of the *katcinas* heaped each tray with the sweet-corn meal (*tosi*) concealed behind the screen's front partition, and passed the tray around to all the spectators.

Throughout this performance, in order to make sure that there would be enough light, a large blaze was kept going in the firepit. As a result, the kiva became uncomfortably warm.

Then the fire was again covered, the screen and the dolls were carried out of the kiva in the dark, but the clay mounds with sprouts were purposely left behind to be handed out to the onlookers.

CHAPTER XI

The Changing Scene

[*Impressive changes have taken place at Old Oraibi since 1932. Few young adults continue to live in the village, yet, thanks to vastly improved medical care, the total population has increased somewhat. Farming, once the principal occupation of all Hopi men, is gradually losing its importance, and the formerly widespread practice of sheepherding has become virtually extinct. Automotive vehicles have made the keeping of livestock unnecessary, and few animals of any kind are now to be seen. In general terms, the Hopi are shifting from a subsistence economy to one based on cash earned from jobs in nearby cities.*

Changes in material culture have been matched by important nonmaterial changes. At Old Oraibi, not a single major ceremony has been performed since the early 1950s.

Many factors have contributed to the collapse of Old Oraibi's traditional way of life, but none has had a more telling effect than the building of paved, all-weather roads. These have broken down the comparative isolation of the Hopi towns and have caused the inhabitants to look outward to the "White" cities instead of inward toward their own pueblos.]

In the early 1930s traditional Hopi culture was very much a going concern at Old Oraibi. Tawaqwaptiwa was active as Village chief; the ceremonial calendar was reasonably full; *katcina* dances in the open season were of frequent occurrence; communal activities took place quite often; and racing, of one kind or another, was an important activity.

A census, taken on November 24, 1933, showed that about twenty-seven houses (Fig. 20) were permanently occupied.[1] At the same time four kivas—Tawaovi, Hawiovi, Marau, and Powamu—were in regular use. The number of occupied houses remained practically unchanged until about 1953, when a noticeable tendency developed to build modern structures northeast of the old center of the village, on free land, that is, land unassigned for any purpose by the chief. A son and a daughter of Joe have recently built new houses close to his in the main part of Old Oraibi (Fig. 21, H, G). Joe's daughter and her husband are the only Oraibi couple that was ever readmitted to the old pueblo after living for a time in New Oraibi. As to kivas, Tawaovi remains active; but Hawiovi has been abandoned, and Marau and Powamu are used only sporadically, often forced by lack of numbers to combine their memberships. Of the two, Marau is in greater use as a weaving center and a *katcina* dressing place, but Powamu seems to be headed for extinction.

As shown by a census, Oraibi's population in the fall of 1933 was estimated at about 112,[2] counting children of all ages. Twenty years later there were about 119, and now the figure seems to be approaching 130. In all likelihood, the primary factor that accounts for this upswing is a decline in infant mortality, a decline that more than makes up for the steady loss of young adults who are increasingly moving out of Oraibi. (One must always bear in mind that with each departure it grows ever lonelier for those who remain at Oraibi.) Apparently, the upswing in the number of young children has been caused by a greater willingness on the part of prospective mothers to take advantage of government hospitals and other facets of "White" medicine. A few native medicine men continue to be active throughout the reservation, but none resides in Old Oraibi. The last one to have lived there, as I was told in 1955, was Poliyestiwa, whose maternal grandfather, Dotuka (see p. 69), was said to have been a member of a long-extinct curing society at Walpi. Since Poliyestiwa was capable of "extracting" foreign substances from a patient's body, he was regarded as a reformed witch. He died in 1960.

In the old days babies were born at home, but an investigation conducted in 1955 revealed that eight women had borne a total of twelve children in hospitals. A slight tendency was noted for younger mothers to have only their first babies in hospitals; and older women seemed to prefer home confinements unless there was some complication. Thus, one mature woman gave birth to a premature infant in a hospital, and another was delivered while she was hospitalized with diarrhea.

Traditionally, it has long been believed that no sunlight should fall on a newborn child for twenty days.[3] In keeping with this belief, it has become customary for mothers to subtract from the required period whatever number of days has been spent in a hospital.

A baby, until it had learned to walk, formerly lived much of its life tied and wrapped in a cradleboard (*ta'pû*), but cradles and cribs have now replaced cradleboards. Moreover, three decades ago it was commonplace to see a child being carried pickaback, tightly bound with a shawl or blanket, by an older female (Fig. 22), but this mode of carriage is now becoming obsolete.

Marriage customs have been drastically modified. Early in the century an occasional Hopi couple was persuaded to go through a "White" ceremony, at the insistence of a missionary, school superintendent, or government official. Now it is customary for couples voluntarily to have a "White" civil or religious ceremony before entering into the protracted rites of a Hopi wedding.[4] This change of custom does not necessarily indicate conversion but is based on a desire for official written records, since the Hopi have no writing. The people realize that documented weddings make it harder than was earlier the case to get a divorce. On the other hand, women, especially, feel that possession of written records simplifies numerous dealings with the American government. For example, legal documents make it easier for wives to get money allotments if their husbands go into the armed services, and women with official papers stand a far better chance of getting financial support in the event of divorce.

Today, Hopi brides, even if they live and work off the reservation, still receive traditional, newly made wedding outfits from their relatives. In other respects, however, modern weddings are modeled on "White" lines. They are often preceded by bridal "showers"; and they have become very lavish affairs. The standard gift is a sack of flour, and most families keep on hand, for such occasions, a large number of sacks. A newlywed is apt to receive so many presents that they have to be brought to the scene of the festivities by a number of trucks, and so ample is the supply of gifts likely to be that brides make a practice of redistributing some of the surplus to chosen guests.

While the citizenship status of the Hopi Indians is unclear, the American government has ruled that their young men are eligible for the draft. As is to be expected, this has aroused a great deal of resentment. Nevertheless, eight Oraibi men, most of whom were already married, were drawn into the armed services in World War II. About six veterans returned as heavy drinkers. This introduced a new problem to Oraibi. Traditionally, the Hopi were complete teetotalers and used to call all intoxicating beverages *honakkuyi* ("crazy water"). None of them even sipped beer in the old days. Gradually, a few schoolboys began to drink a little, then ex-servicemen developed a real taste for hard liquor. From the younger men the custom spread to the older, and now a fair proportion of Hopi men drink in varying amounts. In 1955 even Ned, one of the more conservative elderly men, admitted that he liked a small amount of beer once in a while. In fact, his chief objections to the consumption of liquor were the costs involved and the trouble that drunkards often caused their neighbors. Another middle-aged Oraibi man, who worked frequently on the roads, frankly stated that he used to enjoy going into Winslow for a spree about twice a month. Later, this man gave up drinking, and resumed his abstemious ways. The state of Arizona has legalized the sale of liquor to Indians in its cities and towns, but it remains a federal offense to bring intoxicants onto a reservation. As is true elsewhere under such conditions, bootleggers flourish, and those who want to drink have no trouble in obtaining supplies.

The rising incidence of drunkenness has affected other areas of behavior. For instance, Rebecca Williams used to sleep outdoors in good weather in the yard of her home at Kikötcmovi. In 1954 she was attacked and badly beaten by a drunken man, whom she thought she recognized as a resident of Bakavi. Thereafter, she slept indoors in all seasons of the year. Physical assault was virtually unknown in earlier times.

It is charged that drunkards never participate in the performance of rituals, but that they use ceremonial events only as occasions for getting drunk.

Burial practices, too, have become noticeably altered.[5] There is a greater use of coffins, and farewell speeches that resemble sermons are not uncommon. Then, too, funeral parties with many mourners are becoming customary. There are also times when pagan families let Christian missionaries perform burials for the sake of convenience or economy.

Formerly, in the early 1930s, small children of either sex used to run about naked in the warm months, and liked particularly to wade in mud puddles after a rain; but thirty years later total nakedness was uncommon, although it was occasionally to be seen. Adult nudity has always been distasteful to the Hopi, and middle-aged folk still grumble about "White" tourists, especially women, who appear in shorts or with much of their bodies exposed. As Ned once phrased it, " 'White' people like to go around naked."

Long ago, whenever a child at play noticed a strange Caucasoid coming into the village, he was expected to raise a warning cry of "Bahana" (" 'White' man"), which was invariably echoed throughout the pueblo, but "White" visits are now so frequent that no warning shouts are ever heard. As a matter of fact, in the summer of 1957, on a day that Snake dances were being held on First and Second Mesas, Greyhound buses brought loads of tourists right into Old Oraibi. Their coming was neither unexpected nor unwelcome. A few adult villagers and a great many youngsters sold plaques and other small items on every hand. Chief Tawaqwaptiwa's adopted daughter Margaret had cleaned up one of the town's squares for her adoptive father. Old as he was, the chief had erected an outdoor counter at which he did a brisk business, primarily from the sale of *katcina* dolls.

There has been a significant increase in the use of English by children. Some speak that language even while playing with their fellow Hopi. This is unquestionably the result of "White" schooling, but even some of the older folk, who speak only their native tongue and have never gone to school, have become so accustomed to calling youngsters by their English names that they cannot recall the Hopi names. Practically everyone who is now middle-aged or younger has been to school and knows some English. About thirty years ago every resident of Oraibi who had outside correspondents had to adopt an Anglicized version of his Hopi name and had to purchase a box—for one dollar per year— at the local post office in New Oraibi. Most people spelled their names as they had learned to do at school.

One of the principal feminine occupations of former years was the grinding of cornmeal on old-fashioned *metates*. These are essentially slabs of sandstone, set upright in small, wooden bins, in the manner of old-fashioned washboards. Each household used to have several *metates* for making meal in varying degrees of fineness. (After Ruth received $10,000 for the death of George, late in World War II, she became lazy and hired Louise to grind for her at $1.00 per day. Later, Louise and her husband separated, and it is rumored that, for her dependent children, she gets a large monthly check from the American government. She no longer grinds corn for Ruth, and she does not seem to lack material goods.)

Nowadays, Oraibi women spend little time at *metates*. Much corn is ground at home in meat choppers with special attachments. In addition, for those who can afford his services, Lorenzo Yoyoki, of New Oraibi, brother of Horace, Hubbell's workman, serves as a professional miller. He uses a power-driven machine and charges $1.00 for making about a hundred pounds of meal. From one point of view these changes provide a great advantage. Fine particles of sandstone invariably used to become mixed with whatever cornmeal was prepared on a *metate*, but the use of modern implements has eliminated grit from the diet.

Piki bread is still baked in the old-fashioned way, however, and remains a universally favorite food.[6] Even Ruth, who has given up grinding, continues to bake *piki*. At the same time, as we discovered when we watched Martha making *piki* in 1955, a few innovations have crept in, for she kept the batter in a "china" dish and used Wesson oil in place of native shortening. In the same vein, we were told that many women have begun to use store-bought soda for leavening instead of using freshly made ashes of juniper, sage, or spruce.

On the whole, traditional foods continue in favor despite the increased use of canned goods and store-bought beef, fruits, and vegetables.

Diners generally sit on chairs, and meals are eaten from individual, purchased dishes that are set on linoleum- or plastic-covered tables. Only when the number of guests is so large that it exceeds the number of available place settings are meals served in the old way, in large pottery bowls that are placed on pieces of linoleum on the floor or set directly on the bare floor. In such cases, Hopi diners sit on sheepskins or rugs and customarily take food out of large, common bowls with the hands and fingers. "White" visitors have always been expected to perch on small wooden stools, about a foot high, and to eat with the help of a teaspoon.

Coffee, which was formerly the well-nigh universal drink, has been replaced in the summer by Kool-aid, a beverage made from a powder mixed with cold water, which is cheaper and easier to prepare than coffee.

Hardly anyone continues to wear traditional garb. The essential elements of masculine clothing are trousers or blue jeans, shirts open at the throat, and shoes. Even very old men are no more to be seen in long winter underwear, which they once regarded as proper exterior garments for warm weather (Fig. 23). Many women who used to wear Hopi dresses exclusively now appear in cotton prints or other dresses bought in stores, together with shoes and stockings. Permanents and other styles of "White" hairdo are common with younger women, and cosmetics are frequently used. On the eve of a Butterfly dance in 1955 women were observed washing their hair with prepared shampoos instead of in yucca suds.[7]

At the turn of the present century, Oraibi men wore their hair loose and long at the sides and back, and trimmed into short bangs over the forehead. In the 1930s the long hair at the back was gathered up and, with the help of a wooden form, shaped into a large bun that was tied with string about the middle. A brightly colored kerchief, made into a band and knotted at the right, encircled the head. Today, only Martin wears his hair long and in a bun at the rear. Colored headbands, however, remain popular. Since Ned has joined the council at New Oraibi he wears his hair short, in "White" fashion, with a part to one side, no bangs over the forehead, and no headband.

Sexual dichotomy, except for the making of *katcina* dolls, continues to follow its long-established lines in all the traditional pursuits that are still being carried on. Women, as usual, devote most of their time to the care of children and household tasks, but they no longer go to do laundry at the schoolhouse in New Oraibi. That town has a modern laundromat, but many women in Old Oraibi own washing machines, run on kerosene or butane. These are usually purchased on an installment plan. A number of wage earners who live off the reservation like to buy various appliances for female relatives who have remained in the old village. Such purchases and gifts not only show one's devotion and affection but also gain for a donor a measure of prestige and esteem that greatly exceeds what normally accompanies an identical purchase in a city.

As a seasonal activity toward the end of summer, most of Oraibi's women still make twined plaques, trays, or baskets of sun-dried fibers of rabbit brush (*siva'api*) or of leaves of yucca. Painted designs are now made with purchased aniline dyes, and not with earthen or vegetable coloring materials. (Similar objects are made on Second Mesa and elsewhere by a coiling method that does not produce raised centers.)

Pottery-making was never, in the mid-1930s, an important activity at Oraibi. What little there was, was the work of one or two women and was strictly undecorated and utilitarian. It was usually reddish brown in color and, for the most part, was coiled freehand into bowls and water jars.

At the present time, only Anita and her daughters make pottery regularly at Oraibi. Thanks to "White" interest and patronage they sometimes experiment with shapes and sizes, but there are few innovations; and there is no potter's wheel in the village. (Most Hopi pottery is made on First Mesa.)

Sewing classes were once popular and were conducted in Voth's church at Oraibi by the wives of Christian missionaries. Classes were attended as social events by many pagan women. When, around 1942, Voth's church was struck by lightning and fell into ruin, sewing classes were held in the home of Dorothy, a poor non-Christian who needed whatever small sums of money she could get for the use of her house. In the course of time, Dorothy's husband began to make ample money as an excellent carver of *katcina* dolls, and sewing classes are no longer held in her house. Sometimes, the gap is filled by the sewing of quilts in Fred Johnson's church at New Oraibi, but regular sewing bees have been abandoned.

(Dorothy used to shuttle between her house in Old Oraibi [Fig. 21, #12] and another one in Kikötcmovi. Recently, Jack, as the husband of Oraibi's alleged chieftainess, told Dorothy that she would have to live permanently in one pueblo or the other. She chose to stay in New Oraibi.)

Strange as it may seem, Oraibi women have been known to carve and sell *katcina* dolls. This is an unexpected intrusion into what was formerly an exclusively masculine occupation. In fact, the late chief had established this activity as a monopoly for himself, and those Oraibi men who could also make dolls had had to sell them surreptitiously. Old-fashioned *katcina* dolls were always carved from a knot of drifted cottonwood (*ba'ko*) and were painted with natural colors. In later years, only the chief made his dolls according to traditional methods, but as he grew old, his dolls tended to be poorly carved and badly painted.

Those Oraibi men who have not turned for their livelihood to nonorthodox pursuits, such as roadwork or carpentry,[8] still devote themselves mainly to farming; and even the men who work outside the reservation raise a good deal of their food by farming on weekends with the aid of wives, children, or hired help. For a time, about three decades ago, the herding of sheep was extremely important and seemed to be the most important of masculine occupations. Sheep provided meat and cash from surplus animals, lambs, and wool. However, it may well be that the spread of a money economy, and the attendant urge to work for cash, have had a fatal impact on many aspects of the old culture. Contemporary young men are disinterested in farming and particularly disillusioned with sheepherding. They do not care to work outdoors seven days a week, in all kinds of weather, and for very little gain. Nowadays when a Hopi inherits or is given a flock of sheep, he usually sells it for cash in preference to herding.

Occasionally, the women of a modern family raise a few pigs, but the practice is rare and never long-lasting.

Some of the men who know the old-fashioned arts and crafts continue to practice weaving. It is the older males who work most at looms, and only one young man at Oraibi engages in this pursuit. He does just a little miscellaneous work. In all, a variety of garments and accessories are woven, but some workmen limit their weaving to wedding robes, belts, and sashes.

Jack is the only elderly silversmith in the town; but three of the younger men work in silver.

Since 1953 cinder blocks and cement have become popular building materials, replacing chipped local stone and adobe mud. Large roof beams, transported by truck, may be brought in from a radius of one hundred miles. They make possible the construction of larger rooms than were ever known before. At first, some traditionalists opposed the building of new style houses, especially in the old inhabited portions of Old Oraibi, but in the end they were forced to yield.

The major tasks of house building and repair, regardless of construction methods or materials used, continue to be done by men but, as usual, such lighter operations as plastering are still performed by women. Moreover, there has been little change in the Hopi convention that finished houses belong only to females. Consequently, the traditional system of matrilocal residence has been retained, but postmarital residence is no longer unilocal. Not in a single instance does a married woman at Oraibi live in the same house with her mother. On the contrary, young wives like to own more than one house in the pueblo, and to move between them, especially for convenience on ceremonial occasions. At such times, an occupant is required to remain in one house for four days after an event.

One might think that the Split of 1906, coupled with the increasing tendency of some Oraibi families to live off the reservation, has resulted in a great surplus of houses. This has not been the case; partly because most of the buildings that were abandoned in 1906 have been allowed to crumble into ruin, and partly because each nuclear family now occupies a separate dwelling.

Nevertheless, house ownership by clans continues to follow traditional lines. The principal exceptions pertain to cases in which a woman chooses to occupy a house belonging to the clan of her father or husband rather than one that belongs to her own clan. The potential for a change in clan ownership is always present when such a choice is made, but in only a single instance has a decision of this kind actually resulted in a transfer of clan ownership.

Other potential irregularities may result from rentals or gifts. Hopi rentals usually entail an owner's permission rather than a payment, but an owner from one clan is free to rent her house to someone from an unrelated clan. The same is true of gifts. For instance, Martin, of the Parrot clan, lives alone in House #18 (Fig. 21), which was given to him by an *ikya'a* from the Butterfly clan. Not only is it extraordinary for a Hopi man to own a house, but no one knows what will happen to this house when Martin dies.

Traditional household furnishings have given way to modern tables, chairs, beds, sofas, and bureaus. Sheepskins whose use was once widespread are no longer in evidence.

Appliances of "White" manufacture are becoming increasingly common. A count made about a dozen years ago revealed that even at that time Oraibi's houses contained one oil stove, one gas range, four refrigerators, eleven washing machines, fifteen radios, and two phonographs. Since the pueblo has always lacked gas and electricity, these contrivances are powered by batteries, kerosene, or butane.

When such appliances were first introduced, a curious situation, judged by our own standards, arose. Prestige was gained by ownership, without concern for utility or practicality. Hence, many a refrigerator or radio stood idle even if the owner could afford to replace batteries or buy additional tanks of gas. Furthermore, it should be remembered that many early radios had outside antennae, which mischievous boys delighted in pulling out of place, and tired owners soon came to prefer silence to the constant need of readjusting misplaced antennae.

Today, the situation is entirely different, and radios blare forth on every side.

Toilet habits have changed markedly. In the 1930s young boys, in particular, did not hesitate to urinate on the terraces before their houses. They were warned only not to wet and thus weaken the walls. At present they go to the edge of the mesa to relieve themselves, and house terraces no longer reek of stale urine. As for defecation, members of both sexes used to resort to the outskirts of the pueblo and trusted to cultural blindness to preserve their modesty. These conditions no longer prevail. In the last few years Old Oraibi has become ringed with out-houses. Over a dozen wooden structures have been built, and practically every family has access to one. (Indeed, some Hopi villages, as Dr. E. A. Kennard has told me, even have an official, known half-jokingly as an "outhouse chief," whose duty it is to inspect these buildings.) As it happens, Old Oraibi is located on rocky ground, so that it is often impossible to dig trenches under the privies. Consequently, more than one outhouse teeters over the mesa's edge. Not everyone, apparently, resorts to the use of a privy, for human excrement may still be seen occasionally in the village streets. Once in a while, too, one may observe one of the older men urinating against a woodpile close by his home; and, on rare occasions, one may even see old women urinating in public. As in times past they bend over but do not raise their dresses.

Beyond doubt, some of the most drastic changes affecting the material culture of Old Oraibi have been the results of new roads. Since the economic depression of 1929, the government of the United States has sponsored the building of all-weather highways across the reservation, making it possible for the pueblo's inhabitants to drive into cities, such as Holbrook, Flagstaff, or Winslow in about three hours. At least sixteen cars or trucks are to be found at Oraibi. This means that there are about half as many automotive vehicles as there are inhabited houses. Therefore, even if a householder does not own a car or truck, he can readily arrange to hire one. By contrast, about three decades ago at Oraibi, only Bert and Allen had small trucks.

In 1932 many burros (Fig. 24) roamed the pueblo's streets and served as scavengers when they were not in use; there was much horseback riding; and wagons drawn by mules or horses were common. Men used to spend many hours taking their animals out in order to hobble them beyond the limits of the town's cultivated lands. Then, when the beasts were again wanted, it required a considerable effort, usually involving a great deal of running, to round them up. Now, the last burro is gone;[9] horseback riding is rare; and in 1961 only about ten men, usually in partnerships, owned a total of twenty-one mules and horses of every sort.[10] No individual or combination of partners owned more than three such animals.

Communal work parties, once a regular part of life at Oraibi, are becoming extinct. In June, 1952, Ned took charge of the cleaning and repair of Lenva ("Flute Spring"), one of the town's principal reservoirs. In keeping with orthodox practice, he named Kane to succeed him as sponsor, but so much rain fell in 1953 that Kane never held his work party. Since then, scarcely any communal work has been done. Yet, so important were these activities in former times that they used to be officially announced by the Tca'akmongwi ("Crier chief"). (When the last official crier, Poliyestiwa, grew too old for the task, Ned took over, but he made only secular announcements from his own house.)

The new and ever-improved roads, combined with the increasing number of gasoline-powered vehicles, have had many profound effects on life at Oraibi. Above all, the inhabitants no longer feel isolated, and no longer are they impelled to direct their energies inward toward the village and to develop internal strength through self-reliance, pueblo-wide ceremonies, local amusements, and communal enterprises. Instead, people now turn their attention outward and away from the pueblo, especially in such matters as jobs, shopping, and entertainment.[11] There is also a growing number of men who dwell in rent- and tax-free homes at Oraibi but commute daily to work in a town like many suburbanites in our own culture. Such men have neither the time nor willingness to memorize long ritual speeches, to learn new songs, or to rehearse meticulously the complicated dance steps that were once an integral part of ceremonial life. Small wonder that the once-elaborate calendar of rites has shrunk so drastically, that dances tend to be held on weekends, and that the most popular performances are those in which a workingman can readily join a group of singers. So little of a serious religious nature takes place at Oraibi that qualified residents who like to participate in traditional ceremonies are led to take part in the rituals of other pueblos, particularly those of their natal villages.

All informants agree that the collapse of the ceremonial calendar is the most drastic aspect of culture change at Old Oraibi. Not only do the orthodox lament the passing of traditional beliefs and practices, but they also miss the color, excitement, and entertainment that the rituals used to provide. Consciously or not, many Hopi now sense what a tremendously binding effect used to be exerted by large-scale participation in ceremonial events; and nostalgically they point to the great pleasure that the ceremonies used to give to participants and spectators alike.

Directly linked to the extinction of Old Oraibi's ceremonial calendar is the marked indifference of the younger generation toward the perpetuation of old Hopi customs and beliefs. As a rule, they have little concern with orthodoxy and are content, for the most part, to forego active participation in anything but an occasional *katcina* dance. Furthermore, as improved technology and knowledge has brought more and more desired results under human control, there has been less and less *reliance* on the super-natural to bring about whatever is wanted.[12] Thus, when ample water can be readily obtained by turning a faucet, it is felt to be unnecessary to dance or pray for rain.

Yet, the extinction of rites is not a new phenomenon among the Hopi, for some ceremonies are known to have lapsed in times past. In the 1930s there were occasional references to a Ladder dance (Lamati) and other rites that had long ago been given up; and at Oraibi the Wuwutcim, Flute, and Snake-Antelope ceremonies have not been held for over half a century.

Even the great Soyal in which participation was once a badge of manhood and the goal of every male's ceremonial life has been abandoned.[13] At Old Oraibi its leadership used to go hand in hand with the Village chieftainship, but when Tawaqwap-tiwa began to relinquish that office, he turned more and more Soyal duties over to Martin. By 1950, Martin had become the leader of the Soyal, and Tawaqwaptiwa was serving as one of his assistants. By this time, too, the ceremony had become greatly reduced, and the only other participants in the esoteric rites per-formed in Tawaovi were Tom, formerly Tobacco chief; Tom's wife, Anita, who acted as Soyalmana, an office once held by her mother; and three Moenkopi men. In the winter of 1953 even this small number shrank drastically (Ned claims that at different times Tom and he had simply been ordered out), and only Martin and one Moenkopi man, probably Qopilvuh, kept alive a few aspects of the traditional rites. By 1955 the Soyal had virtually disappeared except that Ned and Martin had continued to stay up all night and to make prayer sticks for the Sun.

Entirely gone are all the customs that once bound the vil-lagers together by providing opportunities for pueblo-wide par-ticipation. No longer do Soyal men rush out of Tawaovi late in the afternoon of the fourth day to smear freshly made medicine on relatives, friends, neighbors, domestic animals, and sundry pieces of property. No more do messengers go from door to door, urging one and all to breathe on cornhusks, *hihikwispi* ("objects-to-be-breathed-upon"), that are later to be deposited at shrines as col-lective prayers. Scarcely remembered are the colorfully dressed Soyal men who used to collect from each householder a previously prepared bundle of corn which was to be blessed in the kiva and used for seed the next spring; and gone, too, are the antic Mastop *katcinas* who hopped and jumped about as they bestowed fer-tility on all females. Hardly anything remains of the prayer-stick distribution by Soyal men, which used to be followed by a "never-to-be-forgotten picture" as women ran at daybreak to deposit their *pahos* ("prayer sticks") at the Sowika shrine for children, and men hastened to put down their sticks at Tcupki, a shrine devoted to hunting. No longer do the droll Qöqöqlom *katcinas* appear in shabby and assorted garments to open all the kivas for the later use of their fellow *katcinas*. What a contrast there is between the hustle and bustle of the old Soyal and the present observance when one or two old men pray alone and make a few prayer offerings.

On the other hand, social or pleasure dances that never had important ceremonial connotations are still immensely popular. For instance, a two-day Butterfly dance was held at Oraibi on August 20 and 21, 1955. It was sponsored by Tom and Anita, who had vowed to assume this responsibility if a daughter and granddaughter returned nonpregnant from a year's stay at a government-run boarding school in Albuquerque. Sidney was invited to act as cosponsor because he is well versed in such matters, capable of providing mutton and sharing the expenses involved, and certain to get the help of his Sun clanswomen in running the affair. Songs were composed for the occasion by Louis, Harold, Sidney, and Andrew. Louis beat a large kettle-shaped drum, and practically all of the older men clustered about him and sang, while Harold led about two-dozen younger people of both sexes who, gaily costumed and painted but unmasked, performed the dance steps. The dance plaza alongside Tom's house was freshly swept and sanded for the occasion. The singers wore their "Sunday" pants, colorful shirts, bright headbands, belts of silver, and long strings of turquoise; and some carried in their hands twigs of spruce with which they gesticulated as they sang. The male dancers, in keeping with orthodox custom, wore gay shirts of velvet with varicolored ribbons attached, dance kilts, red moccasins, silver bracelets, and strings of beads; carried gourd rattles in the right hand; and had "sleigh" bells bound about their calves. They had "warriors' markings" (*Pûkong kûkû,* i.e., "footprints of Pûkong," elder of the Little War Twins or gods) drawn in two vertical stripes across their cheekbones with red lipstick.

Their partners, in former times always girls from the father's clan (*ikya'as,* conventionally translated as "paternal aunts"), were dressed in homespun, woolen dresses (*mantas*). They were gaily beribboned and wore bright scarfs. Their heads were crowned with carved and painted boards known as *tablitas,* and their foreheads were covered by fringes of false, black hair; their bare feet were daubed with yellow clay; they wore many ornaments; and in their hands they carried pieces of spruce with which they kept time to the rhythmic beating of the drum (Fig. 25).

Late in the second day, as custom decrees, some of the "paternal aunts" who had not been chosen to dance intruded into the dance line and, pretending jealousy, jostled aside the girls who were dancing with their beloved "nephews." All these women had hitherto been mere spectators. They were clothed in print dresses, several had on high-heeled shoes, and some were city dwellers who had never before taken part in a Butterfly dance. However, the pull of the traditional observance was so strong that ignorance of the proper steps was no deterrent. In their enthusiasm some "aunts" drew a number of singers into the dance line for a few measures; and one woman even forced the drummer to dance a little, but this was regarded as too extreme by the older men, who felt that lack of a drumbeat disrupted the performance.

So much enjoyment did the inhabitants of Oraibi get out of the dance that Mary, who was quite ill, put off entering the hospital at Keam's Canyon in order not to be deprived of the pleasure of dancing for a few moments with her "nephews."

Ada, Sidney's niece, came all the way from Barstow, California, in order to share in the fun; and Ida, Sidney's younger sister, came from the Grand Canyon at considerable inconvenience. Nor did the men take the festivities lightly. Just before the dance Sidney had suffered a sore throat and a severe bronchial infection, but he did not allow his ailments to keep him from playing his full part as cosponsor and singer.

At the noon rest periods on both days Tom and Anita served a huge meal of mutton stew, *piki*, wheat bread, corn, and watermelon for all participants, villagers, and visitors.

It was rather expensive to hold open house for so many people, and we were told that Anita had refused an offer from her brother Cedric to swell the ranks of singers and dancers by bringing a Moenkopi contingent to Oraibi. Anita felt that she could not afford the expense of lodging and feeding so large a number of extra people.

Katcina dances, as has already been noted, continue to be staged in the open season, but they are held rarely at Oraibi.[14] When they are given, they are regarded as plain dances, in the sense that they have no connections with other parts of the former ritual calendar. Men whose daughters had had Hopi marriages within the preceding year like to put on Niman ("Homegoing") dances so that, as in the past, their daughters may appear in public in their wedding finery.

The dwindling in number of outdoor *katcina* dances seems to result not only from widespread loss of interest in carrying on former rites, but also from a shortage of sponsors. Few Oraibi residents are wealthy enough to assume the heavy costs involved, and people are reluctant to shoulder the responsibilities of sponsorship unless they are reasonably sure that they will get the necessary cooperation of their fellows.

On the other hand, there is a universal feeling that the *katcina* cult itself must never be allowed to lapse. Consequently, a *katcina* initiation takes place every few years. It has been greatly modified and abbreviated in recent times, and neophytes may be several years younger than they once were, but the outlines of the old pattern may still be discerned.

Traditionally, the entire *katcina* cult was intricately bound to the great Powamu ceremony. Youngsters who were being inducted into the Powamu society's rites found themselves simultaneously being initiated into the *katcina* cult as well. They were taken into the kiva where *katcina* initiations were taking place, and they looked on, unwhipped, while the children who were joining *only* the *katcina* cult were severely lashed. In addition to remaining unwhipped, a masculine member of the Powamu society could, in later life, be chosen to serve as the "father of the *katcinas*," an extremely important official in all *katcina* performances. This post cannot be held by one who has been initiated only into the *katcina* cult. Since the Powamu society has become extinct at Oraibi, parents who want their children to join the *katcina* cult without a whipping and who want them to become eligible, ultimately, to serve as a "father of the *katcinas*" send them to be initiated to a village which still performs the Powamu rites. It is probably from this source that Oraibi will some day draw its "fathers."

(Not until he was about sixty-five years old had Ned been inducted into the Powamu by Panimptiwa, as part of a treatment for "rheumatism." In June of 1957, Ned was asked to serve as "father of the *katcinas*" during a dance at Oraibi. He was very proud to have been chosen, especially because he had hitherto been ineligible for the office. Although he is said to have performed his duties reasonably well, he was never again chosen to be a "father.")

Oraibi's recent method of initiating children into the *katcina* cult may be illustrated by describing the initiation that took place in the winter of 1954, when five youngsters were admitted. Whippings were administered by two Hu *katcinas,* but there was no Hahai'i impersonator. Each of the initiates, accompanied by his ceremonial father, stood on a heap of plain sand that had not been fashioned into the conventional dry painting,[15] and Panimptiwa made a short speech about the origin of the *katcina* cult and warned the children never to reveal to uninitiated juniors what they had just learned. That night, for the first time, the initiates saw a traditional Bean dance with unmasked *katcinas.* (See pp. 313–26.)

At present, Oraibi is modeling its *katcina* initiation along the lines of Kikötcmovi's procedure (at which Oraibi inhabitants once used to scoff), namely, a fully costumed *katcina* rests his mask for a moment on the head of each male candidate. Since Hopi females *never* wear masks, the girls simply look on. Inasmuch as there are no more Powamu (Bean dance) *katcinas,* the initiates are taken that night to an ordinary kiva dance at the end of which the *katcinas* unmask to show that ordinary men impersonate these supernaturals.

For a time an effort had been made at Oraibi to keep the Powamu rites going. As long as Siletstiwa, the traditional chief from the Real Badger clan, was alive, he came annually from his home in Moenkopi to conduct the ceremony in the Powamu kiva of the mother village. Unfortunately, Siletstiwa died suddenly around 1947, without having trained a successor. Accordingly, after his death his younger brother, Panimptiwa, an Oraibi man then in his middle sixties, voluntarily assumed the leadership. But Panimptiwa had never been trained for the office and did not know all the details of the complicated observances. Ironically, he was forced to follow the text published by Voth,[16] whom the orthodox Hopi hated because they held him responsible for having spread so many of their most cherished ceremonial secrets to the world at large. Because Panimptiwa could not read English, Voth's account used to be translated to him by his grandson Edmond, one of Kane's sons. Consequently, the ceremony had to be given up when Edmond died in 1952.

Another factor contributing to the collapse of the Powamu is said to have been the unwillingness of Ruth to continue the feminine duties associated with the rites. Panimptiwa, in his old age, had come to board with Ned and Ruth (later he boarded with his son Harold), and to humor him she used to prepare *wotaka* ("salt-free gravy") (see p. 313) and other foods that were customarily eaten in the kiva during Powamu. Since Ruth was of the Masau'û clan, whose women did not ordinarily perform this function, and since she herself had no personal connection with Powamu, she refused to participate after four or five years.

Regardless of how one may choose to interpret the cause, the ceremony was thereafter all but given up. The only vestiges remaining at present are the making of some prayer offerings in the Powamu kiva at the appropriate time, and the forced growing of beans by most men in their kivas or at home. Beyond that nothing persists but a sentimental or nostalgic feeling for the color and excitement that had formerly accompanied the Powamu (see pp. 311–13).

Long ago, it was customary for the Powamu chief to extend his rites by the addition of a Patcava ceremony in years when novices had been inducted into the Wuwutcim (Tribal Initiation) societies (O.O., pp. 222–26). In 1946 or 1947, just prior to his death, Siletstiwa had supervised the last of Oraibi's Patcava rituals. It was only faintly connected with the long-extinct Tribal Initiation observances, and it was an abbreviated affair, with only two participating kivas and two Patcava maidens.

Although the effects of the new road system are so plainly evident in matters of ritual, they have by no means been limited to the ceremonial side of life at Old Oraibi. Even in such an activity as farming have good roads induced important changes. For instance, in earlier times it was pointless for a farmer to raise a large surplus, particularly if it concerned a product, such as watermelon, that could not be easily preserved. At present, the more one raises of anything the more he can sell in town.[17] Conversely, it was amazing, during the drought year of 1953, to see a peddler from Phoenix selling corn to the Hopi at Oraibi.[18]

Women's duties too have not remained unaffected by the development of new roads. In past times, as occasion demanded, they were expected to haul water, in huge pottery jars (*ollas*), up the steep incline of Third Mesa. Now, almost any truck owner, either as a favor or for a small charge, will haul water for a householder.

Several impressive changes, not necessarily related even to "White" contact, have taken place internally in the social and political fields. What has been called Phratry IX,[19] comprising the Chicken-hawk, Crane, and Squash clans, had become extinct prior to 1932. By 1950 the Bow, Real Coyote, Patki, and Navaho Badger clans had also disappeared. The Bear clan died out in 1960, and today the Sand, Reed (Bakab), Water Coyote, Real Badger, and Gray Badger clans have only masculine representatives. In this matrilocal society, it follows that they are destined soon to die out unless new members move into Oraibi at marriage.

The political situation at Oraibi is still incompletely settled. Tawaqwaptiwa, the late Village chief, who died on April 30, 1960, was buried by Margaret and Jack. He had belonged to the proper clan (Bear) for chiefs; but since he and his wife, Nasingönsi (Parrot), were childless and since there were no other Bear people at Oraibi, it was understood that the succession would pass to the Parrot clan through his wife's sister Masamösi. This impression was strengthened when Tawaqwaptiwa adopted three of Masamösi's children, Martin, Sam, and Margaret, all of whom belonged, of course, to the Parrot clan.

In 1932 Tawaqwaptiwa began to groom Sam and Martin for various pueblo offices. Inasmuch as Sam was only a boy, most of the functions associated with the Village chieftainship were performed by Martin, and around 1948 the chief let it be known that he was retiring in favor of Martin. Thereupon, most of the residents, except Ned, objected violently. They charged Martin with being selfish and quarrelsome, and they claimed that he lacked the proper temperament to be a good leader. To support their arguments they pointed out that after years of stormy marriage his wife had just left him. Many of those who refused to acknowledge Martin's leadership insisted that their true chief was Sam, even though he was living in Hollywood, California, and in recent years had had only slight contacts with the pueblo.

While the problem of Oraibi's leadership was so badly tangled, Tawaqwaptiwa, around 1956, suddenly announced that he was resuming the Village chieftainship. Since he was then losing his memory, no one could tell whether he was acting out of mere forgetfulness or out of a recognition of Martin's unpopularity.

By the time Tawaqwaptiwa had died, Margaret, his adopted daughter, had also laid claim to the Village chieftainship. From the outset, it was understood that her husband, Jack, of the Gray Badger clan, would carry out the masculine duties of the office. There was opposition to this arrangement because it involved a chief of the wrong sex and a male of the wrong clan. Then, in 1966, the situation changed. Sam voluntarily withdrew his candidacy; and Martin, who had not been especially diligent in the past, began to spend more and more of his time at his sheep camp, outside the pueblo. Like any typical Hopi, he was "waiting to see" what his rivals might do. (Compare p. 138.)

Finally, when Martin and Ned, his principal backer, joined the Kikötcmovi council, the remaining people of Oraibi rather reluctantly accepted Margaret's leadership. Thus, for the first time in the pueblo's long history, did most of its inhabitants come to be headed by a feminine chief.

Although this study is based, essentially, on data pertaining to Old Oraibi, it appears that all the Hopi villages are, to different degrees, undergoing similar culture change. Certainly, this is true of all the pueblos of Third Mesa, whose inhabitants originally came from Old Oraibi.

For example, at New Oraibi, where the first residents chose to retain their traditional Oraibi farmlands but to live away from the ancient town, the people conduct no orthodox ceremonies and only a few social dances, such as the Butterfly. They are administered by a "governor" and a council that only came into existence in the 1930s. They keep open all their three kivas, but they use them mainly for weaving and as masculine workshops and clubhouses.

The only relic of traditional ceremonialism that is still to be found at Kikötcmovi is a modified and quite unorthodox *katcina* initiation.

Hotevilla, founded in 1906 by a dissentient group of Oraibi conservatives, has preserved, as might have been expected, a fairly large number of traditional customs among the older inhabitants. In fact, in 1950 its leaders would not allow the American government to construct a paved highway across the pueblo's boundaries. Consequently, the new road skirts Hotevilla. Similarly, the headmen blocked the use of a water pump that had already been built on the mesa top, for fear that its operation might cause the drying up of the pueblo's traditional spring at the foot of the mesa.

Yet, even at conservative Hotevilla, the old way of life is disappearing. All of its six kivas still operate to some extent, but no ritual has preserved its integrity in full detail. Perhaps, the *katcina* cult comes closest to having retained its old forms, but even its rites have been somewhat abbreviated. Something yet remains of the Soyal, Wuwutcim (Tribal Initiation), and the Powamu ceremonies, but they have greatly shrunk. The Flute rituals have been entirely given up, although the proprietary Spider clan is well represented in the village; and, over ten years ago, it was openly being said that the Snake-Antelope observances were on the verge of extinction. Nevertheless, as late as on the afternoon of August 21, 1966, Hotevilla staged "a Snake dance" before a huge audience, consisting largely of "White" tourists. Twelve men, none of them very young, represented the Snake society, and there were between fifteen and twenty Antelope men.

In the early 1930s Hotevilla was so orthodox that no stoves or lamps were permitted in the kivas, which depended entirely for heat and light on old-fashioned open fire pits and skillful fire tenders. Around 1940, however, lamps and stoves began to displace open fireplaces.

By the 1960s, more and more conservative men from Lower Moenkopi were beginning to participate in Hotevilla ceremonies. Traditionally, Moenkopi had been geared to Oraibi's ceremonial calender, but since this has almost totally collapsed, Moenkopi conservatives have no choice but to join Hotevilla, since Hotevilla is known to have split off from Oraibi and to have inherited some of Oraibi's fetishes and ceremonies.

One of contemporary Hotevilla's main problems is its inability to agree upon a Village chief. It should be remembered that at the time of its establishment its leaders were the Conservatives: Yokioma, of the Kokop clan, and the elderly "Uncle Joe" Lomahongyoma, of the Spider clan. "Uncle Joe" left Hotevilla within a few months, returned to Oraibi, was driven out again in October of 1907, and went with his "nephew" Kuwannimptiwa to found the new pueblo of Bakavi. "Uncle Joe's" withdrawal left Yokioma the undisputed chief of Hotevilla until he died in 1929. He was succeeded by "Uncle Joe's" sister's son Poliwuhioma, of the Spider clan, who was Hotevilla's Soyal chief and, in keeping with Third Mesa practice, directly linked with the Village chieftainship. Trouble began when Poliwuhioma died many years ago. In those days, in accordance with established usage, the chieftainship was claimed by Yokioma's maternal nephew James Pongyayauoma, of the Kokop clan. However, Yokioma's own son Dan Qötchongva (Sun), who was not a proper Hopi heir, argued that he was more conservative and therefore ought to be chief of Hotevilla. This statement so angered James Pongyayauoma that, in a fit of temper, he turned all his paraphernalia over to Dan Qötchongva and went off to live at San Felipe. Soon after, Dan, himself, lost interest in the post, left the pueblo, and, despite his claims to conservatism, began to reside and work in various "White" towns. It is true that Dan later returned and now claims to be one of Hotevilla's most authoritative leaders, but the truth is that the pueblo has no completely accepted chief who might hold it together, and is steadily disintegrating.

Hotevilla's populace, in even larger numbers than Oraibi's, owns many cars and trucks. It has ready access to good roads at the village limits, and the residents are far more interested in working for cash than they are in continuing orthodox pursuits. There is little likelihood that Hotevilla will ever regain its former position in Hopi culture.

Bakavi, too, is beset with unsolved problems. Until the death of its original chief, Kuwannimptiwa (Sand), around 1940, it had managed to be reasonably independent and to maintain a fairly full schedule of its own religious and secular affairs. As the pueblo's ceremonial calendar began to shrink, a few men from Bakavi formed the habit of taking part in some of nearby Hotevilla's rites; but such associations proved to be neither satisfactory nor long-lasting.

Upon Kuwannimptiwa's death, his own son refused to become Bakavi's new chief. Thereupon, the office fell to Howard Talaiyamptiwa (Water Coyote), who is married to a Bear clanswoman. Howard seldom acts as a leader, and since 1959, Bakavi's affairs have been run by a council. In reality, Bakavi has become little more than a place in which to live.

Moenkopi, last of the Hopi pueblos to have drawn its original populace from Old Oraibi, is situated on the plain about forty miles northwest of Third Mesa. It is only about one mile from the Navaho center at Tuba City, and about seventy-five miles, over good roads, from Flagstaff.

Far back in the past Oraibi farmers used Moenkopi land for growing cotton, and by 1912 enough permanent residences had been built to give the settlement the appearance of a village. Throughout his life Tawaqwaptiwa regarded Moenkopi as a farming colony of Oraibi, and he was in the habit of calling its chief, Frank Siemptiwa (Pikyas), his "lieutenant." In the 1930s a few folk still grew cotton at Moenkopi and other crops at Oraibi. Even as late as 1952 Lawrence, son of Martin, managed to maintain farms in both places. This practice has been given up, and there are now scant economic ties between the two villages.

Although the Moenkopi people built three kivas, they habitually staged only *katcina* and social dances. For major rituals they used to travel to Oraibi, where they would stay with relatives while they were taking part in religious events.

Inasmuch as Moenkopi has always had ready access to a "White" city and has always received powerful external influences, it was inevitable that its inhabitants would steadily have lost their interest in perpetuating the old Hopi culture. By 1930, under the leadership of a man named Poli Payestiwa, those residents who favored "White" American ways began to occupy a section called Upper Moenkopi, while their more conservative fellows resided in Lower Moenkopi. For a while the two factions continued to use the same kivas and dance plaza, but about ten years ago they stopped sharing one another's facilities.

In the course of time Louis Hongnimptiwa, of the Greasewood clan, succeeded to the leadership of Upper Moenkopi; while Qopilvuh (Pikyas), brother of the late Frank Siemptiwa, headed the Lower village. At present, it seems that the gulf between the two factions will not soon be bridged.

Although the writer has, of late, made only a limited number of widely spaced visits to First and Second Mesa towns, enough was seen to suggest that pressures for change, with an attendant decline of traditional customs, have begun to work throughout the entire Hopi domain. At Shipaulovi, on Second Mesa, for instance, there was a Niman ("Homegoing") *katcina* dance on Sunday, July 31, 1955. The impersonation was Angya ("Long-haired") *katcina*. Only a few songs seemed to have been composed, for there were excessively long waits between dances. Many of the *katcina* dancers had such "foreign" objects as cigarette lighters for hair weights; and ice cream and cold drinks were being sold at a stand near the dance plaza. Similarly, signs of change were to be noted at the Antelope and Snake dances that were performed at Mishongnovi on Friday and Saturday, August 19 and 20, 1955. Apparently, members of the participating societies had lowered the age of initiation to seven or so, for many of the dancers were little children, too young to understand what was happening. Moreover, aspects of acculturation had worked right into the details of ceremonial performance, for the Snake chief carried sacred cornmeal in a percale bag; and the feminine members of the Snake clan, who sprinkle the reptiles with meal as the dance ends, used plastic bowls in place of woven plaques. Similar innovations were observed in 1957.

A visit to Chimopovy (Shongopavi), probably the most conservative of the Hopi pueblos on Second Mesa, also revealed numerous signs of change. The purpose of the visit was to observe the race held on the morning of the Flute observances on August 25, 1955. The race did not begin exactly at sunrise, as was once the rule, but long after the sun was high in the sky. Only a single man, instead of a mass of spectators, hallooed from the mesa's edge to signal for the start of the competition; and no runner carried a gourd of water. Afterwards, as custom demands, a few boys, carrying green vegetation, ran *ñötiwa* half-heartedly and self-consciously, and the women made only desultory efforts to catch them.

Several Second Mesa kivas are in a state of bad repair, and proposals to have them fixed by communal work parties have met with no response. The hiring of a private contractor to fix one of them has been considered at Chimopovy, and it was even suggested that funds for paying him might be raised either by charging an admission fee to "White" spectators at Hopi dances or else by holding a raffle. These plans did not materialize, and the kiva in question was ultimately repaired by members of the Kwan society.

It cannot be denied that on the whole the pueblos of Second Mesa have retained more traditional ways than have the Third Mesa villages. For example, a young woman recently came from Phoenix to go through her natal town's rites of feminine adolescence (O.O., pp. 203–4); and three young men were brought home a few years ago, in order to be initiated into the Wuwut-cim. These two ceremonies have long been extinct at Old Oraibi.

First Mesa, too, does not seem to be free of change. Most amusing of all was the appearance, below Walpi, of two out-houses marked "His" and "Hers" that had been erected for the convenience of tourists who had come to see the Snake-Antelope dance on Saturday, August 27, 1955.

Scant though these observations are, they tend to support the thesis that Old Oraibi is not unique in regard to change. Good roads run throughout the reservation, and each pueblo has its share of cars and trucks. Wherever one looks, he is sure to find aboriginal Hopi culture steadily disintegrating under the con-tinuous pressure of irresistible forces of change. The workings of these forces combine to make up an inevitable process that is probably worldwide in its distribution.

CHAPTER XII

Conclusion

Work on this monograph has given rise to some thoughts about the study of culture change in general. Unfortunately, at the present time there is no agreement either on objectives or procedures. Changes that affect only single individuals are often undifferentiated from those that apply to entire societies; the *forces* that bring about changes of culture are generally confused with the end products that they bring into being; and the conditions under which such forces remain quiescent or become rampant are not properly understood.[1] Furthermore, while it is commonly recognized that cultural changes have different effects on people of different age, sex, occupation, and socioeconomic status, little effort has been made to deal specifically with these differences.

It is disconcerting, too, to find that existing studies are invariably ethnocentric, at least in the sense that all emphases and judgments are made in terms of the observer's own culture. The viewpoint of the person living within the changing society is seldom given any consideration. This is not to argue that a native's analysis is necessarily more valid, but it should not be completely brushed aside, even when it differs widely from the observer's point of view. How different these viewpoints may be became clear on an occasion when I was discussing matters of culture change with a Hopi man. At one point I was astounded to hear him link installment-plan buying with the proper reciprocal behavior of kinsfolk. His reasoning ran along the following lines: Formerly, a son was taught never to bring any of his problems to his father.[2] Today, when a young man cannot meet an installment payment, he is very likely to go directly to his father for help. Hence, there is a direct link between purchases on the installment plan and the altered relations between a son and his father. This is the kind of tie-up that no outsider is apt to make.

The existence of such divergent viewpoints makes it all the more difficult for an outside observer to know in advance which changes are likely to be accepted and which ones rejected. For example, during the summer of 1964 I met a young Hopi woman who appeared to be thoroughly acculturated to the ways of the "White" man. She lived off the reservation, ate a standard "American" diet, spoke excellent English, and taught in one of Flagstaff's elementary schools. During the course of our conversation she remarked that she had lent her car to a nephew who had a date, and that when he returned it, she would have to have it fumigated. This pointed reference to the traditional love that is supposed to exist between a boy and his father's clanswomen (*ikya'as*), together with an allusion to the "dislike" a "paternal aunt" is supposed to have for any of her darling "nephew's" girl friends (pp. 16–17), startled me. How was one to anticipate that this particular segment of traditional behavior would have been retained by a young woman who had given up so many other parts of her tribal culture?

It would be presumptuous to try to dictate the lines that future studies ought to follow, but it may be proper to make a few comments and suggestions. There is a marked need to make clear a distinction between those changes that originate from an outside source and those that result from the play of purely internal forces. Thus, among the Hopi, the use of pickup trucks represents an *external* change; while the extinction of certain clans is, assuredly, an *internal* change.

Of course, external changes, which always imply contact situations, must continue to be studied; but it should not be forgotten that it is the processes of internal change that constantly remain in operation, even at those times when there is no outside contact. It is true that internal changes are often gradual and undramatic; yet they are of vital importance. They may function even in areas, such as that of food preferences, which are usually regarded as resistant to change. Many years ago, the Hopi enjoyed eating the head of a roasted prairie dog (*dukyatpe*);[3] but by 1933 the younger people, most of whom had never even seen the dish, spoke of it with repugnance; and today nothing but a faint memory of this food remains. There is *no evidence* to show that this change of taste was even remotely the result of outside influences.

Without standardized criteria it is not always possible to tell whether a particular change should be classified as external or internal. For example, it is an observable fact that the former practice of unilocal, matrilocal residence no longer prevails at Old Oraibi (pp. 45–46), but does the refusal of modern brides to live in their mothers' houses stem from an internal or external source?

There is an interesting corollary to this aspect of culture change. It concerns the length of time that it takes, as well as the conditions under which an originally alien (external) trait loses its foreignness and becomes an accepted part of a "traditional" way of life. Knowledge of these factors is essential for a complete understanding of culture change. This knowledge may also serve to illuminate such a case as that of the elderly Hopi woman who explained that she had to refuse canned sausages and condensed milk because she ate only "traditional" foods. She then proceeded to take a slice of wheat bread and a cup of black coffee (p. 273). After how long a lapse of time, and under what conditions, had she come to regard two of these once-alien foods as "foreign" and two others as "traditional"?

Current studies of culture change lack rigor and precision. There is no scale of measurement by means of which one can accurately distinguish a major change from a very minor one. Yet, it may be possible to devise such a scale based, perhaps, on the number of people who are simultaneously affected by a given change, together with the extent to which other areas of their total behavior are also affected. Categories could thus be established for separating *trivial* changes from those that were *moderately important* or *highly significant*. As these categories apply at Old Oraibi, one could classify as *trivial* the abandonment of long underwear as an exterior summer garment for old men (p. 331). Such a change affected only one individual at a time and had little bearing on the rest of his conduct. On the other hand, when small knots of women stopped making day-long, yucca-gathering excursions because it was more convenient to buy shampoo preparations (p. 332, and n. 7, p. 369), the change was *moderately important* because the former custom had required small groups of women to forego their usual duties for several hours. And when men gave up making long arduous expeditions for natural salt (n. 4, p. 359) in favor of buying packaged salt, it brought about a *highly significant* change, inasmuch as it freed parties of able-bodied men for the pursuit of many other tasks over a period of several days.

Long ago, it was recognized that various elements of culture undergo change at differing rates of speed. At Oraibi, the traits that have changed most slowly, in the order of their apparent resistance, are: the use of the native language in the home; witchcraft beliefs; food preferences; faith in folk "explanations" of seemingly inexplicable phenomena; and active participation in ancient ceremonies.

On the whole, such a list serves to support the commonly held notion that material things change faster than people's ideas or religious concepts. There are, however, some disturbing exceptions to this generalization. Thus, when the village of New Oraibi was established around 1911, it closely resembled Old Oraibi, its parent pueblo, in material respects. Its settlers built their houses and kivas with the same kinds of materials, used identical tools, wore similar clothes, engaged in the same occupations, and ate the same kind of foods. However, New Oraibi never developed a ceremonial calendar, and its residents never performed a single one of the traditional rites, with the exception of a few that were connected with the *katcina* cult. Here we have a specific example of a whole town whose inhabitants forsook most of their former religious practices but continued to carry on their old material culture.

It is extremely important to note that certain material changes, far from occurring at random, seem to result from consistent obedience to an underlying principle or law. Whenever a society is confronted with a choice of things designed for similar purposes, it will unfailingly choose that contrivance whose use will result in the greatest saving of human muscular effort, a reduction of time, or both.[4] Once it has been selected, the favored device will ultimately become a part of a receiving society's "traditional" pattern of culture.

Admittedly, the twin laws of time reduction and the conservation of human muscular energy can apply only to appropriate parts of the material realm. Nevertheless, their recognition serves to explain many of the changes that have taken place in the past and helps to provide a sound basis for the prediction of certain changes in the future. A search for additional guiding principles may well furnish a common objective for further studies of culture change and may also go far toward supplying that sense of order and coherence which is now so obviously lacking.[5]

Notes

PREFACE

1. The unexpurgated and unchanged original diary is in the archives of the Museum of Northern Arizona in Flagstaff.
2. For a recent study of the Hopi language, primarily lexical in its emphasis, see Charles F. and Florence M. Voegelin, "Hopi Domains," *International Journal of American Linguistics,* supplement to vol. 23, no. 2 (April, 1957). In the same journal see also E. A. Kennard, "Linguistic Acculturation in Hopi," *I.J.A.L.,* vol. 29, no. 1 (January, 1963).
3. Oraibi and Old Oraibi will be used interchangeably to designate the ancient pueblo that is situated on top of Third Mesa. Either New Oraibi or Kikötcmovi is the name for the settlement at the foot of Third Mesa. It became an independent village around 1911.
4. Because the easternmost of three inhabited mesas on the Hopi reservation was always the first to be seen in former times, it has long been known as First Mesa. Second and Third Mesas lie in a generally westward direction, at intervals of ten or eleven miles each. First Mesa holds the Hopi village of Walpi, its "suburb" Sitcumovi, and the Tewa-speaking pueblo of Hano. Second Mesa holds the Hopi towns of Mishongnovi, Shipaulovi, and Chimopovy (Shongopavi). Oraibi was the only pueblo on Third Mesa until the Split of September 7, 1906. Thereafter, some of its former inhabitants founded Hotevilla and Bakavi atop Third Mesa, New Oraibi at its foot; and also helped to swell the populace of Moenkopi. Moenkopi, until 1912 a farming colony of Old Oraibi, stands on the plain, about forty miles northwest of Third Mesa. It has long had ready access to the city of Flagstaff.

CHAPTER I

1. In those years the Laboratory of Anthropology sponsored annual expeditions, each under an experienced leader, in archaeology,

ethnology, and physical anthropology. Four students were selected for each party with the purpose of providing them with
opportunities for fieldwork in their branches of major interest.

2. The Reverend H. R. Voth lived and worked at Oraibi for about
twenty-five years, beginning some two decades prior to the
turn of this century. He was a zealous churchman and was directly responsible in 1901 for the building of the Mennonite
Mission Church atop Third Mesa, on the southwest outskirts of
Old Oraibi. The church was later abandoned. In 1942 it was
struck by lightning, and has now crumbled into ruin.

   Voth learned to speak Hopi fluently. In addition to his
religious duties, he was persuaded by Dr. G. A. Dorsey, of
the Field Columbian Museum at Chicago, to make ethnographic
collections and investigations. Although he was untrained in
anthropology, he was amazingly diligent in the pursuit of ethnographic details, even to the point of defying native prohibi-
tions. His publications are, accordingly, filled with details that
are priceless, but meaningful only to specialists.

3. Mrs. Williams was greatly influenced by the Reverend Mr. Fry,
a later Mennonite missionary to the Hopi, who did most of his
work at Moenkopi.

4. Full details of "The Split at Oraibi," are given in Mischa Titiev,
"Old Oraibi: A Study of the Hopi Indians of Third Mesa,"
*Papers of the Peabody Museum of American Archaeology and
Ethnology*, vol. 22, no. 1 (Cambridge, Mass., 1944), chap. 6, pp.
69–95. (Hereafter, this work will be cited in the notes as "Old
Oraibi.")

5. Ned's tenacious memory is evidenced by the abundant autobiographical detail contained in Leo W. Simmons, editor, *Sun
Chief* (New Haven: Yale University Press, 1942). (This book
will be cited hereafter as *Sun Chief*.) Ned is the Sun Chief.

   While nonliterate peoples may have excellent memories for
whatever interests them deeply, such as religious details, they
may have poor memories in other regards. Apparently, memories are compartmentalized and may work well in some areas
and badly in others.

CHAPTER II

1. Homer used to clerk at Hubbell's trading post in New Oraibi, but
later opened a store there for himself. He is reputed to have
been dissolute and lives apart from his wife, Eva Talashönim,
at Kikötcmovi. Although he was not popular with the Old

Oraibi folk, partly because he had inherited the Kwan society fetishes but had never acted as a Kwan chief, several residents of the ancient pueblo invested money in his store. Thus, around 1950, he still owed $224 to Ned; over $600 to Ruth; and $250 to Kane. Several years ago, Homer's mother accidentally set fire to his trading post, which burned to the ground. At present he farms, runs cattle, and deals in wool. He pays some of his debts with meat or by hauling wood, but there is little chance that he will ever pay back his supporters in full.

2. Horace farmed in his free time, but his principal occupation was clerking. He used to work in Hubbell's warehouse at Kikötcmovi, but was employed by the Babbitt Company when they purchased Hubbell's trading post. He retired around 1960.

3. Edna was alleged to have been licentious and was constantly at odds with her family. In 1934 she was the only Hopi woman at Oraibi who had to do the greater part of her own farming.

In 1966, Moe, old and unwell, was living as a bachelor at New Oraibi, in the home of another single man. He had once been married to an Apache woman, but was separated from her. For other details about this family, abnormal in Hopi eyes, see "Old Oraibi," p. 40, fnn. pp. 57, 196; Chart XI, *et passim*. For a time Allen lived at Hotevilla and had charge of dynamiting on a road crew, but he now lives and works in town.

4. A different story of a Hopi-Navaho fight is presented, explained, and analyzed, in Fred Eggan, "From History to Myth: A Hopi Example," *Studies in Southwestern Ethnolinguistics* (The Hague and Paris: Mouton and Co., 1967), pp. 33–35.

5. Every Hopi youngster begins his ceremonial career by being inducted into the Katcina cult. As a child nears the customary initiation age, the parents look about for some worthwhile neighbor to serve as its ceremonial father or in the case of a girl as a ceremonial mother. Ceremonial parents may not be chosen either from the novice's own or his father's phratry.

6. See "Old Oraibi," p. 87, fn. 154. Although Lololoma and Yokioma were leaders on opposite sides of the dispute that culminated in the Split of 1906, Coin interpreted for both men. Their pictures are shown as Pl. 5 and 7 of the German edition of *Sun Chief*. Don C. Talayesva, *Sonnenhäuptling Sitzende Rispe* (Kassel, Hungary: Röth Press, 1964).

7. Ned feared lest his beloved mother should lure him to join her in the realm of the dead. This was the overt reason why he wondered if she were a witch. Cf. his statement in *Sun Chief*, pp. 326–27.

8. Allen was considered the laziest man in Oraibi. "Old Oraibi," fn. 13, p. 19; n. 3, Chart XI, p. 196.

9. This episode is mentioned in P. Beaglehole, "Census Data from Two Hopi Villages," *American Anthropologist,* vol. 37, no. 1 (1935), p. 51.

10. See Mischa Titiev, "Notes on Hopi Witchcraft," *Papers of the Michigan Academy of Science, Arts, and Letters,* vol. 28 (1942) (1943), pp. 553–54. (This work will hereafter be referred to as "Hopi Witchcraft.")

11. According to Hopi convention a Village chief is the owner of all the *katcinas* that appear in his village. In 1933, it should not be forgotten, the Oraibi chief still had real jurisdiction over Moenkopi.

12. These data are summarized in "Old Oraibi," Chart XI, p. 196.

13. All witches are supposed to have two hearts. This is the basis of the widely used euphemism by which a witch is called "a two-hearted person." See Titiev, "Hopi Witchcraft," p. 550.

14. Those who intrude on the secret parts of a ritual, whether by accident or design, are automatically inducted into the ceremony. This is called initiation by trespass.

15. While a boy is being married, his father's clanswomen, *ikya'as,* stage a "mud-fight" during which they revile and befoul the bride and the parents of the groom. This expresses their "resentment" because the groom is marrying outside their ranks.
     For a description and analysis of this custom, see M. Titiev, "The Problem of Cross-Cousin Marriage among the Hopi," *American Anthropologist,* vol. 40, no. 1 (1938).

16. Additional details are given in M. Titiev, "Hopi Racing Customs at Oraibi, Arizona," *Papers of the Michigan Academy of Science, Arts, and Letters,* vol. 24 pt. iv (1938) (1939), pp. 33–42. (This work will hereafter be cited as "Hopi Racing.")

17. Traditionally, the gatherers at a Snake dance sprinkle meal toward the head of a released reptile and swoop it up with a flourish after it has had a few moments of freedom on the dance plaza. At the close of the dance the Snake society chief emerges from the booth and at the opposite end of the plaza and, using sacred cornmeal, draws and dissects into quadrants a large circle. Into this all the gatherers drop their snakes. The squirming reptiles are sprinkled by ceremonially clad Snake (?) clanswomen, after which four swift dancers carry them to distant shrines in all directions, where they are released with prayers for rain, crops, and good health.

18. The Hopi do not take lightly the use of terms of kinship. Cf. M. Titiev, "The Hopi Use of Kinship Terms for Expressing Sociocultural Values," *Anthropological Linguistics* (May, 1967), pp. 44–49.

19. In *Sun Chief,* pp. 121–29, 380, *et passim,* Ned reports dreams in which his "spirit guide" appears. He makes much more use of this concept than does any other Hopi.

    Hopi dreams have been carefully studied by Dorothy Eggan. See her article, "Hopi Dreams in Cultural Perspective," *The Dream and Human Societies,* ed. G. E. von Grunebaum and R. Caillois (Berkeley and Los Angeles: University of California Press, 1966), pp. 237–65. For a bibliography, consult the references on pp. 264–65.

20. The Hopi believe that not everyone consciously knows if he has acquired a second heart. Also, people accused of being witches sometimes find it convenient to scare off attackers by claiming that they really *are* witches who can harm their detractors.

21. A sketch of Tawaqwaptiwa's character is given in Mischa Titiev, "An Historic Figure, Writ Small," *Michigan Quarterly Review* (August, 1956), pp. 325–30.

22. It seems to be an old procedure of Hopi medicine men to "extract" insects from patients. When Stephen was treated at Walpi in 1894, a medicine man named Sikyahonavuh "extracted" from him an insect that looked like a headless centipede. See E. C. Parsons, ed., "The Hopi Journal of Alexander M. Stephen," *Columbia University Occasional Contributions to Anthropology,* vol. 23 (New York, 1936), pp. 862–63, Fig. 464. (Hereafter this work will be cited as "Stephen's Hopi Journal.") In a footnote on p. 862, Dr. Parsons notes that a Zuñi medicine man had once "sucked" a similar insect from a patient.

23. Men who go *dumaiya* usually call clandestinely, for sexual purposes, on girls who sleep well apart from their parents. In the eyes of the Hopi such affairs are taken lightly. They are, however, seriously condemned if either of the parties has ever gone through a marriage ceremony while the other has not. The violator who has never been wed becomes a "basket-carrier" in the afterlife and is doomed to carry a heavy basket which an offended spouse, whether alive or dead at the time of the affair, loads with gravel. To some extent this belief serves to keep apart people of different age levels.

    Although most people have lost faith in punishments that are supposed to take place in the hereafter, even thoroughly modernized Hopi are apt to feel ill at ease about violations of the "basket-carrying" code.

24. Valjean broke his earlier partnership partly because, being a young man, he wanted to go to tribal dances and resented having to herd instead. Kane promised to have him relieved on ceremonial occasions.

25. Boys, too, were often soothed by having the penis stroked. See *Sun Chief,* p. 34.

26. Missionaries have long been connected with boarding schools. Some details are given in *Sun Chief*, pp. 116–17. Hence Christianity and schooling are often linked.

CHAPTER III

1. See Mischa Titiev, "Shamans, Witches, and Chiefs among the Hopi," *To-morrow*, vol. 4, no. 3 (New York, 1956), pp. 51–56.

2. Further details of shared *katcina* control are given in "Old Oraibi," pp. 120–29, fn. 66.

3. See *Sun Chief*, pp. 294, 296. Ned's impotence led him into a frenzied search for a cure. All facts regarding the cause and true nature of his ailment are obscure, but in later years he professed to be entirely cured. It is not at all certain that he ever had gonorrhea, but there is no doubt that he was impotent for a time.

4. For more detailed accounts of these former journeys from Oraibi, see Mischa Titiev, "A Hopi Salt Expedition," *American Anthropologist*, vol. 39, no. 2 (1937); and *Sun Chief*, pp. 232–47. Oraibi folk gave up going for salt long ago. Around 1951 a number of Hotevilla men set out for the Salt Canyon, but they could not find the spot and returned empty-handed. I know of no later salt-gathering expeditions from Third Mesa. People from the other Mesas are said to go to Zuñi Salt Lake occasionally by truck.

5. For a full account of the proceedings, see Mischa Titiev, "The Hopi Method of Baking Sweet Corn," *Papers of the Michigan Academy of Science, Arts, and Letters*, vol. 23 (1937) (1938), pp. 87–94 (hereafter cited as "The Hopi Method of Baking Sweet Corn"); and *Sun Chief*, pp. 247–48. Families regard sweet-corn baking as a kind of picnic.

6. Patjiro refers to a bird with a yellowish neck. As the first syllable of its name implies, it is associated with water; and in several ceremonies it is asked to bring rain.

7. The behavior of people who live in pueblos where there is little space or privacy needs very much to be studied further. Some of the effects of a lack of privacy on social organization have begun to be investigated. See Alan F. Westin, *Privacy and Freedom* (New York: Atheneum Publishers, 1967). The first two chapters have many references to the works of anthropologists.

8. See Titiev, "Hopi Witchcraft," p. 554.

9. *Ibid.*, p. 556; and Titiev, "The Hopi Method of Baking Sweet Corn," pp. 87–88.

10. On another occasion Ned lost his temper and struck George. This event had serious consequences for Ned and has aroused much

discussion on the part of Dr. Simmons and other social scientists. See *Sun Chief*, pp. 357–61, 401–15.

11. "Poison arrows" is Ned's term for disease-causing objects that a witch is supposed to send into a victim's body. See Titiev, "Hopi Witchcraft," p. 551. Cf. *Sun Chief*, p. 293.

12. With the shrinkage of clans and secret societies at Oraibi many substitutions have been made. As nearly as could be made out Ned (later replaced by Sidney) functioned as a Sun Watcher until about 1963, and the rites he mentions resemble those once done by the Flute societies. The relationship of the Flute society to the Sun is shown by the fact that Flute men at Oraibi used to wear Sun-shields on their backs. See Pls. 19 and 20 in Don C. Talayesva, *Sonnenhäuptling Sitzende Rispe* (Kassel, Hungary: Röth Press, 1964).

The traditional way of determining the correct times for planting various crops is described in M. Titiev, "Dates of Planting at . . . Oraibi," *Museum Notes, Museum of Northern Arizona*, vol. 11, no. 5 (Flagstaff, 1938). It is based on the apparent journeys of the sun.

13. Ned's use of the word *symbol* may have been a consequence of his long association with "Whites." Many Hopi attribute the outcome of their deeds to the gods. This may be a way of avoiding responsibility.

14. For comparative details see the index to Parsons, "Stephen's Hopi Journal," s.v. Yayatu society.

15. Some of the teasing that goes on between Marau women and Wuwutcim men is attributed to the fact that these societies are supposed to stand in a brother-sister relationship, and that siblings often tease one another.

CHAPTER IV

1. Ned was reluctant to regard adultery as ground for divorce. Cf. *Sun Chief*, p. 276.

2. For legends about Matcito, see "Old Oraibi," pp. 60 ff. The sacred stone is pictured as Fig. 4, p. 60. In 1933 the chief claimed that the sacred stone had no connection with Hopi ceremonies, but several other informants said that it was used at Monglavaiya ("Chiefs' Talk") in conjunction with the Soyal. See "Old Oraibi," p. 61. Now that the Soyal ceremony is extinct, the sacred stone is not used. For references to Bahana, see "Old Oraibi," p. 71, fn. 29.

3. Ma'ovi is a yellow snakeweed, *Gutierrezia sarothrae* (Pursh) B. & R. It is sometimes used in making prayer offerings. It is also attached to "mother" ears when baking sweet corn. See Titiev, "The Hopi Method of Baking Sweet Corn," p. 89, n. 1, *et passim*.

4. Chief Tawaqwaptiwa once said that Voth had come into Tawaovi while a secret rite (Soyal?) was in progress. The warrior (*kaletaka*) on duty to prevent intrusions carried Voth up the ladder and dropped him outside, but Voth promptly came in again. This time he was permitted to remain, on condition that he stay on the spectators' platform, behind the ladder. Voth obeyed, but preached in Hopi throughout the rite, saying that the pagan ceremony was "no good" and that all the participants would be burned in a big fire.

   For other Hopi attitudes toward Voth, see *Sun Chief*, p. 252.

5. Relatives of a pregnant girl often object to her marrying the alleged father of her child.

6. Fearing to lose Ned's valuable help and support at Oraibi, I quickly sent an advance letter explaining my plight to the Museum's director. I then wrote a letter of inquiry for Ned. The reply stated, as I had suggested, that the Soyal group in Chicago was made up entirely of reconstructions based on Voth's notes; and that the Museum authorities had never heard of Ned and had had no dealings with him. This reply satisfied Ned, who had begun to wonder if he were a witch unbeknown to himself. He happily translated his letter to the chief and to his accusers. Interestingly enough, his principal enemy was Panimptiwa, whom he later befriended (p. 342). This episode is reported in *Sun Chief*, pp. 309–11.

   Siding with Panimptiwa were his stepdaughters, Jacob's Clara and Fern. (They both died many years ago. They were children of the chief's wife's sister and rather loose in their conduct.)

   Panimptiwa was a clan brother to Ruth's father. One of his stepdaughters, Clara, had stayed with Ruth and Ned while Fern had gone to Chicago.

7. This method of cure is reminiscent of the discharming procedure employed to neutralize the power of objects used in ceremonies.

8. A discussion of Dr. Parsons's ideas of Hopi lineages may be found in "Old Oraibi," pp. 44–46. See also Robin Fox, *The Keresan Bridge* (London: The Athlone Press, 1967).

9. At the time, I did not fully realize the extent of Ned's anguish over his impotence. See *Sun Chief*, pp. 293–94, *et passim*.

10. A recent study, entitled "Modern Transformations of Moenkopi Pueblo," expands the doctoral dissertation of Shuichi Nagata. This thesis was done in 1966 at the University of Illinois, under the direction of Prof. Julian H. Steward, as part of his project: "Studies of Cultural Regularities."

    Most of Nagata's data were obtained in the field. He states that some orthodox men from Moenkopi now participate in Hotevilla rites.

11. It may be that Joe meant to say Oaqöl instead of Lakon. The founder of the Oaqöl society is customarily branded a witch. She is accused of having somehow "stolen" some of the most hidden parts of several secret ceremonies.

12. Participants in rites must abstain from sex for varying periods of time.

   The headmen of the Pikyas clan play important parts in the Soyal ceremony.

13. A recent study has been made of Hopi albinism. See G. M. Woolf and R. B. Grant, "Albinism among the Hopi Indians of Arizona," *Yearbook of Physical Anthropology,* ed. J. Kelso and G. W. Lasker (Boulder, Colo., 1962), pp. 13–22.

14. This custom, somewhat differently reported on the basis of data supplied by other informants, is to be found described in "Old Oraibi," p. 135, fn. 44. Also, see Julian H. Steward, "Notes on Hopi Ceremonies in Their Initiatory Form," *American Anthropologist,* vol. 33, no. 1 (1931).

15. Criers' calls have been studied by C. F. Voegelin and R. C. Euler in "Introduction to Hopi Chants," *International Journal of American Linguistics,* vol. 7, no. 276 (1957).

16. Patcava ceremonies were generally held in years when the Wuwutcim society sponsored initiations. These initiations took place in November, at which season Dennis places the Patcava. However, I am under the impression that Patcava was always given in February–March in conjunction with the Powamu. See "Old Oraibi," pp. 119, 222–26, for details.

   The Patcava, now extinct on Third Mesa, was last held after the Powamu at Old Oraibi around 1945. It was performed to satisfy the nostalgic desires of some and the curiosity of others.

17. F. Waters, *Book of the Hopi* (New York: Viking Press, 1963), p. 140, shows a Horn (Al) chiefs' stick (*mongkoho*).

18. Ned's "death" story is reported in Mischa Titiev, "A Hopi Visit to the Afterworld," *Papers of the Michigan Academy of Science, Arts, and Letters,* vol. 26, pt. IV (1940) (1941), pp. 495–504. Another version occurs in *Sun Chief,* pp. 119–29.

CHAPTER V

1. See H. R. Voth, "The Traditions of the Hopi," *Anthropological Series, Field Columbian Museum,* vol. 8, no. 35 (Chicago, 1905).

2. Ultimately, it became clear that premarital sexual relations are commonplace, but every woman needs a wedding outfit for the otherworld.

3. Jemez dances always begin by having the *katcinas* shake their gourd rattles before singing. Later, the men who are impersonating females (*manas*) kneel on quilts while they scrape notched sticks, placed on gourd resonators, with sheep scapulae

(shoulder blades). [The sound made by scraping notched sticks is sometimes interpreted as imitating the croaking of frogs whose association with water is self-evident.]

4. There seems to be no other way to interpret such remarks except by postulating a former practice of cross-cousin marriage in which a boy married a woman of his father's clan.

5. This mud-fight is described and discussed in M. Titiev, "The Problem of Cross-Cousin Marriage among the Hopi," *American Anthropologist*, vol. 40, no. 1 (1938), pp. 101–10.

6. This 1933 performance of the Soyal *katcina* is also described in "Old Oraibi," p. 110.

   Since the part is customarily played by Oraibi's chief, it is noteworthy that Tawaqwaptiwa allowed Martin to play the part while he "rested." Martin continued to impersonate the Soyal *katcina* until the ceremony lapsed around 1953. He bases much of his claim to Oraibi's chieftainship on this fact.

7. Momtcit society procedures are described in "Old Oraibi," pp. 156–59. According to H. R. Voth, "The Oraibi Powamu Ceremony," *Anthropological Series, Field Columbian Museum*, vol. 3, no. 2 (Chicago, 1901), p. 109, fn. 2 (hereafter cited as "The Oraibi Powamu Ceremony"), Momtcit used to cure sore throat; but Ned claimed that this "whip" belonged to the Nakyawimi, its ceremonial partner, whose members "swallowed" long sticks, while the Momtcit dealt with such things as frights and scares.

8. Bert gave two words for scalp, *yovuta* and *kapukna*. It was later explained that the word *yovuta* might possibly indicate anything that can be peeled, whereas *kapukinta* may refer specifically to scalping.

9. Tihkuyi Wuhti ("Childbirth-water Woman") is also known commonly as Tuwapongwuhti ("Sand-altar Woman") and Tuwapongtumsi ("Sand-altar Female"). She is the supernatural patron of all game animals. See H. R. Voth, "The Traditions of the Hopi," *Anthropological Series, Field Columbian Museum*, vol. 8, no. 37 (Chicago, 1905), p. 136.

10. This behavior is reported in Mischa Titiev, "A Hopi Salt Expedition," *American Anthropologist*, vol. 39, no. 2 (1937).

11. For more details see Mischa Titiev, "Dates of Planting at . . . Oraibi," *Museum Notes, Museum of Northern Arizona*, vol. 11, no. 5 (Flagstaff, 1938).

12. An account and discussion of this incident appears in "Old Oraibi," pp. 76–79.

13. A description and analysis of racing is given in Titiev, "Hopi Racing," pp. 33–42.

14. Sunlight is not supposed to fall on a neonate for the first twenty days of its life. For this reason, blankets or other coverings are hung over doorways and windows when a child is born.

CHAPTER VI

1. The reference is to A. B. Thomas, *Forgotten Frontiers* (Norman: University of Oklahoma Press, 1932).

2. This story is told in Mischa Titiev, "Two Hopi Tales from Oraibi," *Papers of the Michigan Academy of Science, Arts, and Letters,* vol. 29 (1943) (1944), pp. 425–30. (Cited hereafter as "Two Hopi Tales.")

3. The Village crier's remarks are printed in H. R. Voth, "The Oraibi Summer Snake Ceremony," *Anthropological Series, Field Columbian Museum,* vol. 3, no. 4 (Chicago, 1903), p. 276.
   The speech used during the cornbake is given in Titiev, "The Hopi Method of Baking Sweet Corn," p. 90.

4. An extremely detailed account of the entire ritual may be found in G. A. Dorsey and H. R. Voth, "The Oraibi Soyal Ceremony," *Anthropological Series, Field Columbian Museum,* vol. 3, no. 1 (Chicago, 1901). (This work will hereafter be cited as "The Oraibi Soyal.")

5. The conventional pattern of courtship, long out of date, consists of a lover talking to his sweetheart through the window of a house in which she is grinding corn at night.

6. Girls may propose marriage by giving a large loaf of *qömi* to a sweetheart.

7. See Dorsey and Voth, "The Oraibi Soyal," p. 43, Pls. XIX (b, d), XX.

8. Details are given in Dorsey and Voth, "The Oraibi Soyal," pp 44–45, Pl. XXII. The full name of the spring where the offerings are made is Lenangva. It lies in the western outskirts of Oraibi. Its water is still used, particularly as a solvent when prayer sticks are being painted.

9. The full Niman observance is reported in detail in "Old Oraibi," pp. 227–35.

10. Regular terms of kinship or ceremonial terms are used. Poliyestiwa and Charles called each other grandfather–grandson; Kane and Poliyestiwa used father–son; and so did Humiletstiwa and Kane. For an account of this custom see Mischa Titiev, "The Use of Kinship Terms in Hopi Ritual," *Museum Notes, Museum of Northern Arizona,* vol. 10, no. 3 (Flagstaff, 1937). A possible explanation is offered in M. Titiev, "The Hopi Use of Kinship Terms for Expressing Sociocultural Values," *Anthropological Linguistics* (May, 1967), p. 48.

11. See Dorsey and Voth, "The Oraibi Soyal," pp. 58–59, Pls. XXXV–XXXVII. The caption for Pl. XXXVI says simply, "Soyal Priests." Actually, they are shown being doused at the home of a Soyal *mana.*

12. It is possible, too, that the rattlesnakes of this area do not secrete enough venom to cause a fatal bite. The entire topic is reviewed in M. Titiev, "Hopi Snake Handling," *Scientific Monthly*, vol. 57, no. 1 (Lancaster, 1943).

CHAPTER VII

1. This story, concerning the anguish of a young man who was a very poor hunter, may be found in Titiev, "Two Hopi Tales," pp. 425–37.
2. Note that invitations to dine are customarily extended by males, but that the houses themselves can be owned only by females.

   While there is no doubt that solidarity and friendship are increased when people share a meal, realism dictates that attention should also be called to the fact that there was no refrigeration at Oraibi in 1933–34, and that all perishable items had to be consumed lest they spoil.
3. The quotation is from A. B. Thomas, *Forgotten Frontiers* (Norman: University of Oklahoma Press, 1932), p. 237.
4. Information regarding the custom of keeping eagles and "sending them home" after the Niman *katcina* dance is to be found in H. R. Voth, "Brief Miscellaneous Hopi Papers," *Anthropological Series, Field Columbian Museum*, vol. 11, no. 2 (Chicago, 1912), pp. 105–9.
5. A picture of a Soyalmana sitting on seed corn may be found in F. Waters, *Book of the Hopi* (New York: Viking Press, 1963), following p. 190.
6. This event is described in Titiev, "Hopi Witchcraft," p. 555. In this account only one woman is supposed to have been a witness.

CHAPTER VIII

1. The Marau society, at least, is reported formerly to have sent a messenger to Aponivi to invite the participation of the dead. Some informants were of the opinion that the Kwan society, whose patron was the god of death, also sent a messenger on a similar errand. Some Hopi believed that a Kwan spirit from Aponivi directed souls of the dead along the road to the Otherworld (Maski).
2. See Titiev, "Hopi Racing," pp. 33–42.
3. See K. Bryan, "Flood-water Farming," *Geographical Review*, vol. 19, no. 3 (New York, 1929).
4. For a discussion of this point, see M. Titiev, "The Hopi Use of Kinship Terms for Expressing Sociocultural Values," *Anthropological Linguistics* (May, 1967), pp. 44–49. See especially pp. 45, 47.
5. The basic material may be found in M. Titiev, "A Hopi Salt Expedition," *American Anthropologist*, vol. 39, no. 2 (1937). The

social links pertain chiefly to the possibility of a former practice of cross-cousin marriage and are discussed in M. Titiev, "The Problem of Cross-Cousin Marriage among the Hopi," *American Anthropologist,* vol. 40, no. 1 (1938).

6. See M. Titiev, *The Science of Man,* rev. ed. (New York: Holt, Rinehart and Winston, Inc., 1963), pp. 378–79.

7. A similar object is pictured in Voth, "The Oraibi Powamu Ceremony," Pl. XLVI.

CHAPTER IX

1. Ned states that during the Split of 1906 some people were surprised to see him opposing the Conservatives. *Sun Chief,* p. 110.

2. The chief's version of this story appears in M. Titiev, "Two Hopi Myths and Rites," *Journal of American Folklore* (Jan.–Mar., 1948), pp. 31 ff.

3. Encores are gotten by the simple expedient of having a spectator, usually an elderly woman, direct a soloist or the first man in a line *around* a kiva ladder, instead of permitting him to clamber *up.*

4. It should be remembered that by Hopi custom anyone who trespasses on any part of an esoteric rite must be initiated. Apparently, the Marau society was short of members and that was why they had tried to trick Qöyawaisi into trespassing after which she would have been forced to join the group. It is not known why the Marau was so desperate for new members nor why Qöyawaisi and her family had such an aversion for that society. One guess is that they were on bad terms with the officers who had charge of the Marau.

5. The story and the actions of this *katcina* are given in M. Titiev, "The Story of Kokopele," *American Anthropologist,* vol. 41, no. 1 (1939).

6. A. M. Stephen, "Hopi Tales," *Journal of American Folklore,* vol. 42, no. 163 (New York, 1929).

7. This entire question is discussed in M. Titiev, "The Problem of Cross-Cousin Marriage among the Hopi," *American Anthropologist,* vol. 40, no. 1 (1938).

CHAPTER X

1. For other accounts of birth and naming rites see J. G. Owens, "Natal Ceremonies of the Hopi Indians," *Journal of American Ethnology and Archaeology,* vol. 2, no. 2 (Boston, 1892); and H. R. Voth, "Oraibi Natal Customs and Ceremonies," *Anthropological Series, Field Columbian Museum,* vol. 6, no. 2 (Chicago, 1905).

2. Comparative material may be found in R. H. Lowie, "A Women's Ceremony among the Hopi," *Natural History,* vol. 25 (New York, 1925).

   For Third Mesa performance, see H. R. Voth, "The Oraibi Marau Ceremony," *Anthropological Series, Field Columbian Museum,* vol. 11, no. 1 (Chicago, 1912).

3. The three feminine societies among the Hopi are Marau, Oaqöl, and Lakon. The Marau is the most popular and widespread. Thus, for instance, both Hotevilla and Chimopovy have the Marau, but Hotevilla has no Oaqöl and Chimopovy lacks the Lakon.

4. For pictures of Marau boards at Oraibi, consult H. R. Voth, *op. cit.,* note 2 above, Pls. XVII, XVIII b. Muyingwa is the main germination god.

5. For comparative material, see Parsons, "Stephen's Hopi Journal," pt. I, p. 343, *et passim;* pt. II, pp. 818–23, Fig. 446.

   In addition to being performed on First Mesa by Hano and Walpi, the dance (and the society that performs it) is known at Mishongnovi on Second Mesa, whose performance is said to be the best of all. The Ya-ya society cures sore eyes and has a large membership because everyone they treat must join their society.

6. The colors associated with the cardinal directions in all Hopi rites, in the order of the usual ritual (counterclockwise) circuit, are yellow for north, blue or green for west, red for south, white for east; black for above or zenith; and mixed or speckled for below or nadir. The Maya and others also associated colors with directions, but their system differed from that of the Hopi.

7. Comparative data may be found in J. W. Fewkes and J. G. Owen, "The Lalakonta: A Tusayan Dance," *American Anthropologist,* o.s., vol. V, no. 2 (Washington, 1892).

8. Readers are reminded that in orthodox Hopi belief the *katcinas* are locked up to sleep and rest between approximately mid-July and the end of the year. This constitutes the "closed" season during which no *katcinas,* except Masau, are supposed to appear in the villages.

9. The Wuwutcim, or Tribal Initiation rites, are performed jointly by the Wuwutcim, Tao, Al, and Kwan societies. For a description of these observances, see "Old Oraibi," pp. 130–41. The last Wuwutcim ever performed at Oraibi was held in 1912. No observer has ever seen or published an account of the entire ceremony.

10. The average Hopi man dreads the Kwan society because its patron is Masau'û, the god of death, and its members are supposed to fear neither death nor the dead. Note that some of

their duties are performed by warrior groups in a number of primitive societies.

11. In keeping with their ties to the god of death, the Kwan men's markings reverse those of other chiefs.

12. It is amazing how often the features of one ceremony duplicate parts of other rites.

13. Two men with Al headdresses are pictured in F. Waters, *Book of the Hopi* (New York: Viking Press, 1963), p. 191.

14. At Oraibi before 1906, as at Hotevilla, only Wuwutcim men who had gone through the rites in the Chief kiva (Sakwalenvi) were eligible for unrestricted participation in the esoteric portions of the Soyal.

    Hotevilla practice seems to mirror what used to be the procedure at Oraibi.

15. Consult H. R. Voth, "The Traditions of the Hopi," *Anthropological Series, Field Columbian Museum,* vol. 8, no. 35 (Chicago, 1905), p. 260.

16. For a description of *wotaka* see Dorsey and Voth, "The Oraibi Soyal," p. 58.

17. Cf. Voth, "The Oraibi Powamu Ceremony," p. 121.

18. *Ibid.* See Pls. LXI and LXV for pictures of dolls and men with these masks.

19. An abbreviated account of this performance may be found in M. Titiev, "A Dance for Beans," *Michigan Quarterly Review* (July, 1962), pp. 197–99.

20. A kicking ball made of piñon sap is also called *qöyune.*

21. Comparative material may be found in Dorothy Eggan, "Hopi Dreams in Cultural Perspective," in *The Dream and Human Societies,* ed. G. E. von Grunebaum and R. Caillois (Berkeley and Los Angeles: University of California Press, 1966), pp. 257–60, and in Parsons, "Stephen's Hopi Journal," pp. 284–307.

22. A variant picture is shown on p. 258 of the Eggan article cited in note 21 above.

CHAPTER XI

1. It is impossible to give the precise number of occupied houses at Oraibi at any given date because the inhabitants shift about in unpredictable ways. Some structures are occupied at one time and vacant at another; some residents come to own more than one house; at times, dwellings become converted to storehouses and storehouses to dwellings; and there is a considerable amount of rebuilding.

2. No population figures for the Hopi are ever exact because there is no restriction on the movements of villagers, who are free to come and go whenever they wish. Thus, Oraibi's population is always in a state of flux.

3. Data on old-fashioned natal and naming practices are to be found in J. G. Owens, "Natal Ceremonies of the Hopi Indians," *Journal of American Ethnology and Archaeology,* vol. 2, no. 2 (Boston, 1892); and in H. R. Voth, "Oraibi Natal Customs and Ceremonies," *Anthropological Series, Field Columbian Museum,* vol. 6, no. 2 (Chicago, 1905).

4. For a study of the traditional marriage ceremony at Oraibi, see H. R. Voth, "Oraibi Marriage Customs," *American Anthropologist,* vol. 2, no. 2 (1900).

5. Oraibi's former burial customs are reported in H. R. Voth, "Brief Miscellaneous Papers," *Anthropological Series, Field Columbian Museum,* vol. 11, no. 2 (Chicago, 1912).

6. *Piki* is made from a batter of finely ground cornmeal and water, generally leavened with fresh ashes of sage, spruce, or juniper. An oil pressed from watermelon seed was traditionally used for shortening. Females learn early to apply the batter, with the palm and fingers of the right hand, from a bowl to a very hot stone (*duma*). The batter quickly bakes into crisp, paper-thin sheets, which are rolled or folded into elongated, multilayered loaves that are about 12 inches long and about 1½ inches wide. Ordinary *piki* is blue gray, but by adding a suitable dye, colored *piki* may be produced for a *katcina* dance or for some other festivity.

7. Suds used to be made by women from water mixed with yucca roots that they had dug up, dried, and pounded. These have become so scarce that it takes a long and difficult journey to secure them. Nowadays, store soaps or prepared shampoos are used except on the most important of ceremonial or traditional occasions.

8. Kane works as a carpenter. He is the only Hopi at Oraibi to have joined a union and is reputed to be the wealthiest man in the village. (Other Hopi are loath or forbidden [?] to join unions.) Kane built himself a new house on top of Third Mesa (Fig. 21, D) in conjunction with a filling station, which was to have been run by his son, Edmond. When Edmond died in 1952, Kane gradually lost interest in the station and soon had it closed. He plans to run it again when he retires at sixty-five and begins to draw social security. Meantime, he supplements his carpentry earnings by farming in his free time.

9. The last burro in Oraibi belonged to Panimptiwa. He rode it daily when he went sheepherding.

   Actually the popularity of burros began to fade around 1840 when wagons were first introduced. Men quickly found out that burros were poor draft animals and that mules and horses were far superior for pulling wagons.

For more information on these topics, consult "Old Oraibi," pp. 194–95.

10. It is interesting to note that Ned and Sidney, who are among the last to keep horses and to use a wagon, are the sons of the arch-conservative Duvenimptiwa, who would not even ride in a wagon because wagons were not a part of the ancient Hopi way.

11. Kennard estimates, "In the summer of 1962, there were 38 Hopi families [presumably from all the villages] living and working in Flagstaff alone." E. A. Kennard, "Post-War Economic Changes among the Hopi," *Proceedings of the American Ethnological Society* (Spring, 1965), pp. 26–27.

12. This idea, treated as a principle of general culture growth, is to be found in M. Titiev, *The Science of Man*, rev. ed. (New York: Holt, Rinehart and Winston, Inc., 1963), pp. 516–19.

13. A meticulously detailed account of the Soyal as it was performed at Oraibi at the turn of the century is given in Dorsey and Voth, "The Oraibi Soyal."

14. The scarcity of out-of-door *katcina* dances is somewhat compensated by the fact that contemporary performances, unlike those of former times, are likely to continue for two successive days during a weekend. In such cases, participants are expected to remain awake all night before the first day only.

15. For a picture of a traditional *katcina* initiation including the whipping *katcinas* and sand-painting, see Voth, "The Oraibi Powamu Ceremony," Pl. LXIII. This work describes in detail all that took place during a *katcina* initiation.

    The impact of the *katcina* whipping on a child's personality is discussed by Dorothy Eggan, in "The General Problem of Hopi Adjustment," *American Anthropologist*, vol. 45 (1943), pp. 357–73. See also *Sun Chief*, pp. 79–85.

16. Allusion is made here to Voth, "The Oraibi Powamu Ceremony." Not only does this work give a detailed account of the Powamu, but it contains many Hopi texts with English lettering.

17. Even in the days when travel was slow and difficult, an enterprising farmer occasionally made his way into a "White" town in order to hawk such things as peaches.

18. Since the peddler stocked and sold a variety of fruits and vegetables, he may have served as an agent of diffusion, introducing to the Hopi such new items as grapes, which a few native farmers now grow.

19. A list of former clans and phratries may be found in "Old Oraibi," p. 53. The same phratry numbers that are used in "Old Oraibi" are retained in this work.

    References to a Fire clan have been made of late. These are probably in error. Fire is one of the *wuyas* ("ancients") of the

Masau'û clan, but it is not an independent clan in its own right. It is to be doubted if there ever was a Fire clan at Oraibi.

CHAPTER XII

1. Compare M. Ginsberg, "Social Change," *British Journal of Sociology,* vol. 9, no. 3 (1958), pp. 205–29.
2. For details of traditional father-son behavior see "Old Oraibi," pp. 17–18.
3. This is one of the archaic foods that Masau *katcinas* sometimes force spectators to eat in public.
4. These laws are set forth and discussed in terms of the general development of culture in M. Titiev, *The Science of Man,* rev. ed. (New York: Holt, Rinehart and Winston, Inc., 1963), pp. 378–79.
5. As the late Dr. Keesing has written with respect to studies of culture change, "The disconcerting fact . . . [is] that standardization and operational clarity does not exist. . . ." F. M. Keesing, *Culture Change* (Stanford: Stanford University Press, 1952), p. 70. It is true that Dr. Keesing's statement was published in 1952 but, unfortunately, it is still valid today.

Topical Index and Glossary
of Hopi Terms

[*Hopi personal names and clan affiliations; the names of the Hopi villages and most other place-names; and the material in the Notes are not included.*]

Adultery, 30, 51, 68, 302, 303
Age-grades, 109, 111
Al ("Bow" or "Horn") society, 80, 81, 98, 142, 144, 151, 166, 167, 203, 228, 231, 298–99, 300, 301; *see also* Wuwutcim rites
Albino, 88, 89
Albuquerque Indian school, 30, 76, 159, 164, 261, 339
Anktioni ("Repeat") announcements and dances, 219, 222, 229, 231–32, 244, 247–48, 252, 258, 259–60, 324–25; *see also* Kiva night-dances
Antelope society, 148, 228; *see also* Snake-Antelope Dance
Apache, 229–30, 249, 271
Aphrodisiac, 152
Archaic foods, 122, 273, 351, 352
Ashes, 73, 85, 249, 331
atühöya ("small ceremonial mantle," worn by women)
atü'ü ("ceremonial mantle" for women)
aya ("gourd rattle")

Bahana (" 'White' person"), 68–69, 110, 133, 134, 232, 330

bakap ("reed")
banda ("headband")
Banquette, 305
Baptism by Kwans, 231
Bartlett, Katharine, 88
Basket-carrier, 54, 89, 93, 111, 180
Bastard, 23, 71, 77, 83, 111, 142, 154, 265
Bean Dance, 71, 91, 189, 201, 202, 213, 217, 218, 219, 220, 221, 224, 225, 313–21, 342
Bisexualism, 99–100, 153, 158, 215, 293, 299, 309, 310
Bone "doctor," 44, 69, 190, 245
Bow and arrow, 20, 69, 127, 150, 288, 302, 309, 310
Buffalo Dance, 37, 166, 184, 189, 191, 198, 200, 202, 204, 206, 208, 232, 302, 309–11
Burial, 9, 39, 49, 69, 102, 124, 142, 258, 281, 327
Burro, 22, 104, 227, 281, 336
Butterfly Dance, 4, 20, 23, 30, 32, 38–39, 60, 107, 202, 286, 289, 339–40, 345
Butterfly "wings," 213, 267

Calendar, viii, 29, 49, 95, 96, 146, 157, 166, 174, 179–80,